Food Policy in the United Kingdom

T0292831

This book provides an introduction to food policy in the United Kingdom, examining policy development, implementation, influences and current issues.

The book begins by providing a wide-ranging introduction to food policy in the UK, situating it within wider global debates and establishing key drivers, such as issues related to global citizenship, trade and finance. The use of food control as a policy lever is also discussed and contrasted with alternative approaches based on behaviour change. The book presents an overview of the history of UK food policy, from which there is much to be learned, before moving onto current challenges posed by political instability, both at home and abroad, global pandemics and cost of living crises. Foremost is the need to manage public health, including both malnutrition and obesity, while promoting sustainable and healthy diets, as well as the broader issues around addressing food security and food poverty. The book also examines public sector food initiatives, such as school food and early childhood provisions, and food regulation. As a part of food regulation, chapters examine food scares and food fraud, from chalk in flour to "horsegate". The role of media, marketing and advertising is also considered within a policy perspective. Taking a wider lens, the book also discusses the impact of global food trade and the financialisation of food on food policy in the UK and vice versa. The book is supported by instructor eResources on the Routledge website, designed to support student learning as well as provide regular updates on UK food policy developments. The eResources include student activities, group exercises and links to further reading and additional resources.

This book serves as a key introduction to UK food and agricultural policy for students, scholars, policymakers and professionals, as well as those interested in food systems, public health and social policy more widely.

Martin Caraher is Emeritus Professor of Food and Health Policy in the Centre for Food Policy at City, University of London, UK. He was a founding member of the London Food Board and has sat on the National Institute for Health and Clinical Excellence (NICE) advisory board. He has published five books, including *The Economics of Emergency Food Aid Provision* (2018) and *Food Poverty and Insecurity* (2016).

Sinéad Furey is a senior lecturer in Consumer Management and Food Innovation at Ulster University Business School, UK. She previously worked in food and consumer policy roles for the Consumer Council, Education and Training Inspectorate, and the Food Standards Agency in Northern Ireland.

Rebecca Wells is a senior lecturer in Food Policy in the Centre for Food Policy at City, University of London, UK, and the programme director for the Centre's MSc in Food Policy. She previously worked as a producer and food journalist on radio programmes for the BBC, including BBC Radio 4's *The Food Programme*.

Earthscan Food and Agriculture

Net Zero, Food and Farming
Climate Change and the UK Agri-Food System
Neil Ward

Conservation Agriculture in India
A Paradigm Shift for Sustainable Production
Edited by A.R. Sharma

Agricultural Commercialization, Gender Equality and the Right to Food
Insights from Ghana and Cambodia
*Edited by Joanna Bourke Martignoni, Christophe Gironde, Christophe Golay,
Elisabeth Prügl and Dzodzi Tsikata*

The Sociology of Farming
Concepts and Methods
Jan Douwe van der Ploeg

Genetically Modified Crops and Food Security
Commercial, Ethical and Health Considerations
Edited by Jasmeet Kour, Vishal Sharma and Imtiyaz Khanday

Climate Neutral and Resilient Farming Systems
Practical Solutions for Climate Mitigation and Adaptation
Edited by Sekhar Udaya Nagothu

Sustainable Apple Breeding and Cultivation in Germany
Commons-Based Agriculture and Social-Ecological Resilience
Hendrik Wolter

Food Policy in the United Kingdom
An Introduction
Martin Caraher, Sinéad Furey and Rebecca Wells

For more information about this series, please visit: www.routledge.com/books/series/ECEFA/

Food Policy in the United Kingdom

An Introduction

Martin Caraher, Sinéad Furey and Rebecca Wells

LONDON AND NEW YORK

from Routledge

Designed cover image: © Oscar Wong / Getty Images

First published 2023
by Routledge
4 Park Square, Milton Park, Abingdon, Oxon OX14 4RN

and by Routledge
605 Third Avenue, New York, NY 10158

Routledge is an imprint of the Taylor & Francis Group, an informa business

British Library Cataloguing-in-Publication Data
A catalogue record for this book is available from the British Library

Library of Congress Cataloging-in-Publication Data
Names: Caraher, Martin, author. | Furey, Sinéad, author. | Wells, Rebecca
(Policy scientist), author.
Title: Food policy in the United Kingdom : an introduction / Martin Caraher, Sinéad Furey, and Rebecca Wells.
Description: New York, NY : Routledge, 2024 | Includes bibliographical references and index.
Identifiers: LCCN 2023005718 (print) | LCCN 2023005719 (ebook) | ISBN 9781032196824 (hardback) | ISBN 9781032196770 (paperback) | ISBN 9781003260301 (ebook)
Subjects: LCSH: Food industry and trade—Government Policy—Great Britain. | Food supply—Government Policy—Great Britain. | Nutrition policy—Great Britain.
Classification: LCC TX360.G7 C29 2023 (print) | LCC TX360.G7 (ebook) | DDC 363.80941—dc23/eng/20230210
LC record available at https://lccn.loc.gov/2023005718
LC ebook record available at https://lccn.loc.gov/2023005719

ISBN: 978-1-032-19682-4 (hbk)
ISBN: 978-1-032-19677-0 (pbk)
ISBN: 978-1-003-26030-1 (ebk)

DOI: 10.4324/9781003260301

Typeset in Times New Roman
by codeMantra

Access the Support Material: www.routledge.com/9781032196770

Lest we forget

Minnie Weaving, a mother of seven children in southeast London, died in 1933. Her husband was unemployed and received 48 shillings a week benefit. She fed her husband and children but starved herself in order to do so, which contributed to her death. Her death sparked a prolonged debate under the headline "Hungry England". A large public outcry coincided with the hunger or protest marches and this became known as the "Hungry England" debate.

To all those in the UK who currently are experiencing food insecurity: from the families who grow our food to the mothers who self-sacrifice on behalf of their families and go hungry, to the activists and policymakers who attempt to make this world a better place. Keep on trying. We hope this book goes some way to making the world a better place and helps establish a new debate about food in our society.

Dedicated to the memory of Jane Dixon, who was an inspirational academic and friend and who provided insights into food systems and food insecurity.

Contents

Acknowledgements   ix
List of figures   xi
List of tables   xiii
List of abbreviations   xv

1 Introduction   1

2 Food policy in the UK: from public health and nutrition to sustainable diets   13

3 Food policy and nutrition: the triple burden of modern diets   44

4 The growth of food insecurity: the new face of food poverty   65

5 Sustainable diets: linking nutrition and environment   92

6 Food media, marketing and advertising   112

7 The UK food industry   129

8 Global food trade and commodities: the financialisation of food   157

9 Public sector food initiatives: the case of school food and early
   childhood provision   171

10 Food scares, food safety and food fraud from chalk in flour to "horsegate"   197

11 Examples of success in UK food policy   215

12 Conclusions, reflections and the future for food policy   231

Index   241

Acknowledgements

When we undertook to write this book, the world was a different place: no COVID, no lockdowns and no global economic depression. The world was not perfect by any means, but since then, the situation has deteriorated with more many in the UK suffering from food poverty and hunger re-emerging. To all those we work with – academics, practitioners and those in the front line of food policy responses – we remain in awe of your work and dedication.

Martin, Sinéad and Rebecca

Martin would like to thank Sinéad and Rebecca for their patience in responding to his constant demands for edits, reviews and cries for help. As always, love to Maggie who put up with my having to write in lockdown and even further isolate myself in a year when we had planned to travel and see friends, neither of which was possible. To all of those who I have been lucky to work with over the years.

My background reading and research for this book has reunited me with many of the giants of food policy and the inspirations for my initial move into food policy. Standing on the shoulders of giants like Richard Titmus, Peter Townsend, John Boyd Orr, Tim Lang and Lizzie Collingham has been indeed humbling and convinced me of one of the central themes of this book: that there is much to be learned from the past, if only we listen and act.

Sinéad would like to thank Martin for inviting me to join him on this book writing adventure. Reading his writing is inspirational in itself and his impressive list of recommended texts reminds me not only of the great minds that have shaped the field of food policy and those issues the three of us care so much about, but also that Martin is most definitely one of them. Martin is my humble "food hero" whose opinions and logic help me fathom so many of the big issues within this book and discipline. Thanks too to Rebecca for widening my food policy world and mentoring me through food media, marketing and advertising.

I would particularly like to thank my Father, Matthew, for instilling in me the importance of education and voicing one's opinion with the courage of your convictions. Little wonder, then, that I would enter a world of academia and consumer advocacy where the voice of the *experts by experience* is so compelling and the most powerful words I will ever write and read.

Rebecca would like to thank Martin and Sinéad for inviting me to work with them on this project, for their wisdom, insights and infinite patience. I am indebted to Martin, Tim Lang and Sheila Dillon for inspiring and encouraging me to work in the field of food policy. Working with colleagues and students at the Centre for Food Policy invigorates and rewards me every day, and motivates me to continue working for a better, more sustainable and healthy food system for everyone.

My heartfelt thanks go to my husband Jonathan and my two wonderful children, Hannah and Evie, for making everything better.

Figures

2.1   Depiction of the food system   14
2.2   Public health levels of intervention   22
2.3   The Overton Window with an example of tackling obesity interventions   23
4.1   Well-being of Future Generations (Wales) Act 2015   81
4.2   Independent Food Aid Network hierarchy of responses to food insecurity 2021   83
7.1   The UK food chain   132
7.2   Ten most common changes in eating habits in the last 12 months   142
10.1 Timeline of the emergence of the horsemeat scandal   206

Tables

2.1	A list of definitions of food policy	16
2.2	Models of policy development	19
2.3	Some examples of the focus on individual behaviour and household skills	28
2.4	Ultra-processed food (UPF) or NOVA classification	32
3.1	Some key examples of nutrition policy and influences	45
3.2	Some examples of key health- and food-related policies in the past 50 years	47
3.3	Examples of assumptions regarding the reduction of dietary intake linked to a lack of skills, knowledge and "ignorance"	54
4.1	Childhood under- and over-nutrition in the UK	67
4.2	References to poverty in National Food Strategy: the plan	79
5.1	Five models of public health	94
5.2	Policy examples of sustainable diet approaches	96
5.3	UN progress towards the Sustainable Development Goals	99
5.4	The Sustainable Development Goals	100
7.1	The range of the food industry	130
7.2	Summary of future scenarios for agricultural production	137
7.3	List of some defunct supermarkets (since the 1960s) and who purchased them	138
7.4	Shifting power in the food value-added chain	140
8.1	Some examples of concentration in global trade	159
9.1	Some key dates for school food policy	175
11.1	List of some important websites for local food projects	224
11.2	Examples of academic policy influencers	225

Abbreviations

AFN	alternative food networks
AMR	anti-microbial resistance
ANU	Australian National University
ASA	Advertising Standards Authority
AWB	Australian Wheat Board
b-a-u	business as usual
BIS	basic income support
BMI	Body Mass Index
BNPL	buy now, pay later
Brexit	this is a combination of Britain and exit used to describe the withdrawal process of the United Kingdom from the European Union.
BRIC	economies of Brazil, Russia, India and China
BRICS	economics of Brazil, Russia, India, China and South Africa
BSE	Bovine Spongiform Encephalopathy (mad cow disease)
CA	conservation agriculture
CAP	Common Agricultural Policy
CAPO(s)	Concentrated Animal Feeding Operation(s)
CCIs	Community Cooking Interventions
CHD	coronary heart disease
CJD	Creutzfeldt-Jakob Disease
CME	Chicago Mercantile Exchange
COS	Charitable Organisation Society
COVID-19	Coronavirus 2019
CPAG	Child Poverty Action Group
CSR	Corporate Social Responsibility
CWFS	Committee on World Food Security
DEFRA	Department for Environment, Food & Rural Affairs
DETR	Department of the Environment, Transport and the Regions
DfE	Department for the Economy
DfEE	Department for Education and Employment
DoH	Department of Health
DR-NCDs	diet-related non-communicable diseases
DWP	Department for Work and Pensions
EC	European Commission
ELMS	Environmental Land Management Scheme
EU	European Union

EU-SILC	The European Union Statistics on Income and Living Conditions
FAO	Food and Agricultural Organization of the United Nations
FB	food banks
FDI	foreign direct investment
FHRS	Food Hygiene Rating Scheme
FI	food insecurity
FIIN	Food Industry Intelligence Network
FMD	foot and mouth disease
FNI	food and nutrition insecurity
FNS	food and nutrition security
FOPNL	front of pack nutrition labels
FSA	Food Standards Agency (UK)
FSM	free school meals
GDP	gross domestic product
GHG	greenhouse gases
GM	genetically modified (foods)
GNTs	Global Nutrition Targets
GUFP	Grow up Free from Poverty Coalition
HFCS	high fructose corn syrup
HFSS	(foods) high in fat, salt and sugar
HFSSM	Household Food Security Survey Module
ICESCR	International Covenant on Economic, Social and Cultural Rights 1966
IFAD	International Fund for Agricultural Development
IFAN	Independent Food Aid Network
JIT	just in time retailing
LCA	life cycle assessment
LCC	life cycle costing
M&As	mergers and acquisitions
MAFF	Ministry of Agriculture, Fisheries and Food
MDGs	Millennium Development Goals
MIG	minimum income guarantee
MNCs	multinational corporations
MTL	multiple traffic light (labels)
NACNE	National Advisory Committee on Nutrition Education
NCDs	non-communicable diseases
NDPB	non-departmental public body
NFS	The National Food Strategy
NFU	National Farmers' Union of England and Wales
NGOs	non-governmental organisations
NI	Northern Ireland
OECD	Organization for Economic Cooperation and Development
Ofcom	Office of Communications
OIE	World Organisation for Animal Health (formerly the Office International des Epizooties
ONS	Office for National Statistics
OPEC	Organization of the Petroleum Exporting Countries
PHRD	Public Health Responsibility Deal
PM	Prime Minister

PPPs	public-private partnerships
REHIS	Royal Environmental Health Institute of Scotland
RSA	Royal Society of Arts
RUTF	ready to use therapeutic food – milk-based ready to use food
SDIL	Soft Drinks Industry Levy
SI	sustainable intensification
SNAP	Supplemental Nutrition Assistance Program
SNP	Scottish National Party
SONA	State of Nation Address
TNC(s)	Trans National Corporation(s)
UBI	universal basic income
UC	Universal Credit
UCIs	unhealthy commodity industries
UIF	unemployment insurance funds
UK	United Kingdom
UMB	Universal Monthly Benefit
UN	United Nations
UNDHR	The Universal Declaration of Human Rights
UNEP	The United Nations Environment Programme
UPFs	ultra-processed foods
USA	United States of America
USSR	Union of Soviet Socialist Republics (the Soviet Union)
VSA	voluntary service agreements
VSS	voluntary sustainability standards
WFP	World Food Programme
WFS	World Food Security
WRAP	Waste and Resources Action Programme
WHO	World Health Organization
WTO	World Trade Organization
WWI	World War I
WWII	World War II

1 Introduction

Introduction: modern concerns with food policy

Food policy has, in recent times, become a topic of both policy and public concern driven by factors such as food scandals, rising rates of obesity, food poverty and insecurity, the UK leaving the European Union (Brexit), the COVID-19 crisis, the climate and weather crises, the possible relaxing of food standards posed by new bilateral trade deals in a post-Brexit world and geopolitical issues such as the war in Ukraine (Lang, 2020, Lang & McKee, 2022).

Such concerns have led to reviews of the food system: the first, called "Food Matters" in 2008 commissioned by a Labour government, and in 2019, two National Food Strategy (NFS) reports (Cabinet Office, 2008, Dimbleby, 2020, 2021), both of which failed to gain policy traction and achieve widespread policy change or action. The 2021 "National Food Strategy: The Plan" (NFS) and its recommendations were considered by the government in March 2022. The NFS was the second report in a two-part series and sets out 14 recommendations for governmental consideration. Suggested remedies include addressing diet-related inequality with the majority being rejected (Dimbleby & Lewis, 2023), breaking the "junk food cycle" and the impact of current agricultural practices on land and health as well as changes in legislation and the food system. It also contains a considerable amount of detail on trade and trade agreements and outlines the implications for British agriculture and national food security. In many ways, the report is ambitious and sometimes radical in its recommendations, such as the tax on sugar and salt which could raise £3 billion annually as well as push food companies to reformulate their products. Within days of the NFS being published the Prime Minister (PM) Boris Johnson indicated that "I am not, I must say, attracted to the idea of extra taxes on hard-working people" (Smyth, 2021). This despite the tax being primarily designed to encourage reformulation by manufacturers. The government response was muted, and in the midst of a political leadership crisis, we saw some PMs, three in 2022,[1] not only disregarding the conclusions and recommendations of the NFS but also threatening to roll back other already implemented and promised reforms such as the soda tax and restrictions on advertising and labelling (Food Ethics Council, 2022, Lang, 2022a, White, 2022, Yap, 2022).

There are developments in Northern Ireland and Scotland with a Food Strategy Consultation in 2021 and a Food and Drink Good Nation Policy, respectively. So, while there is a lot of white noise about food policy, we remain to see the practical results of this in terms of policy and legislation implementation. In many ways this book explores the gap between talk about and action for food policy.

This chapter sets out a broad perspective for food policy in the UK, which includes Wales, Scotland and Northern Ireland. This includes issues related to global citizenship, trade and finance as drivers of policy and how they operate at the micro, meso and macro levels of influence. The chapter finishes by providing a broad overview of the remaining 11 book chapters.

DOI: 10.4324/9781003260301-1

British food policy in a global context

The focus of this book is food policy in the United Kingdom of Great Britain and Northern Ireland,[2] but of course the UK does not exist in a vacuum; it is dependent on other countries for trade and some foods and other countries rely on both trade and aid from the UK; this is the issue of global citizenship. Concerns with food cross many areas of interest from agriculture to health outcomes and have links with trade, global warming and foreign policy and aid. There are internal or domestic issues for the UK in terms of governance of its food production and growing as well as its place in a global world where interconnections are complex; the UK has a strong reliance on imports of food, especially fruit and vegetables, as its own horticultural sector is weak (Dimbleby, 2021, Lang, 2020). This issue of foreign aid is important in terms of the role of the UK as global citizen and its contribution to the United Nations Sustainable Development Goals (SDGs) and climate change agenda (Biermann, Kanie & Kim, 2017, World Health Organization, 2021). The plight of growers/producers in developing and emerging economies, are also being impacted by decisions to cut aid budgets. In the UK, the foreign aid budget in 2021 was reduced from 0.7% to 0.5% of gross national income (Kobayashi, Heinrich & Bryant, 2021). This follows a growing movement by developed nations as they move from food aid to food trade and economic liberalisation to tackle global food supply issues such as food insecurity (Barrett & Maxwell, 2005, Hebinck et al., 2018, Moyo, 2010, Nunn & Qian, 2014). In early 2022, with the invasion of Ukraine, there were global concerns over the world supply of wheat; 23% of global trade in wheat originated from Ukraine. Much of its exports went to North Africa, a region already suffering from political upheavals and economic crises.

Following the 2008 Great Recession, food-related riots in North Africa gave rise to political upheaval and the Arab Spring. There were fears for food security in Yemen, Tunisia and Egypt because of the Ukrainian crisis. As countries such as the UK and the US roll back on foreign aid budgets, their role is being replaced by private companies who under the heading of corporate social responsibility (CSR) are providing support to growers in Africa and Asia (McGoey, 2015). The aid aspect is epitomised by the Gates Foundation, but many companies now operate their own internal polices generally under the guise of CSR commitments (Rieff, 2016, 2015, Various Public Interest, Health, and Citizens' Groups, 2017). These issues are picked up in Chapter 8.

These concerns with food policy have been dealt with by policies within separate areas, sometimes referred to as "silo policymaking". This often resulted in fallout from one area to another and a lack of coherence: for example, foreign policy very rarely considered the issue of food access and how food trade deals might impact on foreign policy. The City of London is one of the global centres for trade in food products, yet this trade is lightly regulated and has little relevance to the SDGs and reducing food insecurity and the livelihoods of small farmers.

There was a shift in health policy to attempts to incorporate health in all policies, and now with food policy, a similar emphasis is to have food in all policies or at a minimum for all policies to be "food proofed" (Kickbusch & Buckett, 2010, Parsons & Hawkes, 2019). Likewise, there have been attempts to develop a comprehensive approach to food policy by linking different areas: obesity with food poverty, hunger and obesity and links with the food supply system (Peña & Bacallao, 2000), food production and healthy dietary consumption in the area of eco-nutrition (Lang & Mason, 2018, Mason & Lang, 2017). These approaches will be explored in the chapters that follow. While arguing for a comprehensive approach to policymaking and food policy, there needs to be pragmatic tactics taking the chance for change where possible. So, if the focus is obesity, as it often is with current concerns with overweight and diet-related non-communicable diseases (DR-NCDs), then this can be the fulcrum for policy change. In practical terms, we should remember that food policy is the art of the possible and needs to take its opportunities when they arise. We will see in Chapters 2, 3, 9 and 11 that a health and nutrition focus has traditionally been at the core of food policy and Chapters 2, 3 and 4 set out the issues related to eco-nutrition and poverty. The linking of healthy eating with sustainable food production offers a way forward, linking issues from farm to fork, and offers a possible link to how policy can be comprehensively formulated.

In all of this, the UK has contributed significantly to the development of food policy in practice and as an academic discipline. The Centre for Food Policy at City, University of London, has the world's first dedicated centre for food policy along with masters and PhD programmes. The origins of this can be found in the focus on food policy in World War I (WWI) and World War II (WWII). The writings of John Boyd Orr were influential in proposing a social side to nutrition and a wider approach to food and nutrition (Orr, 1936, Orr & Lubbock, 1940). He suggested to the US President Franklin D. Roosevelt the idea of a "world food plan" which resulted in the establishment of the FAO (Food and Agriculture Organization) in 1945 (Orr, 1966). These aspects will be dealt with in more detail in Chapters 2, 3, 8 and 9.

The domestic UK food policy scenario is concerned with providing affordable, healthy, acceptable and sustainable food to the UK population; a second role is, or should be, concerned with that of the UK as a global citizen and its contribution to food producers in other countries and contribution to the SDGs (Biermann, Kanie & Kim, 2017). We cannot and should not aim for the first if it compromises the health of those in emerging nations; this is simply off-shoring the problem. This perspective will appear throughout the chapters in using the idea "Nobody Wins Unless Everybody Wins" attributed to Bruce Springsteen in the fiscally conservative US Reagan years (Taylor, 2010).

Global equity and food policy

So, providing affordable, healthy, acceptable and sustainable food to the UK population must not come at the expense of others. Collingham points out that "From the mid-nineteenth century, the country looked to its trading empire to supply it with staple foods" (Collingham, 2017, pp. 217–218). The long-term impacts of such a policy have given rise to the development of "ghost acres"; this is another aspect of off-shoring.[3] This is land, often in poor and developing nations of the world, which is used to grow feed for cattle in richer nations as well as fresh fruit and vegetables. They are called ghost as they are not seen by consumers. But more than this, such a policy shifts the burden of environmental damage and risks to those countries. In the nineteenth century, such policies were driven by cheap labour and the absence of "expensive" labour standards (Kropotkin, 2008).

In the early stages of Empire (mid-nineteenth century), this was driven by the need to supply "cheap" food to the rapidly expanding urban classes and ensure political stability. Cheap food was deemed necessary to avoid the food riots of the 1800s and to help power the industrial revolution by ensuring that the workers had at least the basic minimum necessary for bodily health. Some argue that the modern equivalent of these riots are the emergence of food banks and queues for food; the last food riots were in 1932 in Belfast (Cooper & Dumpleton, 2013, Mitchell, 2017, Power, 2022). The modern shift in UK relationships has been from commonwealth countries and former colonies to more global trading – globalisation (Collingham, 2017, McKeon, 2021). The point here is not an anti-trade perspective but an equity one, where those growing food for us in the UK are often not adequately compensated for their labours and the requirements of production often result in localised damage to the environment and a shift from growing local indigenous food to dependency on growing crops for cash (George, 2010, 1986, McKeon, 2021).

Moves towards a neoliberal economic approach result in low regulation, low tax economy, with little taxable income available to spend on public infrastructure and food companies. Large transnational companies (TNCs) concerned about their supply chains have begun to invest in local infrastructures and agricultural support systems. The move away from traditional public policy by national governments which involved providing food welfare, whether direct (provision of food) or indirect (cash transfers), has created a space which "Big Food" and charity have stepped in to fill, often reluctantly. This move to company-funded is welfare referred to as "welfare capitalism", which again reflects the retreat of government from making welfare policy to a focus on private and NGO sector governance (Lacy-Nichols & Williams, 2021, Richards, Kjærnes & Vik, 2016, Riches & Silvasti, 2014). At a global level, TNCs see this as investment in their futures and support training for farmers and capital investment projects. There are some positives to such moves. Often, corporations have resources bigger than many nation states and can move faster than state institutions, thus ensuring action is prompt and directed at the problem.

In the wake of the 2008 Great Recession, some of the big TNCs were shocked by the lack of global accountability and the fact that the actions of some hedge funds threatened the viability of their supplies. This aspect of "financialisation" will be dealt with in more detail in Chapter 8. This refocus also allows companies an opportunity to rebrand civil activism demands within a consumer activism model, usually under a CSR banner (Belasco, 2007). This gives rise to a new form of food policy which is closely wrapped up and even controlled by trade and food industry interests (Blas & Farchy, 2021).

The downside of a food policy based on welfare capitalism is the unregulated nature of such policy developments, with the food industry investing where they can gain most and only investing in commodities that they trade in such as coffee, cocoa, sugar or cereals. Such an approach also limits benefits to those who fall within the commercial interests of the sponsoring company and does not guarantee an increase in income for growers/producers. For example, while cocoa production is concentrated in 30 countries with 90% grown on plots of less than ten hectares, the percentage price of the finished chocolate bar going to cocoa farmers over the last 30 years has decreased from 6% to 3% (Leissle, 2018). Cases such as this are not confined to low-income and emerging economies: dairy and beef farmers in the Global North, including the UK, have experienced similar problems with falling farm incomes. Another danger is the lack or limited investment in infrastructures such as transport and education, which are in essence publicly owned assets (Goodbody, 2022, Schneider, 2022). This shift in governmentality from the state to the private sector is a concept which will be explored across various chapters (Marston & McDonald, 2006). Such developments, while welcome, should not and cannot replace public-based food policy. Such schemes should run parallel to government-based food policy and may require regulation. Beveridge said in 1928 in his reflections on WWI that it was feasible to substitute "managed for automated provisioning of the people" (Beveridge, 1928, pp. 337–338). However, the notion of controlling or even regulating the food industry has become an anathema to governments, including that of the UK, as they pursue policies based on neoliberal economics with low-tax, low-wage, low-regulation and "small state" economies (Chang, 2022).

Finance versus well-being and healthy eating

A strong influence (even counter-influence) on food policy has always been the financial aspect and the contribution of food growing, production and consumption to Gross Domestic Product

(GDP). Scientific data on nutrition and health are appreciated by policymakers, but these data have to compete with other evidence, including the financial and political aspects. For the UK, agriculture gradually over time ceased to be considered important as its percentage contribution to GDP sank: by the end of the 1980s it was 3%, by the early 2000s it was less than 1% and it is now estimated to be 0.5% of the GDP. There are arguments from those on the political right and those advocates of free trade who contend that the UK should not invest in food production and farming but import its food needs. The case hinges on the argument that the contribution of British agriculture to GDP is minuscule and that, as argued by a senior government advisor, the food sector is not "critically important" to the economy – and that agriculture and fishery production "certainly isn't" (Owen, 2020). For the UK, WWII was an exception to this when national security and the concern with food supplies convinced the government to take control of the food supply system (Collingham, 2017, Hammond, 1954). The establishment of the Ministry of Food in WWII introduced a form of food policy which was referred to as "food control" (Fearnley-Whittingstall, 2010, Hammond, 1954, Sitwell, 2017). This period is often regarded by policymakers as the golden era of food policy. It is important to distinguish the different social context that WWII introduced; restrictions on food choice through rationing and a points system were accepted as part of the greater good and the view that the measures were applied to all in the population (Kynaston, 2007). Hammond (1954), as one who was party to much of this policymaking, considers that improvements to health from rationing in WWII were incidental and not planned.

Food control as food policy

There is a long tradition of UK "food control" ranging from the repeal of the Corn Laws in 1846 through both World Wars which saw the creation of a post called the "Food Controller" and a Ministry of Food to, in modern times, a more liberal and freedom of choice approach to food policy. The reasons for this food control vary but in essence seem to be enacted when there is (1) a humanitarian crisis (Corn Laws and The Great Irish famine, An Górta Mór); (2) the state is in peril (e.g. poor health of recruits to the army for the Boer War, feeding the population in WWII) (Hammond, 1951, Kinealy & Moran, 2020, Woodham-Smith, 1962); or (3) vested interests are threatened. In times of peace, there seems to be less state intervention in food policy. The food poverty of the interwar years and the "Hungry 1930s" saw little direct intervention in tackling food poverty and hunger (Smith & Nicolson, 1995, Vernon, 2007). Food control was deemed to be suitable for the war years but judged to be unacceptable in peace time.

Food control does in many senses mean some restrictions on choice, and in times of peace, this seems to be an unacceptable intrusion for the majority. The tension is that many may be suffering from nutritional inadequacies and food insecurity, and food control could help benefit them. But, this is often deemed to be less important than the issue of choice. In 2022 with global crises in food supply, food price increases and the war in Ukraine, there may be a need to revisit, and perhaps implement, some aspects of "food control" (Lang, 2022b, Lang & McKee, 2022).

The first official use of the term food policy was around WWI when there were calls for a national "food policy". This was repeated for WWII where the term used was food control; this involved the state through the Ministry of Food taking control of the food supply chain from growing and buying of food stocks to rationing and the provision of food in workplaces. A Ministry of Food was established in both World Wars and in the first instance lasted until 1921 and then from 1939 to 1954. The interwar years ignored the lessons learned from WWI for food policy to alleviate poverty and hunger (Beveridge 1928, Hammond 1951). The advent of WWII saw an increased focus on food policies driven by a concern with national food security and the reliance on imports (Le Gros Clark & Titmuss, 1939). In 1939/1940, a Subcommittee on Food Policy led to the establishment of a Food (Defence Plans) Department. This was located as a subcommittee of the Committee of Imperial Defence and the focus was on national security and a concern with imports of food and disruptions to food supply due to U-boat activity. Health and nutrition were secondary issues and improvements in diet were the fallout from rationing and pricing controls which were based on an austere but healthy diet (Hammond, 1954). Hammond (1951) in his conclusions and reflections on food control during WWII says:

> The present volume might well have been entitled "The Expansion of Food Policy". That theme, or perhaps one should say succession of themes, must not be allowed to obscure another, less spectacular but scarcely less important in the whole work of the Ministry of Food: the continuous adaptation of both old and new control machinery to the fortunes of war and to the inexorable fact of economic change.
>
> (Hammond, 1951, p. 375)

Yet, even Hammond saw little from the experience of WWII that could be applied or be acceptable in peacetime as the memory of rationing and privation were seen as "controls" to escape. Rationing and food control were acceptable to the public as the visible effects of rationing were apparent from reductions in food queues with a flat rate of rationing which was the same allowance for everyone, with some special consideration for at-risk groups such as children and pregnant women.

National food education

From an early stage, food policy initiatives driven by concerns with national food security were supported by measures to educate the masses; this has remained a constant feature of UK-based food policy. The initial approaches to education were crude and a form of indoctrination or propaganda. For example, at the end of WWI, the Food Advice Division of the Ministry of Food established food advice centres and food advice organisers; there were 50 centres and 150 advisors, and by 1946, there were centres in nearly every major town and 22,000 wore a badge proclaiming them as "food leaders". The focus in the centres was on basic cooking and "motherliness", designed to meet the national interest (Vernon, 2007). This approach to food policy was based on behaviour change and a view of the working classes as lacking skills and knowledge necessary for the management of the household. As we will see in Chapter 2, such views were contrasted with those that argued the issues were those of income and inequality. The view of poverty as an individual and moral failing is one that has carried over into modern developments (Seabrook, 2013, Wells & Caraher, 2014), albeit it is tackled in a more sophisticated way as is the case with psychological nudges (Thaler & Sunstein, 2009).

There have been calls for the reinstitution of a Ministry of Food or at least a clear structure to govern food policy implementation (Parsons & Barling, 2022, Stitt & Prisk, 1997). WWII food control involved the state in controlling and managing areas of international trade, stockpiling foods to control price and access, setting up state-controlled restaurants (known as *British Restaurants* or *National Kitchens*) and rationing. Modern concerns seem to be with finding easy ways to deliver food policy with a light touch from government, whereas what is becoming more apparent is that a complete overhaul of our food system is needed from "farm to flush" or "farm to fork" (Dimbleby, 2021, Slater, Baker & Lawrence, 2022). Soft or downstream policy options which rely on behaviour change on their own are no longer sufficient to deliver the necessary changes to safeguard health and the environment. We will see in Chapters 2 and 3 how some are attempting to move to a model of food policy which incorporates or links environment and well-being (Mason & Lang, 2017).

Food policy and equity: a recurring theme

Food policy has long had a concern with inequality and how to provide equity around food. Since the 1930s, the social nutrition movement was concerned with broadening the reach of food policies (Orr, 1936 and Brockway, 1936). This was continued in the 1980s, 1990s and 2000s through the work of pioneering social activists and researchers such as Caroline Walker, Suzi Leather, Elizabeth Dowler and Tim Lang (Lang, Barling & Caraher, 2009). Today, this work continues through a network of food aware groups and individuals. An underpinning concern throughout this book is inequality and how the current food system does not serve everyone equally and indeed fails many. The COVID-19 pandemic exposed many of the weaknesses in the food system – it did not cause them. Inequality and poverty monitoring along with nutrition inequality measurement remain concerns and are addressed throughout the chapters in this volume, for example, in Chapter 4. The amount spent on food in the household budget, known as Engel's law, is an observation that as income rises, the proportion of income spent on food falls, even if absolute expenditure on food rises (Clements & Si, 2018, Torres Pabón, 2019, Zimmerman, 1932). So the income elasticity of demand for food oscillates between 0 and 1. Of course, this is not true for all income groups and those in the lower income brackets can spend up to 30% of their income on food while those in higher income brackets spend as low as 6% (Barosh et al., 2014). Hence an inequality and one that with Brexit and the COVID-19 pandemic has seen the gap increase (Barosh et al., 2014, Food Foundation, 2021).

Agriculture is the basis of the food supply chain, yet in many ways is one of the "losers" in the food supply chain. In sub-Saharan Africa, agriculture accounts for 53% of total global employment and food security and poverty reduction is correlated to the agricultural production (Giller et al., 2021). Following the global economic crisis in 2008, there were major impacts on global food poverty levels and political unrest; for example, the Arab Spring was triggered by concerns and riots over rising food prices (Ansani & Daniele, 2012, Johnstone & Mazo, 2011). The crises we now see (as of 2022–2023) are extensive and more far-reaching than that of 2008; extremes of food insecurity leading to famine are threatened because of the breakdown in global food supply chains (Lang & McKee, 2022).

The COVID-19 pandemic and subsequent global crises

Since starting this book, we have gone through two major global crises: the COVID-19 lockdowns and the war in Ukraine. Just as we thought we were recovering from the COVID-19 pandemic with the removal of lockdowns, the invasion of Ukraine introduced another crisis. A new word was introduced into dictionaries in 2022 and this was "permacrises" to indicate the perilous state of world affairs. The price volatility seen in the early stages of the COVID-19 pandemic began to level out, but in 2022 the war in Ukraine, along with a number of other global factors (climate, COVID, trade wars), resulted in food price increases. For example, futures for wheat rose by 20% in the first three months of 2022 and then 70% in the next three. The Oxfam report concluded that the COVID-19 crisis and the cost of living crisis triggered by the war in Ukraine have resulted in increases in extreme poverty while the profits of large food corporations and the wealth of individuals increased (Oxfam, 2022). Some global trading companies have seen their fortune increase by almost USD$ 20 million a day since the start of the COVID-19 pandemic (Oxfam, 2022). Price volatility (the range of price movements over a particular period of time) has been at its highest level in the past 50 years (Oxfam, 2022, p. 2). The report shows that "billionaires and corporations in the food, energy, pharmaceutical, and technology sectors are reaping huge rewards at the same time as the soaring cost of living is hurting so many worldwide". The report goes on to say that the pandemic has resulted in a new billionaire every 30 hours while a million people "fall into extreme poverty" (Oxfam, 2022, p. 3). Price volatility may be good for financial markets but is bad for farmers – especially small farmers – and producers and ultimately for the consumer.

The global food system is complex and has many inter-relationships with other industries. As an example, take what is generally referred to as the "Haber-Bosch" process[4]: this involves chemical firms making ammonia which goes towards the making of fertilisers; the by-products of the process then are used in other fertiliser production as well as disinfectant, diesel exhaust fluid, carbon dioxide (CO_2) used in the food industry for stunning pigs and chickens, for fizzy drinks as well as a preservative in some bagged food products. Rises in energy prices have resulted in some plants shutting down or cutting back production. Thus, fertiliser is in short supply, leading to price rises, leading to farmers applying less to crops, leading to smaller yields, all contributing to food price increases. Shortages of CO_2 supplies have meant that there is a problem with the slaughter of pigs and chickens, where it has resulted in a shortage of some goods on supermarket shelves.

The impacts within global food commodity chains are direct and indirect, the latter can be seen from reductions in the "Haber-Bosch" process. An indirect example comes from Australia where shortages of food on supermarket shelves were due to a lack of one of the by-products from the "Haber-Bosch" process, the diesel additive AdBlue. So, food deliveries in Australia were under threat due to a lack of uric acid from China and the policy of self-sufficiency being pursued by the Chinese government (Lau, 2022). All this shows the global reach and interconnectedness of the food system.

In previous food crises, the solution was often to shift supply from one area of the globe to another; so, a poor harvest of grain in Canada could be supplemented by grain from the Black Sea area. These options are seriously curtailed by poor harvests, the war in Ukraine and countries limiting exports to protect their own populations. For example, China has launched a self-sufficiency food policy and restricted exports, introduced tariffs on imports and is engaged in trade wars with Australia and the USA (Lau, 2022). All this forms a part of future food policy and shows how fragile the food system is and how food policy needs to adopt a broad palate to address problems such as climate change and war.

This book

This book has a UK focus but draws on global food policy literature to help frame the debate. This book consists of 12 chapters and these are as far as possible designed to stand alone. The UK has a long tradition of food policy, although perhaps not always effective and in certain instances benefitting those for whom it was intended. There is an abundant academic literature, both past and present, on the UK. This will, as appropriate, be supplemented by international citation where this supports or adds to the UK-based literature. This chapter has set out a broad background introduction to food policy in the UK within a global framework. A broad route map to the other chapters is provided below. Chapters will contain models and theories related to food policy, so Chapter 2 sets out some of the key principles, concepts and models underpinning food policy. This chapter, we recommend reading as the basis for other chapters, particularly the Overton Window and some examples of history repeating itself. This is followed by a chapter on "Food Policy and nutrition: the triple burden of modern diets". This sets out a short history of how nutrition has been key and often kept food policy in the public eye and led to the development of food policies. The concept of the triple burden of malnutrition and new developments with respect to development of eco-nutrition/sustainable diets is discussed. Chapters 4–6 deal with the issue of food insecurity followed by sustainable diets and then Chapter 6 on the influence of food media and advertising. The UK food system is set out in Chapter 7 using the headings of agriculture, retail and hospitality to explain the UK food supply chain. Given the UK reliance on food imports and exports as well as the importance of London as a financial trading centre for foodstuffs, the international perspective is the focus of Chapter 8, specifically the "financialisation" of food as a commodity. Chapter 9 sets out public sector food initiatives that have been initiated in the UK, focusing on school meals. Food safety and related issues of food fraud and food scares are focused on in Chapter 10. Successful exemplars of food policy advocacy and implementation are the concern of Chapter 11. Finally, Chapter 12 sets out some issues for the future, and how food policy might develop or have to adapt to the future is, of course, hard to predict, but new technologies and changes in the food system will pose new challenges for food policy. Each chapter is supported by instructor eResources on the Routledge website to aid student learning as well as provide updates on UK food policy developments. The eResources include student activities, group exercises and links to further reading: www.routledge.com/9781032196770.

Notes

1 Conservative PMs from 2016: Theresa May July 2016–July 2019, Boris Johnson July 2019–September 2022, Liz Truss September 2022–October 2022, Rishi Sunak October 2022.
2 UK will be used as a shorthand for the United Kingdom of Great Britain and Northern Ireland in the rest of this book.
3 Used to refer to when a business or country transfers growing or production process to another country where regulation, land, labour and taxes are lower.
4 This involves the extraction of ammonia from the air of which Nitrogen is a key component. Carbon dioxide (CO_2) is a by-product of this process. The process uses large amounts of energy and the increase in energy prices linked to the war in Ukraine has increased costs significantly.

References

Ansani, A. & Daniele, V. 2012, "The economic motivations of the Arab Spring", *International Journal of Development and Conflict*, vol. 18, no. 2(03), p. 1250013. https://doi.org/10.1142/S2010269012500135

Barosh, L., Friel, S., Engelhardt, K. & Chan, L. 2014, "The cost of a healthy and sustainable diet – who can afford it?", *Australian and New Zealand Journal of Public Health*, vol. 38, no. 1, pp. 7–12. https://doi.org/10.1111/1753-6405.12158

Barrett, C.B. & Maxwell, D.G. 2005, *Food Aid After Fifty Years: Recasting Its Role*, Routledge, London.

Belasco, W. 2007, *Appetite for Change: How the Counteculture Took on the Food Industry and Won*. 2nd edn, Cornell University Press, New York.

Beveridge, W.H. 1928, *British Food Control*, Humphrey Milford, London.

Biermann, F., Kanie, N. & Kim, R.E. 2017, "Global governance by goal-setting: the novel approach of the UN Sustainable Development Goals", *Current Opinion in Environmental Sustainability*, vol. 26–27, pp. 26–31. https://doi.org/10.1016/j.cosust.2017.01.010

Blas, J. & Farchy, J. 2021, *The World for Sale: Money, Power and the Traders Who Barter the Earth's Resources*, Random House Business, London.

Brockway, A.F. 1932, *Hungry England*, Victor Gollancz, London.

Cabinet Office 2008, *Food Matters Towards a Strategy for the 21st Century*, Cabinet Office, HM Government, London.

Chang, H. 2022, *Edible Economics: A Hungry Economist Explains the World*, Allen Lane, Great Britian.

Clements, K.W. & Si, J. 2018, "Engel's law, diet diversity, and the quality of food consumption", *American Journal of Agricultural Economics*, vol. 100, no. 1, pp. 1–22. https://doi.org/10.1093/ajae/aax053

Collingham, L. 2017, *The Hungry Empire: How Britain's Quest for Food Shaped the Modern World*, The Bodley Head, London.

Cooper, N. & Dumpleton, S. 2013, *Walking the Breadline: The Scandal of Food Poverty in 21st-Century Britain*, Church Action on Poverty, Oxford.

Dimbleby, H. 2021, *National Food Strategy, Independent Review: The Plan*, https://www.nationalfoodstrategy.org.

Dimbleby, H. 2020, *The National Food Strategy: Part One – July 2020*, DEFRA, London.

Dimbleby, H. & Lewis, J. 2023, *Ravenous: How to get ourselves and our planet into shape*, Profile Books, London.

Fearnley-Whittingstall, J. 2010, *The Ministry of Food*, Hodder and Stoughton, Frome.

Food Ethics Council 2022, *Responding to the Government Food Strategy*, Food Ethics Council, https://www.foodethicscouncil.org/resource/government-food-strategy-response/.

Food Foundation 2021, *A Crisis within a Crisis: The Impact of Covid-19 on Household Food Security*, Food Foundation, London.

George, S. 2010, *Whose Crises, Whose Future? Towards a Greener, Fairer, Richer World*, Polity Press, Cambridge.

George, S. 1986, *How the Other Half Dies: The Real Reasons for World Hunger*, Penguin, Harmondsworth.

Giller, K.E., Delaune, T., Silva, J.V., Descheemaeker, K., van de Ven, G., Schut, A.G.T., van Wijk, M., Hammond, J., Hochman, Z., Taulya, G., Chikowo, R., Narayanan, S., Kishore, A., Bresciani, F., Teixeira, H.M., Andersson, J.A. & van Ittersum, M.K. 2021, "The future of farming: who will produce our food?", *Food Security*, vol. 13, no. 5, pp. 1073–1099. https://doi.org/10.1007/s12571-021-01184-6

Goodbody, W. 2022, *Nestlé to Pay Cocoa Growers to Keep Children in School*, Radió Telefís Éireann (RTE), https://www.rte.ie/news/business/2022/0127/1276133-nestle/.

Hammond, R.J. 1954, *Food and Agriculture in Britain 1939–45: Aspects of Wartime Control*, Stanfoprd University Press, Stanford, CA.

Hammond, R.J. 1951, *Food, Volume 1. The Growth of Policy*, H.M.S.O., London.

Hebinck, A., Galli, F., Arcuri, S., Carroll, B., O'Connor, D. & Oostindie, H. 2018, "Capturing change in European food assistance practices: a transformative social innovation perspective", *Local Environment*, vol. 23, no. 4, pp. 398–413. https://doi.org/10.1080/13549839.2017.1423046

Johnstone, S. & Mazo, J. 2011, "Global warming and the Arab Spring", *Survival*, vol. 53, no. 2, pp. 11–17. https://doi.org/10.1080/00396338.2011.571006

Kickbusch, I. & Buckett, K. 2010, *Implementing Health in All Polcies*, Government of South Australia, Adelaide.

Kinealy, C. & Moran, G. 2020, *Irish Famines before and after the Great Hunger*, Quinnipiac University Press, Spain.

Kobayashi, Y., Heinrich, T. & Bryant, K.A. 2021, "Public support for development aid during the COVID-19 pandemic", *World Development*, no. 138, p. 105248. https://doi.org/10.1016/j.worlddev.2020.105248

Kropotkin, P. 2008, *The Conquest of Bread*, AK Press, Oakland, CA.

Kynaston, D. 2007, *Austerity Britian 1945–51*, Bloomsbury, London.

Lacy-Nichols, J. & Williams, O. 2021, "'Part of the solution': food corporation strategies for regulatory capture and legitimacy", *International Journal of Health Policy Management*, vol. 10, no. 12, pp. 845–856. https://doi.org/10.34172/ijhpm.2021.111

Lang, T. 2022a, "Boris Johnson's food strategy fails to address food poverty and the cost-of-living crisis", *The New Statesman*, [Online], vol. 13th June, pp. 15th June. Available from: https://www.newstatesman.com/environment/food-farming/2022/06/boris-johnsons-food-strategy-fails-to-address-food-poverty-and-the-cost-of-living-crisis.

Lang, T. 2022b, "Food Policy in a changing world: implications for nutritionists", *Proceedings of the Nutrition Society*, pp. 1–26, https://doi.org/10.1017/S0029665122000817

Lang, T. 2020, *Feeding Britain: Our Food Problems and How to Fix Them*, Pelican, London.

Lang, T., Barling, D. & Caraher, M. 2009, *Food Policy: Integrating Health, Environment and Society*, Oxford University Press, Oxford.

Lang, T. & Mason, P. 2018, "Sustainable diet policy development: implications of multi-criteria and other approaches, 2008–2017", *Proceedings of the Nutrition Society*, vol. 77, no. 3, pp. 331–346. https://doi.org/10.1017/S0029665117004074

Lang, T. & McKee, M. 2022, "The reinvasion of Ukraine threatens global food supplies", *BMJ*, vol. 376, p. o676.

Lau, M. 2022, *China can't count on global markets for food security, Xi Jinping says*, 7th March edn, South China Morning Post, https://www.scmp.com/news/china/politics/article/3169467/china-cant-count-global-markets-food-security-xi-jinping-says.

Le Gros Clark, F. & Titmuss, R. 1939, *Our Food Problem: A Study of National Security*, Penguin Books, Harmondsworth.

Leissle, K. 2018, *Cocoa*, Polity, Cambridge, UK.

Marston, G. & McDonald, C. 2006, *Analysing Social Policy: A Governmental Approach*, Edward Elgar, Cheltenham.

Mason, P. & Lang, T. 2017, *Sustainable Diets: How Ecological Nutrition Can Transform Consumption and the Food System*, Routledge, London.

McGoey, K. 2015, *No Such Thing as a Free Gift: The Gates Foundation and the Price of Philanthropy*, Verso, London.

McKeon, N. 2021, "Global Food Governance", *Development*, vol. 64, pp. 172–180. https://doi.org/10.1057/s41301-021-00299-9

Mitchell, S. 2017, *Struggle or Starve: Working-Class Unity in Belfast's 1932 Outdoor Relief Riots*, Haymarket Books, Chicago, IL.

Moyo, D. 2010, *Dead Aid: Why Aid Is Not Working and How There Is a Better Way for Africa*, Penguin, London.

Nunn, N. & Qian, N. 2014, "US Food Aid and Civil Conflict", *American Economic Review*, vol. 104, no. 6, pp. 1630–1666.

Orr, J.B. 1966, *As I Recall*, MacGibbon & Kee, London.

Orr, J.B. 1936, *Food, Health and Income: Report on a Survey of Adequacy of Diet in Relation to Income*, MacMillan & Co, London.

Orr, J.B. & Lubbock, D. 1940, *Feeding the People in War-Time*, MacMillan and Co, London.

Owen, G. 2020, *'Britain doesn't need farmers', leaked emails claim: Major new Whitehall storm erupts over incendiary suggestions made by Dominic Cummings' adviser after Number 10 brands senior mandarin who quit over Priti Patel row 'Sir Calamity*, [Online edn], MailOnline, https://www.dailymail.co.uk/news/article-8060473/Britain-doesnt-need-farmers-reveal-leaked-emails-senior-government-official.html.

Oxfam. 2022, *Profiting from Pain*, Oxfam, https://oi-files-d8-prod.s3.eu-west-2.amazonaws.com/s3fs-public/2022-05/Oxfam%20Media%20Brief%20-%20EN%20-%20Profiting%20From%20Pain%2C%20Davos%202022%20Part%202.pdf.

Parsons, K. & Barling, D. 2022, "England's food policy coordination and the Covid-19 response", *Food Security*, https://doi.org/10.1007/s12571-022-01280-1

Parsons, K. & Hawkes, C. 2019, *Brief 4: Embedding Food in All Policies*, Centre for Food Policy, London.

Peña, M. & Bacallao, J. 2000, *Obesity and Poverty: A New Public Health Challenge. Scientific Publication no 576*, Pan American Health Organization, Washington, DC.

Power, M. 2022, *Hunger, Whiteness and Religion in Neoliberal Britain: An Inequality of Power*, Policy Press, Bristol.

Richards, C., Kjærnes, U. & Vik, J. 2016, "Food security in welfare capitalism: comparing social entitlements to food in Australia and Norway", *Journal of Rural Studies*, vol. 43, pp. 61–70.

Riches, G. & Silvasti, T. 2014, *First World Hunger Revisited: Food Charity or the Right to Food?* 2nd edn, Palgrave Macmillan, Basingstoke.

Rieff, D. 2016, *The Reproach of Hunger: Food, Justice and Money in the 21st Century*, Verso, London.

Rieff, D. 2015, *Philanthrocapitalism: A Self-Love Story: Why Do Super-Rich Activists Mock Their Critics Instead of Listening to Them?*, 1st October edn, The Nation, https://www.thenation.com/article/archive/philanthrocapitalism-a-self-love-story/.

Schneider, M. 2022, *How a living income can help remake cocoa farming*, Nestlé, https://www.nestle.com/stories/living-income-cocoa-farming-responsible-sourcing.

Seabrook, J. 2013, *Pauperland: Poverty and the Poor in Britain*, Hurst and Co., London.

Sitwell, W. 2017, *Eggs or Anarchy: The Remarkable Story of the Man Tasked with the Impossible: To Feed a Nation at War*, Simon and Schuster, London.

Slater, S., Baker, P. & Lawrence, M. 2022, "An analysis of the transformative potential of major food system report recommendations", *Global Food Security*, vol. 32, p. 100610.

Smith, D. & Nicolson, M. 1995, "Nutrtion, Education, Ignorance and Income: A Twentieth Century Debate" in *The Science and Culture of Nutrition 1840–1940*, eds. H. Kamminga & A. Cunningham, Rodopi, Amsterdam, pp. 288–318.

Smyth, C. 2021, *Johnson sours hopes of a sugar tax*, Friday July 16th, No 73625, page 6 edn, *The Times*, London.

Stitt, S. & Prisk, E. 1997, "A Ministry of Food for Britain for 21st Century?", *Nutr Health*, vol. 12, no. 1, pp. 1–15. https://doi.org/10.1177/026010609701200101

Taylor, B. 2010, "Why nobody wins unless everybody wins", *Harvard Business Review*, https://hbr.org/2010/12/why-nobody-wins-unless-everybo.

Thaler, R.H. & Sunstein, C.R. 2009, *Nudge: Improving Decisions about Health, Wealth and Happiness*, New international edn, Penguin, London.

Torres Pabón, G. 2019, "What food do we buy and how much do we spend on it? Socioeconomic conditions and budget for food consumption (Colombia, 1993–2014)", *Revista Colombiana de Sociología*, vol. 42, no. 2, pp. 191–228.

Various Public Interest, Health, and Citizens' Groups 2017, *Open Letter to the Executive Board of the World Health Organization: Re: Conflict of interest safeguards far too weak to protect WHO from influence of regulated industries (the case of the Bill and Melinda Gates Foundation)*, Open Letter, http://healthscienceandlaw.ca/wp-content/uploads/2017/01/Public-Interest-Position.WHO_.FENSAGates.Jan2017.pdf.

Vernon, J. 2007, *Hunger: A Modern History*, The Belknap Press of Harvard University Press, Cambridge, MA; London.

Wells, R. & Caraher, M. 2014, "UK print media coverage of the food bank phenomenon: from food welfare to food charity?", *British Food Journal*, vol. 116, no. 9, pp. 1426–1445. https://doi.org/10.1108/BFJ-03-2014-0123

White, M. 2022, "Half hearted and half baked: the government's new food strategy", *BMJ*, vol. 377, p. o1520. doi: https://doi.org/10.1136/bmj.o1520

Woodham-Smith, C. 1962, *The Great Hunger: Ireland 1845–1849,* 1st edn, Harper and Row, New York.

World Health Organization 2021, *COP26 Special Report on Climate Change and Health: The Health Argument for Climate Action*, World Health Organization, Geneva.

Yap, C. 2022, *Leaked Food Strategy vs Published Strategy: A Side by Side Analysis*, https://fixourfood.org/leaked-strategy-vs-published-strategy-a-side-by-side-analysis/.

Zimmerman, C.C. 1932, "Ernst Engel's law of expenditures for food", *The Quarterly Journal of Economics*, vol. 47, no. 1, pp. 78–101.

2 Food policy in the UK

From public health and nutrition to sustainable diets

Introduction

This chapter provides a background to the origins of food policy in the UK detailing influences at different epochs and how social, commercial and financial conditions and views have influenced the form and degree of intervention that currently modern food policy takes. This helps establish the basis for the other chapters by providing some underpinning, using examples of past influences and key theoretical concepts. It also details some models of food policy which are distinguished by the differences between "research for food policy" and "research on and of food policy". These are essentially two different perspectives: the former is where research is used to inform food policy initiatives; the latter is then an examination of how, in practice, food policy is formulated and enacted. The Overton Window will be used in this and other chapters to help make sense of the changing and sometimes not changing nature of food policy. Signposts to a number of food policy models are provided to show how food policy is currently developing (Newman, 2013, Szałek, 2013, Hawkes & Parsons, 2019, Parsons, 2019, 2022, Parsons & Hawkes, 2019a, 2019b, Parsons, Hawkes & Wells, 2019).

We all eat, and food policy has an ambition to cover the gamut of activities from farm to fork (paddock to plate, farm to flush, soil to society), and this includes a concern with the control of food systems at a global level (Newman, 2013). Food policy, as an academic subject, lays claim to the study of the relationship between all these areas and how policies are developed or not developed despite the weight of the evidence. Food policy can cover enormous and diverse terrains with numerous claims to being inter- or multidisciplinary (Lang, Barling & Caraher, 2009). Existing food policies can be broadly divided into two groups; the first are those that have nutritional health as their focus and the second group is agricultural/processing policies (Bronner, 1997, Milo & Helsing 1998). This is despite calls for the development of joint food and nutrition policies by the World Health Organization following the 1992 International Conference on Nutrition (World Health Organization, Food and Agricultural Organization, 1992). Egger and Swinburn make the link between nutrition and the planetary issues in the subtitle of their book *How we're eating ourselves and the planet to death* (Egger & Swinburn, 2010). There is another argument that food policy should not become a distinct area of endeavour seeking instead to become part of, and embedded in, other policies. Like the concept of health in all policies, the argument is that food should be in all policies (Kickbusch & Buckett, 2010, Lawless et al., 2012). This in reality is difficult to achieve and the fallback position is often to develop a separate food policy to act as an umbrella for actions in different spheres. This often takes the form of a nutrition-based policy and/or a separate agricultural one, often with some cross reference to other policies (Milo & Helsing, 1998, Caraher & Coveney, 2004). Of course, the greater the overlap between these two areas, the more an integrated approach is achieved. In practice,

DOI: 10.4324/9781003260301-2

production and consumption are often separated in the real world of policymaking. Part of the function of the academic discipline of food policy is to analyse and explain why this is to provide ways forward in policymaking.

This breadth of potential coverage of food policy is both its strength and also its weakness, as it struggles to build its evidence base both "for" and "of" food policy. Actions in the name of one area of interest can have a knock-on effect elsewhere. Food policy from the 1950s onwards has been marked by a patchwork of policies in issues as wide ranging as trade policy, price controls, nutrition and agriculture. There have been attempts to link healthy diets with sustainable production. Mason and Lang propose a multi-criteria, six-pronged approach to sustainable diets, giving equal weight to nutrition and public health, the environment, sociocultural issues, food quality, economics and governance (Mason & Lang, 2017, Lang & Mason, 2018). This latter perspective can also be incorporated under the taxonomy of ultra-processed foods (UPFs) called the NOVA classification. For England, the food systems diagram (Figure 2.1) from Parsons,

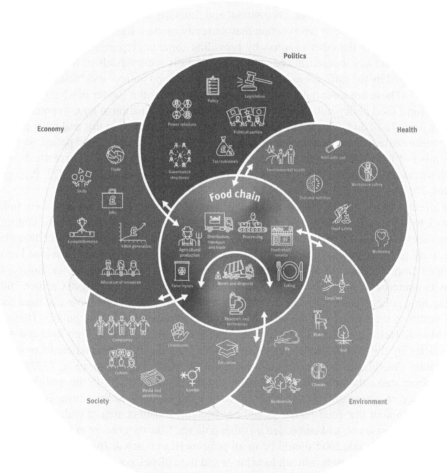

Figure 2.1 Depiction of the food system.

Source: Parsons, Hawkes and Wells (2019).

Hawkes and Wells (2019) considers how the food system food policy can attempt to escape food policy silos for more on this see chapter 5.

Parsons identified 16 English government departments that have a say in food policy (Sharpe, Parsons & Hawkes, 2020, Parsons, 2021). The lead agency is the Department for Environment, Food and Rural Affairs (DEFRA). In 2002, following the foot-and-mouth disease outbreak among cattle, DEFRA was established and took over the functions of the Ministry of Agriculture, Fisheries and Food combined with some other food functions from the Department of the Environment, Transport and the Regions (DETR) and the Home Office (National Audit Office, 2002).

For England, in 2020 and 2021, independent reports from Henry Dimbleby, non-executive director at DEFRA, were produced (Dimbleby, 2020, 2021). The 2021 "National Food Strategy: The Plan" (NFS) made a plea for an integrated approach to food policy. The response to the final strategy document has been weak, and not just that, but the formal response has been weak with many of the suggested ideas being ignored (Dimbleby & Lewis, 2023). At the same time, due to political turbulence in Parliament, some previously enacted pieces of legislation were threatened with being withdrawn[1] (Department for Environment Food & Rural Affairs (DEFRA), 2022, Food Ethics Council, 2022, Goodwin, 2022, White, 2022).

Plans to tackle obesity continue to be released as drip-feed initiatives; there are concerns that obesity policy is not fit for purpose and that despite "government-proposed obesity policies in England (n = 689) within obesity strategies (n =14) over almost three decades (1992–2020) there has been a failure to learn lessons from policy failures" (Theis & White, 2021). This process of drip-feeding initiatives continued in February 2022, with a commitment to ensuring school lunches in England meet national standards contained in a White Paper on tackling inequality between the regions; but we know that the existing school food standards are not being met or monitored (Dimbleby & Vincent, 2013, Dimbleby, 2021). Additionally, there are plans as part of a "levelling-up agenda" to allow GPs "to prescribe vouchers for fresh fruit and vegetables" and "cooking lessons and nutritional education". Close reading of these proposals makes it clear that these are to be pilots and not widespread initiatives across the UK. The NFS was ambitious and in some instances radical in its proposals (the introduction of sugar and fat taxes) and clearly called for an integrated approach to food policy, but the scenario described above shows the difficulty in achieving coherence in policymaking as policy drip feeds from different departments and linked to different agendas.

The author of the NFS resigned his official role as a government advisor and said the "so-called 'Government Food Strategy that was unveiled in June 2022, in response to my review, is not a strategy at all. It is merely a handful of disparate policy ideas, many of them chosen because they are unlikely to raise much of a media storm" (Dimbleby, Lewis, 2023, page 17) .

So what is food policy or what should it be?

It is more and more recognised that food policy is, or should be, the set of policies that influence the food system, not separate nutrition or agricultural policies. This is captured in the following definition by Pinstrup-Andersen and Watson who said:

> Food policies are plans of action related to the food system. More specifically, food policy consists of the setting of goals for the food system or its parts, including natural resources, production, processing, marketing, food consumption & safety, & nutrition, and determining the processes of achieving these goals.
>
> (Pinstrup-Andersen & Watson II, 2011, p. 29)

A lot of academic work has focussed on food policy within a public policy context, and this is certainly where its roots lie. Guba (1984) identified eight different types of policy:

1 An assertion of intents or goals.
2 The accumulated decision of a governing body to guide that which is within its sphere of control (directly/indirectly).
3 A guide to discretionary action.
4 A strategy used to solve or ameliorate a problem.
5 Sanctioned behaviour, either informally or formally.
6 A norm of conduct.
7 An output of the policy making system.
8 The effect of the policy making and policy implementation system.

Birkland identifies multiple definitions of what constitutes public policy and that public policies have several common characteristics, such as (i) they are decisions of the government to implement or not; (ii) they involve governmental and non-governmental actors; (iii) they are motivated by public welfare; and (iv) they are oriented towards a general objective, such as the solution of a social problem (Birkland, 2015). So, to the eight above, we add that of non-intervention or the decision not to implement a policy.

Table 2.1 contains a list of definitions of food policy. Many of the definitions assume a logical approach to food policy development and do not fully acknowledge the influence of powerful players such as "Big Food" or the fact that non-action can itself be a policy approach. They are, in fact, what food policy should be and not what it is in practice. Again, think of the distinction between research of policy "for" food policy and research "on or of" food policy in practice.

Table 2.1 A list of definitions of food policy

Definition
Food policy is a strategy that views the food economy and policies relating to it in an integrated way and in a broad economic and political context (Organization for Economic Co-Operation and Development, 1981).
Food policy encompasses the collective efforts of governments to influence the decision-making environment of food producers, food consumers and food marketing agents in order to further social objectives (Timmer, Falcon & Pearson, 1983).
Food policy and nutrition policy can best be considered together, as they both concern the food supply. Food and nutrition policy as a whole may be defined as a concerted set of actions based on scientific principles, intended to ensure the safety and nutritional quality of the food supply and the accessibility of affordable and properly labelled food to all population groups and that encourage and facilitate the healthy use of food (Milo & *Helsing*, 1998).
The decision-making that shapes the way the world of food operates and is controlled (Lang & Heasman, 2004).
Food policy constitutes the policies that shape who eats what, when, where and how much (Lang, Barling & Caraher, 2009).
Food policy encompasses laws, regulations, decisions and actions by governments and other institutions that influence food production, distribution and consumption (Wilde, 2018).
"Food policy" comprises the policies that influence and shape the food system – everything and everybody involved in producing, storing, packing, processing, distributing, consuming and disposing of food. Integrated food policies take account of the interconnections in the food system to enable nutrition, health, environmental, social and economic goals to be delivered more coherently. Inclusive food policies take account of people's voices and experiences across the food system to enable goals to be delivered more effectively and equitably (Centre for Food Policy, n.d.).

The process of policymaking is influenced by powerful lobbies and financial interests (Clapp & Scrinis, 2017, Nestle, 2018, Sacks et al., 2018, Wood, Ruskin & Sacks, 2020, Baker et al., 2021, Lauber, Rutter & Gilmore, 2021). As we noted in Chapter 1, large corporations or trans-national companies (TNCs) are developing welfare policies for their suppliers, including setting up pension schemes and paying growers to send their children to school. In welfare studies, this is referred to as welfare economies or welfare capitalism. For food policy, this may represent a new dimension for study (Goodbody, 2022). The involvement of vested interests such as the food industry in policymaking is contentious, especially when it involves unhealthy commodity industries (UCIs). This development by the private sector moves beyond being involved and influencing public or government food policy to the industry developing its own set of food policies.

What the definitions in Table 2.1 have in common is that food policies should *intervene* and *influence* some aspect of the food system. But, in many instances, they are not specific about the range of influences. Milo and Helsing, (1998) referring to policymaking in the WHO European region, point out that the problem is often one of linking different departments:

> The gap between the departments of agriculture and health, however, often seemed dif-ficult to bridge. There is nevertheless hope that, with more consumer concern about food and health, common interests will bring these sectors together again.
>
> (p. 1)

We see the continuation of this divide in the development of food policies in the UK. Parsons (2020) refers to DEFRA in England and its role in food policy as a "super ministry". The fact that the NFS was coordinated through DEFRA supports this contention and is reinforced by its broad remit for food, farming, environment and rural affairs. In many ways, this supports the contention in Chapter 1 that economics and business influence the development of food policies and DEFRA has more links with business and farming than the Department of Health. The inter-connectedness and sometimes even the disconnect between these various areas and departments often form the ground for research on food policy (Panjwani & Caraher, 2014, Knai et al., 2015, Panjwani & Caraher, 2018). Much food policy is still silo policymaking, and often involves battles between government departments and outside agencies over territory and the relative importance of areas such as health versus jobs in the food industry (Lang, Barling & Caraher, 2009, Carey et al., 2016, Lacy-Nichols & Williams, 2021).

Conceptual models of policymaking

There is a wider literature on policy development within the social sciences and this has had an influence on food policy academics. Some, such as Smith (2013), have outlined the following distinctions between different models of policymaking:

1 **Knowledge-driven** model, where research findings provide pressure or evidence for policy, often in health research.
2 **Problem-solving** model, where a policy problem is identified and research is meant to address the gap.
3 **Political model**, where selective research is often used to support predetermined policy, for example, welfare reform.
4 **Tactical model**, research or lack of research is used to delay decision-making.

5   **Two community model** policymakers and experts/academics, although more often lobby and interest groups.
6   **Interactive model**, where research is but one component of a complex process.
7   **Enlightenment model** addresses over a period of time ideas about how policy should be addressed.

There is a more cynical approach among policy influencers who talk about policy action being more of the "whack-a-mole" approach. When a problem appears, devise a policy to solve it; but this lacks a preventive approach. We see this with food scandals such as that related to BSE (mad cow disease) and the scandal over horsemeat in the beef supply chain. There is also a feeling that policymaking can occur in the absence of evidence and that evidence sometimes seeks a policy home as well as policy makers seeking evidence.

Table 2.2 outlines some of the key theoretical models concerned with policymaking that food policy analysts have adopted for their own use. The key references refer to those who have developed the models or theories and are followed by where they have been used for food policy analysis.

Many of the above models are used to frame research work and to help describe the findings from food policy research. They are often used by food policy researchers to frame their research agendas, often as the epistemological basis.

Upstream versus downstream approaches to food policy

Public health-based food policy has much to say about the level of intervention adopted. Geoffrey Rose in his book *The strategy of preventive medicine* pointed out that we do not just have "high risk people", we also have "high risk populations" (Rose, Khaw & Marmot, 2008). A *population strategy* is one that aims to change everybody's behaviour. For example, raising tax on cigarettes is a population strategy to cut down smoking benefiting both smokers and nonsmokers the later from the effects of secondhand or passive smoking. This strategy can also be used in the primary care arena of information and education. Those working in primary care can provide a constant "feed" of information – about cutting down salt intake, cutting down on cigarettes, taking more exercise – not just to people who are thought to be at high risk of heart disease or cancer, but to everybody who comes to the surgery. A "fat tax" or a "food tax" could be introduced to influence behaviour at a population level supported by work at the primary care level to help people make healthier choices.

A *high-risk strategy* means intervening only with those who are seen to be at high risk. The problem is that in order to identify those at high risk, it is necessary first to have some way of either screening *everyone* or filtering out those not at risk. The current, most used measures include high blood pressure, body mass index (BMI) and cholesterol screening.

Reviews of policy evidence show that upstream approaches based on regulation, mandatory reformulation and subsidies are more effective than those that rely on downstream interventions reliant on voluntary agreements, behaviour change and education (see Figure 2.2). The two approaches are not mutually exclusive, but the upstream approaches are population-based (these can be communities, groups or areas such as a city) as compared to downstream approaches which tend to focus on individual behaviour change (Theis & White, 2021). Labelling of takeaway and restaurant food is less effective than reformulation strategies (Adams et al., 2016, Goodman et al., 2018). The focus of public health is prevention by reducing exposure to risk, not treatment or amelioration of existing conditions. This difference can be illustrated by a poem from Joseph Malins, a temperance activist, from 1895 called the "The Ambulance Down in the Valley". This presented as an allegory a community debate whether to build a fence at the top of a cliff to prevent people falling or to provide an ambulance at

Table 2.2 Models of policy development

Theory	Strengths	Limitations
Multiple Streams Theory.	The emphasis is on the role of individual agency. Often does not account for institutional power. Provides simple and practical applications in how alternative policies are selected and agendas are set. Fluid and flexible model. Emphasises the importance of ideas in policy and how they emerge by their adoption and rejection by decision-makers. Likened to paradigm shifts in policy ideas/fashion. Can account for "fashions", e.g. sugar, saturated fats, trans-fats. Based on the work of Kingdon (2010) can take a quantitative form.	May not address collective action and coordination among participants. Downplays the role of institutions in the policymaking process, believes institutions make things possible, but people make things happen. Does not address or fully explain the independence of policy streams and tensions. Often does not account for actors keeping streams apart as a policy process – de facto a policy, albeit policy aversion.

Key references
Zahariadis (2007), Kingdon (2010), Cullerton et al. (2016a).

Theory	Strengths	Limitations
Advocacy Coalition Framework.	Can help clarify how interested actors/stakeholders interact to influence public policy or policy change within a specific policy subsystem over time. Highlights the role of scientific and technical information. Explains why conflict is about value differences rather than technical deficiencies.	Provides a complex framework yet does not fully explain policy change, with little explanation on the required conditions for policy-oriented collective action to take place. Places an emphasis on external shocks as the main reason for policy change. Neglects the role of individual choice. Assumes individuals do not act of their own accord, only as part of a coalition. Danger that intergovernmental relations are the only institutional choices recognised, industry power is hidden. Concept of power not operationalised.

Key references
Sabatier and Weible (2014), Zahariadis (2007), Page and Caraher (2020).

(Continued)

Table 2.2 (Continued)

Theory	Strengths	Limitations
Punctuated Equilibrium Theory.	This places dual emphasis on political institutions and boundedly rational decision-making. The attention paid to the dynamics of problem definition, policy images and venues of action is helpful for advocates. Ideas, individual actors and their interests are crucial. Incorporates the role of power. Paradigm shifts in knowledge, fashion or concern are seen as key to providing the fulcrums for policy change.	A general, descriptive theory, in that it does not make specific predictions for particular policy issues. Focuses on bottom-up policymaking, neglecting how preferences can be shaped from above. Limited explanation for change. Assumes there are key points where policy has a greater chance of being implemented. Assumes a Kuhnian perspective on policy change, where a paradigm shift in view or evidence contributes to policy shifts (Kuhn, 1970).

Key references
True, Jones and Baumgartner (2007).

Theory	Strengths	Limitations
Public Policy.	Often based on two community theses of actor networks located around researchers and policymakers. Now expanded to include civil society. Relies on evidence-based policy or the equivalent evidence-based medicine approach.	Assumes interactions between the two policy communities are the key. Oversimplifies policy process. Limited explanation for change built on Caplan's two communities model, now three communities to include civil society (Caplan, 1979).

Key references
O'Connor and Netting (2011), Buse, Mays and Walt (2012), Cairney (2012).

Theory	Strengths	Limitations
Policy Network Analysis.	Combines all of the above but assumes a rational basis for policy decision-making. Assumes interactions between actors. Can account for policy champions and entrepreneurs.	As above, under Public Policy.

Key references
Walt and Gilson (1994), Walt et al. (2008), Cullerton et al. (2016b), Caraher et al. (2013).

Theory	Strengths	Limitations
Food in all policies.	Attempts to locate health in all policies. Often led by public health and nutrition concerns and professionals. Food is clearly identified in policies.	May become a tick box exercise for non-health departments and interests. May fail to achieve coherence and coordination.

(Continued)

Table 2.2 (Continued)

Theory	Strengths	Limitations
Key references Kickbusch and Buckett (2010), Parsons and Hawkes (2019a, 2019b).	A food system approach. Looks at the food system in its entirety.	Can assume an effectiveness and efficiency approach to the dominant food system.
Key references George (1990), Ingram (2011), Fanzo et al. (2020), Parsons, Hawkes and Wells (2019).		
Equity and rights.	What is the outcome of a policy decision, intervention, Marmot and Wilkinson thesis.	Sometimes difficult to operationalise in or for food policy.
Key references Marmot (2020), Lindberg, Rose and Caraher (2016), Wilkinson and Pickett (2018)		
Government versus governance models.	Shift from government (public policy) to "governance", including or by the private sector. Institutions, state and non-state. How governance or non-governance occurs.	Hard to define boundaries.
Key references Keating and Davis (2000), Sabatier and Weible (2014), Rhodes (1997), Cairney (2012), Boswell, Cairney and St Denny (2019).		
Policy as an idea/ Narrative Policy Frameworks.	Core issue is not about the effectiveness or otherwise of evidence on unhealthy foods but the war of ideas. Compelling ideas are often based on notions of individual freedom and the power of the "nanny state". Can account for paradigm shifts in policy ideas/fashion. Places ideas within a network society model.	Abstract and hard to operationalise research.
Key references Smith (2013), Caraher and Perry (2017), McBeth, Jones and Shanahan (2014).		

Source: Adapted from Parsons (2017) and Page (2020).

the bottom to treat the injuries resulting from falls. The call for an ambulance carried the day as it was visible and offered theatre with its flashing lights and drama. Many current debates over food policy reflect this debate, with the emphasis on picking people up after they have fallen as opposed to stopping them falling in the first place. The argument is not an either/or scenario but a reflection on structure versus behaviour and a potential cost argument. Although prevention may be more cost-effective in the long run, it requires an upfront investment and policymakers such as politicians are often reluctant to invest in actions from which they will not see an immediate return. The modern equivalent of the ambulance with its flashing lights is the opening of a new facility to treat those already ill or sick. The preventive fence might be an increase in taxes on unhealthy food or investment in more preventive health services such as community interventions, which are less popular and less visible (Acheson, 1998). The work of Sir Michael Marmot is key in this area, with its focus on structural and commercial determinants (Marmot, 2005, Marmot, 2015). Others have focused on commercial determinants or the impact of the food industry on food policy (Clapp & Scrinis, 2017, Sacks et al., 2018, Lauber, Rutter & Gilmore, 2021).

With its roots in public health and public health nutrition, food policy has a focus on prevention at the primary and secondary levels and less so on tertiary or treatment levels. So, with obesity, the focus on food policy is on food at the level of primary care and early prevention and not on treatment or rehabilitation of those who are obese.

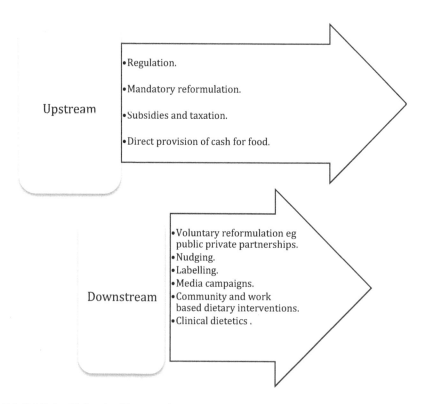

Figure 2.2 Public health levels of intervention.

Source: Adapted from and based on McLaren, McIntyre and Kirkpatrick (2010).

The Overton Window

The Overton Window, named after American political scientist Joseph Overton, can be used as a way of locating policies within different epochs and explaining why at different times different approaches to food policy are more or less acceptable (see Figure 2.3) (Szałek, 2013, Balaji, Seeberger & Hennedige, 2018). Its benefits are that it allows us to see where policymakers and politicians seek consensus over action. The influences can be formal evidence, costs of actions versus cost of not taking action, opinion polls, focus groups or lobbying by vested food industry groups. In past times, the latter might have been the influence of powerful figures such as politicians, landowners or "captains of industry". Smith calls this the "war of ideas" where competing narratives vie for policy space (Smith 2013, Caraher & Perry, 2017). A problem with public health food narratives is they are often negative in orientation; so, messages are often focused around don't consume this, cut back, take more exercise and so on. Food industry narratives on the other hand tend towards the positive, so indulge yourself, just have one more piece, doesn't it taste nice, this is value for money, you deserve it, our industry creates lots of jobs and so on.

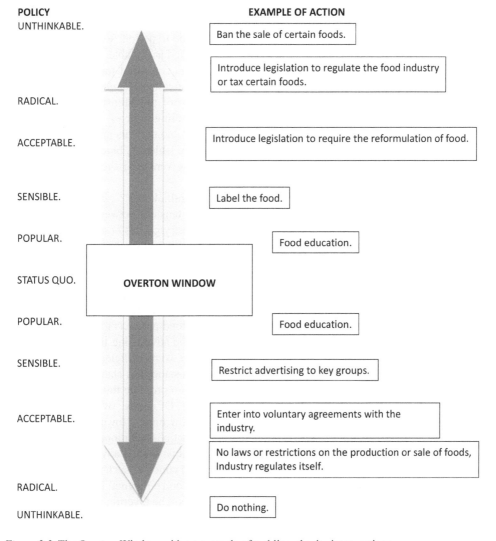

POLICY	EXAMPLE OF ACTION
UNTHINKABLE.	Ban the sale of certain foods.
	Introduce legislation to regulate the food industry or tax certain foods.
RADICAL.	
ACCEPTABLE.	Introduce legislation to require the reformulation of food.
SENSIBLE.	Label the food.
POPULAR.	Food education.
STATUS QUO.	OVERTON WINDOW
POPULAR.	Food education.
SENSIBLE.	Restrict advertising to key groups.
ACCEPTABLE.	Enter into voluntary agreements with the industry.
	No laws or restrictions on the production or sale of foods, Industry regulates itself.
RADICAL.	
UNTHINKABLE.	Do nothing.

Figure 2.3 The Overton Window with an example of tackling obesity interventions.

The usefulness of the Overton Window for food policy analysis is that it helps us understand how policymakers come to a consensus and why policy can change in the light of public opinion and vary in the light of social mores from era to era. With this in mind, the Window can be used to contextualise the impacts of the various models, theories and approaches contained in Table 2.2. We will see in Chapter 4 how this changes over time with respect to food poverty while still maintaining a core view of poverty, its causes and responsibilities; an example is how the concepts of the "deserving" and "undeserving" poor play out, although changing over time to reflect social mores. The "Window" allows us to adopt an approach to policy, which argues that at key points in time, there is a limited range of policy options that are acceptable and that these parameters of acceptability change from time to time. This can be related to the changing social mores and values such as the industry advertising to children.

The Overton Window is not itself a model for policy planning but one that allows us to analyse policy acceptance retrospectively. Such acceptance is, of course, framed by circumstances and the prevailing social milieu; the modern connected world can be influenced by media reporting or political scandal. Acceptance ranges through the following: unthinkable, radical, acceptable, sensible, popular, radical and unthinkable, with the extremes of the vertical axis being represented by more choice/more control to less control/less choice (see Figure 2.3). With respect to the issues of choice, this can shift from period to period; so, during World War II (WWII), controls of food supply and rationing were deemed acceptable, but in the post-war period restrictions on choice were not popular. Rationing and control of food supply in WWII was not devised as a health issue but was an unintended outcome. Hammond in his opus on food control in WWII points out that the primary function of the Ministry of Food was to ensure food supply, not to promote welfare and/or healthy eating policies. Rationing, he says, was "in no way an instrument for promoting better feeding" and that "its motive force was not philanthropy, but conservation; it owed its origin to the fear of isolation, blockade and industrial unrest" (p. 140). He argues that where rationing and subsidies were used, they were deployed as anti-inflationary measures, not to encourage healthy eating.

Such decisions, along vertical axis "unthinkable" to "unthinkable", can be influenced by pre-existing beliefs about the food system and food choices, tensions between health and trade, opinion polls, focus groups or lobbying by vested food industry groups or public concern. Use of the Overton Window does not suggest a reinterpretation of history, but merely provides a context to help us understand why certain food policy decisions were made at key points in time. It does not preclude the issue of alternative or countervailing views but that these did not hold sway in the decision-making process. For instance, the example of obesity and restricting advertising of foods to young people has changed over time. When this debate kicked off in the 1990s, the advertising industry saw it as a right to promote food products to young children on the basis that this prepared them to be future consumers. The advertising industry argued that education initiatives devised by them and taught in schools were sufficient to protect young people (Caraher, Landon & Dalmeny, 2006). Over time, this stance has changed, and while the food and advertising industries might still believe it is okay to promote foods to children, they are less likely to use the same arguments or rhetoric openly. Of course, over time the science of nutrition and food policy has improved, and we now know more. However, this additional scientific knowledge does not always result in appropriate action. Additionally, the social context has changed with the idea of protecting children from unwarranted advertising, now more generally acceptable. This is where the Overton Window and concepts such as that espoused by Smith (2013) about the war of ideas help us to contextualise food policymaking. If evidence was the basis for food policy, we would have lots of food policies. The Overton Window provides a backward look at how food policy has been implemented or avoided.

Historical influences of less eligibility and personal behaviours

To understand contemporary food policy, it helps to have some knowledge of the history of food policy in the UK, the repetitions and changes in emphasis. Although Barack Obama is known for the quote "the past is never dead", he borrowed the quote from William Faulkner who said "The past is never dead. It's not even past". The meaning of this is that the values from one era often transfer to the next, often dressed in new words and social context but still carrying the underlying beliefs of a time past (Faulkner, 2011, Seabrook, 2013). We will see more of this in Chapters 3 and 4, where the ideas about food poverty are passed down from one era to another while still holding the underpinning values of the deserving and undeserving poor, although the language used to describe the situation may change.

For practitioners, policymakers and influencers, it is important to have some knowledge of past failures and successes (Theis & White, 2021). Marx asserted in the last line of his "Theses on Feuerbach" that "the philosophers have only interpreted the world, in various ways. The point, however, is to change it". Despite the changing times, we can see the remnants of past beliefs and values in the formation of food policy. Who is deserving of welfare and why should we feed those who are not prepared to take care of themselves are questions that are continually asked of food policy.

One of the key arguments is that while the rhetoric, social influence and perceptions change over time, there are some issues that remain constant as influences in the Overton Window and its to food policy. So, two of these are the concepts of less eligibility and the focus on the individual within a victim blaming framework (Caraher, 2018).

The example of less eligibility

Those who experienced the stigma of the old and new poor law systems[2] and the workhouses came away stigmatised and determined to escape such institutions. Tressell's novel *The Ragged-Trousered Philanthropists*, published in 1914, captures these times through his description of the lives of working-class painters (Tressell, 2018). The novel's protagonists mainly eat bread and margarine, wear cast-off shoes, pawn their possessions, take in lodgers or take cheaper lodgings to save themselves from destitution. They die young from accidents in the workplace or exhaustion in the workhouse exacerbated by poor diets.

The various poor law acts of the 1840s and the Public Health Act of 1848 reflected concerns with the differences between the deserving and undeserving poor and the principle of "less eligibility", borrowing from their predecessor Elizabethan laws. The standard used for food relief was based on the principle that relief was set below minimum wage and the then known and understood nutritional levels – "less eligibility". The principle underpinning all of this was the prevention of pauperism and people presenting themselves to the workhouse for relief. Food provision in the workhouse was designed to act as a deterrent; the food given to a recipient of charity or welfare was calculated to be inferior to that provided to a member of the lowest significant equivalent social class in that society. This is a concept that can still be found in the operation and delivery of modern-day food policies (Seabrook, 2013). This principle still forms the basis of much policy formation, the mix of science and moral stances over standards related to food. The emerging science of nutrition in the mid-1800s was used to set ceiling standards above which the poor could not rise, as opposed to floor standards below which they should not fall. Those involved in setting standards for food poverty often feel compelled to set minimum standards under pressure from politicians alive to the prospect of the unwaged and those in receipt of food relief (many of whom were seen as the undeserving poor) being better off than the working or deserving poor.

Through the ages there were, of course, dissenting voices. The Quaker response to the Irish famine, An Gortá Mór, recognised the limits of charity relief in the face of an overwhelming crisis (Woodham-Smith, 1962, Kinealy, 2002). Another example of dissention was "The Minority Report of the Royal Commission on the Poor Laws and Relief of Distress". This influenced a generation of academics and thinkers, even if it did not immediately bring about changes in food policy. It did however set the tone for the Beveridge Report of 1942, which is a landmark in policy for the development of the post-WWII British state and welfare systems (Beveridge, 1942, Robson, 1963). The principle of "less eligibility" remained an underpinning principle of many food-related reforms and remained so until 1948 with the establishment of the Welfare state (Timmins, 2017). We will see examples of this in Chapters 3 and 4.

Vernon commenting on the 1942 Beveridge Report which was a key influence on the formation of the welfare state says that:

> Yet Beveridge's foundational text remained caught between the conception of welfare as a necessary social right and the conception of welfare as a form of disciplinary care: the former protecting the innocent from systemic failures beyond their control, the latter disciplining those who had failed to protect themselves from these misfortunes. In many ways it was absolutely 'the last and most glorious flowering of late Victorian philanthropy'.
>
> (Vernon, 2007, p. 256)

And Veit-Wilson in an analysis of the working documents of the same committee says that its proposals for benefit levels were inadequate as it knowingly:

> implemented the principles of minimum subsistence and less-eligibility in the face of inadequate wages, the proposed scales were arguably more austere even than Rowntree's 'primary poverty' standard which both he and Beveridge acknowledged was not sufficient to meet human social needs.
>
> (Veit-Wilson, 1992, p. 269)

The formation of modern food poverty standards still continues to be informed by the principles of the past and the deserving/undeserving poor dichotomy. Welfare relief is constituted so that it does not offer an advantage to those in receipt of welfare over and above those of an equivalent class in work. In 1979, a proponent of the New Right, politician Keith Joseph, suggested that:

> An absolute standard means one defined by reference to the actual needs of the poor and not by reference to the expenditure of those who are not poor. A family is poor if it cannot afford to eat. It is not poor if it cannot afford endless smokes and it does not become poor by the mere fact that other people can afford them.
>
> (Veit-Wilson, 1986)

In saying this, he launched a debate on the issue of the cycle of deprivation and how deprivation is transmitted, which continues to the present day.

Leather in 1992 pointed out that "modern malnutrition" had a new face and had not gone away but largely been hidden from view and went on to say that "there was profound resistance to the concept of food poverty (and poverty in general) at official levels" (p. 32) and that civil servants avoided use of the term along with redefining health inequalities as "health variations". We also contend that some of the early beliefs which underpinned initiatives in the eighteenth and nineteenth centuries have not disappeared but merely gone "underground". An example of this is the concept of the deserving/undeserving poor and the modern interpretation of this as "welfare scroungers" (Shaw, 1987, Hudson & Coukos, 2005, Garthwaite, 2016, Power, 2022).

So while the eighteenth- and nineteenth-century narrative of the deserving/undeserving poor was wrapped up in discourse which related to moral concepts, the modern equivalent is the public debate around the myth that the population divides into those who benefit from the welfare state and those who pay into it – "skivers" and "strivers", "them" and "us", the "deserving" and the "undeserving" in the old language (van der Horst, Pascucci & Bol, 2014, Wells & Caraher, 2014, Geiger, 2016, Hills, 2017, Caraher & Furey, 2018).

Using the Overton Window allows us to see that policymakers and politicians view policy as what is acceptable to the general populace but also to note that while the language used to describe the phenomenon of food poverty changes underlying principles remain remarkably constant.

Individual responsibility and behaviour

There has long been a focus on the role of individuals and behaviour change. As far back as the 1840s, the public health reformer Chadwick shared this view, stating that "ignorance of domestic economy leads to ill health by the purchase of unsuitable and at the same time expensive food" (Chadwick, 1842, p. 140). There was a strong emphasis on education of the working classes around food, hygiene and domestic management with local authorities and education providers running classes for young women (Yoxall, 1965 [1913]). This reoccurs as a feature through the ages reducing differences in health to individual behaviour and ignorance; some examples of this can be seen in Table 2.3.

In the eighteenth and nineteenth centuries, there was a concerted and very influential voice among scientists, physicians, policymakers and charitable organizations promoting the education of "the poor" and the importance of scientifically responsible diets, arguing that those in poverty needed to heed official advice and change their dietary practices while ignoring the limited options available to do this.

This moralising impulse was opposed by dissenting and "politically radical movements and individuals, who saw the eradication of poverty, rather than paternalistic education, as the top priority" (Kamminga & Cunningham, 1995, p. 12). The radical approach was that advanced by social nutritionists in the 1930s who linked income, access to food and scientific approaches to diet (Lang Barling & Caraher, 2009). The work of Orr and the work of M'Gonigle and Kirby was notable in challenging poverty and food insufficiency as being a failure of public morals and skills and was more to do with wider economic determinants and living conditions (M'Gonigle & Kirby, 1936).

A report in the 1930s on pregnant mothers in the Rhondda Valley in Wales found that to reduce maternal death rates from 11.29 per thousand to 4.77 per thousand, what was required was to feed pregnant women nourishing food and that ill health among the poor was related to deficient family income (Vernon, 2007). The report showed that the working poor could not afford to buy sufficient, good-quality, nutritious food. The Ministry of Health dismissed the report's findings (Smith & Nicolson, 1995) as "speculations" and asserted that ignorance, not income, was the root of the problem but the result of "bad cooking, bad marketing, [*and*] bad household economy" (Smith & Nicolson, 1995). The Rowett Institute in Aberdeen undertook a dietary survey of the UK in conjunction with the Ministry of Agriculture. Yet, when the authors

Table 2.3 Some examples of the focus on individual behaviour and household skills

Source	Issue
1906 The Interdepartmental Committee on Physical Deterioration.	Professor Edward Cathcart of Glasgow University and Sir George Newman, the Chief Medical Officer, both consistently emphasised the role of ignorance as a key factor in food inadequacy. Official policy focused on the prevention of undernourishment, not the alleviation of poverty; there was a recommendation for the teaching of cooking to young children (Interdepartmental Committee on Physical Deterioration, 1904).
1986 Edwina Currie, MP.	On high mortality rates in the north of England, she said: "the problem very often for many people is, I think, just ignorance and failing to see that they do have some control over their own lives" (Smith & Nicolson, 1995).
1991 Anne Widdecombe, then junior minister at the Department of Social Security.	Said "to educate those on low incomes how to buy healthy, nutritional food" and suggested that "people receiving Income Support should shop at local markets rather than supermarkets" (Smith & Nicolson, 1995).
1993 Lady Olga Maitland.	During a TV discussion, advised a group of single mothers to "avoid processed foods, to buy in bulk from cut-price stores, to purchase fresh produce from sources other than supermarkets, and to learn to make casseroles and stews from cheaper cuts of meat, augmented with vegetables and pulses" (Smith & Nicolson, 1995).
2013 Jamie Oliver.	Reported as saying: "The fascinating thing for me is that seven times out of ten, the poorest families in this country choose the most expensive way to hydrate and feed their families. The ready meals, the convenience foods" (Deans, 2013).
2013 Michael Gove, MP, then Education Secretary.	Poor forced to use food banks? They've only got themselves to blame for making bad decisions. Education Secretary says families are "unable to manage their finances" (Chorley, 2013).
2014 Conservative peer Lady Jenkins.	The peer told the press conference at the launch of a report examining the rapid rise in numbers of Britons who are reliant on food banks that low-income people who used food banks did so in part because they were not skilled enough in cooking and food management. She said: "we have lost a lot of our cookery skills. Poor people do not know how to cook". She went on to say, "I had a large bowl of porridge today, which cost 4p. A large bowl of sugary cereals will cost you 25p" (Walters, 2014).
2019 Caroline Blaiklock, an ex-City financial trader and hotelier who was the founder and first leader of The Brexit Party.	"The problem is not lack of food or the cost of it in this country: indeed, food has probably never been so relatively cheap or in such vast quantities" (Blaiklock, 2019).
2022 Lee Anderson, Conservative MP.	"We have generation after generation who cannot cook properly—they cannot cook a meal from scratch—and they cannot budget ... When people come for a *food* parcel now, they have to register for a budgeting course and a cooking course. We show them how to cook cheap and nutritious meals on a budget; we can make a meal for about 30p a day, and this is cooking from scratch" (Mendel, 2022).
2023 Brendan Clarke Smith, Conservative MP.	He made comments on Twitter that firefighters earning £32,000 a year who use food banks should "learn how to budget". Brendan Clarke-Smith tweeted that the idea of people on this money using a food bank was the most "ridiculous" thing he had heard. "If true", he added, they should learn "how to budget and prioritise" (BBC News, 2023).

of the report wanted to talk about the report's findings, they were threatened with expulsion from the Medical Register (Orr, 1966). The result was the publication of the report under the name of one of the key authors, John Boyd Orr. This became a landmark report on food poverty and the first of a set of reports that were quashed by governments. Orr attempted to reconcile the differing perspectives in his report by including a chapter on "Consumption of particular foods at different income levels" (Orr, 1936).

In the run-in to WWII, the ethos was still that the poor were ignorant and lacking in the skills necessary to eat a healthy diet. The Chief Medical Officer George Newman regarded an inquiry into the question of poor health among working-class men and women as unnecessary and unwelcome, for the reason that he was certain that it would reveal "a great mass of sickness and impairment attributable to childbirth, which would create a demand for organized treatment by the state" (Mayhew, 1988). He believed that a positive relief programme which addressed health problems on such a scale was beyond the capacity even of "modern civilized nations" (Vernon, 2007). Professor Cathcart of Glasgow University, one of the key advocates of education over income approach, was heartened to hear that a £500 grant from the Carnegie Trust was to be spent on instructing working-class women in different cookery methods as "one of the sanest efforts yet made". He believed that "bad cooking, bad marketing, bad household economy, plays a bigger part than shortage of cash in the majority of cases of malnutrition" (Mayhew, 1988, p. 450). He made these comments in his role as a member of a health department committee and had the support of the Permanent Secretary who wrote that "malnutrition is ignorance quite as much as insufficient income and it is this ignorance on which I want to organise the attack" (Robinson, 1933, Mayhew, 1988). These same debates continued into WWII and continue today over the role of teaching children cooking in the school setting (Keith, 2020, Dimbleby, 2021).

The interwar years saw an increased call for food policies and the need to tackle hunger and food poverty (Le Gros Clark & Titmuss, 1939). Many of the responses were in the area of education and propaganda and not at the level of structure or underlying causes such as work or income.

The principle of individual behaviours and the belief that domestic economy and nutrition knowledge and skills are lacking continue to be features of modern food policy. Table 2.3 sets out some examples of old and more recent pronouncements in this vein.

Of course, if you cannot cook, then there is a double jeopardy effect, but the reasons why you cannot cook may also be structural, such as lack of facilities, money or access to food. But not being able to cook is not the reason people are in food poverty. As Caraher says, to solve the problem, you need to "Fight poverty, not poor people" (Caraher, 2018).

Changing governance for food policy: local and global

The fulcrum of governance has shifted from government through public policy being the instrument of action to partnerships with the food industry, often called public private partnerships (PPPs). Such moves are often accompanied by a shift away from regulation to what are called voluntary agreements. Some see this as a benign influence and argue for extensions of the model (refer to Table 2.2). This represents a move through three stages of food control, from when government directly took action, such as buying and storing stocks of food to controlling supply and prices, through the use of legislation to control the action of others to a situation where it is judged best to have a light touch to food policy through minimum legislation and rules and to allow the food industry to police itself. None of these three stages are absolute in their reach, but represent a dominant focus at key points in time. There are arguments that the governance can flip-flop at points in time to reflect the problem. However, this can be difficult as governance mechanisms and political philosophies, once embedded, take time to shift and to respond to a crisis (de Waal, 2021).

The COVID-19 pandemic and the food crisis that emerged around it show how slow and cumbersome the state can be to respond (Cummins et al., 2020, Boons et al., 2021). For example, the problem of hunger among children and low-income families and the response which was to hand the problem to private firms who were ill-equipped to deliver the solution when they did not have access to local data or the knowledge that local public health teams and community groups possessed of local populations (Noonan-Gunning et al., 2021, Spyreli et al., 2021). de Waal points out that crises are by their very nature unpredictable and the ability to respond must be based on learning from the past while remaining open to new developments. What is important is to have an infrastructure in place which can respond to the problem. The problem facing UK public food policy was that local public health teams had been decimated due to a series of cuts which saw spending of £72.5 million less on public health in 2019–2020 than in 2018–2019 (Buck, 2019, Caraher, 2019). This was mirrored in cuts to education and welfare budgets (Caraher & Furey, 2018). When the COVID-19 crisis hit, there was little capacity in the public health workforce to deal with the fallouts for food access.

Others see the influence of the food and commercial interests as a malign influence and argue for control of the situation (Clapp & Scott, 2018, Lauber, Rutter & Gilmore, 2021). This is especially true of what is called "Big Food" or the unhealthy food commodities industry. The National Food Plan for England attempted to link the various elements in the food chain, but also gives a vaulted place to industry representation through an industry representative Food and Drink Sector Council which will be "a source of close advice and counsel" (Caraher, 2019, Dimbleby, 2020).

As noted above, food policy may also include actions by private sector actors whether on their own or in combination with state actors through the mechanism of the PPPs described earlier (Douglas et al., 2018). This is more than the involvement of private or non-governmental actors in policymaking and can be a situation where private actors set, implement and police the policy on their terms (Panjwani & Caraher, 2018). At a global level, there are many food companies investing in their supply chains by supporting community and infrastructure projects (Chapter 8 deals with this in detail). This arises because of a confluence of concerns: the first is a fear of the supply chain breaking down because of a lack of government support; the second is what some have called caring or welfare capitalism (Richards, Kjærnes & Vik, 2016). The push to neoliberal economics and lack of global governance and the development of low-tax, low-regulation economies have contributed to a diminution of the power and influence of global agencies such as the UN, WHO, FAO and UNICEF; such developments have aided the development to philanthrocapitalism and given voice to solutions which are based on high-tech solutions to producing more food but often do not address the right to food (Rieff, 2015). The aid aspect is epitomised by the Gates Foundation, but many companies now operate their own internal polices, generally under the guise of corporate social responsibility (CSR) commitments (Rieff, 2015, Rieff, 2016, Various Public Interest, Health, and Citizens' Groups, 2017). The fallout from these developments is a growing charity sector (at national and international levels), which supposedly addresses food policy but is dependent on industry support for its continuance.

The above raises important points about the global aspect of food policy and the positioning of the UK as global citizen, the reduction in foreign aid, a significant amount of which was spent on food projects, and its contribution to the Global Sustainable Development Goals (SDGs). The 17 UN SDGs are designed to achieve three primary objectives by 2030:

- Protect the planet;
- End poverty; and
- Create prosperity and peace for all (International Food Policy Research Institute, 2016).

The plight of growers/producers in developing and emerging economies are being impacted by decisions to cut aid budgets. In the UK, the cut is from 0.7% to 0.5% of gross national income (Kobayashi, Heinrich & Bryant, 2021). As countries such as the UK and the US roll back on foreign aid budgets, their role is being replaced by private companies who under the heading of CSR are providing support to growers in Africa and Asia. Many transnational companies see this as investment in their futures by supporting training for farmers and supporting capital investment projects. As a policy, this represents a shift in governmentality from the state to the private sector. There are positives to such moves; often, corporations have resources bigger than many nation states and can move faster than state institutions. The downside is the unregulated nature of such policy developments with the food industry investing where they can gain most and only investing in commodities that they trade in such as coffee, cocoa, sugar or cereals. Such an approach also limits benefits to those who fall within the commercial interests of the sponsoring company and still does not guarantee an increase in income for growers/producers. For example, cocoa production is concentrated in 30 countries with 90% grown on plots of less than ten hectares; the percentage price of the finished chocolate bar going to cocoa farmers over the last 30 years has decreased from 6% to 3% (Leissle, 2018).

The SDG targets offer a way to set goals for both governments and the private sector (Biermann, Kanie & Kim, 2017). The food system has particular relevance to goal numbers: 1 (no poverty), 2 (zero hunger), 3 (good health and well-being), 4 (quality education), 5 (gender equality), 8 (decent work and economic growth), 10 (reduced inequalities), 11 (sustainable cities and communities), 12 (responsible consumption and production), 13 (climate action) and 14 and 15 (life below water and on land, respectively). The goals are interlinked and have relationships with one another: Goal number 2 – zero hunger – has a target to "end hunger, achieve food security and improved nutrition and promote sustainable agriculture" links with goal 6 which is concerned with clean water and sanitation. All this policy noise is not resulting in action to address the SDGs. The poverty reduction targets were already not being met even before the COVID crisis (High Level Panel of Experts on Food Security and Nutrition, 2021).

Can industry be trusted in the absence of government to deliver on the SDGs? A survey by Visual Capitalist ranked companies by their positive or negative contribution to each of the 17 SDGs. The findings were that global companies fell mostly in the middle ranking with approximately 38% aligned and 55% misaligned or neutral. Only 0.2% of companies were strongly aligned to meeting the UN SDGs (Neufeld, 2021). One of the strongly aligned goals was "Responsible Production and Consumption". This indicates that while there is commitment, often under a CSR banner, the obligation is tempered by the demands of shareholders and the markets.

We know from research that the involvement of vested interests, such as the food industry, gives rise to policies that prioritise profit and vested interests above those of public health and sustainability (Clapp & Scrinis, 2017, Cossez, Baker & Mialon, 2022). The evidence for the success of such industry-led policies is weak (Public Health England, 2020, Ollila, 2003). Involvement and lobbying by the private sector have long been features of food policy from the repeal of the Corn Laws in the 1840s to reformulation of food products in the 2000s. Nonetheless, these public–private partnerships (known as PPPs) are now more common and are popular with governments of all political shades (Banerjee, 2008).

The extent of the operation of food policy has given way to new forms of partnerships and new strategies, for example, welfare capitalism and eco-nutrition. Welfare capitalism is an economic model that includes social welfare policies and/or the practice of businesses providing welfare services to their employees and suppliers.

Eco-nutrition: an old approach in new clothing

Eco-nutrition involves the relationships between nutrition and human health, environment, agriculture, economic development and sustainability (Mason & Lang, 2017). There are strong links between sustainable food production and healthy food, and there are also links to food processing and what are called UPFs and the NOVA classification. This classification fits foods into four categories, which are outlined in Table 2.4.

There are links between UPFs and the degree of sustainability inherent in the product. Generally, the more processing a food has undergone, the greater the damage to the environment. The NOVA classification has been used to present information to consumers, which links healthy eating with sustainable sourcing. There are some critics of the classification system claiming that it is too simplistic and arguing that the links with UPFs are tenuous. These operational details can be worked through in much the same way that nutritional profiling was developed for restricting food advertising. The UPF categorisation offers a way of imposing food control over food growing, imports, manufacturing and consumption. It also has the advantage of linking health and eco-sustainability agendas, as outlined by Mason and Lang (2017), under the heading of eco-nutrition or sustainable diets (see Chapter 5). In many ways, our analysis of

Table 2.4 Ultra-processed food (UPF) or NOVA classification

Group	Description
1.	**Unprocessed or natural foods** are the edible parts of plants (fruit, leaves, stems, seeds, roots) or from animals (such as muscle, offal, eggs, milk) and also fungi, algae and water.
2.	**Processed culinary ingredients** include oils, butter, lard, sugar and salt. These are substances derived from group 1 foods from processes such as pressing, refining, grinding, milling and drying.
3.	**Semi-Processed foods** include canned or bottled vegetables or legumes (pulses) preserved in brine; whole fruit preserved in syrup; tinned fish preserved in oil; some types of processed animal foods such as ham, bacon, pastrami and smoked fish; most freshly baked breads; and simple cheeses to which salt is added. They are made by adding salt, oil, sugar or ingredients from groups 1 and 2.
4.	**Ultra-processed foods** are creations of ingredients, produced from a series of industrial techniques and processes. Common ultra-processed products include carbonated soft drinks; sweet, fatty or salty packaged snacks; confectionery; mass-produced packaged bread, biscuits, pastries, cakes and cake mixes; margarine and other spreads; sweetened breakfast "cereals" and fruit yoghurt and "energy" drinks; pre-prepared meat, cheese, pasta and pizza dishes; poultry and fish "nuggets"; sausages, burgers and other reconstituted meat products; powdered and packaged instant soups, noodles and desserts; baby formula.

Sources: Monteiro et al. (2019), Jones (2019).

such an approach using the Overton Window shows that it would be acceptable to the population at large. Research has shown the classification is easily understood, can bring about changes in food purchasing and is acceptable to populations in other countries. While there is a need for some piloting for use in a UK situation and to make it culturally appropriate, its advantage is that it addresses multiple perspectives under the one banner. It offers a system of food control which can be applied at different stages in the food chain. The UK has the highest consumption of UFPs in Europe with consequent outcomes for health and sustainability. The COVID pandemic saw a rise in the consumption of UPFs and changes in the food system related to home delivery (Cummins et al., 2020). Such developments are likely to continue, yet there are no clear plans to tackle this food policy issue. A partial solution is labelling and the provision of information to help inform choice; these are, in public health terms, downstream approaches relying on information provision and consumer behaviour. An upstream approach would be regulating the content of such foods and setting standards for reformulation.

Conclusions

There are debates that the proliferation of policies examining individual areas of poverty, such as food policy and food poverty, dissipate the main focus, which should be poverty in general (Field, 1981). Chakrabortty argues this position and says:

> Like the legendary Inuit people who coined 57 words for snow, we have devised a long list of clever aliases for the stuff that dominates everyday life. Know the ones I mean? Try food poverty. Fuel poverty. Child poverty. Clothing poverty. Transport poverty. Period poverty.
>
> (Chakrabortty, 2021)

So, why food policy and why should it demand special attention? With food policy, wider concerns should also be considered such as obesity, livelihoods, the marketing of unhealthy foods by large corporations to children, damage to the environment, greenhouse gases, workforce productivity, mental health and social and cultural lives. In addition to income, it is concerned with social capital and where people live. These are the reasons it demands our attention. There is also the danger that by relegating it to a place within the pantheon of wider policies, we focus on the outcomes, not the primary determinants of food policy (Caraher & Coveney, 2004). Food is often referred to as the elastic item in the budget; in times of financial stress, people compromise on food purchasing shifting to poor quality diets and even going hungry. So, in times of crisis, you can spend less on food by eating less healthy, less nutrient-dense foods and compensate by eating more filling, energy-dense foods. The fallouts from Brexit, the COVID-19 pandemic and the current global crises triggered by the war in Ukraine all lead to the concomitant rise in food and fuel poverty, so the hard decisions for many low-income households are a choice between heating the house or eating.

Within this perspective, it is necessary, as previously mentioned, to distinguish between research *for* food policy and research *on* and *of* food policy. Why food policy was unsuccessful may relate to a lack of political will; the school experiment in Kingston upon Hull, described in Chapter 9 in the section on schools' meals, is one such example.

A fallout from the formation of the welfare state in 1948 was that policy related to food was set aside as an issue for policy attention. This was partially because the tackling of the five great wants was deemed to be sufficient to tackle the food poverty that was a feature of the "Hungry Thirties" (Renwick, 2017, Timmins, 2017). However, we see mirror images of the 1840s' concept of "less eligibility" and the deserving poor in current developments related to charity provision of food through food banks, soup kitchens and social supermarkets. Government support for food banks in the UK are illustrative of the ways the state chooses to distinguish between the "deserving" and "undeserving", concomitant with funding cuts in both welfare provision and public health services (Taylor-Gooby, 2012, Caraher, 2014, Power, 2022). Evidence is one part of food policy formation, but beliefs about causality are also important. So, policymakers and influencers can agree on evidence but diverge on the reasons why; for example, survey data may indicate households are cooking less but one person can see this as "laziness" and another as a consequence of not teaching cooking in schools.

The first official use of the term food policy was around World War I (WWI), when there were calls for a national "food policy". This was repeated for WWII, where the term used was food control; this involved the state through the Ministry of Food taking control of the food supply chain from growing and buying of food stocks to rationing and the provision of food in workplaces. A Ministry of Food was established in both World Wars, and in the first instance lasted until 1921 and then from 1939 to 1954. The interwar years ignored the lessons learned from WWI for food policy to alleviate poverty and hunger (Hammond, 1951). The advent of WWII saw an increased focus on food policies and a concern with national food security and a concern with imports of food. In many ways, health and nutrition were secondary issues and improvements in diet were a fallout from rationing and pricing controls which were based on an austere but healthy diet. As already noted in the introduction Hammond, in his conclusions and reflections on food control during WWII, said "The present volume might well have been entitled "The Expansion of Food Policy"" (Hammond, 1951, p. 375).

Yet even Hammond saw little from the experience of WWII that could be applied or be acceptable in peacetime – think Overton Window. Control of the food industry was not a priority at a time when the dominant belief was that the food industry (aside from hygiene concerns) needed little regulation (Hammond, 1954). The belief was that the food industry would deliver on prosperity and jobs as well as an adequate supply of food – a belief that continues to inform food policy. In the immediate post-war period, the public wanted to escape the privations of rationing (only finally ended in 1954) and austerity, and again the use of the Overton Window allows us to see what was acceptable to both the public and politicians at different times.

In the UK, these concerns led to the production of an independent report for England (The National Food Strategy: The Plan) produced and written by an independent advisor, which, as we already have noted, has largely been ignored in formal terms by the government (Caraher, 2019, White, 2022). Northern Ireland has a separate approach which was out for consultation in autumn 2021 called Food at the Heart of Our Society: A Prospectus for Change. The "National Food Strategy: The Plan" attempted to bring together many of the above strands and contains little to disagree with, but it does not address the issue of governance in any great depth and some areas of concern were omitted from its remit such as food welfare reform. There are also some areas for concern which relate to the lack of a population or public health focus and the over-reliance on social prescribing by general practice (Adams, 2021). The NFS claimed to be the first food policy since WWII comprehensively dealing with food, either ignoring or not aware of the 2008 Food Matters report (Cabinet Office, 2008, Parsons & Barling, 2021). This is sometimes referred to as policy amnesia. If there is such agreement on the need to tackle food issues, why the need for a consultation document? The reason is that policy is only partially influenced by evidence; the issues of beliefs, values, politics, economics, social values and lobbying all play a part.

Early food policy initiates were largely focused on issues of national food security supported by measures to educate the masses. The approach to education was crude and a form of indoctrination or propaganda. This approach to food policy was based on behaviour change and this influence is one that has carried over into modern developments, albeit in a more sophisticated way, as is the case with psychological nudges (Thaler & Sunstein, 2012). Yet, such approaches remain in the pantheon of policy options limited in their success (Dimbleby, 2021, Theis & White, 2021).

While different terms have been used through the ages to describe policies related to food from public health, food propaganda to food control, they generally fall within the broad rubric of what can be called food policy. They reflect the different concerns in different epochs, ranging from the early science of nutrition (1840s) through agriculture to a modern concern with policies around food which are integrated. One of the effects of the early COVID-19 lockdown was queues for food displaying similarities with the past, as in the queues for food that occurred in 1914, the 1930s, the 1940s, the 2000 fuel blockades and following the Great Recession in 2008. A case can be put forward that the successes of WWII were due to the food control aspect of the approach. So, while there were local and community initiatives, these were supported by control of the food supply from purchasing to distribution via rationing. In effect the Ministry of Food took over procurement for the civilian population.

An issue for food policy is not about the effectiveness or otherwise of evidence for food policy, but about what many call the "war of ideas" (Smith, 2013). The food industry, while calling into account the evidence of impact and outcome, also relies on ideas of personal freedom and the role of the state in restricting choice. Strategies include reframing a fat or soft drinks tax as an issue of consumer rights and a debate over the role of the state in "nannying" or restricting people's choices as opposed to health issues (Mindell et al., 2012). Nixon and colleagues (2015) when talking about the soda industry, talk about "Big Soda's long shadow" The new and powerful influences are the corporate interests and the influence of neoliberal economics above and beyond health, and we need to find ways to monitor and hold such interests to account. One way is for the government to accept this responsibility and the other is for civil society to adopt this role and advocate for citizens where and when the government fails to deliver on its commitments.

The UK food system faces a number of challenges which can be found in disparate polices, both existing and future developments to come. The House of Lords Select Committee on Food, Poverty, Health and the Environment concluded that the evidence received described a:

> food system that is biased towards providing an overabundance of cheap, less healthy food, with adverse consequences for health and the environment. We were told that farmers are trapped in a cycle where there is not enough emphasis or incentive on the need for healthy, environmentally sustainable produce.
> (Select Committee on Food, Poverty, Health and the Environment, 2020)

The negotiated Brexit deal has resulted in no tariffs on food but increases in increased bureaucracy, lorries queuing at the docks and confusion, all of which will add to the cost of food. The Northern Ireland (NI) Protocol, as part of the Brexit negotiations, also introduced some indications of what the future might hold with a border in the Irish Sea, as a trade *border*, between Northern Ireland and Great Britain (H.M. Government, 2020). The paradox is that Brexit, the COVID-19 pandemic and the current global recession offer opportunities to reflect on the adequacy of food systems and to use these legislative actions to change them. The issue seems to be a lack of vision, little joined-up thinking and tensions over what is "right to do" and the demands of "Big Food" and consumers for the status quo. An example of such tensions can be found in consumers' desire for "local food" but also their expectation for a year-round supply of out of season produce. No-deal Brexit food lessons were ignored by the UK government, but more than this, concerns over Brexit seem to have overridden the response to the COVID-19 crisis and food supply to vulnerable communities and households. The atmosphere is a strange mix of complacency, crisis management and a desire for an economic b-a-u (business as usual). There is currently little evidence of a government "appetite" for a policy approach to food or to alleviate food poverty, control obesity or to regulate food supply currently or in the long term (Lang, 2020, 2022).

If we think of the above, there is surely place to use the legal system to challenge food policy development. For example, in the area of environmental concerns, Client Earth (www.clientearth.org), a group of lawyer activists acting to save the earth, provides a model for a way forward by holding governments to account through legal action. So, linking activist lawyers around food systems with food academics and community food activists would combine knowledge, research and activism to generate a new idea around food provision and the right to food for citizens could be one way forward. Some limited models of this approach exist. One such example is the Dullah Omar Institute at the University of the Western Cape in South Africa (https://dullahomarinstitute.org.za). Through advocacy, partnerships and research, it uses the law to hold government agencies to account on food issues.

Notes

1 Between August and October 2022, the UK had three prime ministers – Boris Johnson, Liz Truss and Rishi Sunak – who expressed different views on food policy.
2 The old Poor Law ran from 1601 to 1834 (origin in the Elizabethan laws [*43 Eliz*]) and then new Poor Law from 1834 until 1948 replaced with the establishment of the Welfare State.

References

Acheson, D. 1998, *Independent Inquiry into Inequalities in Health Report*, The Stationery Office, London.

Adams, J. 2021, "National food strategy: what's in it for population health?", *BMJ*, vol. 374, p. n1865. https://doi.org/10.1136/bmj.n1865

Adams, J., Mytton, O., White, M. & Monsivais, P. 2016, "Why are some population interventions for diet and obesity more equitable and effective than others? The role of individual agency", *PLoS Medicine*, vol. 13, no. 4, p. e1001990. https://doi.org/10.1371/journal.pmed.1001990

Baker, P., Russ, K., Kang, M., Santos, T.M., Neves, P.A.R., Smith, J., Kingston, G., Mialon, M., Lawrence, M., Wood, B., Moodie, R., Clark, D., Sievert, K., Boatwright, M. & McCoy, D. 2021, "Globalization, first-foods systems transformations and corporate power: a synthesis of literature and data on the market and political practices of the transnational baby food industry", *Globalization and Health*, vol. 17, no. 1, p. 58. https://doi.org/10.1186/s12992-021-00708-1

Balaji, S., Seeberger, G. & Hennedige, O. 2018, "Burden of oral diseases and noncommunicable diseases: an Asia-Pacific perspective", *Indian Journal of Dental Research*, vol. 29, no. 6, pp. 820–829. https://www.ijdr.in/text.asp?2018/29/6/820/248259

Banerjee, S.B. 2008, "Corporate social responsibility: the good, the bad and the ugly", *Critical Sociology*, vol. 34, no. 1, pp. 51–79. https://doi.org/10.1177/0896920507084623

BBC News 2023, *Tory MP Brendan Clarke-Smith defends 'learn how to budget' remarks*, BBC News, https://www.bbc.co.uk/news/uk-politics-64187046.

Beveridge, W.H. 1942, *Social Insurance and Allied Services. Cmd 6404*, His Majesty's Stationery Office, London.

Biermann, F., Kanie, N. & Kim, R.E. 2017, "Global governance by goal-setting: the novel approach of the UN Sustainable Development Goals", *Current Opinion in Environmental Sustainability*, vol. 26–27, pp. 26–31. https://doi.org/10.1016/j.cosust.2017.01.010

Birkland, T.A. 2015, *An Introduction to the Policy Process: Theories, Concepts, and Models of Public Policy Making*, Routledge, New York.

Blaiklock, C. 2019, *Hungry? Let them eat spuds!*, The Conservative Woman, https://www.conservativewoman.co.uk/hungry-let-them-eat-spuds/.

Boons, F., Doherty, B., Köhler, J., Papachristos, G. & Wells, P. 2021, "Disrupting transitions: qualitatively modelling the impact of Covid-19 on UK food and mobility provision", *Environmental Innovation and Societal Transitions*. https://doi.org/10.1016/j.eist.2021.04.003

Boswell, J., Cairney, P. & St Denny, E. 2019, "The politics of institutionalizing preventive health", *Social Science & Medicine*, vol. 228, pp. 202–210. https://doi.org/10.1016/j.socscimed.2019.02.051

Bronner, F. (ed) 1997, *Nutrition Policy in Public Health*, Springer, New York.

Buck, D. 2019, *Public health spending: where prevention rhetoric meets reality* [Homepage of The King's Fund], [Online]. Available from: https://www.kingsfund.org.uk/blog/2019/07/public-health-spending-blog [2019, 09/19].

Buse, K., Mays, N. & Walt, G. 2012, *Making Health Policy*, 2nd edn, Open University Press, Maidenhead.

Cabinet Office 2008, *Food Matters Towards a Strategy for the 21st Century*, Cabinet Office, HM Government, London.

Cairney, P. 2012, *Understanding Public Policy: Theories and Issues*, Palgrave Macmillan, Basingstoke.

Caplan, N. 1979, "The two-communities theory and knowledge utilization", *American Behavioral Scientist*, vol. 22, no. 3, pp. 459–470. https://doi.org/10.1177/000276427902200308

Caraher, M. 2019, "New food strategy for England", *British Medical Journal*, vol. 366. https://doi.org/10.1136/bmj.l5711

Caraher, M. 2018, "Want to solve the obesity crisis? Fight poverty, not poor people", *Wired*, [Online], pp. 1st November. Available from: https://www.wired.co.uk/article/jamie-oliver-food-poverty-obesity-policy-scottish-government.

Caraher, M. 2014, *Food Banks as Indicators of the New 'Tory' Style Poor Law* [Homepage of WAKEUPSCOTLAND], [Online]. Available from: https://wakeupscotland.wordpress.com/2014/12/01/martin-caraher-food-banks-as-indicators-of-the-new-tory-style-poor-law/ [2019, 03/06].

Caraher, M., Carey, R., McConell, K. & Lawrence, M. 2013, "Food Policy Development in the Australian State of Victoria: A Case Study of the Food Alliance", *International Planning Studies*, vol. 18, no. 1, pp. 78–95. https://doi.org/10.1080/13563475.2013.750939

Caraher, M. & Coveney, J. 2004, "Public health nutrition and food policy", *Public Health Nutrition*, vol. 7, no. 5, pp. 591–598. https://doi.org/10.1079/PHN2003575

Caraher, M. & Furey, S. 2018, *The Economics of Emergency Food Aid Provision*, Springer, Cham.

Caraher, M., Landon, J. & Dalmeny, K. 2006, "Television advertising and children: lessons from policy development", *Public Health Nutrition*, vol. 9, no. 5, pp. 596–605. https://doi.org/10.1079/PHN2005879

Caraher, M. & Perry, I. 2017, "Sugar, salt, and the limits of self regulation in the food industry", *BMJ*, vol. 357. https://doi.org/10.1136/bmj.j1709

Carey, R., Caraher, M., Lawrence, M. & Friel, S. 2016, "Opportunities and challenges in developing a whole-of-government national food and nutrition policy: lessons from Australia's National Food Plan", *Public Health Nutrition*, vol. 19, no. 1, pp. 3–14. https://doi.org/10.1017/S1368980015001834

Centre for Food Policy n.d., *Advancing integrated and inclusive food policies that work for everyone*, Centre for Food Policy, https://www.city.ac.uk/__data/assets/pdf_file/0018/364212/The-Centre-for-Food-Policy-brief-final-May-2017.pdf.

Chadwick, E. 1842, *Report on the Sanitary Condition of the Labouring Population and on the Means of its Improvement*, W. Clowes and Sons For Her Majesty's Stationery Office, London.

Chakrabortty, A. 2021, The problem is poverty, however we label it, *The Guardian*, https://www.theguardian.com/commentisfree/2021/jan/21/poverty-food-child-fuel-britons-action.

Chorley, M. 2013, *Poor forced to use food banks? They've only got themselves to blame for making bad decisions, says Michael Gove*, Online edn, Mailonline, http://www.dailymail.co.uk/news/article-2416737/Michael-Gove-food-banks-Poor-got-blame.html.

Clapp, J. & Scott, C. 2018, "The Global Environmental Politics of Food", *Global Environmental Politics*, vol. 18, no. 2, pp. 1–11. https://doi.org/10.1162/glep_a_00464

Clapp, J. & Scrinis, G. 2017, "Big food, nutritionism, and corporate power", *Globalizations*, vol. 14, no. 4, pp. 578–595. https://doi.org/10.1080/14747731.2016.1239806

Cossez, E., Baker, P. & Mialon, M. 2022, "'The second mother': How the baby food industry captures science, health professions and civil society in France", *Maternal & Child Nutrition*, vol. 18, no. 2, p. e13301. https://doi.org/10.1111/mcn.13301

Cullerton, K., Donnet, T., Lee, A. & Gallegos, D. 2016a, "Using political science to progress public health nutrition: a systematic review", *Public Health Nutrition*, pp. 2070–2070. https://doi.org/10.1017/S1368980015002712

Cullerton, K., Donnet, T., Lee, A. & Gallegos, D. 2016b, "Exploring power and influence in nutrition policy in Australia", *Obesity Reviews*, vol. 17, no. 12, pp. 1218–1225. https://doi.org/10.1111/obr.12459

Cummins, S., Berger, N., Cornelsen, L., Eling, J., Er, V., Greener, R., Kalbus, A., Karapici, A., Law, C., Ndlovu, D. & Yau, A. 2020, "COVID-19: impact on the urban food retail system and dietary inequalities in the UK", *Cities & Health*. pp. 1–4. https://doi.org/10.1080/23748834.2020.1785167

Deans, J. 2013, Jamie Oliver bemoans chips, cheese and giant TVs of modern-day poverty, *The Guardian*, https://www.theguardian.com/lifeandstyle/2013/aug/27/jamie-oliver-chips-cheese-modern-day-poverty.

Department for Environment Food & Rural Affairs (DEFRA) 2022, *Government food strategy*, DEFRA, https://www.gov.uk/government/publications/governmentfood- strategy/government-food-strategy.

de Waal, A. 2021, *New Pandemics, Old Politics: Two Hundred Years of War on Disease and its Alternatives*, Polity Press, Cambridge.

Dimbleby, H. 2021, *National Food Strategy, Independent Review: The Plan*, https://www.nationalfoodstrategy.org.

Dimbleby, H. 2020, *The National Food Strategy: Part One – July 2020*, DEFRA, London.

Dimbleby, H. & Lewis, J. 2023, *Ravenous: How to get ourselves and our planet into shape*, Profile Books, London.

Dimbleby, H. & Vincent, J. 2013, *The School Food Plan*, Department of Education, London.

Douglas, N., Knai, C., Petticrew, M., Eastmure, E., Alison Durand, M. & Mays, N. 2018, *How the food, beverage and alcohol industries presented the Public Health Responsibility Deal in UK print and online media reports, Critical Public Health*, vol. 28, no. 4, pp. 377–387. https://doi.org/10.1080/09581596.2018.1467001

Egger, G. & Swinburn, B. 2010, *Planet Obesity: How We're Eating Ourselves and the Planet to Death*, Allen and Unwin, NSW, Australia.

Fanzo, J., Covic, N., Dobermann, A., Henson, S., Herrero, M., Pingali, P. & Staal, S. 2020, "A research vision for food systems in the 2020s: Defying the status quo", *Global Food Security*, vol. 26, pp. 100397–100397. https://doi.org/10.1016/j.gfs.2020.100397

Faulkner, W. 2011, *Requiem for a Nun*, Vintage, London.

Field, F. 1981, *Inequality in Britain: Freedom, Welfare and the State*, Fontana, Glasgow.

Food Ethics Council 2022, *Responding to the Government Food Strategy*, Food Ethics Council, https://www.foodethicscouncil.org/resource/government-food-strategy-response/.

Garthwaite, K. 2016, "Stigma, shame and 'people like us': an ethnographic study of foodbank use in the UK", *Journal of Poverty & Social Justice*, vol. 24, no. 3, pp. 277–289.

Geiger, B. 2016, *Benefit 'myths'?: The accuracy and inaccuracy of public beliefs about the benefits system, CASEpaper 199*, London School of Economics, London.

George, S. 1990, *Ill Fares the Land: Essays on Food, Hunger and Power*, Penguin, Harmondsworth.

Goodbody, W. 2022, *Nestlé to pay cocoa growers to keep children in school*, Radió Telefís Éireann (RTE), https://www.rte.ie/news/business/2022/0127/1276133-nestle/.

Goodman, S., Vanderlee, L., White, C.M. & Hammond, D. 2018, "A quasi-experimental study of a mandatory calorie-labelling policy in restaurants: Impact on use of nutrition information among youth and young adults in Canada", *Preventive Medicine*, vol. 116, pp. 166–172. https://doi.org/10.1016/j.ypmed.2018.09.013

Goodwin, S. 2022, "A cursory National Food Strategy lacks substance and joined up thinking on food insecurity", *BMJ*, vol. 377, p. o1549. https://doi.org/10.1136/bmj.o1549

Guba, E.G. 1984, "The effect of definitions of policy on the nature and outcomes of the policy process", *Educational Leadership*, vol. 42, pp. 63–70.

Hammond, R.J. 1954, *Food and Agriculture in Britain 1939–45: Aspects of Wartime Control*, Stanford University Press, Stanford, CA.

Hammond, R.J. 1951, *Food, Volume 1. The growth of policy*, H.M.S.O., London.

Hawkes, C. & Parsons, K. 2019, *Brief 1: Tackling Food System Challenges: The Role of Food Policy*, Centre for Food Policy, City, University of London.

High Level Panel of Experts on Food Security and Nutrition 2021, *Food security and nutrition: building a global narrative towards 2030. A report by the High Level Panel of Experts on Food Security and Nutrition of the Committee on World Food Security, Rome*, High Level Panel of Experts on Food Security and Nutrition of the Committee on World Food Security, Rome.

Hills, J. 2017, *Good Times, Bad Times: The Welfare Myth of Them and Us*, 2nd edn, Policy Press, Bristol.

H.M. Government 2020, *Trade and Cooperation Agreement between the European Union and the European Atomic Energy Community, of the One Part, and the United Kingdom of Great Britain and Northern Ireland, of the Other Partners*, www.gov.uk, https://assets.publishing.service.gov.uk/.

Hudson, K. & Coukos, A. 2005, "The dark side of the protestant ethic: a comparative analysis of welfare reform", *Sociological Theory*, vol. 23, no. 1, pp. 1–24. https://doi.org/10.1111/j.0735-2751.2005.00240.x

Ingram, J. 2011, "A food systems approach to researching food security and its interactions with global environmental change", *Food Security*, vol. 3, no. 4, pp. 417–431. https://doi.org/10.1007/s12571-011-0149-9

Interdepartmental Committee on Physical Deterioration 1904, *Report of the Interdepartmental Committee on Physical Deterioration*, H.M.S.O., London.

International Food Policy Research Institute 2016, *Global Nutrtion Report 2016: From Promise to Impact: Ending Malnutrition by 2030*, International Food Policy Research Institute, Washington, DC.

Jones, J.M. 2019, "Food processing: criteria for dietary guidance and public health?", *The Proceedings of the Nutrition Society*, vol. 78, no. 1, pp. 4–18.

Kamminga, H. & Cunningham, A. (eds) 1995, *The Science and Culture of Nutrition 1840–1940*, Rodopi, Amsterdam.

Keating, M. & Davis, G. 2000, *The Future of Governance*, Allen & Unwin, St Leonards.

Keith, R. 2020, *Marcus Rashford: a brief history of free school meals in the UK*, The Conversation, https://theconversation.com/marcus-rashford-a-brief-history-of-free-school-meals-in-the-uk-140896#comment_2255411.

Kickbusch, I. & Buckett, K. 2010, *Implementing Health in All Polcies*, Government of South Australia, Adelaide.

Kinealy, C. 2002, *The Great Irish Famine: Impact, Ideology and Rebellion*, Macmillan, Basingstoke.

Kingdon, J.W. 2010, *Agendas, Alternatives, and Public Policies, Update Edition, with an Epilogue on Health Care*, 2nd edn, Pearson.

Knai, C., Petticrew, M., Durand, M.A., Eastmure, E., James, L., Mehrotra, A., Scott, C. & Mays, N. 2015, "Has a public–private partnership resulted in action on healthier diets in England? An analysis of the Public Health Responsibility Deal food pledges", *Food Policy*, vol. 54, pp. 1–10.

Kobayashi, Y., Heinrich, T. & Bryant, K.A. 2021, "Public support for development aid during the COVID-19 pandemic", *World Development*, no. 138, p. 105248.

Kuhn, T.S. 1970, *The Structure of Scientific Revolutions*, 2nd edn, Enlarged edn, University of Chicago Press, Chicago, IL.

Lacy-Nichols, J. & Williams, O. 2021, "'Part of the solution': food corporation strategies for regulatory capture and legitimacy", *International Journal of Health Policy Management*, vol. 10, no. 12, pp. 845–856. https://doi.org/10.34172/ijhpm.2021.111

Lang, T. 2022, "Boris Johnson's food strategy fails to address food poverty and the cost-of-living crisis", *The New Statesman*, [Online], vol. 13th June, 15th June. Available from: https://

www.newstatesman.com/environment/food-farming/2022/06/boris-johnsons-food-strategy-fails-to-address-food-poverty-and-the-cost-of-living-crisis.

Lang, T. 2020, *Feeding Britain: Our Food Problems and How to Fix Them*, Pelican, London.

Lang, T., Barling, D. & Caraher, M. 2009, *Food Policy: Integrating Health, Environment and Society*, Oxford University Press, Oxford.

Lang, T. & Heasman, M. 2004, *Food Wars: The Global Battle for Mouths, Minds and Markets*, Earthscan, London.

Lang, T. & Mason, P. 2018, "Sustainable diet policy development: implications of multi-criteria and other approaches, 2008–2017", *Proceedings of the Nutrition Society*, vol. 77, no. 3, pp. 331–346. https://doi.org/10.1017/S0029665117004074

Lauber, K., Rutter, H. & Gilmore, A.B. 2021, "Big food and the World Health Organization: a qualitative study of industry attempts to influence global-level non-communicable disease policy", *BMJ Global Health*, vol. 6, p. e005216. https://doi.org/10.1136/bmjgh-2021-005216

Lawless, A.P., Williams, C., Hurley, C., Wildgoose, D., Sawford, A. & Kickbusch, I. 2012, "Health in all policies: evaluating the South Australian approach to intersectoral action for health", *Canadian Journal of Public Health*, vol. 103, no. 7 Suppl 1, pp. eS15–eS19. https://doi.org/10.1007/BF03404454

Le Gros Clark, F. & Titmuss, R. 1939, *Our Food Problem: A Study of National Security*, Penguin Books, Harmondsworth.

Leissle, K. 2018, *Cocoa*, Polity, Cambridge, UK.

Lindberg, R., Rose, N. & Caraher, M. 2016, "The human right to food", *Parity*, vol. 29, no. 2, pp. 13–15.

Marmot, M. 2020, *Health Equity in England: The Marmot Review 10 Years On*, Health Foundation and UCL Institute of Health Equity, London.

Marmot, M. 2015, *The Health Gap: The Challenge of an Unequal World*, Bloomsbury, London.

Marmot, M. 2005, *Status Syndrome: How Your Social Status Standing Directly affects Your Health*, Bloomsbury, London.

Mason, P. & Lang, T. 2017, *Sustainable Diets: How Ecological Nutrition Can Transform Consumption and the Food System*, Routledge, London.

Mayhew, M. 1988, "The 1930s nutrition controversy", *Journal of Contemporary History*, vol. 23, no. 3, pp. 445–464. https://doi.org/10.1177/002200948802300307

McBeth, M.K., Jones, M.D. & Shanahan, E.A. 2014, "The narrative policy framework" in *Theories of the Policy Process*, eds. P. Sabatier & C.M. Weible, 3rd edn, Westview Press, Boulder, CO, pp. 225–266.

McLaren, L., McIntyre, L. & Kirkpatrick, S. 2010, "Rose's population strategy of prevention need not increase social inequalities in health", *International Journal of Epidemiology*, vol. 39, no. 2, pp. 372–377. https://doi.org/10.1093/ije/dyp315

Mendel, J. 2022, *Tory MP claims food bank users 'cannot cook or budget properly' and meals cost 30p a day*, 11th May edn, City A.M., https://www.cityam.com/tory-mp-claims-food-bank-users-cannot-cook-or-budget-properly-and-meals-cost-30p-a-day/.

M'Gonigle, G.C.M. & Kirby, J. 1936, *Poverty and Public Health*, Victor Gollanz, London.

Milo, N. & Helsing, E. (eds) 1998, *European Food and Nutrition Polices in Action*, World Health Organization, Copenhagen.

Mindell, J.S., Reynolds, L., Cohen, D.L. & McKee, M. 2012, "All in this together: the corporate capture of public health", *BMJ*, vol. 345, p. e8082.

Monteiro, C.A., Cannon, G., Levy, R.B., Moubarac, J., Louzada, M.L., Rauber, F., Khandpur, N., Cediel, G., Neri, D., Martinez-Steele, E., Baraldi, L.G. & Jaime, P.C. 2019, "Ultra-processed foods: what they are and how to identify them", *Public Health Nutrition*, vol. 22, no. 5, pp. 936–941.

National Audit Office 2002, *The 2001 Outbreak of Foot and Mouth Disease: Report by the Comptroller and Auditor General*, The Stationary Office, London.

Nestle, M. 2018, *Unsavory Truths: How Food Companies Skew the Science of What We Eat*, Basic Books, New York.

Neufeld, D. 2021, *UN Sustainable Development Goals: How Companies Stack Up*, March 16th edn, Visual Capitalist, https://www.visualcapitalist.com/sustainable-development-goals/.

Newman, K. 2013, *The Secret Financial Life of Food: From Commodities Markets to Supermarkets*, Columbia University Press, New York.

Nixon, L., Mejia, P., Cheyne, A. & Dorfman, L. 2015, "Big Soda's long shadow: news coverage of local proposals to tax sugar-sweetened beverages in Richmond, El Monte and Telluride", *Critical Public Health*, vol. 25, no. 3, pp. 333–347. https://doi.org/10.1080/09581596.2014.987729

Noonan-Gunning, S., Lewis, K., Kennedy, L., Swann, J., Arora, G. & Keith, R. 2021, "Is England's public health nutrition system in crisis? A qualitative analysis of the capacity to feed all in need during the COVID-19 pandemic", *World Nutrtion*, vol. 12, no. 2, pp. 83–103. https://doi.org/10.26596/wn.202112283-103

O'Connor, M.K. & Netting, F.E. 2011, *Analyzing Social Policy: Multiple Perspectives for Critically Understanding and Evaluating Policy*, Wiley, Hoboken, NJ.

Ollila, E. 2003, *Global Health-Related Public Private Partnerships and the United Nations*, Ministry for Foreign Affairs of Finland, Helsinki.

Organization for Economic Co-operation and Development 1981, *Food Policy*, Organization for Economic Co-operation and Development, Paris.

Orr, J.B. 1966, *As I Recall*, MacGibbon & Kee, London.

Orr, J.B. 1936, *Food, Health and Income: Report on a Survey of Adequacy of Diet in Relation to Income*, MacMillan & Co, London.

Page, D. 2020, *"Get More People Growing Food in More Gardens" Local Food Production and Sustainability in Local-Level Food Strategies: An Examination of Five UK Cases*, Unpublished PhD thesis, City, University of London, London.

Page, D. & Caraher, M. 2020, "A Novel Approach to Local Level Food Policy Case Studies: Application of the Advocacy Coalition Framework", *Novel Techniques in Nutrition & Food Science*, vol. 4, no. 5. https://doi.org/:10.31031/ntnf.2020.04.000597

Panjwani, C. & Caraher, M. 2018, "CASE 11 Voluntary agreements and the power of the food industry: the Public Health Responsibility Deal in England" in *Public Health and the Food and Drinks Industry: The Governance and Ethics of Interaction. Lessons from Research, Policy and Practice*, ed. M. Mwatsama, UK Health Forum, London, pp. 110–120.

Panjwani, C. & Caraher, M. 2014, "The public health responsibility deal: brokering a deal for public health, but on whose terms?", *Health Policy*, vol. 114, no. 2, pp. 163–173. https://doi.org/10.1016/j.healthpol.2013.11.002

Parsons, K. 2022, *12 tools for connecting food policy: A typology of mechanisms. Rethinking Food Governance Report 3*, Food Research Collaboration, London.

Parsons, K. 2021, *How connected is national food policy in England? Mapping cross-government work on food system issues. Rethinking Food Governance Report 2*, Food Research Collaboration, London.

Parsons, K. 2020, *Food Research Collaboration – Rethinking Food Governance Who Makes Food Policy in England?* Food Research Collaboration an initiative of the Centre for Food Policy, London.

Parsons, K. 2019, *Brief 3: Rethinking Food Policy: A Fresh Approach to Policy and Practice*, Centre for Food Policy, London.

Parsons, K. 2017, *Constructing a National Food Policy: Integration Challenges in Australia and the UK*, Unpublished doctoral thesis edn, City, University of London, London.

Parsons, K. & Barling, D. 2021, *Policy and governance questions about the National Food Strategy. Briefing paper by the Food Systems and Policy Research Group*, Food Systems and Policy Research Group, University of Hertfordshire. https://doi.org/10.18745/pb.24766

Parsons, K. & Hawkes, C. 2019a, *Brief 4: Embedding Food in All Policies*, Centre for Food Policy, London.

Parsons, K. & Hawkes, C. 2019b, *Brief 5: Policy Coherence in Food Systems*, Centre for Food Policy, London.

Parsons, K., Hawkes, C. & Wells, R. 2019, *Brief 2: What is the Food System? A Food Policy Perspective*, Centre for Food Policy, London.

Pinstrup-Andersen, P. & Watson II, D.D. 2011, *Food Policy for Developing Countries*, Cornell University Press, Ithaca, NY.

Power, M. 2022, *Hunger, Whiteness and Religion in Neoliberal Britain: An Inequality of Power*, Policy Press, Bristol.

Public Health England 2020, *Sugar Reduction: Report on Progress between 2015 and 2019*, Public Health England, London.

Renwick, C. 2017, *Bread for All: The Origins of the Welfare State*, Aleen Lane, London.

Rhodes, R. 1997, *Understanding Governance: Policy Networks, Governance, Reflexivity and Accountability.* Open University Press, Buckingham.

Richards, C., Kjærnes, U. & Vik, J. 2016, "Food security in welfare capitalism: Comparing social entitlements to food in Australia and Norway", *Journal of Rural Studies*, vol. 43, pp. 61–70.

Rieff, D. 2016, *The Reproach of Hunger: Food, Justice and Money in the 21st Century*, Verso, London.

Rieff, D. 2015, *Philanthrocapitalism: a self-love story: why do super-rich activists mock their critics instead of listening to them?*, 1st October edn, The Nation, https://www.thenation.com/article/archive/philanthrocapitalism-a-self-love-story/.

Robinson, A. 1933, *Memorandum from Robinson to Hilton Young*, 18th December edn, PRO MH 56/53.

Robson, W.A. 1963, "New introduction" in *English Poor Law History*, eds. S. Webb & B. Webb, Longmans, Green and Company, Edinburgh, pp. V–XX.

Rose, G., Khaw, K. & Marmot, M. 2008, *Rose's Strategy of Preventive Medicine*, Oxford University Press, Oxford.

Sabatier, P.A. & Weible, C.M. (eds) 2014, *Theories of the Policy Process*, 3rd edn, Westview Press, Boulder, CO.

Sacks, G., Swinburn, B.A., Cameron, A.J. & Ruskin, G. 2018, "How food companies influence evidence and opinion – straight from the horse's mouth", *Critical Public Health*, vol. 28, no. 2, pp. 253–256.

Seabrook, J. 2013, *Pauperland: Poverty and the Poor in Britain*, Hurst and Co., London.

Select Committee on Food, Poverty, Health and the Environment 2020, *Hungry for change: fixing the failures in food. HL Paper 85*, Parliamentary Copyright, https://publications.parliament.uk/pa/ld5801/ldselect/ldfphe/85/8502.htm.

Sharpe, R., Parsons, K. & Hawkes, C. 2020, *Coordination must be key to how governments respond to Covid-19 food impacts: a view from England. Rethinking Food Governance Guidance Note*, Food Research Collaboration, London.

Shaw, C. 1987, "Eliminating the Yahoo eugenics, social Darwinism and five Fabians", *History of Political Thought*, vol. 8, no. 3, pp. 521–544.

Smith, K. 2013, *Beyond Evidence-Based Policy in Public Health: The Interplay of Ideas*, Palgrave Macmillan, London.

Smith, D. & Nicolson, M. 1995, "Nutrition, education, ignorance and income: a twentieth century debate" in *The Science and Culture of Nutrition 1840–1940*, eds. H. Kamminga & A. Cunningham, Rodopi, Amsterdam, pp. 288–318.

Spyreli, E., McKinley, M.C., Woodside, J.V. & Kelly, C. 2021, "A qualitative exploration of the impact of COVID-19 on food decisions of economically disadvantaged families in Northern Ireland", *BMC Public Health*, vol. 21, p. 2291. https://doi.org/10.1186/s12889-021-12307-1

Szałek, B.Z. 2013, "Some praxiological reflections on the so called 'overton window of political possibilities', 'framing' and related problems", *Reality of Politics: Estimates - Comments - Forecasts*, no. 4, pp. 237–257.

Taylor-Gooby, P. 2012, "Root and branch restructuring to achieve major cuts: The social policy programme of the 2010 UK coalition government", *Social Policy & Administration*, vol. 46, no. 1, pp. 61–82. https://doi.org/10.1111/j.1467-9515.2011.00797.x

Thaler, R.H. & Sunstein, C.R. 2012, *Nudge: Improving Decisions about Health, Wealth and Happiness*, Penguin.

Theis, D.R.Z. & White, M. 2021, "Is Obesity Policy in England Fit for Purpose? Analysis of Government Strategies and Policies, 1992–2020", *The Milbank Quarterly*, vol. 99, no. 1, pp. 126–170. https://doi.org/10.1111/1468-0009.12498

Timmer, C.P., Falcon, W.P. & Pearson, S.R. 1983, *Food Policy Analysis*, Johns Hopkins University Press & World Bank, Baltimore, MD.

Timmins, N. 2017, *The Five Giants: A Biography of the Welfare State*, New edn, Harper Collins, London.

Tressell, R. 2018, *The Ragged Trousered Philanthropists*, BoD–Books on Demand.

True, J., Jones, B. & Baumgartner, F. 2007, "Punctuated-equilibrium theory" in *Theories of the Policy Process*, ed. P. Sabatier, 2nd edn, Westview Press, Boulder, CO, pp. 155–188.

van der Horst, H., Pascucci, S. & Bol, W. 2014, "The "dark side" of food banks? Exploring emotional responses of food bank receivers in the Netherlands", *British Food Journal*, vol. 116, no. 9, pp. 1506–1520.

Various Public Interest, Health, and Citizens' Groups. 2017, *Open Letter to the Executive Board of the World Health Organization: Re: Conflict of interest safeguards far too weak to protect WHO from influence of regulated industries (the case of the Bill and Melinda Gates Foundation)*, Open Letter, http://healthscienceandlaw.ca/wp-content/uploads/2017/01/Public-Interest-Position.WHO_.FENSAGates.Jan2017.pdf.

Veit-Wilson, J.H. 1992, "Muddle or mendacity? The Beveridge committee and the poverty line", *Journal of Social Policy*, vol. 21, no. 3, pp. 269–301. https://doi.org/10.1017/S0047279400019954

Veit-Wilson, J.H. 1986, "Paradigms of poverty: a rehabilitation of B.S. Rowntree", *Journal of Social Policy*, vol. 15, no. 1, pp. 69–99. https://doi.org/10.1017/S0047279400023114

Vernon, J. 2007, *Hunger: A Modern History*, The Belknap Press of Harvard University Press, Cambridge, MA; London.

Walt, G., Shiffman, J., Schneider, H., Murray, S.F., Brugha, R. & Gilson, L. 2008, "'Doing' health policy analysis: methodological and conceptual reflections and challenges", *Health Policy and Planning*, vol. 23, no. 5, pp. 308–317. https://doi.org/10.1093/heapol/czn024

Walt, G. & Gilson, L. 1994, "Reforming the health sector in developing countries: the central role of policy analysis", *Health Policy and Planning*, vol. 9, no. 4, pp. 353–370.

Walters, S. 2014, How I dined on 4p-a-bowl porridge... with Baroness who said poor can't cook, *Mail on Sunday*, https://www.dailymail.co.uk/femail/article-2872969/How-dined-4p-bowl-porridge-Baroness-said-poor-t-cook.html.

Wells, R. & Caraher, M. 2014, "Print media coverage of the food bank phenomenon: from food welfare to food charity?", *British Food Journal*, vol. 116. https://doi.org/10.1108/BFJ-03-2014-0123

White, M. 2022, "Half hearted and half baked: the government's new food strategy", *BMJ*, vol. 377, p. o1520. doi: https://doi.org/10.1136/bmj.o1520

Wilde, P. 2018, *Food Policy in the United States: An Introduction*, 2nd edn, Routledge, London.

Wilkinson, R. & Pickett, K. 2018, *The Inner Level: How More Equal Societies Reduce Stress, Restore Sanity and Improve Everyone's Well-being*, Allen Lane, London.

Wood, B., Ruskin, G. & Sacks, G. 2020, "How Coca-Cola Shaped the International Congress on Physical Activity and Public Health: An Analysis of Email Exchanges between 2012 and 2014", *International Journal of Environmental Research and Public Health*, vol. 17, no. 23, p. 8996. https://doi.org/10.3390/ijerph17238996

Woodham-Smith, C. 1962, *The Great Hunger: Ireland 1845–1849*, 1st edn, Harper and Row, New York.

World Health Organization & Food and Agricultural Organization 1992, *World Declaration and Plan of Action for Nutrition. FAO/WHO International Conference on Nutrition*, Food and Agriculture Organization, Rome.

Yoxall, A. 1965 [1913], *A History of the Teaching of Domestic Economy*, Cedric Chivers, Bath.

Zahariadis, N. 2007, "The multiple streams framework", in *Theories of the Policy Process*, ed. P. Sabatier, 2nd edn, Westview Press, Boulder, CO, pp. 65–92.

3 Food policy and nutrition

The triple burden of modern diets

Introduction

As indicated in Chapters 1 and 2, there is a strong relationship and history of the involvement of health and specifically nutrition as a driver for food policy in the UK. This has happened at the level of interventions directed at healthy eating, with health departments often leading food policy development (Milo & Helsing, 1998). At one level of reasoning, the motivations for this are clear: unhealthy food consumption and deteriorating health of the population related to an increase in diet-related non-communicable diseases (DR-NCDs). The weakness of such an approach is that it sometimes precludes intervention in the social, cultural and economic determinants of the food system, as these are judged as beyond the remit of health and nutrition-based policies (Milo & Helsing, 1998, Lacy-Nichols & Williams, 2021).

Food policy has since the 1840s been engaged in the battle for healthy eating for the population. This has been an important feature of food policy down through the ages. This chapter traces the origins of nutrition science and its role in food policy. This is reflected in a move from a scientific approach to attempts to have a more social nutrition or critical dietetics perspective. The internal battles for the direction of food policy and nutrition represent an ongoing debate begun in the 1930s (Coveney & Booth, 2019). Some key UK time points which have influenced debates on nutrition policy have been extracted and are listed in Table 3.1.

The 1904 *Interdepartmental Committee on Physical Deterioration* was established to determine why the health of recruits to the army for the Boer War (1899–1902) was so poor. They heard witness statements which claimed that working-class housewives were idle, uninterested and more likely to spend their limited resources in fish and chip shops or on tinned food (Interdepartmental Committee on Physical Deterioration, 1904). Concerns with the health of children and young people contributed to the establishment of Education (Provision of Meals) Act 1906 (H.M. Government, 1906). The 1905–1909 *Royal Commission on Poor Laws* resulted in two reports: the Minority and Majority Reports (Poor Law Commission, 1909, Wakefield et al., 1909). At that time, the Majority Report held more policy sway than that of the Minority Report. The Majority report called for limited reforms and focused on changes in administration to deliver a more cost-effective system. The Minority Report saw the causes of poor diet and unemployment as economic rather than moral or behavioural and had a longer lasting impact on policy influencers such as Beveridge and Orr (Wakefield et al., 1909). The Minority Report was influenced by Fabian socialism under the influence of Beatrice Webb and was more influential in the long run, but did not have an immediate impact (Webb, 1910, Robson, 1963).

This chapter traces the origins of the nutrition profession and nutrition science and their contributions in food policy. This is underpinned by a move from a scientific approach to

DOI: 10.4324/9781003260301-3

Table 3.1 Some key examples of nutrition policy and influences

Date	Key influence
1904.	Committee on Physical Deterioration on the issue of recruits to the Boer War and their poor health status.
1918.	WWI Rationing started as a result of food shortages, queues and evidence of malnutrition; note how late in the war rationing was introduced.
1920s to 1930s.	Hunger protest marches.
1934.	Introduction of free milk for "needy" children.
1936.	Nutrition reports from Fenner Brockway and John Boyd Orr.
1936.	The Jarrow March.
1939.	Publication of "Our Food Problem" by Le Gros Clark and Titmuss.
1939.	Ministry of Food established and assumes wide-ranging power for food control.
1939/1940.	Rationing introduced.
1941.	First nutritional standards for school meals established.
1946.	Free school milk for all attending children.
1964.	Retail price maintenance ended.
1960s.	Number of meals consumed at work canteens decreases.
1970.	Cessation of the provision of free school milk scheme.
1980.	The Education Act (1980) reduced the requirement for meal provision by schools only to those children eligible for a free school meal.
1991.	Committee on Medical Aspects of Food Policy (COMA) report on dietary reference values published.
1992.	The Caroline Walker Trust expert panel report on nutritional guidelines for school meals published.
1995.	"Report of the Low-Income Project Team of the Nutrition Taskforce" published.
2000s.	The re-emergence and rise of eco-nutrition linking food growing to healthy eating or sustainable diets.
2000s.	Industry-based voluntary sustainability standards (VSS) become more popular.
2000s.	Local food projects emerge as a way of tackling food-based problems.
2000.	Establishment of the Food Standards Agency.
2007.	Foresight report on obesity highlights future costs.
2013.	"School Food Plan" published.
2020.	"The National Food Strategy – Part 1" published.
2021.	"The National Food Strategy: The Plan" published.

attempts to combine this with a social nutrition or critical dietetics perspective. The internal battles for the direction of food policy and nutrition represent an ongoing debate for the profession of nutrition (Coveney & Booth, 2019). The latest developments which concern a link between nutrition with sustainable ethical food growing and production will be addressed in more detail in Chapter 5.

Involvement of health departments in food policy

Milo and Helsing, (1998) point out that the involvement of health departments in the formation of food policy was often limited by not being "part of the negotiations that effectively shape the food supply, nor do they currently have the organizational capacity to prepare nutrition-related interventions". This in many ways remains a problem as nutrition struggles for (both the science and the professionals) to find a place in the pantheon of food policy. The National Food Strategy (NFS) for England was strong on the big influences on food supply and choice but was critiqued for not including a primary care and public health focus (Adams, 2021, Dimbleby, 2021). Public health and primary care have been reduced to a "walk-on role" that is concerned largely with social prescribing lifestyle interventions such as exercise and healthy eating as opposed to tackling the wider determinants of health (Gopal et al., 2021).

Health services have traditionally played an important part in developing food policy and have often led when other sectors and departments of state have prevaricated. Table 3.2 shows some of the key UK health-related food polices in the last 50 years.

Health departments have often filled gaps in food activities left by others. In 1998, the teaching of cooking skills in schools was removed from the school curriculum by the Department of Education and employment (Lang & Caraher, 2001). This was partially influenced by a number of industry-dominated reports which called for the teaching of skills for those who would go on to work in the food and catering industries and required different skills than domestic cooking skills. These latter skills were not deemed to be hands-on cooking skills but much more around management of food preparation processes and included marketing and promotion of foods (ACARD, 1982, Caraher et al., 1999). All these concerns contributed to the development of a Design and Technology curriculum within which food was located and which replaced the old domestic science curriculum (Leith, 1998). This meant that practical hands-on cooking was removed from the National Curriculum in English and Welsh schools. A consequence of this was that as the education department removed cooking from the school curriculum, the health department began to fund community cooking classes to fill the gap (Caraher & Lang, 1999, Caraher & Seeley, 2010, McCloat & Caraher, 2016).

As health budgets and staffing levels began to shrink, the voluntary sector began to fill a gap with cooking classes being offered to schools, young people and in community settings often partially supported by public health monies to compensate for a neglect in education policy (Blamey et al., 2017). There is a track record of nutrition-based, community-based cooking classes since the 1990s, ranging from the Royal Society of Arts (RSA), Waitrose-funded Focus on Food campaign headed by Prue Leith through to the Chefs Adopt a School initiative to the current "TasteEd" campaign headed by Bee Wilson (RSA, 1998, Caraher, Wu & Seeley, 2010, Wilson & Lee, 2015). The academic literature agrees that the best way to pass on cooking skills is through the family, followed by education in schools if the former route of transmission breaks down (Caraher et al., 1996, Caraher et al., 1999, Lavelle et al., 2016). The evidence for community-based solutions to the problem of population-level deskilling are weak and unproven (Rees et al., 2012, Blamey & Gordon, 2015, McGowan et al., 2017); that is not to say such classes don't have a role – they are *part* of a solution, not *the* solution to a wider problem with culinary deskilling or healthy eating. As a policy approach, these are cheap alternatives for government, as they don't have to provide specialist spaces in schools or invest in specialist teacher training (discussed in Chapter 2 downstream approaches; see Figure 2.2). So, if challenged, those in power can point to action and praise the voluntary nature of the initiatives. Deskilling is a multifaceted problem and there are those who argue that the food system itself contributed to this through the provision of processed foods and the increasing popularity of eating out (Stitt et al., 1997).

This is a trend that continues up to the present time and can be said to represent the schizophrenic nature of food policy, as one proven source of intervention is pulled by government, it is patched up with a less effective approach by a sister department. The NFS identified this as a major gap and calls for education of food and nutrition to be formalised in the school setting (Dimbleby, 2021). In Scotland and Wales, the health sector plays a major lead on community cooking classes (Blamey et al., 2017).[1,2]

The above shows the shifting governmentally from the state to the third sector, including charity and voluntary provision. Gaps in provision are filled because of a lack of clear policy.

Table 3.2 Some examples of key health- and food-related policies in the past 50 years

Year	Title	Department
1976.	Prevention and Health.	Department of Health and Social Security.
1991.	Dietary reference values for Food Energy and Nutrients for the UK.	Department of Health.
1992.	Health of the Nation.	Department of Health.
1996.	Eating for Health: The Scottish Diet Action Plan.	The Scottish Office.
1998.	Food Standards Agency: A Force for Change.	Department of Health and Ministry of Agriculture, Fisheries and Food.
2000.	National Service Framework Coronary Health Disease.	Department of Health.
2001.	National Service Framework Diabetes.	Department of Health.
2001.	Investing for Health Strategy (NI).	Department of Health for Northern Ireland.
2003.	Food and Well-Being (Wales).	Department of Health for Wales.
2004.	Choosing Health: Making Healthy Choices Easier.	Department of Health.
2004.	A Healthier Future – A 20-Year Vision for Health and Well-Being in Northern Ireland 2005–2025.	Department of Health, Social Services and Public Safety.
2004.	Fit Futures: Focus on food, activity and young people.	Department of Health, Social Services and Public Safety.
2005.	Choosing a Better Diet: Food and Health Action Plan.	Department of Health.
2008.	Quality of Food.	Department of Health, Welsh Government.
2008.	Healthy Weight, Healthy Lives: A Cross-Government Strategy for England.	Cross-Government Obesity Unit.
2009.	Recipe for Success – Scotland's National Food and Drink Policy.	Scottish Government.
2009.	Every School a Good School – A Policy for School Improvement.	Department of Education.
2009.	Nutritional standards for school lunches: A guide for implementation: School Food Top Marks.	Health Promotion Agency for Northern Ireland, Department of Education and Department of Health, Social Services and Public Safety.
2010.	Healthy Lives, Healthy People: Our Strategy for Public Health in England.	Department of Health.
2012.	A Fitter Future for All Framework for Preventing and Addressing Overweight and Obesity in Northern Ireland 2012–2022.	Department of Health, Social Services and Public Safety.
2012.	Food in Schools Policy.	Department of Education and Department of Health, Social Services and Public Safety.
2013.	From 2010 to 2015 government policy: obesity and healthy eating.	Department of Health.
2014.	Good Food Nation.	The Scottish Government.
2015.	Food Standards Agency Strategy 2015–2020.	Department of Health.
2016.	Childhood obesity: a plan for action.	Department of Health.
2018.	Childhood obesity: a plan for action Chapter 2.	Department of Health.
2020/21.	National food Strategy (NFS) 1 and 2.	Department for Environment, Food & Rural Affairs (DEFRA).
2021.	Food at the Heart of our Society – A Prospectus for Change Public Consultation Document.	Department of Agriculture, Environment and Rural Affairs.

The origins of nutrition science

The origins of nutrition science can be found in the work of Liebig (1803–1873) in Germany, who introduced an analytical perspective via organic analysis. He is now perhaps better known for his Liebig's extract of meat compound, the forerunner of Oxo cubes (Kamminga & Cunningham, 1995a, 1995b). Liebig's theory of rational analysis contrasted with that of his contemporary Moleschott (1822–1893), who advocated for the development of a humanist science (Kamminga, 1995). Kamminga points out that the former was concerned with the quantity of food intake while the latter was concerned with both quantity and quality of the diet. Moleschott's texts have constant references to social justice, economic policy and political change. In the end, Moleschott's social nutrition lost out to the rational science approach advocated by Liebig and others. Nutrition science thus became an instrument to set intake standards which were sometimes devoid of social context. In many ways, these debates re-emerged in the 1930s, 1970s and in the 1990s on the issues of social nutrition, minimum income standards and household budgets (Veit-Wilson, 1986, Veit-Wilson, 1998, Deeming, 2010).

There were attempts in the 1930s to reintroduce a social element to nutrition-based food policy as espoused by Orr, Fenner Brockway and others (Vernon, 2007). They fought for a place in a debate where the dominant position was that poor diet was self-induced by women who did not know how to manage the family or to cook (Smith & Nicolson, 1995). During this time, many reports on nutrition were ignored and, in some cases, subject to censorship if they did not fit this prevailing trend. Reports on changing food habits, rising inequalities and health outcomes were produced regularly, yet government responses were muted. Other examples of attempts to ignore reports include the release of the Black Report over a Bank Holiday weekend in 1980. This was an attempt to bury the report and it was not formally published, but a number of photocopies were distributed by the government. The report had been commissioned in 1977 by a Labour Secretary of State, but by the time it was reported, there was a Conservative government in power. This is an example of non-action in policy terms (see Chapter 2 for further discussion on this; Birkland, 2015). A similar fate met the Health Divide in 1987, commissioned to determine what, if any, progress had been made since the Black Report seven years previously. The then Conservative government refused to sanction an official launch and an impromptu release was organised in a pub in New Oxford Street. Despite the lack of official recognition of these reports and any subsequent policy action, these reports influenced a generation of researchers, especially in the area of health and nutrition (Townsend, Whitehead & Davidson, 1992).

In 1984, the nutritionist Caroline Walker co-authored with Geoffrey Cannon *The Food Scandal: What's Wrong with the British Diet and How to Put it Right* (Walker & Cannon, 1984). It became a UK number one bestselling book and challenged the Department of Health's official 1981 statement that "nutrition in Britain is generally good". The background to the book was an official National Advisory Committee on Nutrition Education (NACNE) report (referred to as the James Report) on the British diet (James, 1983). NACNE was a committee of physicians and nutrition scientists commissioned by the British government to produce a report on food and health in the UK. Walker was the committee's secretary. The report was delayed and suppressed for two and a half years, after lobbying from the food manufacturing industry and its representative organisations (Cannon, 1989). When the report finally appeared, its message was that the British population would be much healthier if their diet contained less fat and sugar. *The Food Scandal* took the findings of the NACNE report and "challenged the unholy trinity of British processed food: saturated fat, commercial sugar, added salt. It was rude about specific branded products". Walker said, "as a general rule, the more heavily a food is advertised, the worse it is liable to be for your health". Caroline Walker died in 1988 and the Caroline Walker Trust was established in her memory. The Trust continues to campaign and produce reports on diet and inequality (see www.cwt.org.uk).

Buss showed that from the 1950s to the 1970s, the British diet remained remarkably consistent for a majority of the population with milk, bread, cereals, meat and potatoes, despite the end of rationing and other changes in 1954 (Buss, 1993). Yet the 1970s show the cracks beginning to appear in traditional food practices, with new tastes and food and technology influencing changes, not all for the better. This period is characterised by a move towards more pre-prepared food and convenience foods (Hardyment, 1995). This coincides with modern concerns with obesity, which were further fuelled by a report in 2007 predicting massive rises in obesity, increasing costs of treatment and wider (hidden) costs to the economy (Foresight, 2007b, McPherson, Marsh & Brown, 2007). We have seen 14 obesity strategies in England from 1992 to 2020 without any reduction in the prevalence of obesity or a clear policy focus on nutrition (Theis & White, 2021). The focus on obesity is easy to rationalise: it is measurable, visible and potentially preventable, given the correct interventions. The use of behavioural interventions based around persuading people to eat healthier foods has proved to be insufficient to address the rise in obesity. The failure to address structural determinants such as the power of the food industry and introduce legal requirements is a clear failure of UK policy (Dimbleby & Lewis, 2023).

There have been some individual UK nutrition-focused food policy successes; the introduction of a soda tax has resulted in reformulation by producers and a reduction in sugar intake via soft drinks (Bandy et al., 2020, 2021). This was done under pressure from the celebrity chef Jamie Oliver and needed to be written into tax law and thus became a policy introduced by the Treasury (Caraher & Perry, 2017). The Overton Widow (see Chapter 2 and Figure 2.3) helps explain the policy implementation and why a previously unpopular approach became acceptable. More "hard" regulation and upstream policies are required to encourage healthy eating. A reframing of the problem to a focus on preventing obesity among children contributed to a swing in public attitudes towards restrictions on choice. There is a saying in public health that there are three possible responses to a crisis: do nothing, introduce large-scale social change or do some health education. The latter is not likely to be effective but, in many instances, may be the acceptable option compared to doing nothing or large-scale social change. The education approach also has the advantage of focussing on the individual or family level and locating responsibility and blame for failure at this level (Blaxter, 1997, Caraher, 2018). In essence, nutrition or health-driven policies struggle to influence wider aspects of the food system such as taxes, subsidies or growing policies which are harder to gain support for and to implement (Milo & Helsing, 1998).

The Acheson Report of 1998 did have some purchase with a newly elected Labour government and resulted in some actions such as the Public Health Strategy for England, "Saving lives: Our healthier nation" (Acheson, 1998). The Acheson Report and the health strategy strengthened and re-energised initiatives such as the five-a-day fruit and vegetable and school meals campaigns (Sharp, 1996). The report also highlighted the role of primary care professionals as key in any prevention strategy. Outcomes included the setting up of Sure Start centres aimed at early years' interventions. The role of midwives and health visitors in promoting healthy eating with their access to families was emphasised. What has occurred since then has been a major reduction in both these services due to budget cuts (Buck, 2019, Caraher, 2019a, 2019b).

The triple burden of diet-related ill health

Concerns with national health status have acted as spurs for food policy through the eras, often prompted by a national crisis or scandal. In the early twentieth century, the concern was that inadequate nutrition was related to the lack of healthy recruits for the Boer War; in the last

20 years, the focus is on the cost of inadequate diets to the NHS, the wider economy and the contribution to rising obesity rates (Foresight, 2007a, Burges Watson, Draper & Wills, 2021, Theis & White, 2021). Many now refer to the triple burden of DR-NCDs, which includes over- and under-nutrition as well as micro-nutrient deficiency (Gómez et al., 2013, Luo, Zyba & Webb, 2020). Diet is also part of the broader triple challenge of health (which includes nutrition), environment and social justice (World Health Organization, 2021).

So the inadequacy of diet has shifted from a concern with undernourishment to the triple burden of malnutrition, which, in practice, involves the co-existence of under-nutrition with hunger and micro-nutrient deficiencies. The co-existence also occurs in the same populations. So those groups that periodically go hungry also suffer from obesity (Peña & Bacallao, 2000). There is evidence of weight gain across the population, but the association is greatest with those who are in the lower-income groups (Dimbleby & Lewis, 2023).

Modern malnutrition in the UK manifests itself primarily in the form of obesity, and policy has tended to focus on this one aspect without examining the wider influences such as poverty and income or indeed any linking of the strands. The critique levelled at modern nutrition-driven policy is its lack of focus on upstream factors and too much on individual lifestyle decisions (Coveney & Booth, 2019).

There are policies for obesity and some policies for food poverty, but there are few links despite their common roots – "never the twain shall meet" (Caraher, 2018, Caraher & Davison, 2019). The COVID-19 pandemic and the war in Ukraine have exposed weaknesses in the food system which have had major impacts on obesity during lockdown as well as food choice and hunger. There is evidence emerging of increases in obesity and widening inequalities during the COVID-19 lockdown (Connors et al., 2020, Cummins et al., 2020, Murphy et al., 2021). The Food Foundation in its ongoing tracking of food insecurity found that one million people had gone without food for one day in the month of January 2022 (see https://foodfoundation.org.uk/initiatives/food-insecurity-tracking). By September, the tracking indicated that 18% of households (9.7 million adults) have experienced food insecurity in the past month – more than double since January.

The issue of food security and food poverty will be dealt with in more detail in Chapter 4; here, we focus on the fact that "hunger" and the associated nutrition problems have not disappeared, and with rising food prices, stagnant incomes and increases in fuel costs are likely to rise even further.

The "Hunger-Obesity Paradox"

Food poverty is not a constant state for all families; there may be times of the month when money is less of a problem and other times when you are hunting down the side of the couch for spare change to buy food. The new marker of food poverty is obesity, punctuated with periods of hunger, which means, for many, cutting down on or going without food – referred to as the "Hunger-Obesity Paradox". The paradox is that the want and abundance in terms of over- and under-consumption exist in the same cohorts (Peña & Bacallao 2000). Within this, there is a gender issue, with women often eating less so other family members can eat. In feeding the family or household, there is a need to consider filling them up, and this comes from energy-dense as opposed to nutrient-dense foods.

While the whole population is gaining weight, the trend is more acute in lower-income groups. Lacking resources determines the (poor) quality of diets and increases the likelihood of consuming energy-dense food. As food prices increase, food is the "elastic item" in the budget.

People can compromise and trade down in their food choices, often with health consequences; but for most people in straitened circumstances, the key issue is hunger and particularly not seeing their children go hungry. Unfortunately, the energy-dense food that wards off hunger has long-term negative health consequences. The same people who are overweight are also likely to go hungry at intervals. The group is also more likely to be poor, whether those in receipt of welfare or the working poor. Links between nutrition approaches and welfare and working conditions are therefore necessary for effective food policy. But, what we see is often a response to a crisis and a response not rooted in cross-department preventive activities but located within the powers and functions of individual government departments (Peña & Bacallao, 2000). Interventions are also likely to be aimed at picking up the pieces as opposed to tackling the real causes (Caraher & Furey, 2018).

From the early work of Rowntree and Orr on to Leather's work on "modern malnutrition", we can see there has been a shift from the inadequacy of diet to the inappropriateness of diet and a concern with over consumption, with hunger being hidden from view or assumed to have disappeared in modern Britain (Rowntree, 1902, Orr, 1936, Rowntree & Lavers, 1951, Orr, 1966, Leather, 1996). Debates from the early days of the public health movement have uncanny continuity, with hunger being denied or ascribed to poor domestic skills. Leather in 1996 pointed out that "modern malnutrition" had a new face and that "there was profound resistance to the concept of food poverty (and poverty in general) at official levels" (p. 32).

Food standards: a floor or ceiling approach

In the early days of nutrition science, the measurement of food adequacy drew on the embryonic science of nutrition for the setting of standards. These standards were not simply technical standards but were designed to be punitive, and nutrition science was used in the pursuit of this aim. Standards were used to discourage those seeking food relief and welfare from becoming dependent on charity or local aid through the Poor Laws (Vernon, 2007). The practice arose from the Speenhamland Scale or System which was established in Newbury in 1795 and resulted from the decision not to fix a minimum wage, but instead to draw up a table to determine locally the minimum income necessary to maintain a labourer and his family "at a given price of bread" (Rose, 1971, p. 33).[3] The general principle was to set the standard at a lower level than that of the lowest paid agricultural worker. This is often referred to as the principle of "less eligibility" (see wider discussion of this principle in Chapter 2). This was passed into law in the Poor Law Amendment Act 1834. It specified that conditions in workhouses had to be worse than conditions available outside so that there was a deterrence to claiming relief, although workhouses often operated a system which was more generous than this. This was on the basis that poor food was likely to cause unrest among workhouse inmates, and this outweighed the principles of less eligibility and deterrence. With the ascent of organic analysis, as espoused by Liebig, and the fading of the social view, as offered by Moleschott (discussed above in the section "The origins of nutrition science"), nutrition became subject to a narrow scientific view and of being used to set social norms.

This setting of minimum subsistence levels was established as the ceiling above which the poor could not rise (rather than the floor below which they could not fall) and has remained a central, but often hidden, plank of provision to the current day in government policy. Contemporary right-wing political commentators have adopted the absolutist view with enthusiasm. In 1979, the then Secretary of State for Education and a guru of the New Right, Keith Joseph, attacked relative standard setting when he said:

> An absolute standard means one defined by reference to the actual needs of the poor and not by reference to the expenditure of those who are not poor. A family is poor if it cannot afford to eat. It is not poor if it cannot afford endless smokes and it does not become poor by the mere fact that other people can afford them.
>
> (Joseph & Sumption, 1979, pp. 27–28)

This emphasis on absolute standards and the exclusion of social and psychological needs which dominates the measurement of poverty leads to the claim by Veit-Wilson that:

> In short, the concept of absolute poverty is literally an absolute nonsense. Its use in debate always means no more than a decision by some non poor people to allow the poor only certain shared human needs and not others.
>
> (Veit-Wilson, 1989)

The use of nutrition to set minimum standards for those in receipt of welfare and on low incomes is often used to determine ceiling levels, which to attain more requires them to seek employment, unless, of course, they are judged to be one of the "deserving poor".

In many ways such approaches are still the central planks of government policy and can be seen in the focus on personal responsibility and behaviour. Again, using the Overton Window, the narrative has changed to reflect modern mores but the underpinning principle is one of a focus on behaviour and individual culpability often closely linked to assumptions about poor skills (Caraher, 2016, Caraher, 2018, Barrie, 2019).

Nutrition standard setting

The overwhelming views of the "experts" in the early twentieth century were that poverty was not a key factor in poor nutrition so much as ignorance of domestic economy and degenerative habits as the reasons for poor physical physique. One of the witnesses to the Committee on Physical Deterioration, Dr Robert Jones, said:

> The main point lies in education, especially of women, who should be taught how to choose and cook proper food. I have visited places in remote country districts as well as in congested metropolitan areas and I have seen provision shops retailing tinned rabbits, tinned fish, tinned milk and even tinned 'madeira' and other cakes, most of which could be served fresh and clean locally by the housewives.
>
> (Interdepartmental Committee on Physical Deterioration, volume 2, 1904, p. 398)

The Committee recommended domestic education for working-class girls as its preferred long-term solution to the nutritional problems of the poor. Smith and Nicolson give the examples of Professor Edward Cathcart of Glasgow University and of Sir George Newman, the Chief Medical Officer (from 1919 to 1935), who both consistently emphasised the role of ignorance as a key factor in food inadequacy (Smith & Nicolson, 1995). Official policy focussed on the prevention of undernourishment, not the alleviation of poverty as a causal factor; there was a recommendation for the teaching of cooking to young children in 1907 (Board of Education, 1907). This prevention was to be achieved through education of working-class women (Smith & Nicolson, 1995).

The use of the embryonic science of nutrition was used to set minimum standards for a healthy diet devoid of social and family context. The proposed diets were bland and monotonous and often took no account of the lack of storage and cooking facilities available to working-class families. Working-class women often shopped, or "marketed" as it was then called, daily due to lack of storage. There were, of course, dissenting voices which stressed poverty as the prime determinant of inadequate diets, but these were highly contested. The work of John Orr and the work of M'Gonigle and Kirby were notable in challenging poverty and food insufficiency as being a failure of public morals and skills (M'Gonigle & Kirby, 1936, Orr, 1936). A full discussion of these tensions and battles can be found in the work of Smith and Nicolson (1995).

The Hungry 30s and legacy

An abundance of technical standards emerged with little agreement between them, hence why the era of the 1930s was referred to as the "Nutrition Controversy" and the "Hungry 30s" (Mayhew, 1988, Vernon, 2007). Malcolm Muggeridge observed that the:

> under nourished soon got forgotten in the excitement of deciding what was the measure of their under-nourishment … [If] it had been possible to make a meal of Nutrition, many who went hungry would have been fed; but, alas, Nutrition allayed no hunger, except for self-importance and self-righteousness.
>
> (Muggeridge, 1940, pp. 281–282)

The Ministry of Health through the 1920s and 1930s continued to dismiss any findings that located income as an influence on poor diet, instead dismissing them as "speculations", and asserted that ignorance, not income, was the root of the problem. Poor diet and ill health were the result of "bad cooking, bad marketing, [*and*] bad household economy", according to the Ministry of Health (Vernon, 2007). Mayhew (1988) says of the 1930s "nutrition controversy", government ministers and their advisers were unwilling to admit that existing help such as the 1911 insurance scheme and its subsequent amendments were failing to provide for those who needed care the most: the wives and children of working men and the unemployed.

Orr attempted to reconcile the differing perspectives in his 1936 report by including a chapter on "Consumption of particular foods at different income levels". This report marks what Deeming called the modern development of family budgetary standards begun by Booth and Rowntree (Deeming, 2010). This can be related to the debates, in Chapter 2, concerning the make-up of food policy, which are formed not just by scientific factors but beliefs and values. An example can be found in the work of Orwell, who in *The Road to Wigan Pier* commented that:

> English working people everywhere, so far as I know, refuse brown bread; it is usually impossible to buy wholemeal bread in a working-class district. They sometimes give the reason that brown bread is 'dirty'. I suspect the real reason is that in the past brown bread has been confused with black bread, which is traditionally associated with Popery and wooden shoes. (They have plenty of Popery and wooden shoes in Lancashire. A pity they haven't the black bread as well!) But the English palate, especially the working-class palate, now rejects good food almost automatically. The number of people who prefer tinned peas and tinned fish to real peas and real fish must be increasing every year, and plenty of people who could afford real milk in their tea would much sooner have tinned milk—even that dreadful tinned milk.
>
> (Orwell, 2001 [1937], pp. 91–92)

Official denials of the findings of reports on the influence of poverty and income on food choice and nutrition shifted responsibility onto the poor. The Chief Medical Officer Newman regarded an inquiry into the question of poor health among working-class men and women as unnecessary and unwelcome for the reason that he was certain that it would reveal "a great mass of sickness and impairment attributable to childbirth, which would create a demand for organized treatment by the state". He believed that a positive relief programme which addressed health problems on such a scale was beyond the capacity even of "modern civilized nations" (Vernon, 2007). The result of this was that in the run-in to World War II the ethos was still that the poor were ignorant and lacking in the skills necessary to eat a healthy diet. Professor Cathcart of Glasgow University, already mentioned, one of the key advocates of education over income approach, was heartened to hear that a £500 grant from the Carnegie Trust was to be spent on instructing working-class women in different cookery methods as "one of the sanest efforts yet made". He believed that "bad cooking, bad marketing, bad household economy, plays a bigger part than shortage of cash in the majority of cases of malnutrition" (Mayhew, 1988, p. 450). He made these comments in his role as a member of a health department committee and had the support of the Permanent Secretary who wrote: "malnutrition is ignorance quite as much as insufficient income and it is this ignorance on which I want to organise the attack" (Robinson, 1933, Mayhew, 1988).

Solutions in the 1930s were further complicated by the lack of lead agency to drive forward the findings from research: was it a health issue, a Poor Law responsibility or that of the new Unemployment Assistance Board or, as outlined above, simply one of educating the "ignorant"? Between 1920 and 1934, there were 21 separate pieces of legislation enacted related to unemployment insurance, creating confusion among delivery agencies and relegating food to a minor role in all of this. Table 2.3 in Chapter 2 showed some examples of this tendency to reduce food and diet to individual failings of skills as opposed to being structural in origin (some more examples are provided in Table 3.3).

Table 3.3 Examples of assumptions regarding the reduction of dietary intake linked to a lack of skills, knowledge and "ignorance"

Source	Issue
1984, Dr Rhodes Boyson, as Minister for Social Security, gave his view of "relative poverty" to the House of Commons in a debate on the rich and the poor called by the opposition.	"The fact that the poor in Britain today are better off than the poor of the past, and than the poor of other countries today, is seen to devalue their problems. Those on the poverty line in the United States earn more than 50 times the average income of someone in India. That is what relative poverty is all about.... Apparently, the more people earn, the more they believe poverty exists, presumably so that they can be pleased about the fact that it is not themselves who are poor" (Hansard, 28 June 1984). Quoted in Mack and Lansley (1985).
2022, Conservative MP Lee Anderson "blames food poverty on lack of cooking skills".	In the House of Commons, he invited "opposition MPs to visit an unnamed food bank in his constituency, where he helps out." And in parliament, he said: "When people come now for a food parcel, they have to register for a budgeting course and a cooking course … And what we do at the food bank, we teach them how to cook cheap and nutritious meals on a budget. We can make a meal for about 30p a day, which is cooking from scratch" (Walker, 2022).

Nutrition-based food policy has an important part to play in encouraging skills development, but it needs to look broader to fulfil its potential and to influence upstream social and economic determinants on food choice and subsequent nutritional health.

The nutrition transition

As the background to the changing nature of dietary intake, the world is experiencing a "nutrition transition" (Popkin, Adair & Ng, 2012, Monteiro et al., 2018, Adams et al., 2020) with diseases, such as obesity and type II or late-onset diabetes, previously associated with affluence, middle age and lifestyle factors, now skipping a generation and occurring amongst younger members of society and in low-income and marginalised groups. Obesity, heart disease and cancers related to food intake are now issues of major concern. The nutrition transition helps introduce an analysis of decision-making at an upstream level (see Figure 2.2 in Chapter 2).

A major nutrition food policy development in this area was the realisation that the dominant food systems, while delivering benefits in terms of "cheapness", convenience and consumer choice, had a downside and that was the emergence of DR-NCDs. In the UK these changes have occurred over a period of 50 plus years; in developing and emerging economies, they are happening within shorter and shorter periods of time. The overall result is the consumption of more processed and ultra-processed foods (UPFs) (Baker et al., 2020). This is true for the UK which has the highest level of consumption of UPFs in Europe (Lam & Adams, 2017, Monteiro et al., 2018). UPFs, of course, fit well with modern lifestyles: they are cheap, store well and are generally easily prepared with minimum fuss. The approach preferred by UK-based policy is on individual behaviour exhortations and the use of labels to inform consumers of the health and nutrition content of the foods. This is in contrast to upstream approaches which could encompass taxes, mandatory reformulation and even banning certain foods or ingredients.

The issue of individual choice is not diminished by the application of the nutrition transition. It does, however, help to explain the context of choice and decision-making. It also enables us to see that certain changes in the food system result from a global pattern of cultural changes that accompany the globalisation processes related to food and food systems (Clapp, 2021, Fanzo & Davis, 2021, McKeon, 2021). This can be characterised by the increasing urbanisation and the adoption of habits and lifestyle behaviours which involve the consumption of more processed foods (Baker et al., 2020). There are four stages to the nutrition transition, which can be summarised as follow:

- Stage 1 Hunter-Gatherer: individuals live active lives, hunting and foraging for food.
- Stage 2 Early Agriculture: famine is common, slowing individuals' growth and decreasing body fat.
- Stage 3 End of Famine: famine recedes as income rises and nutrition improves, population numbers increase.
- Stage 3 to Stage 4, that is, the moves away from traditional indigenous diets towards foods higher in fats, meats and sugar, and the rise in food behaviours as countries become more urbanised and industrialised.

The last stage of the transition from 3 to 4 is what is common in developed and emerging nations and is driven by changes in the food system. For the UK, this transition has been happening since industrialisation in the 1840s, influenced at different times by new foods and technologies as well as changing tastes (Mennell, 1996, Collingham, 2017). These processes contribute to the "triple burden" of DR-NCDs.

The changes in any society are complex and subject to mediation from local food culture and customs; some like Italy and France have sought to protect their food cultures (Mennell, 1996, Helstosky, 2004, Dickie, 2007). However, the nutrition transition tends to follow a pattern, whereby in the first stages of development, the rich adopt the food habits of convenience, eating processed and novelty foods. This can take the form of consumption of takeaways and processed foods, all of which can contribute to chronic diseases such as heart disease and cancers (Popkin & Reardon, 2018). The reasons for this are twofold – these lifestyle choices are culturally aspirational but also expensive and often only the well-off can afford them in the early stages of the transition. The second stage of the transition is rooted in the food system becoming more industrial and concentrated so that processed foods and fast food become more affordable to all. Fast food is "fast" thanks to modern technology and suits modern lifestyles, and in many instances is a viable option for those on low incomes (the Big Mac index is an indicator of how much time you have to work to afford a Big Mac; see www.bigmacindex.org). In fact, the use of takeaways and fast food (or street food) often becomes an important money- and labour-saving mechanism for many who are engaged in piecemeal work. In the third stage of the transition, the rich classes return to eating more basic foods due to the health implications while poor quality food becomes more available and affordable to those on low incomes. An oxymoron is that as cooking assumed a leisure aspect, many see this period as being about culinary deskilling and the loss of role models in the home to pass on cooking skills and knowledge (Leith, 1998, Spencer, 2002). Fieldhouse asked, "if prepared food is so easily accessible, why bother to learn to cook?" and his follow-on question "are those new skills label reading and the assembly of pre-prepared ingredients?" captured the common zeitgeist where convenience and ready prepared foods were rapidly becoming the norm (Fieldhouse, 1995). Short argues that what was occurring was a restructuring of skills and not demise in skills *per se* (Short, 2006). New technological developments in food processing and the domestic kitchen, according to Spencer (2002), allowed the factory to extend its reach into the home and allow people to prepare food with "minimum ability", and that by the "1990s Britain had become a society where in order to eat people were not obliged to cook at all" (p. 331).

The first stages of the UK post-war evolution of the new technologies of frozen foods and kitchen design benefited the rich, while the "poor" ate a local – inadequate – diet; the second sub-stage of the transition leads to the rich reverting their dietary and purchasing habits to local (organic etc.) food, while the disadvantaged become dependent on processed foods (Caraher, 2011). This shifts the burden of disease from the rich to the poor. An example may help to illustrate this point: the development of allotments was intended to aid the diet of the urban poor and working classes; recent interest in "growing your own" has resulted in more middle-class allotment owners and waiting lists, shifting the purpose of allotments.

The second sub-stage of the nutrition transition change is rooted in the food system becoming more industrial and concentrated so that processed foods and fast food become more affordable to all (Caraher, 2019a, 2019b). So, less time in the kitchen, less time shopping, convenience food and eating all became facets of lifestyle and modern diets in the 1970s. Here, we begin to see the emergence of the catering and hospitality sector as a rival to the major retailers; their share of the food budget continued to grow in the 1980s and 1990s. It also marks the beginnings of the shift to cooking as a leisure activity; so, dinner parties, the growth of TV cooking programmes and cookbooks can be seen to be growing in this period (Hardyment, 1995, Sherman, 2010).

The overall dietary impacts of the nutrition transition are an increase in the fat, salt and sugar (HFSS) content of these foods with long-term consequences for health burdens. Food or nutrition policy that focuses on one aspect is bound to be only partial in its scope and effectiveness.

Obesity and coronary heart disease (CHD) have, until relatively recently, been viewed as diseases of affluence/food choice and less of a problem in low and middle income countries than in rich, industrialised ones. This is no longer true in low and middle income countries; obesity now exists alongside more traditional problems of under-nutrition, the triple burden phenomena discussed above. These changes have taken root in the UK over a long period, and this has become part of the cultural landscape and thus harder to shift, an issue identified in the NFS for England where it is referred to as the "junk food cycle" (Dimbleby, 2021).

All this has in the past been preceded by changes in the make-up of population demographics and influenced by better health status due to infectious diseases being controlled and improvements in nutrition, housing, maternal health and health care, so a shift from communicable to non-communicable diseases of which food intake forms a large part. The "nutrition transition" model helps explain some of these effects with overabundance and want existing in the same society; so, in the UK, the link between hunger and obesity.

At a time when well-off consumers are moving away from the dominant system, the dominant (industrialised processed food) system is being brought closer to the poor. Gopnik asks:

> who is likelier to eat the healthier today the diet of the American farmer or the Russian peasant of the Old Country-brown bread and freshly grown local vegetables, free-range chicken and raw milk cheese – the farmers' great-grandchildren, or the professor of comparative literature at the nearby liberal arts college?
>
> (Gopnik, 2012)

But this may not be an option for those on low incomes or disenfranchised in other ways (Kingsolver, 2007).

At the same time as the nutrition transition, the face of food poverty is changing with under-nutrition and micro-nutrient deficiencies now existing alongside the problems of over-nutrition. Eating seasonally was once the preserve of the poor; now, with the development of what Gopnik called the modern "moral taste" or Caraher the "new austerity" (Caraher, 2011, Gopnik, 2012), seasonality and eating locally are fast becoming the terrain of those with resources. The price of food poverty or insecurity in the past was seasonal eating; now, the rich pay money to eat seasonal and local food while the "poor" eat processed foods which have often travelled many miles on their journey to the supermarket shelf. The modern food system and new technologies have allowed us to eat a wide range of foods and to prepare multiple different servings at the same meal; the downside is that with such choices, many choose to eat what they like a lot and not to eat what they don't like, resulting in a narrow dietary range.

Such upstream influences as the food supply and distribution system, fast food availability and increasing urbanisation are often outside the remit of nutrition-focused food policy.

Conclusion

What the Great Recession of 2008, COVID-19 and the war in Ukraine crises have exposed is the lack of a state plan and willingness to intervene directly in nutrition along with the frailty of the current system to address the dietary needs of vulnerable groups. This situation has resulted because of cuts in the guise of austerity following the 2008 Great Recession: in essence, we have seen cuts to public health, community health and welfare services (Buck, 2019, Noonan-Gunning et al., 2021). These cuts were driven by an ideological belief in the small state with a low-tax, low-welfare, low-regulation economy, where the welfare system is not about protecting welfare and health but moving people to seek work and sanctioning them if they do not, and setting food intake standards at minimum or below minimum levels is part of this process (Taylor-Gooby, 2012). The referral of those in need to food banks where the foods they are likely to receive does not in most instances meet social or nutrition standards necessary for healthy living is part of the punishment for being poor (Anonymous, 2017, Caraher & Furey, 2018, Fallaize et al., 2020).

There is an argument that nutrition-led food policy is necessary but insufficient on its own to deliver better nutrition to the population. It needs to have a wider focus and set of partnerships to deliver a meaningful and effective food policy. In many instances, it has been forced to explore individual lifestyle issues such as skills and food literacy. The point is not that these are not important, but they rarely operate in isolation from wider social and economic determinants. Public health nutrition needs to be focussed on both ends of the spectrum: the macro and the micro. The model of the nutrition transition and a reflection on the uses of nutrition science to set minimum standards should encourage reflexive practice on how this is used. Public health nutrition can extend its focus by addressing wider issues. Mason and Lang have developed the concept of eco-nutrition or sustainable diets. They set out a multi-criteria, six-pronged approach to sustainable diets, giving equal weight to (1) nutrition and public health, (2) the environment, (3) sociocultural issues, (4) food quality, (5) economics and (6) governance (Mason & Lang, 2017, Lang & Mason, 2018). Chapter 2 discussed this and how it might be linked to the NOVA measurement system of UPFs (under the heading eco-nutrition: an old approach in new clothing). The overlap between the NOVA classification and eco/sustainable diets is strong with an emphasis on processing and how food is produced along with its impact on health. This may offer a way forward for public health nutrition. This should, of course, be linked with issues of equity and the right to food, which will be picked up in Chapter 4 under food poverty and food security.

Obesity and food poverty have the same underpinning causes yet result in differing policy streams. While the post-war years show great changes in the UK across the population, what had not changed was the gap between the meals of the rich and the "poor" (Hope, 1990, Buss, 1993). The important point is the difference in diets: what we see with the nutrition transition is a gap which is not narrowing but increasing (Baker et al., 2020, Lang, 2020, Lang & Caraher, 2020).

Using the optic of the Overton Window, we see these earlier views for the causes of poor diet being repeated in different epochs where the nutrition science evidence for food policy is clear but the political and popular will is not sufficiently strong. A major omission from diets of the 1950s through to today are fruit and vegetables, which under the food controls of the 1940s were included in meals that were provided by the state through schools and restaurants as well as being used as substitutes for meat or to bulk out dishes in everyday life. With post-war austerity (which lasted until 1954), the British diet of the 1950s was limited: a 1999 study comparing the diets of four-year-olds from the 1950s with those in the 1990s found the 1950s' diet closer to healthy eating guidelines (Prynne et al., 1999). The irony is that with more choice of foods and new technologies, our nutrition status at the population level appears to dis-improve. Among the reasons for this are that with more choice and new cooking and food preparation techniques, we can eat what we like more often. In the past, there were set routines to meals and fewer opportunities to prepare different options for the same meal occasion; in one sense, the household ate out of the "one pot". Now with the advent of processed and pre-prepared meals and microwaves, we can prepare many menu options for the same meal time to cater for different tastes and preferences.

We said at the beginning of the chapter that in 1904, evidence to the *Interdepartmental Committee on Physical Deterioration* focussed on working-class housewives as idle, uninterested and more likely to spend their limited resources in fish and chip shops or on tinned food than on fresh food. The evidence was highly tainted being based on assumptions as opposed to empirical data (Table 3.2 provides modern examples of this sentiment or belief). The evidence indicates that there has been too much of a focus on individual behaviour to tackle nutrition problems (Institute for Government, 2023, Theis & White, 2021). Nutrition-based policy, often within public health frameworks, has a lot to offer but is on its own not sufficient to bring about improvements in dietary health; it needs to embrace wider principles and focus more on upstream determinants. This is what Smith calls the war of ideas in relation to policy development. Formal academic evidence has to compete against common tropes and beliefs (Smith, 2013, Smith, 2013). It is not enough to have good intentions or even robust evidence; policy influencers must also have a good story or narrative. If we take the position that policy is the art of the possible, then it is clear that nutrition should not abandon its efforts or not argue its case.

Notes

1 https://www.communityfoodandhealth.org.uk/advice-resources/good-practice-ideas/cooking-sessions/.
2 https://www.agored.cymru/Units-and-Qualifications/Unit?opusid=BSD959; https://sbuhb.nhs.wales/community-primary-care/nutrition-skills-for-life/nsl-sub-pages/nutrition-skills-for-life-information-for-staff-and-volunteers/.
3 The general term "Bread Scale" was applied to these eligibility criteria as bread was a major component of the diets of the "poor" and of the allowance in institutions such as the workhouses.

References

ACARD 1982, *The food industry and technology*, HMSO, Cabinet Office, London.
Acheson, D. 1998, *Independent Inquiry into Inequalities in Health Report*, The Stationery Office, London.
Adams, J. 2021, "National food strategy: what's in it for population health?", *BMJ*, vol. 374, p. n1865. https://doi.org/10.1136/bmj.n1865
Adams, J., Hofman, K., Moubarac, J. & Thow, A.M. 2020, "Public health response to ultra-processed food and drinks", *BMJ*, vol. 369, p. m2391. https://doi.org/10.1136/bmj.m2391
All-Party Parliamentary Inquiry into Hunger and Food Poverty 2014, *Feeding Britain: A Strategy for Zero Hunger in England, Wales, Scotland and Northern Ireland*, Archbishop of Canterbury's Charitable Trust, London.
Anonymous 2017, "Foodbanks and food poverty in Austerity Britain", *The Pluto Press*, [Online], pp. 1st November. Available from: https://www.plutobooks.com/blog/foodbanks-food-poverty-austerity-britain/.
Baker, P., Machado, P., Santos, T., Sievert, K., Backholer, K., Hadjikakou, M., Russell, C., Huse, O., Bell, C., Scrinis, G., Worsley, A., Friel, S. & Lawrence, M. 2020, "Ultra-processed foods and the nutrition transition: Global, regional and national trends, food systems transformations and political economy drivers", *Obesity Reviews*, vol. 21, p. e13126. https://doi.org/10.1111/obr.13126
Bandy, L.K., Hollowell, S., Harrington, R., Scarborough, P., Jebb, S. & Rayner, M. 2021, "Assessing the healthiness of UK food companies' product portfolios using food sales and nutrient composition data", *PLoS ONE*, vol. 16, no. 8, p. e0254833. https://doi.org/10.1371/journal.pone.0254833
Bandy, L.K., Scarborough, P., Harrington, R.A., Rayner, M. & Jebb, S.A. 2020, "Reductions in sugar sales from soft drinks in the UK from 2015 to 2018", *BMC Medicine*, vol. 18, no. 1, p. 20. https://doi.org/10.1186/s12916-019-1477-4
Barrie, J. 2019, 02/14-last update, *People are sharing this open letter to MPs from a food bank volunteer about the struggles of people who rely on it* [Homepage of News The Essential Daily Briefing], [Online]. Available from: https://inews.co.uk/news/politics/food-bank-volunteer-open-letter-mps-frank-field-heidi-allen/ [2019, 03/06].

Birkland, T.A. 2015, *An Introduction to the Policy Process: Theories, Concepts, and Models of Public Policy Making*, Routledge, New York.

Blamey, A. & Gordon, J. 2015, *A Review of Practical Cooking Skills Activities Which Focus on Promoting an Affordable Healthy Balanced Diet for Adults, Young People and Their Families within Low-Income Communities in Scotland*, NHS Health Scotland, Edinburgh.

Blamey, A., Gordon, J., Newstead, K. & McDowell, J. 2017, "Strengthening adult community-based cooking skills interventions using realist principles", *British Food Journal*, vol. 119, no. 5, pp. 1130–1146. https://doi.org/10.1108/BFJ-09-2016-0432

Blaxter, M. 1997, "Whose fault is it? People's own conceptions of the reasons for health inequalities", *Social Science & Medicine*, vol. 44, no. 6, pp. 747–756. https://doi.org/10.1016/S0277-9536(96)00192-X

Board of Education 1907, *Special Report on the Teaching of Cookery to Public Elementary School Children*, H.M.S.O., London.

Buck, D. 2019, *Public health spending: where prevention rhetoric meets reality* [Homepage of The King's Fund], [Online]. Available from: https://www.kingsfund.org.uk/blog/2019/07/public-health-spending-blog [2019, 09/19].

Burges Watson, D.L., Draper, A. & Wills, W. 2021, "The chimera of choice in UK food policy 1976–2018", *British Food Journal*, ahead-of-print. https://doi.org/10.1108/BFJ-10-2020-0982

Buss, D.H. 1993, "The British diet since the end of food rationing" in *Food, Diet and Economic Change Past and Present*, eds. C. Geissler & D.J. Oddy, Leicester University Press, Leicester, pp. 121–132.

Cannon, G. 1989, *The Food Fight: The life and work of Caroline Walker*, Ebury Press, London.

Caraher, M. 2019a, "New food strategy for England", *British Medical Journal*, vol. 366. https://doi.org/10.1136/bmj.l5711

Caraher, M. 2019b, "High cost cheap food" in *The Blackwell Encyclopedia of Sociology*, ed. G. Ritzer, Blackwell, pp. 1–3. https://doi.org/10.1002/9781405165518.wbeos1494

Caraher, M. 2018, "Want to solve the obesity crisis? Fight poverty, not poor people", *Wired*, [Online], pp. 1st November. Available from: https://www.wired.co.uk/article/jamie-oliver-food-poverty-obesity-policy-scottish-government.

Caraher, M. 2016, "Food literacy beyond the individual: The nexus between personal skills and victim blaming" in *Food Literacy: Key Concepts for Health and Education*, ed. H. Vidgen, Routledge, London, pp. 118–133.

Caraher, M. 2011, "Food Austerity: A lifestyle choice for whom!", *Journal of the Home Economics Institute of Australia*, vol. 18, no. 2, pp. 17–25.

Caraher, M. & Davison, R. 2019, "The normalisation of Food Aid: What happened to feeding people well? *Emerald Open Research*, vol. 1, no. 3. https://doi.org/10.12688/emeraldopenres.12842.2

Caraher, M., Dixon, P., Lang, T. & Carr-Hill, R. 1999, "The state of cooking in England: the relationship of cooking skills to food choice", *British Food Journal*, vol. 101, no. 8, pp. 590–609. https://doi.org/10.1108/00070709910288289

Caraher, M. & Furey, S. 2018, *The Economics of Emergency Food Aid Provision: A Financial, Social and Cultural Perspective*, Palgrave Macmillan, Cham, Switzerland.

Caraher, M. & Lang, T. 1999, "Can't cook, won't cook: a review of cooking skills and their relevance to health promotion", *International Journal of Health Promotion and Education*, vol. 37, no. 3, pp. 89–100.

Caraher, M., Lang, T., Dixon, P. & Carr-Hill, R. 1996, "Buying, eating and cooking food: a review of a national data set on food attitudes, skills and behavioural change", *A Report to the Health Education Authority on Variations in Health: Implications for Health Promotion Policy*.

Caraher, M. & Seeley, A. 2010, "Cooking in schools: lessons from the UK", *Journal of the Home Economics Institute of Australia*, vol. 17, no. 1, pp. 2–9.

Caraher, M. & Perry, I. 2017, "Sugar, salt, and the limits of self regulation in the food industry", *BMJ*, vol. 357. https://doi.org/10.1136/bmj.j1709

Caraher, M., Wu, M. & Seeley, A. 2010, "Should we teach cooking in schools? A systematic review of the literature of school-based cooking interventions", *Journal of the Home Economics Institute of Australia*, vol. 17, no. 1, pp. 10–19.

Clapp, J. 2021, "The problem with growing corporate concentration and power in the global food system", *Nature Food*, vol. 2, pp. 404–408.

Collingham, L. 2017, *The Hungry Empire: How Britain's Quest for Food Shaped the Modern World*, The Bodley Head, London.

Connors, C., Malan, L., Canavan, S., Sissoko, F., Carmo, M., Sheppard, C. & Cook, F. 2020, *The lived experience of food insecurity under Covid-19*, Bright Harbour, Food Standards Agency, https://www.brightharbour.co.uk.

Coveney, J. & Booth, S. 2019, *Critical Dietetics and Critical Nutrition Studies*, Springer, Cham, Switzerland.

Cummins, S., Berger, N., Cornelsen, L., Eling, J., Er, V., Greener, R., Kalbus, A., Karapici, A., Law, C., Ndlovu, D. & Yau, A. 2020, "COVID-19: impact on the urban food retail system and dietary inequalities in the UK", *Cities & Health*, pp. 1–4. https://doi.org/10.1080/23748834.2020.1785167

Deeming, C. 2010, "The Historical Development of Family Budget Standards in Britain, from the 17th Century to the Present", *Social Policy & Administration*, vol. 44, no. 7, pp. 765–788. https://doi.org/10.1111/j.1467-9515.2010.00743.x

Dickie, J. 2007, *Delizia! The Epic History of the Italians and Their Food*, Hodder and Stoughton, London.

Dimbleby, H. 2021, *National Food Strategy, Independent Review: The Plan*, https://www.nationalfoodstrategy.org.

Dimbleby, H. & Lewis, J. 2023, *Ravenous: How to get ourselves and our planet into shape*, Profile Books, London.

Fallaize, R., Newlove, J., White, A. & Lovegrove, J.A. 2020, "Nutritional adequacy and content of food bank parcels in Oxfordshire, UK: a comparative analysis of independent and organisational provision", *Journal of Human Nutrition and Dietetics*, vol. 33, pp. 477–486. https://doi.org/10.1111/jhn.12740

Fanzo, J. & Davis, C. 2021, *Global Food Systems, Diets, and Nutrition*, Palgrave Macmillan, Cham.

Fieldhouse, P. 1995, *Food and Nutrition: Customs and Culture*, Chapman and Hall, London.

Foresight. 2007a, *Foresight. Tackling Obesities: Future Choices – Project Report*, The Stationery Office, London.

Foresight. 2007b, *Tackling Obesities: Future Choices—Project Report*, The Stationery Office, London, http://www.foresight.gov.uk/Obesity/obesity_final/Index.html.

Gómez, M.I., Barrett, C.B., Raney, T., Pinstrup-Andersen, P., Meerman, J., Croppenstedt, A., Carisma, B. & Thompson, B. 2013, "Post-green revolution food systems and the triple burden of malnutrition", *Food Policy*, vol. 42, pp. 129–138. https://doi.org/10.1016/j.foodpol.2013.06.009

Gopal, D.P., Beardon, S., Caraher, M., Woodhead, C. & Taylor, S.J. 2021, "Should we screen for poverty in primary care?", *British Journal of General Practice*, vol. 71, no. 711, pp. 468–469. https://doi.org/10.3399/bjgp21X717317

Gopnik, A. 2012, *The Table Comes First: Family, France and the Meaning of Food*, Quercus, London.

Hardyment, C. 1995, *Slice of Life: The British Way of Eating Since 1945*, BBC Books, London.

Helstosky, C. 2004, *Garlic and Oil: Politics and Food in Italy*, English edn, Berg, Oxford.

H.M. Government 1906, *Education (Provision of Meals) Act 190*. Chapter 57, Rowland Bailey Esq, London.

Hope, A. 1990, Institute for Government. 2023, *Tackling Obesity: Improving policy making on food and health*, Institute for Government, https://www.instituteforgovernment.org.uk/sites/default/files/2023-04/tackling-obesity.pdf. *A Londoners' Larder. English Cuisine from Chaucer to the Present*, Mainstream Publishing, Edinburgh.

Interdepartmental Committee on Physical Deterioration 1904, *Report of the Interdepartmental Committee on Physical Deterioration*, H.M.S.O., London.

James, W.P.T. 1983, *National Advisory Committee on Nutrition Education (NACNE)*, Health Education Council, London.

Joseph, K. & Sumption, J. 1979, *Equality*, John Murray, London.

Kamminga, H. 1995, "Nutrition for the People, or the Fate of Jacob Moleschott's Contest for a Humanist Science" in *The Science and Culture of Nutrition 1840–1940*, eds. H. Kamminga & A. Cunningham, Rodopi, Amsterdam, pp. 15–47.

Kamminga, H. & Cunningham, A. 1995a, "Introduction: The Science and Culture of Nutrition 1840–1940" in *The Science and Culture of Nutrition 1840–1940*, eds. H. Kamminga & A. Cunningham, Rodopi, Amsterdam, pp. 1–15.

Kamminga, H. & Cunningham, A. (eds) 1995b, *The Science and Culture of Nutrition 1840–1940*, Rodopi, Amsterdam.

Kingsolver, B. 2007, *Animal, Vegetable, Miracle: Our Year of Seasonal Living*, Harper Collins, London.

Lacy-Nichols, J. & Williams, O. 2021, "'Part of the Solution': Food Corporation Strategies for Regulatory Capture and Legitimacy", *International Journal of Health Policy Management*, vol. 10, no. 12, pp. 845–856. https://doi.org/10.34172/ijhpm.2021.111

Lam, M.C.L. & Adams, J. 2017, "Association between home food preparation skills and behaviour, and consumption of ultra-processed foods: cross-sectional analysis of the UK National Diet and nutrition survey (2008–2009)", *The International Journal of Behavioral Nutrition and Physical Activity*, vol. 14, no. 1. https://doi.org/10.1186/s12966-017-0524-9

Lang, T. 2020, *Feeding Britain: Our Food Problems and How to Fix Them*, Pelican, London.

Lang, T. & Caraher, M. 2020, "Influencing International Policy" in *Oxford Handbook of Public Health Practice*, eds. I. Kawachi, I. Lang & W. Ricciardi, 4th edn, Oxford University Press, Oxford, https://oxfordmedicine.com/view/10.1093/med/9780198800125.001.0001/med-9780198800125-chapter-32.

Lang, T. & Caraher, M. 2001, "Is there a culinary skills transition? Data and debate from the UK about changes in cooking culture", *Journal of the HEIA*, vol. 8, no 2, pp. 2–14.

Lang, T. & Mason, P. 2018, "Sustainable diet policy development: implications of multi-criteria and other approaches, 2008–2017", *Proceedings of the Nutrition Society*, vol. 77, no. 3, pp. 331–346. https://doi.org/10.1017/S0029665117004074

Lavelle, F., Spence, M., Hollywood, L., McGowan, L., Surgenor, D., McCloat, A., Mooney, E., Caraher, M., Raats, M. & Dean, M. 2016, "Learning cooking skills at different ages: a cross-sectional study", *International Journal of Behavioral Nutrition and Physical Activity*, vol. 13. https://doi.org/10.1186/s12966-016-0446-y

Leather, S. 1996, *The Making of Modern Malnutrition: An Overview of Food Poverty in the UK*, Caroline Walker Trust, London.

Leith, P. 1998, "Cooking with Kids" in *Consuming Passions: Food in the Age of Anxiety*, eds. S. Griffiths & J. Wallace, Mandolin Press, Manchester, pp. 58–65.

Luo, H., Zyba, S.J. & Webb, P. 2020, "Measuring malnutrition in all its forms: an update of the net state of nutrition index to track the global burden of malnutrition at country level", *Global Food Security*, vol. 26, p. 100453. https://doi.org/10.1016/j.gfs.2020.100453

Mack, J. & Lansley, S. 1985, *Poor Britain*, Allen & Unwin, London.

Mason, P. & Lang, T. 2017, *Sustainable Diets: How Ecological Nutrition Can Transform Consumption and the Food System.* Routledge, London.

Mayhew, M. 1988, "The 1930s nutrition controversy", *Journal of Contemporary History*, vol. 23, no. 3, pp. 445–464. https://doi.org/10.1177/002200948802300307

McCloat, A. & Caraher, M. 2016, "Home Economics as a food education intervention: lessons from the Irish secondary education context", *Education & Health*, vol. 34, no. 4, pp. 104–110.

McGowan, L., Caraher, M., Raats, M., Lavelle, F., Hollywood, L., McDowell, D., Spence, M., McCloat, A., Mooney, E. & Dean, M. 2017, "Domestic cooking and food skills: a review", *Critical Reviews in Food Science and Nutrition*, vol. 57, no. 11, pp. 2412–2431. https://doi.org/10.1080/10408398.2015.1072495

McKeon, N. 2021, "Global food governance", *Development*, vol. 64, pp. 172–180. https://doi.org/10.1057/s41301-021-00299-9.

McPherson, K., Marsh, T. & Brown, M. 2007, "Foresight report on obesity", *The Lancet*, vol. 370, no. 9601, p. 1755. https://doi.org/10.1016/S0140-6736(07)61740-1

Mennell, S. 1996, *All Manners of Food: Eating and Taste in England and France from the Middle Ages to the Present*, 2nd edn, University of Illinois Press, Urbana.

M'Gonigle, G.C.M. & Kirby, J. 1936, *Poverty and Public Health*, Victor Gollanz, London.

Milo, N. & Helsing, E. (eds) 1998, *European Food and Nutrition Polices in Action*, World Health Organization, Copenhagen.

Monteiro, C.A., Moubarac, J.C., Levy, R.B., Canella, D.S., Louzada, M.L.D.C. & Cannon, G. 2018, "Household availability of ultra-processed foods and obesity in nineteen European countries", *Public Health Nutrition*, vol. 21, no. 1, pp. 18–26. https://doi.org/10.1017/S1368980017001379

Muggeridge, M. 1940, *The Thirties: 1930—1940 in Great Britain*, Hamish Hamilton, London.

Murphy, B., Benson, T., McCloat, A., Mooney, E., Elliott, C., Dean, M. & Lavelle, F. 2021, "Changes in consumers' food practices during the COVID-19 lockdown, implications for diet quality and the food system: a cross-continental comparison", *Nutrients*, vol. 13, no. 1, p. 20. https://doi.org/10.3390/nu13010020

Noonan-Gunning, S., Lewis, K., Kennedy, L., Swann, J., Arora, G. & Keith, R. 2021, "Is England's public health nutrition system in crisis? A qualitative analysis of the capacity to feed all in need during the COVID-19 pandemic", *World Nutrition*, vol. 12, no. 2, pp. 83–103. https://doi.org/10.26596/wn.202112283-103

Orr, J.B. 1966, *As I Recall*, MacGibbon & Kee, London.

Orr, J.B. 1936, *Food, Health and Income: Report on a Survey of Adequacy of Diet in Relation to Income*, MacMillan & Co, London.

Orwell, G. 2001 [1937], *The Road to Wigan Pier*, Penguin, London.

Peña, M. & Bacallao, J. 2000, *Obesity and Poverty: A New Public Health Challenge. Scientific Publication no 576*, Pan American Health Organization, Washington, DC.

Poor Law Commission 1909, *Report of the Royal Commission on the Poor Laws and relief of Distress, 3 vols (the Minority Report is vol 3), Cd 4499*, HMSO, London.

Popkin, B.M., Adair, L.S. & Ng, S.W. 2012, "NOW AND THEN: the global nutrition transition: the pandemic of obesity in developing countries", *Nutrition Reviews*, vol. 70. https://doi.org/10.1111/j.1753-4887.2011.00456.x

Popkin, B. & Reardon, T. 2018, "Obesity and the food system transformation in Latin America", *Obesity Reviews*, vol. 19, no. 8, pp. 1028–1064. https://doi.org/10.1111/obr.12694

Prynne, C., Paul, A., Price, G., Day, K., Hilder, W. & Wadsworth, M. 1999, "Food and nutrient intake of a national sample of 4-year-old children in 1950: comparison with the 1990s", *Public Health Nutrition*, vol. 2, no. 4, pp. 537–547. https://doi.org/10.1017/S1368980099000725

Rees, R., Hinds, K., Dickson, K., O'Mara-Eves, A. & Thomas, J. 2012, *Communities that Cook: A Systematic Review of the Effectiveness and Appropriateness of Interventions to Introduce Adults to Home Cooking*, EPPI-Centre, Social Science, Research Unit, Institute of Education, University of London, London.

Robinson, A. 1933, *Memorandum from Robinson to Hilton Young*, 18th December, PRO MH 56/53.

Robson, W.A. 1963, "New Introduction" in *English Poor Law History*, eds. S. Webb & B. Webb, Longmans, Green and Company, Edinburgh, pp. V–XX.

Rose, M.E. 1971, *The English Poor Law 1780–1930*, David & Charles, Newton Abbot.

Rowntree, S. 1902, *Poverty: A Study of Town Life*, Macmillan, London.

Rowntree, B.S. & Lavers, G.R. 1951, *Poverty and the Welfare State*, Longmans Green, London.

RSA 1998, *The RSA Focus on Food Campaign: An Update*, The Royal Society for the Encouragement of Arts, Manufacturers and Commerce, Dean Clough. Halifax, UK.

Sharp, I. 1996, *At Least Five a Day Strategies to Increase Vegetable and Fruit Consumption*, National Heart Forum, London.

Sherman, S. 2010, *Invention of the Modern Cookbook*, Greenwood, Santa Barbara, CA.

Short, F. 2006, *Kitchen Secrets: The Meaning of Cooking in Everyday Life*, Berg, New York; Oxford.

Smith, A. 2013, *Beyond Evidence-Based Policy in Public Health: The Interplay of Ideas.* Palgrave Macmillan, London.

Smith, D.F. 2013, "The Politics of Food and Nutrition Policies" in *The Handbook of Food Research*, eds. A. Murcott, W. Belasco & P. Jackson, Bloomsbury Academic, London, pp. 398–409.

Smith, D. & Nicolson, M. 1995, "Nutrition, Education, Ignorance and Income: A Twentieth Century Debate" in *The Science and Culture of Nutrition 1840–1940*, eds. H. Kamminga & A. Cunningham, Rodopi, Amsterdam, pp. 288–318.

Spencer, C. 2002, *British Food: An Extraordinary Thousand Years of History*, Grubb Street, London.

Stitt, S., Jepson, M., Paulson-Box, E. & Prisk, E. 1997, "Schooling for Capitalism: Cooking and the National Curriculum" in *Poverty and Food in Welfare Societies*, eds. B.M. Köhler, E. Feichtinger, E. Barlösius & E. Dowler, WZB, Berlin, pp. 363–374.

Taylor-Gooby, P. 2012, "Root and branch restructuring to achieve major cuts: the social policy programme of the 2010 UK coalition government", *Social Policy & Administration*, vol. 46, no. 1, pp. 61–82. https://doi.org/10.1111/j.1467-9515.2011.00797.x

Theis, D.R.Z. & White, M. 2021, "Is obesity policy in England fit for purpose? Analysis of government strategies and policies, 1992–2020", *The Milbank Quarterly*, vol. 99, no. 1, pp. 126–170. https://doi.org/10.1111/1468-0009.12498

Townsend, P.B., Whitehead, M. & Davidson, N. 1992, *Inequalities in Health: The Black Report & the Health Divide*, 3rd edn, Penguin Books, London.

Veit-Wilson, J.H. 1998, *Setting Adequacy Standards: How Governments Define Minimum Incomes*, The Policy Press, Bristol.

Veit-Wilson, J.H. 1989, "The Concept of Minimum Income and the Basis of Income Support" in *Minimum Income: Memoranda Laid before the Committee, House of Commons Paper 579*, ed. House of Commons Social Services Committee, House of Commons, London, pp. 74–95.

Veit-Wilson, J.H. 1986, "Paradigms of poverty: a rehabilitation of B.S. Rowntree", *Journal of Social Policy*, vol. 15, no. 1, pp. 69–99. https://doi.org/10.1017/S0047279400023114

Vernon, J. 2007, *Hunger: A Modern History*, The Belknap Press of Harvard University Press, Cambridge, MA; London.

Wakefield, R.R., Chandler, F., Lansbury, G. & Webb, S.M. 1909, *The Minority Report of the Poor Law Commission: Part I The Break-up of the Poor Law*, The National Committee to Promote the Break-up of the Poor Law, London.

Walker, P. 2022, *Tory MP blames food poverty on lack of cooking skills*, 11th May edn, The Guardian, https://www.theguardian.com/uk-news/2022/may/11/tory-mp-condemned-after-blaming-food-poverty-on-lack-of-cooking-skills. Accessed 22nd March, 2023

Walker, C. & Cannon, G. 1984, *The Food Scandal: What's Wrong with the British Diet and How to Put it Right*, Century Publishing, London.

Webb, B. 1910, *The Minority Report in its relation to Public Health and the Medical Profession*, The National Committee to Promote the Break-up of the Poor Law, London.

Wilson, B. & Lee, A. 2015, *First Bite: How We Learn to Eat*, Fourth Estate, London.

World Health Organization. 2021, *COP26 Special Report on Climate Change and Health: The Health Argument for Climate Action*, World Health Organization, Geneva.

4   The growth of food insecurity

The new face of food poverty

Rediscovering food poverty

Access to sufficient food is a global challenge whereby 811+ million people in the world are under-nourished and/or hungry (Action Against Hunger, 2021). However, discussing food poverty in high income countries remains problematic, as there endures an opinion by some (O'Hagan, 2013, Lanchester, 2014) that food poverty does not truly exist in the Global North, or at least that it does not manifest to the extent that it occurs in low and middle income countries (Beacom et al., 2020). Yet, food poverty has been highlighted as a rising problem in developed nations (Davis & Geiger, 2017) and is experiencing a high research and policy profile in the UK (DEFRA, 2010, Dowler & O'Connor, 2012). Lambie-Mumford (2013) cited the emergence of this interest in policy circles while Dowler et al. (2011, p. 407) argued that UK household food security has played "no part in policy formulation until the last few years". It is an important issue of interest to policymakers, practitioners and academics around the world due to its far-reaching consequences for society, households and individuals. It is particularly apt in the UK, which is recognised as the sixth richest world economy in 2020 (Statista, 2022). Its causes include insufficient income, benefit delays, benefit changes, debt, and increasing essential cost of living (housing and utility bills). Food poverty "remains a major priority and a typical issue that requires immediate international solutions" (Mihoreanu et al., 2019, p. 38). It has received growing attention in the food policy arena and been declared a public health emergency (Taylor-Robinson et al., 2013). Yet, despite this, the National Food Strategy (NFS) for England did not address food poverty in any comprehensive way. The author of the report, when questioned, said, "he had not included because it had become politically polarising" (Environment, Food and Rural Affairs Committee, 2021).

Food poverty is often considered to be interchangeable with "food insecurity", since food security in the US' vernacular often equates to EU references to food safety and food supply chain regulation of food hygiene, toxicity and traceability (European Commission, 2009). Food security was popularly defined by the 1995 World Food Summit:

> Food security, at the individual, household, national, regional and global levels [*is achieved*] when all people, at all times, have physical and economic access to sufficient safe and nutritious food to meet their dietary needs and food preferences for an active and healthy life.
>
> (FAO, 1996)

Food poverty refers to "the insufficient economic access to an adequate quantity and quality of food to maintain a nutritionally satisfactory and socially acceptable diet" (O'Connor et al.,

DOI: 10.4324/9781003260301-4

2016, p. 429). In fact, there are multiple definitions of food poverty. According to Maxwell and Smith (1992), about 200 definitions of the concept of food security circulated during 1970–1990. The term "food insecurity" is becoming increasingly familiar in the UK literature (see Purdy et al., 2007, Dowler & O'Connor, 2012, Kneafsey et al., 2013), and both terms are now often used synonymously (Dowler & O'Connor, 2012, Borsch & Kjaernes, 2016, Thompson et al., 2018). However, there is currently no UK government-endorsed definition of food poverty (O'Connor et al., 2016, O'Connell et al., 2019).

Food poverty: past and present

There has been hunger in the UK throughout history attributable to wars and famine. Different attempts to ameliorate it ranged between welfare and charity. For example, in the nineteenth century, the Charitable Organisation Society provided charitable relief to exceptional cases and those judged to be deserving of help. The overlap between welfare provision provided by the Boards of Guardians under the Poor Laws and that provided by the COS was not always clear. In Scotland, the vast majority of relief relied on the private charity. Charity here was seen as a moral duty and was influenced by the Protestant work ethic (Weber, 1976 [1930]). The COS was influential in establishing the principles for charity provision. This influence continued right up to the time of the production of the *Majority Report* on the *Poor Law* in 1909, which advocated for more use of voluntary effort and a distinction between the cases that should be covered by the Poor Law and those who were deserving of charity, and indeed into the 1930s. This enshrined relief as a charity provision as opposed to a right, since charity was seen by some as a duty, sometimes referred to as the moral economy, exemplified by the work of Rowntree and others. The Protestant work ethic was an important force behind the emergence of modern capitalism and the role of charity and philanthropy and how these developed alongside government provision of food welfare. Where such benevolence was not employed, this required action on behalf of the state, leading to the development of some of the public health and work-based legislation which were, in part, designed to protect the vulnerable. However, the state did so without establishing a right to food for the populace.

Official concerns over the recommendations in the Minority Report led to the limited introduction of social insurance in 1911, but overall charity continued to play a prominent part in providing food to those in need (Webb, 1910, Robson, 1963).

In 1857, Ernst Engel published a law (referred to as Engel's law), accepted as an empirical regularity, concerning production and consumption epitomised through food expenditure as a proportion of income (Houthakker, 1957, 1992). The measurement of poverty proceeded to gain significant attention as poverty researchers such as Booth (1902), Orr (1936) and Rowntree (1941) discussed the inefficiencies of social policy and its failings of the poor to date. This led to considerations of what constituted food poverty. There were numerous reports in the 1930s on the inadequate diet of many low-income groups in the UK, yet little policy action with the reasons for food poverty being located within the frameworks of individual culpability (Mayhew, 1988, Deeming, 2010). Throughout the 1930s malnutrition, "officials maintained there was no connection between low income and malnutrition: if sections of the population were malnourished, then the fault lay with individual idiosyncrasies or ignorant housewives" (Mayhew, 1988, p. 452). Similar debates occurred over the publication of reports on poverty to the extent that the reports were "buried" (see Chapter 3 Introduction for more information on the Minority and Majority Reports).

Food poverty (re-)emerged as a concern in the 1970s when Caroline Walker and Geoffrey Cannon highlighted the issues, and the work of Peter Townsend led to a refocus on poverty (Deeming, 2010). What comes to mind is the old adage that the "poor will always be with us" with the appendage *but hidden from view*. In the US, the American war on poverty, begun by the Kennedys but completed by Lyndon Johnson had a huge formal policy element and different from that in the UK where it was done without government support or major policy development (Caraher & Furey, 2018). The developments were led by non-governmental organisations (NGOs) and the period saw the establishment of a number of campaigning NGOs. Government responses to poverty can be seen with many of the shadows of nineteenth-century thinking here with the portrayal of food poverty as a failure of lifestyle and skills.

An example of such NGO development is the Child Poverty Action Group (CPAG). The Group was established on 5 March 1965 following the publication of Brian Abel-Smith and Peter Townsend's 1965 work *The Poor and the Poorest*: both men were founding members of the CPAG. The group became politically active in the 1970s, spurred on by a series of reports on poverty which showed a new face to poverty. A series of articles and research culminated in Townsend's classic 1979 text *Poverty in the United Kingdom*. He argued for the construction of a food poverty line, to address multiple dimensions of need: for food, this could be based on the minimum amount of money a household needs to purchase a basic needs (defined in different ways) food bundle and nothing more. He proposed that if the cost of basic non-food needs is estimated, the food poverty line can be added to the non-food needs to create an overall poverty line. This set the ground for a series of food-based researchers such as Caroline Walker and Elizabeth Dowler. The reality of such developments and research was that it was difficult to get policy purchase and the 1970s onwards are characterised by the emergence of campaigning NGOs to fill the gap.

Between the 1970s and the 1990s, food poverty had changed: from the 1970s images of hungry and energy-deprived children to one concerned with obesity – the malnutrition of over-consumption (Peña & Bacallao, 2000). This issue of the triple burden of disease is dealt with in more detail in Chapter 3. We see the re-emergence of food aid as a charity or philanthropic endeavour (food banks and soup kitchens) and of the moral concepts of the deserving and undeserving poor which were dominant in Victorian times and heavily influenced the Poor Laws of the time. Suzi Leather in 1996 pointed out that "modern malnutrition" has a new face and had not gone away but largely been hidden from view. It is an interesting observation because the underpinning contributory factors for food poverty and obesity are the same, yet we see little joined-up policy thinking between welfare and obesity policies; this is a hot potato of modern food policy. The two issues of obesity and poverty are related in terms of having the same underlying causes but are treated separately in policy terms: so one policy for obesity and one for food poverty and "never the twain shall meet".

The same trend continues today. Given the prevalence of over- and under-nutrition in the UK, it has proven difficult to "address malnutrition in all its forms" with "food insecurity and obesity rising". The nutrition paradox is evident in the UK with "high and growing levels of obesity and diet related disease, and among the highest levels of household food insecurity in Europe" (UKSSD, 2018, p. 19) (Table 4.1).

Table 4.1 Childhood under- and over-nutrition in the UK

UK region	Prevalence of over-nutrition	Prevalence of under-nutrition
England.	10% of children aged 4–5 (2016).	1% of children (2016).
Scotland.	6% of children aged 4–6 (2015).	0.4% of children (2015).
Wales.	12% of children aged 4–5 (2016).	0.8% of children (2016).
Northern Ireland.	5% of children aged 4–5 (2014).	No data.

Source: ONS (2018).

Leather went on to say that "there was profound resistance to the concept of food poverty (and poverty in general) at official levels" (1996, p. 32) and that civil servants avoided use of the term along with redefining health inequalities as "health variations". There are a number of key people from this era, Tim Lang, Liz Dowler, Caroline Walker and Suzi Leather, who pioneered the exposure of food poverty.

In the mid-1990s, John Beaumont advised the then Conservative government on food poverty as chair of the *Low-Income Project Team of the Nutrition Taskforce* (Beaumont et al., 1995). He was the CEO of the Institute of Grocery Distribution and was probably judged to be a "safe pair of hands". In his role as Chair of the project team, Beaumont visited many deprived communities and was disturbed by the extent of poverty, and food poverty in particular. Through his industry links, he helped establish FareShare as an industry-led NGO to use surplus food from the food sector to help those in need. Its primary aim was the use and redistribution of surplus food to help organisations, such as supper clubs and community kitchens. His experiences of visiting poverty-stricken areas impacted hugely on him and the findings and recommendations of the project team, which were largely ignored by the then Conservative government.

Despite this report and the evidence being produced by campaigners and academics, the policy remained agnostic on these issues and we saw not a government response but the growth of community and charity provision in the area of food poverty, a progression from the philanthropy described by Dowler and Caraher which focused on community projects and self-help. This straddled the communitarian politics of a newly elected Labour government and the red Tory policies of the Conservatives (Dowler & Caraher 2003, Kisby, 2010, Norman, 2010, Sage, 2012).

COVID-19 is recognised as "a health threat that poses a challenge to food security, from both an actual and a perceptual basis" (Deaton & Deaton, 2020, p. 144). COVID-19 undermines food security directly by disrupting food systems and indirectly through the impacts of lockdowns on household incomes and physical access to food (Devereux et al., 2020, p. 769). Worryingly:

> the income shock triggered by COVID-19 is expected to increase the prevalence of household food insecurity. But an important additional consideration is how the distribution of food insecurity changes across the three categories: marginal, moderate, and severe … Given that COVID-19 is expected to lead to both losses as well as shifts in employment, the likely effect will be to skew the distribution of food insecurity towards the more harmful experiences of 'moderate' and 'severe'.
>
> (Deaton & Deaton, 2020, p. 146)

The COVID-19 pandemic has exacerbated food insecurity among vulnerable groups and led to a newly food insecure population (Loopstra, 2020), moving a substantial group of lowest paid households into acute food insecurity and further increasing demand for emergency food relief (Barker & Russell, 2020, p. 866).

The drive for measurement: *how many* and *who* are food insecure?

A difficulty arises because before 2019 food poverty had not been officially measured in the UK. In the absence of an agreed measure, proxy measures for food insecurity identified in the literature include the use of food banks; economic markers showing general economic trends; household income; measures of income-related poverty; changes in social security; benefit sanctions and conditionality; housing costs; the costs of food; and trends in malnutrition and dietary markers (Boyle & Power, 2021).

Fortunately, standardised data on the prevalence of food poverty for the financial year 2019–2020 across the UK have been available from April 2021 in the Family Resources Survey (DWP, 2021). These data identified 14% of the UK population (9.3 million people) to be food insecure or marginally food insecure before the onset of COVID-19: low household food insecurity (4%); very low household food security (4%); marginally food secure (6%). Single parent households, those in receipt of Universal Credit (UC); African/Caribbean/Black British households and households with one or more disabled adults experienced disproportionately higher prevalence of food insecurity.

Meanwhile, data from the Food Standards Agency's *Food and You* (2) Wave 3 survey of 6,271 adults from 4,338 households (fieldwork from April to June 2021) reported that approximately one in six respondents were food insecure (i.e. had low or very low food security) in England (15%), Wales (18%) and Northern Ireland (16%) (Food Standards Agency, 2022a).

The survey concluded that food insecurity is associated with groups such as younger, lower-income consumers and those with children aged under 16 years, lower occupation grades and those with long-term health conditions. The survey also collated data on food bank use and found that 4% of respondents reported using food banks. It would be interesting to understand why these respondents are categorised in the "very low food security" status. The data provide further evidence that food bank use is a coping mechanism of last resort and that stigma/shame/reticence to claim charitable food aid continues to exist, lending additional credence to the need for a cash first approach to support those in food insecurity to extradite themselves from acute and chronic vulnerability.

The most recent data available (fieldwork between October 2021 and January 2022) found that 82% of respondents were classified as food secure across England, Wales and Northern Ireland (70% high, 12% marginal) and 18% of respondents were classified as food insecure (10% low, 7% very low), with food security levels being comparable across England, Wales and Northern Ireland (Food Standards Agency, 2022b).

The provision of food banks and other emergency food aid provision has been reviewed elsewhere (Caraher & Furey, 2018) with a specific focus on the UK, wherein it is argued that food banks must not be institutionalised as a permanent form of assistance in the UK as they have been in North America. Poppendieck in the USA (1998) and Riches in Canada (2018) have written extensively about how food insecurity has not been addressed in over 30 years of food banks existing in North America. This is paralleled in the UK, with the most recent data unveiling that the Trussell Trust's 1,468 distribution centres in its network distributed 2,537,198 food parcels in 2020/2021, representing a 33% increase in the number of parcels needed compared to the previous financial year (1,906,625 in 2019/2020) (Trussell Trust, 2021).

Food banks in the Trussell Trust's network experienced unprecedented increases during 2020, as the economic impact of the COVID-19 pandemic drove people to food banks. These latest data are lower than those seen in the equivalent period in 2020 but remain higher than 2019 and a 74% increase during the same period in 2016 (Trussell Trust, 2021). Trussell Trust's most recent data reported that 1.3m emergency food parcels were provided to people between April and September 2022 by food banks in the charity's UK network and almost half a million of these went to children. These figures represent one-third more food parcels than were provided during the same period in 2021 and an increase of more than 50% compared to pre-pandemic levels (Trussell Trust, 2022). It should be noted that these data do not include independent food banks, of which there have been at least 1,124 identified by the Independent Food Aid Network (IFAN), nor do they include food banks operated by schools, hospitals and the Salvation Army or other food aid providers such as soup kitchens and social supermarkets. Furthermore, UK data from 2016 show that 17 times the number using Trussell Trust food banks were food insecure, explainable in part because people may use non-Trussell Trust food banks or more likely because many people do not access food aid (Taylor & Loopstra, 2016). Therefore, food bank use is a poor proxy that underestimates the total number in food insecurity since not everyone who is food insecure accesses support from a food bank and there are other food aid distributors outside of Trussell Trust.

In order to understand the prevalence and severity of food insecurity, it is incumbent on governments to measure and report on food insecurity at national, regional and global levels. Until 2019, the UK had no agreed measure for food insecurity and it has been problematic to identify those who are unable to afford and access sufficient food. However, since 2019, food insecurity is now measured across all four regions of the UK using the North American ten-question Household Food Security Survey Module with results available from April 2021 (Butler, 2019).

Different cohorts of food insecurity

Food insecurity has been witnessed historically by (generally) the same cohorts of people, but the impact of COVID-19 has widened the inequality and manifested new subgroups of citizens reporting food insecurity for the first time.

Pre-COVID-19

Research has been undertaken to understand the subgroups of consumers who are more likely to experience food insecurity than others. Perhaps unsurprisingly, food insecurity is most common among low-income households (Deeming, 2011, Carman & Zamarro, 2016, Godrich et al., 2017). Various studies in high income countries (Australia, Canada and USA) have uncovered underlying characteristics and pre-determinants for food insecurity, including poor financial literacy (Carman & Zamarro, 2016) and delayed bill payments and seeking financial help from friends and family (Tarasuk et al., 2019). However, income alone is not sufficient to explain the prerequisites for food insecurity, the cost and consequences of attending to mental health issues, for example, maternal depression (Olson et al., 2004) and poor physical health, including self-reported health status. Furey et al. (2019) concluded that respondents with self-reported poorer health status were more likely to be in food-poor households. Other predictors of food insecurity included black and minority ethnic groups and men living alone (Deeming, 2011), limitations in activities of daily living (Deeming, 2011, Gundersen & Ziliak, 2015) and food consumption behaviours, for example, higher rates of parental overweight and obesity, less healthy foods served at meals, barriers to accessing fruits and vegetables and higher rates of binge eating (Bruening et al., 2012); and poor food skills surrounding managing bills, making a budget, stretching groceries and preparing meals (Olson et al., 2004).

Furey et al. (2019) found that households with more children were also an indicator of increased risk of food insecurity. This finding has agreement in the literature, where research has highlighted the growing numbers of children in the UK who are experiencing food insecurity (Garthwaite, 2016, Lambie-Mumford & Green, 2017, Knight et al., 2018, Lambie-Mumford & Sims, 2018, Mott et al., 2018, Wills et al., 2018). Furey et al. (2019) also found that food insecurity was less likely to be reported among older respondents, those who owned their property and those with higher household incomes. There are predictions that the elderly will be subject to increasing food insecurity in the near future as protections on pensions are removed and we see rises in heating and food bills (Berry, 2021). Food insecurity in Australia was also five times more evident among tertiary-level students than was previously reported for the general population (Gallegos et al., 2014).

Interestingly, it is only a minority of those experiencing food insecurity who access support from food banks (Tarasuk et al., 2019), endeavouring instead to access support from family, friends and other community organisations. Lambie-Mumford and Dowler (2014) concluded that food bank use was precipitated by "crises" which induce sudden reductions in household income, for example, job loss or problems with social security payments, prolonged low income or indebtedness. In understanding the socio-demographics of food bank clients, UK research (Power et al., 2017) typifies food bank guests as white British men aged between 30 and 50 years, living in insecure housing tenure or homeless, with many having a history of alcohol and substance abuse and mental ill health. There is an over-representation from the armed forces among food bank users. The same study reported an increase in attendees in part-time, low-income work in receipt of social security and people with children. Some reported experiencing an acute financial crisis requiring immediate food assistance, while other reasons for accessing a food bank included loneliness and inability to afford a balanced diet.

Since COVID-19

Research since the emergence of COVID-19 among the population has unanimously concluded that food insecurity has increased during the pandemic. The Food Foundation in the UK has tracked food insecurity nine times (with occasionally different emphases) through-out COVID-19 between March 2020 and January 2021 to understand how the prevalence of hunger has changed during the COVID-19 pandemic and found that more people are food insecure now than before the pandemic. At the beginning of the pandemic (April 2020), the number of adults who were food insecure in Britain was estimated to have quadrupled under the COVID-19 lockdown. The report found that about 16.2% of adults surveyed (equivalent to more than three million people) reported experiences of food insecurity since GB went into official lockdown: a three-week period since 23 March 2020. An additional 21.6% of adults reported feeling very worried or fairly worried about getting the food they need during the COVID-19 outbreak (Loopstra, 2020). Adults who are unemployed, adults with disabilities, adults with children and black and ethnic minority groups were found to be particularly vul-nerable to food insecurity. However, there were also newly emerging subgroups of vulnerabil-ity, notably those who experienced income losses and self-isolation as a result of COVID-19 (Loopstra, 2020).

The third wave of the Food Foundation's research (*n*=2,248) included Northern Ireland and focused on households with children, between 24 and 29 April 2020. While the small sample size for Northern Ireland (*n* = 78) should be noted, the data concluded that 13% of Northern Ireland respondents reported experiencing one or more symptoms of food insecurity (compared to the UK average of 17%). Eleven per cent of Northern Ireland respondents had smaller meals than usual or skipped meals because they couldn't afford or get access to food (compared to the UK average of 15%); 6% of Northern Ireland respondents had someone in their households who had been hungry but not eaten because they couldn't afford or get access to food (com-pared to the UK average of 9%): and 1% of Northern Ireland respondents had someone in their household who had not eaten for a whole day because they couldn't afford or get access to food (compared to the UK average of 4%). Furthermore, 4% (UK average = 7%) had relied on only a few kinds of low-cost food to feed the child(ren) because they had run out of food and been unable to get more; and 4% (UK average = 7%) of households had child(ren) who had not had balanced meals because they had run out of food and been unable to get more.

The fourth wave of data (*n* = 4,352, inclusive of Northern Ireland) reported that between 14 and 17 May 4.9 million people (9%) were still experiencing food insecurity, meaning that levels of food insecurity in the UK in May 2020 were almost 250% higher than pre-COVID-19 levels (Food Foundation, 2020a). More recent data (Food Foundation, 2020b) reported that four million people (14% of UK families with children) had experienced food insecurity in the past six months.

Furey et al. (2020) reproduced the Food Foundation survey for Northern Ireland respondents in September 2020 and found that one in eight respondents reported being fairly or very worried currently about having the essential foods their household needs. One in five respondents answered that they had experienced a symptom of food poverty at some point before, during the early lockdown period or during the past month. More than one in ten confirmed that they experienced food impoverishment during the past month, meaning that approximately 35% more households are experiencing food poverty during the past month compared to before the pandemic (when measured against five symptoms of food poverty: (1) eating smaller meals or skipping meals; (2) being hungry but being unable to eat; (3) not eating for a whole day because they could not afford food or because they could not get access to food; (4) relying only on a few kinds of low-cost food because they couldn't afford or get access to food; and (5) relying on support from others to enable them to afford or get access to food). Those who were not working (by reason of unemployment, retired, full time student etc.), those whose daily activities were limited by a persistent health condition and those who were self-isolating were significantly more likely to report food poverty symptoms among the cohort generally.

Food Foundation data collected during January 2021 found that 4.7 million adults (9%) have experienced food insecurity and 2.3 million children (12% of households with children) live in households that have experienced food insecurity in the past six months. The data also concluded that extremely clinically vulnerable people were more than twice as likely to be food insecure than other vulnerable groups. At the same time, people with health problems and disabilities have experienced increasing inequality compared to their healthier counterparts (Food Foundation, 2021).

Food workers are not exempt from food insecurity

Those who work in the food production/retail industry should, one would assume, be protected from food insecurity, yet our food sector workers have experienced higher levels of food insecurity despite being employed. However, there is growing evidence that such food sector workers are struggling to afford basic foodstuffs. A recent Bakers, Food and Allied Workers' Union (BFAWU) study (2021) reported that out of 227 respondents, 40% had eaten less than they thought they should have at some point during the pandemic due to a lack of money. Almost one in five (19%) reported that there had been a time during the pandemic when their household had run out of food due to a lack of money and a similar number (more than one-fifth) had required the support of friends and family to put enough food on the table and 7.5% had required the services of a food bank to provide meals. More than one in three (35%) reported they had gone without enough food to make sure others in the house could be fed properly. An even greater proportion reported that they have had concerns about running out of food. They rightly identified that the public would be disbelieving that people helping produce food for the country can often be priced out of the products they produce!

Similarly, in November 2021, the Living Wage Foundation reported a new real living wage, which is independently calculated every year to accurately reflect the true cost of living in the UK. Their "Life on Low Pay" report reinforced the link between low pay and food insecurity and found that 27% of workers (more than one million people) earning below the real living wage regularly skipped meals and 73% reported struggling to afford essentials like food and bills. The IFAN has confirmed the widening of the spectrum of clients relying on food banks to include supermarket workers at the same time as increasing interest from supermarkets to support the end of food poverty (https://endchildfoodpoverty.org/). However, no UK supermarket is accredited with the Living Wage Foundation.

While it is necessary to monitor food insecurity in order to plan and inform cross-sectoral government policy and appropriate policy and other interventions, in and of itself it does not provide solutions but contributes importantly to understanding the extent and severity of food poverty (Furey, 2019). Critically, we need research and policy solutions that complement each other so that we do not merely continue to describe food poverty occurrences but effect meaningful change amidst our communities to make life better in a timely way for those experiencing acute and chronic hunger.

Campaigners have called for a statutory requirement for the government to routinely measure and report on the incidence, severity and impact of food poverty in the UK. In the words of the BFAWU (2021, p. 12), which has called for a Food Poverty Impact Assessment to accompany every budget and Queen's speech:

> If the pandemic has taught us anything we must test, trace and eliminate threats to help society as a whole. By properly measuring and recording, governments could be held far more accountable for their performance with regards to the health of the nation, in particular the number of people being lifted out of food poverty each year.
>
> (2022, p. 12)

The right to food

The Nobel Prize winner in economics Amartya Sen's arguments that food shortages are not the result of a lack of food due to natural catastrophes but one of access to available food holds true in the UK today with the food queues and shortages experienced during the COVID-19 crisis. There was no overall shortage of food, yet many go without (Sen, 1981). Sen's arguments about how food is accessed and how that right is conceived are important issues for food policy. On its own, a rights-based approach cannot solve the problems of hunger and hunger catastrophes but they can help define the responses. Sen and Drèze's work has been influential in focusing food policy on how the "poor" can share the benefits of economic growth, pro-poor growth strategies and food distribution programmes targeted at vulnerable communities, not just food aid (Sen & Drèze, 1999).

There is a growing momentum around situating food insecurity in rights-based language. Fundamentally, food poverty is embedded in human rights language and access to "sufficient, safe and nutritious food" (FAO, 2006) is a human right (FAO-OHCHR, 2010). Since 1948, food has been recognised in the Universal Declaration of Human Rights (UNDHR Article 25) because "Everyone has the right to a standard of living adequate for the health and wellbeing of himself and of his family, including food …", and updated in 1999 as the right to adequate food (Garner Gruber, 2006). While not legally binding, it has been succeeded and supported by several international legal instruments that are legally binding, wherein there has been a "general consensus among the nations that provision of this basic human right would be the primary responsibility of the States towards their citizens" (Bagchi & Ghosh, 2018, p. 953), in particular, the 1966 International Covenant on Economic, Social and Cultural Rights (ICESCR Article 11) and the 1989 Convention on the Rights of the Child. Both explicitly name adequate food and housing as basic human rights (Caraher & Furey, 2018, p. 37). More recently, the UK is a signatory to the Sustainable Development Goals (SDGs) that call for an end to poverty (SDG1: No Poverty) in all its forms everywhere to end hunger, achieve food security and improve nutrition (SDG2: Zero Hunger) (Caraher & Furey, 2018, p. 38). The human rights literature (The Universal Declaration of Human Rights, 1948, World Food Summit, 1996, World Summit on Food Security, 2009) actively promotes access to food. The academic literature (Chilton & Rose, 2009, Dowler & O'Connor, 2012, Anderson, 2013, Shannon, 2016) similarly discusses the right to food. Additionally, UN rapporteurs, Special Rapporteur on the Right to Food (de Shutter [Committee on World Food Security, 2009]) and the Special Rapporteur on Extreme Poverty and Human Rights (Alston [UN-OCHR, 2018]) have emphasised the importance of not having to struggle to afford adequate food. The former UN Special Rapporteur on the Right to Food, de Schutter, in his final report (2014) discussed the explicit, implicit and framework laws to implement the *constitutional* right to food (Caraher & Furey, 2018). In some countries, the right to food has been legally enforced through the courts, providing citizens an opportunity to hold their governments to account. Of particular interest from the UK perspective is Scotland, whose government is pursuing a policy to address food poverty based on dignity and the right to food as opposed to one based on charity and food aid (The Scottish Government, 2016).

Indeed, several of the SDGs have direct human rights relevance (e.g. good health and well-being, quality education and clean water). The Zero Hunger Challenge, which preceded the SDGs, included an ambition for zero food loss (Meybeck & Gitz, 2017). Zero food loss is interesting because interest now lies in the redistribution of "surplus" food to the charitable sector to feed our vulnerable. In other words, it has become common practice for saleable food which is approaching its end of shelf life to be diverted from landfill and disseminated to charities to supplement their food provisions and free funds for other charitable giving.

Many have stated that food insecurity is a complex issue and requires a multifaceted and coherent strategy to address it globally (Godfray & Charles, 2010, Dharmasena et al., 2016, Saab, 2018). However, efforts to eradicate food poverty thus far have tended to be downstream rather than policy-level responses (Chapter 2 discusses upstream versus downstream approaches to food policy in more detail). For example, food banks and the redistribution of surplus saleable food as emergency food supplies are increasingly viewed as the default solutions to food poverty. They have become emblematic of modern society and now stand as a metaphor for poverty in society. The provision of food banks and other emergency food aid provision have been reviewed elsewhere (Caraher & Furey, 2018), with a specific focus on the UK, wherein it is argued that food banks must not be institutionalised as a permanent form of assistance in the UK as they have been in North America. For example, Trussell Trust's food parcel distribution increased by more than 50% in 2022 compared to pre-pandemic levels (Trussell Trust, 2022).

The proliferation of food banks has meant that the state is no longer the primary duty bearer and instead food aid is dispensed by the charitable sector, distracting from the causes of food insecurity without addressing the contributory factors creating this public health emergency. Caraher and Furey (2018, p. 76) estimated that upwards of £22–25 million is being spent on providing food to citizens through charities. This shows clearly our retreat from the post- World War II (WWII) concept of the greater good and the social contract to the current situation depicting food banks as the answer to food poverty and the displacement of the welfare state by charity provision (Dowler & O'Connor, 2012, Briggs & Foord, 2017), reflecting the shifting governmentality of food aid.

The principles of "laissez-faire" and "caveat emptor" permeate current-day policies on food welfare, with statements from UK government ministers ranging from enthusiasm for charity food provision (i.e. food banks) to blaming "the poor" for making poor decisions, as in:

"[T]hey've only got themselves to blame 'for making bad decisions'" as in poor budgeting decisions (Chorley, 2013). Some have likened this not to Victorian food policy but to the Elizabethan ones of the "old" Poor Law (Rose, 1971, Thane, 2018, Caraher & Cavicchi, 2014). The Victorian reform of the public health laws of 1834 and 1848 were based on the principles of "less eligibility" and the prevention of pauperism (Finer, 1952), principles which we can find in modern food welfare policies (see the discussion on the principle of "less eligibility" in Chapter 2).

Against this background, food banks have become "successful failures": successful because of their large number and growing demand for their services; failures because they serve to distract from the causes of food insecurity without addressing them. Essentially, the "governmentality" around food has shifted from the state to the charity sector (Caraher & Furey, 2018).

A Food Research Collaboration briefing paper (Caraher & Furey, 2017) set out the argument that the use of surplus, saleable food should not be viewed as the default solution for food poverty. To do so may be viewed as serving "leftover food to left behind people" (Riches, 2018), which represents a two-tier approach to a rights-based food issue.

The incongruity between food waste and food security data calls for an integrated approach to these two issues, particularly in high income countries, where the strategic management of food waste is increasingly acknowledged as a mitigation of food insecurity (Kantor et al., 1997). Michelini et al. (2019) explain that the problem is compounded by the fact that one-third of the food produced for human consumption is wasted every year (FAO, 2017), indicating that food poverty is "more a question of access (related to purchasing power and prices of food) than a supply problem" (Papargyropoulou et al., 2014, p. 109). The co-existence of food poverty along with food spoilage and waste is paradoxical, and therefore, the two issues have become inextricably linked in the academic literature. However, it does not naturally follow that diverting food waste is the solution to food insecurity, irrespective of the political and legal momentum to present the two issues as complementary. Popular and political media need to disaggregate the two distinct separate issues (food insecurity and food waste) and consider each as sufficiently significant as to merit its own informed and sophisticated debate (Caraher & Furey, 2017). The juxtaposition of so much waste alongside high rates of food insecurity presents an ethical conundrum, with "concerns stemming from the ethics of waste at one level through to the imbalance of provision that results in malnutrition at another" (Irani & Sharif, 2018, p. 5), and goes some way to explain why food waste and food insecurity have been linked in the popular and political mind sets. Increasingly, the redistribution of surplus, saleable food is heralded as the panacea for food insecurity; yet the issue is controversial and introduces a policy tension between those who argue that it undermines the concept of public welfare and those who argue for action in the face of hunger (Caraher & Furey, 2018).

According to Sert et al. (2018, p. 1629), many authors have described corporate donations as a form of "strategic philanthropy", where donations of corporate resources are motivated by profit considerations which simultaneously legitimise and benefit the company's reputation and maximise value creation (Fry et al., 1982, Porter & Kramer, 2002, Saiia et al., 2003, Brammer & Millington, 2005, Chen et al., 2008). Alternatively, Brief and Motowidlo (1986), Shaw and Post (1993) and Campbell et al. (1999) proffer that altruistic motivations drive corporate food donations for intrinsic reward reasons such as satisfaction and well-being. Sert et al.'s study (2018, p. 1638) concluded that "motives behind corporate food donations are a combination of strategic, moral and operational efficiency reasons". There is some tension around food waste reduction as a competing and yet complementary mission (Lindberg et al., 2014, p. 1478). Redistribution of surplus food, also known as "food rescue", is used internationally in the emergency food sector to reduce waste and augment food supplies to frontline providers and their clients (Lindberg et al.,

2014, p. 1478). Michelini et al. (2019) report Rombach and Bitsch's (2015) contention of the potential of food sharing for saving edible food waste (surplus food) as a key component of food waste prevention approaches, particularly in high income countries. However, there are tensions between right to food theorists and NGOs' food redistribution charities regarding the use of surplus food as a means of feeding hungry people. At its heart, this is because such redistribution does not address the root causes of poverty and food insecurity (Caraher & Furey, 2017). While not detracting from its current contributory role in mediating hunger on a short-term, acute and emergency basis, there is no evidence to show that it addresses food insecurity in the longer term (Silvasti & Riches, 2014, Riches, 2018). Further, any calls recommending strengthening the diversion of surplus food from landfills to food charities require these types of actions to be critically evaluated before being more widely promoted ultimately as ways to "eliminate hunger" in the UK (All-Party Parliamentary Inquiry into Hunger and Food Poverty, 2014).

The issue may be clarified if we understand that many of these initiatives are designed (laudably) to fight food waste, not poverty. Researchers with a right to food bent (Caplan, 2017, Caraher & Furey, 2017) argue that food insecurity is an income issue and a consequence of political choices and therefore it is the function and imperative of government to impart policy-level, structural solutions for a sustainable resolution of food poverty without recourse to the normalisation of food redistribution services as an inadequate, insecure "sticking plaster" on the gaping wound of (food) poverty (Caraher & Furey, 2017). Accepting that if food waste is ever to be eradicated, all food chain actors will need to create alternative food futures that recognise the importance of ensuring sufficient access to affordable nutritious food while concomitantly appreciating the value of food, so that any excessive, avoidable food waste is rightly deplored. De Schutter (2014) talks about the power of the right to food being about a significant change in food policy at a country level; to date, about half the countries in the world have formally recognised the right to food. Leaders among these are Argentina, Bolivia, Brazil, Ecuador, El Salvador, Guatemala, India, Indonesia, Nicaragua, Peru and Venezuela, with others drafting framework laws on food security or the right to food.

The House of Commons' Environmental Audit Committee, in recognition of the fact that the government has failed to recognise and respond to the issues of hunger, malnutrition and obesity in the UK, recommended the appointment of a Minister for Hunger to ensure action is taken on this agenda (10 January 2019). While appointing a Food Surplus and Waste Champion whose first task is to help ensure the £15 million food waste fund redistributes surplus food that would otherwise be wasted to those most in need (UK Government, 2018); unfortunately, the UK government rejected the Committee's final recommendation for a Hunger Minister thereby missing the opportunity to usefully situate the issue within a singular or lead ministry, with one department ultimately answerable for coordinating efforts from multiple inputs. See the discussion in Chapter 1 on approaches to food policy, including food in all policies. Unfortunately then, we appear consigned to the continuation of the conflation of food waste with food poverty, unless our political leaders are persuaded to indicate their unqualified support for the right to food in recognition of the SDGs and the need for citizens to access food in socially acceptable ways. Caraher and Furey (2017) set out the argument that the use of surplus, saleable food should not be viewed as the default solution for food poverty. To do so may be viewed as serving second-hand food to those in need (Riches, 2018), representing a two-tier approach to a rights-based food issue. Repurposing of wasted food misses the dignity and social justice issues of food poverty, while also being ineffective in reducing hunger or supporting clients out of poverty in the longer term. The use of surplus food as a response to food poverty is problematic because it serves to distract political and popular opinion away from the food waste issue, cannot guarantee a continuous supply of appropriate (socially or healthy) foods and is ultimately demeaning to recipients. This is a crucial point, and one that really needs to be addressed for this community of citizens. Instead, food poverty needs to be located within a context of dignity. It is a disservice to those suffering from poverty to distract from the underlying socio-economic causes of food insecurity. Michelini et al. (2019) cite the "negativities of food rescue" as a way of resolving food poverty and other scholars (e.g. Caraher & Furey, 2017, 2018) have called for the structural causes of food poverty, related to social injustices and inequalities (Cloke et al., 2017), to be addressed. Silvasti and Riches (2014, p. 275) acknowledge the urgent "moral imperative" to feed hungry citizens but counterbalance this with the caution that food aid – in the long term – can undermine food justice and the human right to adequate food. Michelini et al. (2019) conclude that we need to manage the trade-offs of redistribution or surplus food to feed hungry people against the need to eradicate (food) poverty by solving social injustices and inequalities. There are examples from Canada where the power of the food bank lobby has been used to campaign for change (see Freedom 90). There are also examples from Brazil with cities such as Belo Horizonte declaring an official end to hunger (see WWF). In Brazil, there are formal dietary guidelines for food provided for food banks and a mixed economy with some food banks being run by the state and others by charities.

Any reliance on redistributing surplus food undermines calls for purposive actions to be taken that systemically reduce the production of surplus food, address the wider policy issues contributing to food poverty and ensure the right to food. Redistributing surplus food detracts from two significant food system failings, while simultaneously depoliticising hunger and distracting from the calls for policy levers to address the gap between income and food costs. While well intentioned, the practice of redeploying food surpluses absolves the government from its duty to deliver against published *Zero Hunger* and *No Poverty* commitments.

Recent developments

The cost of living crisis and the fact that food is often regarded as the flexible item in the household budget have presented a new, as yet unregulated, opportunity for credit providers that are offering a "buy now, pay later" (BNPL) facility for families to pay for their weekly groceries and other staples. Previously introduced for non-food items, more recently, BNPL has been applied to the food delivery services and now take-home food and beverages. The creditor typically offers interest-free credit with the debtor, repaying the borrowed money paid in three or four instalments over four to six weeks or longer. The sector faces new regulation to catch up with this innovation, but welfare groups warn the new form of credit is a "debt trap" (Ungoed-Thomas, 2022). This is certain to proliferate the prevalence and severity of food insecurity via an insidious debt spiral.

Marcus Rashford: end child food poverty

English Premier League footballer Marcus Rashford, who himself experienced poverty in his childhood, wrote an open letter to Members of Parliament in June 2020 pleading that no child should go to bed hungry. In his letter, he documented his family's experience of food insecurity.

In light of successful campaigning by Rashford and others, in November 2020, the UK government committed to extending free school meals and holiday activities for children from low-income families during Easter, summer and Christmas breaks in England into 2021 (Siddique, 2020). These are short term U-turns by the government and do not represent permanent changes in policy – something for which Rashford had been lobbying with the #EndChildFoodPoverty campaign.

Jack Monroe: the Vimes Boots Index

The UK food poverty campaigner Jack Monroe has influenced ONS to calculate inflation in different ways to illustrate the price rises for different household types and income ranges. Jack is creating a new price index (the "Vimes Boots Index", named after Terry Pratchett's former Boots Theory of Unfairness or Poverty). The purpose of the new price index is intended to document the "insidiously creeping prices" of basic food products over the years (Flood, 2022).

Universal credit

In 2016, the UK saw the roll out of a new benefit system called Universal Credit (UC), which consolidated six legacy benefits – Child Tax Credit, Housing Benefit, Income Support, income-based Jobseeker's Allowance (JSA), income-related Employment and Support Allowance (ESA) and Working Tax Credit – into a single welfare payment. It was introduced with the intention of "making sure work pays" (DWP, 2015). This is a repeat of the concept of "less eligibility" discussed in Chapter 2.

UC was criticised for requiring a six-week lead-in from application before a standard UC claimant would receive their first payment benefit; thereafter, the claimant is paid monthly in arrears. There was significant campaigning by the Trussell Trust and others to reduce the initial six-week wait. In an evidence report, the Committee for Work and Pensions (2017) recommended "the Government aims to reduce the standard waiting time for a first Universal Credit payment to one month". At the time of writing, the official government advice stated that "you may have to wait for around 5 weeks for your first payment" (DWP, n.d.).

In the financial year ending 2017, the UK government spent £264 billion on welfare, which made up 34% of all government spending. However, the 2021 Budget (Frazer, 2021) reported spending on welfare to be £227 billion in 2019/2020 (25.68% of total managed expenditure), £245.4 billion in 2020/2021 (22% of total managed expenditure), £246.7 billion in 2021/2022 (23.61% of total managed expenditure) and forecasted welfare spending to be 25.19% (£300.3 billion) by 2026/2027. Townsend (1979) argued for the construction of a food poverty line to address multiple dimensions of need: for food, this was to be based on the minimum amount of money a household needs to purchase a basic needs (defined in different ways) food bundle and nothing more. This could have been built into UC measures of eligibility and support, but was left off the agenda.

During 2020, the number of people on UC more than doubled to reach unprecedented levels throughout 2021. This served to illuminate much that needs to be improved in our welfare system. A principal point of concern was the loss of the £20 UC uplift that was introduced during the Coronavirus (COVID-19) pandemic. It was introduced as a temporary measure and was withdrawn in October 2021. Food poverty researchers and campaigners objected to its removal, claiming that it reduced significantly what were already inadequate welfare payments on which to exist (Joseph Rowntree Foundation, 2021) and would force people further into debt (Citizens Advice, 2021).

The withdrawal of the £20 UC uplift has provided further impetus to consider a guaranteed income to be able to have a dignified standard of living – whether this be Joseph Rowntree Foundation's (JRF) Minimum Income Standard, a Universal Basic Income providing a regular unconditional payment to everyone, or a Minimum Income Guarantee (MIG) topping up everyone's income to a minimum level (Pollard et al., 2022, p. 2). The current minimum wage has its detractors for reasons that it is not a real living wage. There is scope therefore for the minimum wage to be irreversibly linked to the living wage, but even better would be for the baseline to be lifted to at least £15 per hour (BFAWU, 2021). Whichever model is adopted, ultimately it would serve to ensure a more fit for purpose benefits system.

What are the policy responses?

National Food Strategy (England)

The NFS only applied to England. Its terms of reference included devising a Food Strategy that, among other things, enables people to access "safe, healthy, affordable food; regardless of where they live or how much they earn" (Dimbleby, 2021, p. 63). Part 1 of the Strategy became an urgent response to the COVID-19 pandemic and to prepare for the end of the EU exit with seven recommendations: four of which pertained to expanding free school meals eligibility criteria, extending the Holiday Activity and Food Programme, increasing the value of Healthy Start vouchers and extending the lifetime of the Food and Other Essential Supplies to the Vulnerable Ministerial Task Force to improve the situation for children living in disadvantaged circumstances; and three (sovereignty, standards and scrutiny) referred to trade agreement post the UK's withdrawal from the EU (Dimbleby, 2020, pp. 9–10). As noted earlier, the lead author reported in evidence to a parliamentary committee that the issue of food poverty and insecurity, especially when linked to the welfare system as epitomised by UC, was "politically polarising" (Environment, Food and Rural Affairs Committee, 2021).

Part 2 of the NFS, however, made conspicuously infrequent reference to poverty, insecurity and vulnerability (Table 4.2).

Table 4.2 References to poverty in National Food Strategy: the plan

Terminology	Context in which terminology is used	Number of mentions
Poverty.	Agenda item for Government's Cost of Living Roundtable Eating badly is a "symptom of being lazy", not poverty Department for Work and Pensions has a food poverty remit. Poverty as a stressor (× 2). Poverty and density of fast food outlets. Remit of the Child Food Poverty Taskforce.	7 – plus 9 in references list/endnotes and one advisory panellist's job title.
Food Insecurity.	Measuring food insecurity. Community Eatwell programme (× 2) to prescribe fruit and vegetables to people suffering or at risk of suffering from food insecurity. Food insecurity and free school meals. Food insecurity during school holidays (× 2). Food insecurity increase during the COVID-19 pandemic. Summer food programmes are associated with significantly lower rates of food insecurity. Too narrowly targeted Healthy Start scheme means "over 250,000 children under five living in food insecurity cannot benefit from it".	9 – plus 5, including a definition, reference, footnote, social metric and bar chart title.
Food Poverty.	Department for Work and Pensions has a food poverty remit. Remit of the Child Food Poverty Taskforce.	2 – plus two in references list.

Among its recommendations are "using taxation to encourage corporations to reformulate unhealthy food and using some of that money to help the least affluent access healthy food" (Dimbleby, 2021, p. 63). The recommended interventions for food insecurity include continuation of the three original recommendations from Part 1 (free school meals eligibility; expansion of Holiday Activity and Food programmes and increased value of Healthy Start vouchers), with an additional recommendation around GPs prescribing fruits and vegetables as part of a Community EatWell initiative.

Food Poverty Policy in Wales

The Programme for Government for Wales (https://gov.wales/programme-government) requires the Welsh government to develop a Community Food Strategy in the current political term to advance the Future Generations Wales well-being goals (Welsh Government, 2021c). With particular reference to food poverty and food access, the Welsh government secured £2 million European Transition Funding for local authorities and third sector organisations to work collaboratively to tackle food poverty and address food insecurity in 2021/2022 (Welsh Government, 2021a). Funded initiatives should strengthen existing community food initiatives across each local authority to tackle the root causes of food poverty and food insecurity and develop healthy, sustainable solutions which involve the communities that are affected. Once again, then, the governmentality of food has been shifted, at least in part, to the third sector to resolve.

Other government commitments in Wales include the Programme for Government (2021/2026), which makes no reference to food poverty (food insecurity) and instead references food with respect to developing a greener economy wherein there is a commitment to "acknowledging ecologically sustainable local food production". There is an additional plan to "Develop a Wales Community Food Strategy to encourage the production and supply of locally-sourced food in Wales", referenced under climate and nature emergency commitment.

The Co-Operation Agreement was signed in December 2021 by Welsh Labour and Plaid Cymru to provide all primary school children in Wales free school meals within three years (Welsh Government, 2021b). Many Welsh children living in poverty previously hadn't been eligible to receive free school meals, and so this is a positive and inclusive step forward to reduce health inequalities.

The purpose of the Food (Wales) Bill is to establish a more sustainable food system in Wales to strengthen food security, improve Wales' socioeconomic well-being on a local, regional and national level and enhance consumer choice. It will also help the Welsh government and other public bodies to meet their duties as outlined in the Well-Being of Future Generations (Wales) Act's seven well-being goals and facilitate a more coherent approach to the development of food policy in Wales (Figure 4.1).

While an integrated approach is key to creating a resilient and sustainable food system by providing a framework to help achieve policy targets relating to health and well-being, environmental sustainability, social justice and community resilience, as is the case with the other national food strategies, the Food (Wales) Bill likewise recommends requiring supermarkets and other retailers to donate unwanted and unsold food that is fit for human consumption to charities and food banks to help the most vulnerable in society. The majority of the explanatory rhetoric documents the usefulness of the Bill in meeting environmental targets and obligations, serving once again to conflate food waste and food insecurity in a singular debate.

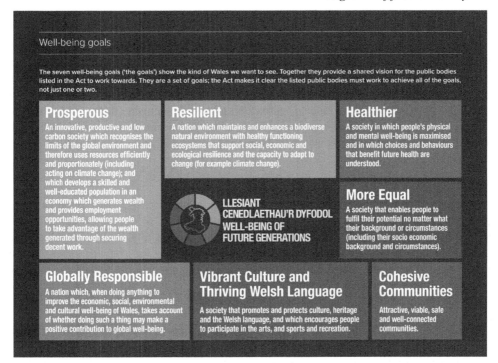

Figure 4.1 Well-being of Future Generations (Wales) Act 2015.

Source: Welsh Government (2015).

Future Food Strategy Framework (Northern Ireland)

The Future Food Strategy Framework for Northern Ireland was consulted upon in autumn 2021. At the time of writing, its vision was articulated as "A transformed food system that protects natural resources for future generations, is economically and environmentally sustainable and provides safe, nourishing, accessible food to people, who make informed healthy choices" (DAERA, 2021, p. 8). The Framework does not explicitly articulate food affordability within its pages, but instead relies on food accessibility, which is defined for the purpose of the Framework as encompassing adequate economic and physical access to nutritious food at household-level food security. Its first strategic priority is "Building connections between health/wellbeing and food" (DAERA, 2021, p. 15), in which it references food poverty as a significant issue in Northern Ireland, with the COVID-19 pandemic having exacerbated the situation. A successful outcome for this strategic priority is foreseen as "a society where everyone has access to safe and nutritious food, where food insecurity and dietary related diseases are in decline, resulting in improved societal health and wellbeing" (DAERA, 2021, p. 16).

The apparently missed opportunity to make explicit reference to "food affordability" in the vision, aim, strategic priorities and principles is concerning and particularly pertinent, given the current strategic economic climate context of a cost-of-living crisis and inflation discussions regarding *Vimes Boots Index*. Additionally, it is problematic to continue the rhetoric of aligning food insecurity with surplus food redistribution. It is imperative that redistribution of surplus food is not seen as a potential solution to food insecurity, for the reasons outlined above in *Right to Food*.

Previous to the Draft Future Food Strategy Framework, Northern Ireland had only one policy document that explicitly referred to food poverty. The *Fitter Future for All Framework for Preventing and Addressing Overweight and Obesity in Northern Ireland 2012–2022* was developed to tackle obesity via a cross-sectoral and cross-government approach on a life course basis. It sought to deliver a coordinated approach to address food poverty through local support, resources and facilities available to those experiencing food poverty, measurable via the percentage of adults experiencing food poverty (DHSSPS, 2012, p. 72).

Good Food Nation Bill (Scotland)

As stated above, the Scottish government is exploring a rights-based approach to food to make good quality food accessible to all (Scottish Government, 2021a). Health boards and local authorities have been tasked with developing wide-ranging plans to help ensure good quality, locally sourced and produced food is a practical everyday reality for everyone under the new legislation. The intention is for the Bill to support social and economic well-being, the environment, health and economic development.

Ending the need for food banks: a draft national plan (Scotland)

Unique to Scotland is the draft National Plan to end the need for food banks. This consultative Plan sets out the Scottish government's vision and approach to ending the need for food banks as a primary response to food insecurity. The Plan affirms that "Food banks are not an appropriate or long-term response to poverty, and where they are the first or only port of call opportunities to strengthen income and prevent future hardship are often missed" (Scottish Government, 2021b, p. 4). Key to the approach is a vision where "Everyone has a sufficient and secure income to be able to access food that meets their needs and preferences … Where help to access food is needed, this is provided in a way that maximises dignity and reduces future need" (Scottish Government, 2021b, p. 4). The Plan reproduces the IFAN's hierarchy of responses, illuminating the superiority of a cash first approach to tackling food insecurity. However, it falls short of articulating an alternate vision that doesn't shift the governmentality of food aid to the charitable sector at all, only going so far as to seek to eradicate the need for food banks as a *primary* response to food aid and could – and should – go further to end the need for charitable food aid as a response to food insecurity with no caveats or qualifications leveraging room for food aid to be a secondary or tertiary response (Figure 4.2).

Importantly, the Plan prioritises a preventative approach to poverty by seeking to improve incomes (whether that be from work that pays a fair income or from social security payments and reduced cost of living) supplemented with a strategy to have solutions on hand other than signposting to food banks, including cash first responses alongside holistic support services. It has as its outcome the intention that everyone has enough income to afford food that meets their needs and preferences (Scottish Government, 2021b, p. 7). The Plan is further situated complementarily alongside the Good Food Nation Bill, Child Poverty Delivery Plan and the right to food in intended attainment of the SDGs.

Conclusions: what are the policy solutions?

The existence of food poverty should not fall to civil society to solve; the primary duty bearer must be government through joined-up, purposive policymaking across government departments

Figure 4.2 Independent Food Aid Network hierarchy of responses to food insecurity 2021.
Source: IFAN (2021, p. 2).

with remits for employment, social security, food, health, housing, transport and education. It is entirely possible to address the rising gap between income and food prices by pursuing policy actions that maximise income and benefit realisation in a sustainable way. Addressing the structural causes of food poverty through economically, socially and culturally fair and appropriate policy levers provide the greatest chance to address the gap between income and food costs and lift our most vulnerable citizens out of food poverty. Governments at the international and national levels must construct policies to address the structural causes that create chronic food poverty. In so doing, these efforts can contribute to the timely achievement of SDG2 ("End hunger, achieve food security and improved nutrition and promote sustainable agriculture") and ensure that the vision for *Zero Hunger* is realised.

The State should guarantee citizens a standard of living by developing a framework approach to protecting and progressing the right to food. This can be achieved by ensuring that policymakers consult with people from the outset, so they can influence actions that would improve the situation of those experiencing food insecurity so that no one presumes to know the answer without first asking the question to the intended beneficiaries.

One solution is that payments should be made directly to households in poverty to adequately protect our vulnerable neighbours at source – the "cash first" approach. It is simply too cost prohibitive not to take action. Government and policymakers must ensure that citizens can afford the cost of living through fit for purpose social security systems and employment schemes that pay a fair day's pay for a fair day's work. We need to act urgently and radically, and re-prioritise and reallocate welfare spending for the greater and common good. Additional awareness raising and signposting is needed to ensure citizens know what help, advice and support they are entitled to and from where to access this assistance in times of need to avoid incidences of unmet need.

A fit for purpose benefit system would require the re-establishment and adequate funding for local discretionary budgets, perhaps with a minimum food element built in. This would support Engel's Law of Expenditure (introduced in Chapter 1) concerning the empirical relationship between income and expenditure on food, whereby the proportion of income spent on food declines as income rises (Güney Işıkara, 2021). It would further provide an important surety that an adequate diet is achievable by all, irrespective of their household income. However, it is complicated by the fact that there is no nationally agreed and regularly costed healthy diet against which household income can be compared (Taylor & Loopstra, 2016). The consensually agreed healthy food basket (*safe*food et al., 2021) that has been costed for the Island of Ireland should be replicated on an annual basis across the UK to inform the adequacy and fitness for purpose of our social security system. These allocations should also be ring-fenced (Caraher & Furey, 2018, p. 105). It is myopic and both morally unacceptable and cost prohibitive not to take meaningful action now.

Sustainable, long-term, pragmatic solutions are needed that address the policy issues under focus: low income, under/unemployment, rising food prices and welfare reform. Food poverty can only be addressed by governments reclaiming their primary duty-bearing status and guaranteeing their citizens a standard of living which includes a right to food, as laid out in the SDGs: *No Poverty* and *Zero Hunger*.

References

Abel-Smith, B. and Townsend, P. 1965, *The Poor and the Poorest*, Bell, London.
Action Against Hunger 2021, *World hunger: key facts and statistics 2021.* Available from: https://www.actionagainsthunger.org/world-hunger-facts-statistics.
All-Party Parliamentary Inquiry into Hunger and Food Poverty 2014, *Feeding Britain: A Strategy for Zero Hunger in England, Wales, Scotland and Northern Ireland*, Children's Society, London.
Anderson, M.D. 2013, "Beyond food security to realizing food rights in the US", *Journal of Rural Studies*, vol. 29, no. 1, pp. 113–122. https://doi.org/10.1016/j.jrurstud.2012.09.004
Bagchi, S. & Ghosh, A. 2018, "A probe into rural households' food accessibility scenario: a micro level study in West Bengal", *Economic Affairs*, vol. 63, no. 4, pp. 953–962. https://doi.org/10.30954/0424-2513.4.2018.19
Bakers Food and Allied Workers' Union (BFAWU) 2022, *The right to food: a law needed by food workers and communities across the UK.* Available from: https://www.bfawu.org/wp-content/uploads/2021/09/BFAWU-Right-to-Food-Report.pdf.
Barker, M. & Russell, J. 2020, "Feeding the food insecure in Britain: learning from the 2020 COVID-19 crisis.", *Food Security*, vol. 12, pp. 65–870. https://doi.org/10.1007/s12571-020-01080-5
Beacom, E., Furey, S., Hollywood, L.E. & Humphreys, P. 2020, "Stakeholder-informed considerations for a food poverty definition", *British Food Journal*, vol. 123, no. 2, pp. 441–454. https://doi.org/10.1108/BFJ-03-2020-0237
Beaumont, J., Lang, T., Leather, S. & Mucklow, C. 1995, *Report on Policy to Low Income Project Team, Nutrition Taskforce*, Institute of Grocery Distribution, Radlett.
Berry, C. 2021, "The missing politics of UK pensions provision", *The Political Quarterly*, vol. 92, no. 4, pp. 707–715. https://doi.org/10.1111/1467-923X.13051
Booth, C. 1902, *Life and Labour of the People in London: The Trades of East London Connected with Poverty* (17 volumes), Macmillan and Co., London.
Borsch, A. & Kjaernes, U. 2016, "Food security and food insecurity in Europe: an analysis of the academic discourse (1975–2013)", *Appetite*, vol. 103, pp. 137–147. https://doi.org/10.1016/j.appet.2016.04.005
Boyle, N.B. & Power, M. 2021, "Proxy longitudinal indicators of household food insecurity in the UK" [version 1; peer review: 1 approved], *Emerald Open Research*, 2021, no. 3, p. 16. https://doi.org/10.35241/emeraldopenres.14311.1
Brammer, S. & Millington, A. 2005, "Corporate reputation and philanthropy: an empirical analysis". *Journal of Business Ethics*, vol. 61, no. 1, pp. 29–44. https://doi.org/10.1007/s10551-005-7443-4
Brief, A.P. & Motowidlo, S.J. 1986, "Prosocial organizational behaviors", *Academy of Management Review*, vol. 11, no. 4, pp. 710–725. https://doi.org/10.5465/amr.1986.4283909

Briggs, S. & Foord, M. 2017, "Food banks and the transformation of British social welfare", *Sociální Práce*, vol. 17, no. 4, pp. 72–86.

Bruening, M., MacLehose, R., Loth, K., Story, M. & Neumark-Sztainer, D. 2012, "Feeding a family in a recession: food insecurity among Minnesota parents", *American Journal of Public Health*, vol. 102, no. 3, pp. 520–526. https://doi.org/10.2105/AJPH.2011.300390

Butler, P. 2019, "UK hunger survey to measure food insecurity", *The Guardian*, London. Available from: https://www.theguardian.com/society/2019/feb/27/government-to-launch-uk-food-insecurity-index.

Campbell, L., Gulas, C.S. & Gruca, T.S. 1999, "Corporate giving behavior and decision-maker social consciousness", *Journal of Business Ethics*, vol. 19, no. 4, pp. 375–383. https://doi.org/10.1023/A:1006080417909

Caplan, P. 2017, *Food poverty and food aid in 21st century UK: a view from anthropology.* Available from: https://blogs.lse.ac.uk/politicsandpolicy/an-anthropological-perspective-on-food-poverty-in-uk/.

Caraher, M. & Cavicchi, A. 2014, "Old crises on new plates or old plates for a new crises? Food banks and food insecurity", *British Food Journal*, vol. 116, no. 9. https://doi.org/10.1108/BFJ-08-2014-0285

Caraher, M. & Furey, S. 2018, *The Economics of Emergency Food Aid Provision: A Financial, Social and Cultural Perspective*, Palgrave Macmillan, Cham.

Caraher, M. & Furey, S. 2017, *Is it appropriate to use surplus food to feed people in hunger? Short-term Band-Aid to more deep rooted problems of poverty.* Food Research Collaboration. Available from: https://foodresearch.org.uk/publications/is-it-appropriate-to-use-surplus-food-to-feed-people-in-hunger/.

Carman, K. G. & Zamarro, G. 2016, "Does financial literacy contribute to food security?" *International Journal of Food and Agricultural Economics*, vol. 4, no. 1, pp. 1–19.

Chen, J.C., Patten, D.M. & Roberts, R.W. 2008, "Corporate charitable contributions: a corporate social performance or legitimacy strategy?" *Journal of Business Ethics*, vol. 82, no. 1, pp. 131–144. https://doi.org/10.1007/s10551-007-9567-1

Chilton, M. & Rose, D. 2009, "A rights-based approach to food insecurity in the United States", *American Journal of Public Health*, vol. 99, no. 7, pp. 1203–1211. https://doi.org/10.2105/AJPH.2007.130229

Chorley, M. 2013, "Poor forced to use food banks? They've only got themselves to blame for making bad decisions, says Michael Gove", *Mail Online* http://www.dailymail.co.uk/news/article-2416737/Michae-Gove-food-banks-Poor-got-blame.html.

Cloke, P., May, J. & Williams, A. 2017, "The geographies of food banks in the meantime", *Progress in Human Geography*, vol. 1, no. 6, pp. 703–726. https://doi.org/10.1177/0309132516655881

Citizens Advice 2021, *2.3 million will be pushed into the red by universal credit cut.* Available from: https://www.citizensadvice.org.uk/about-us/about-us1/media/press-releases/23-million-will-be-pushed-into-the-red-by-universal-credit-cut/.

Committee for Work and Pensions 2017, *The six-week wait.* Available from: https://publications.parliament.uk/pa/cm201719/cmselect/cmworpen/336/33603.htm.

Committee on World Food Security 2009, *Contribution of Mr. Olivier De Schutter Special Rapporteur on the right to food 2nd meeting of the Contact Group to support the Committee on World Food Security (CFS) 22 May 2009, Rome.* Available from: https://www2.ohchr.org/english/issues/food/docs/CFS_reform_note22May09.pdf.

Davis, O. & Geiger, B.B. 2017, "Did food insecurity rise across Europe after the 2008 crisis? An analysis across welfare regimes". *Social Policy and Society*, vol. 16, pp. 343–360. https://doi.org/10.1017/S1474746416000166

Deaton, B.J. & Deaton, B.J. 2020, "Food security and Canada's agricultural system challenged by COVID-19", *Candian Journal of Agricultural Economics*, vol. 68, pp. 143–149. https://doi.org/10.1111/cjag.12227

Deeming, C. 2010, "The historical development of family budget standards in Britain, from the 17th century to the present", *Social Policy & Administration*, vol. 44, pp. 765–788 https://doi.org/10.1111/j.1467-9515.2010.00743.x

Deeming, C. 2011, "Food and nutrition security at risk in later life: evidence from the United Kingdom expenditure & food survey", *Journal of Social Policy*, vol. 40, pp. 471–492. https://doi.org/10.1017/S004727941000070X

DEFRA 2010, *UK Food Security Assessment: Detailed Analysis*, DEFRA, London.

Department for Work and Pensions (DWP) n.d., *Universal credit: new to universal credit.* Available from: https://www.understandinguniversalcredit.gov.uk/new-to-universal-credit/how-and-when-youll-be-paid/#:~:text=4., to%20manage%20during%20this%20period.

Department for Work and Pensions (DWP) 2021, *National statistics: family resources survey: financial year 2019 to 2020.* Available from: https://www.gov.uk/government/statistics/family-resources-survey-financial-year-2019-to-2020/family-resources-survey-financial-year-2019-to-2020.

Department for Work and Pensions (DWP) 2015, *Policy paper: 2010 to 2015 government policy: welfare reform.* Available from: https://www.gov.uk/government/publications/2010-to-2015-government-policy-welfare-reform/2010-to-2015-government-policy-welfare-reform.

Department of Agriculture, Environment and Rural Affairs 2021, *Northern Ireland food strategy framework consultation.* Available from: https://www.daera-ni.gov.uk/sites/default/files/consultations/daera/21.22.076%20NI%20Food%20Strategy%20Framework%20Consultation%20V3.PDF.

DHSSPS, (*Department of Health, Social Services and Public Safety*) 2012, *A fitter future for all: framework for preventing and addressing overweight and obesity in Northern Ireland 2012–2022.* Available from: https://www.health-ni.gov.uk/sites/default/files/publications/dhssps/obesity-fitter-future-framework-ni-2012-22.pdf.

de Schutter, O. 2014, *Final report: the transformative potential of the right to food: report of the Special Rapporteur on the right to food,* United Nations, Washington, DC.

Devereux, S., Béné, C. & Hoddinott, J. 2020, "Conceptualising COVID-19's impacts on household food security", *Food Security*, vol. 12, pp. 769–772. https://doi.org/10.1007/s12571-020-01085-0

Dharmasena, S., Bessler, D.A. & Capps, O., Jr. 2016, "Food environment in the United States as a complex economic system". *Food Policy*, vol. 61, p. 163. https://doi.org/10.1016/j.foodpol.2016.03.003

Dimbleby, D. 2021, *National food strategy – independent review: the plan.* Available from: https://www.nationalfoodstrategy.org/wp-content/uploads/2021/10/25585_1669_NFS_The_Plan_July21_S12_New-1.pdf.

Dimbleby, D. 2020, *National food strategy – part one.* Available from: https://www.nationalfoodstrategy.org/wp-content/uploads/2020/07/NFS-Part-One-SP-CP.pdf.

Dowler, E. 2003, "Food and poverty in Britain: rights and responsibilities" *Social Policy and Administration*, vol. 36, pp. 698–717. https://doi.org/10.1111/1467-9515.00312

Dowler E., Kneafsey M., Lambie, H., Inman, A. & Collier, R. 2011, "Thinking about 'food security': engaging with UK consumers", *Critical Public Health*, vol. 21, pp. 403–416. https://doi.org/10.1080/09581596.2011.620945

Dowler, E.A. & O'Connor, D. 2012, "Rights-based approaches to addressing food poverty and food insecurity in Ireland and UK", *Social Science & Medicine*, vol. 74, no. 1, pp. 44–51. https://doi.org/10.1016/j.socscimed.2011.08.036

Environmental Audit Committee 2019, *Sustainable Development Goals in the UK Follow-Up: Hunger, Malnutrition and Food Insecurity in the UK,* House of Commons, London. https://publications.parliament.uk/pa/cm201719/cmselect/cmenvaud/1491/149102.htm.

Environment, Food and Rural Affairs Committee 2021, *Witness: Henry Dimbleby, lead non-executive board member, Department for Environment, Food and Rural Affairs*, Parliament Live TV. Available from: https://parliamentlive.tv/Event/Index/f27a56f2-119a-4b6b-92b2-dfba6a6120ab.

European Commission 2009, *Food Security: Understanding and Meeting the Challenge of Poverty,* Publications Office of the European Union, Luxembourg.

Finer, S.E. 1952, *The Life and Times of Sir Edwin Chadwick*, Methuen & Co., London.

Flood, A. 2022, Terry Pratchett estate backs Jack Monroe's idea for 'Vimes Boots' poverty index, *The Guardian.* Available from: https://www.theguardian.com/books/2022/jan/26/terry-pratchett-jack-monroe-vimes-boots-poverty-index?utm_source=dlvr.it&utm_medium=twitter.

Food and Agriculture Organization 2017, *Food Loss and Waste Reduction, Measurement and Policy*, FAO, Rome. Available from: https://www.fao.org/platform-food-loss-waste/en/.

Food and Agriculture Organization 2010, *International Scientific Symposium: Biodiversity and Sustainable Diets United Against Hunger,* Food and Agriculture Organization, Rome.

Food and Agriculture Organization 2009, *World Summit on Food Security Bulletin a Summary Report from the World Summit on Food Security,* International Institute for Sustainable Development (IISD) and FAO, Canada.

Food and Agriculture Organization 2006, *Food Security: Policy Brief, vol. 2,* FAO, Rome.

Food and Agriculture Organization (FAO) 1996, *Rome Declaration on World Food Security and World Food Summit Plan of Action,* FAO, Rome.

Food Foundation, 2021, *A Crisis within a Crisis: The Impact of COVID-19 on Household Food Security,* Food Foundation, London. Available from: https://foodfoundation.org.uk/sites/default/files/2021-10/FF_Impact-of-Covid_FINAL.pdf.

Food Foundation 2020a, *Food Insecurity Tracking,* Food Foundation, London. Available from: https://foodfoundation.org.uk/initiatives/food-insecurity-tracking.

Food Foundation 2020b, *Food Insecurity and Debt Are the New Reality under Lockdown,* Food Foundation, London. Available from: https://foodfoundation.org.uk/press-release/food-insecurity-and-debt-are-new-reality-under-lockdown.

Food Sense Wales 2020, *Food for thought: exciting times for Wales' food system.* Available from: https://www.foodsensewales.org.uk/food-for-thought-exciting-times-for-wales-food-system/.

Food Standards Agency 2022a, *Food and you 2 – wave 3.* Available from: https://www.food.gov.uk/research/food-and-you-2/food-and-you-2-wave-3.

Food Standards Agency 2022b, *Food and you 2 – wave 4.* Available from: https://www.food.gov.uk/research/food-and-you-2/food-and-you-2-wave-4

Frazer, L. 2021, *Autumn Budget and Spending Review 2021 a Stronger Economy for the British People,* Her Majesty's Treasury, London. Available from: https://assets.publishing.service.gov.uk/government/uploads/system/uploads/attachment_data/file/1043688/Budget_AB2021_Print.pdf.

Fry, L.W., Keim, G.D. & Meiners, R.E. 1982, "Corporate contributions: altruistic or for-profit?", *Academy of Management Journal,* vol. 25, no. 1, pp. 94–106. https://doi.org/10.5465/256026

Furey, S. 2019, "Food Poverty: Zero Hunger and the Right to Food" in *Encyclopedia of the UN Sustainable Development Goals,* eds. W.L. Filho, A.M. Azul, L. Brandli, P. Gökcin Özuyar & T. Wall, Springer, Cham. https://doi.org/10.1007/978-3-319-69626-3

Furey, S., Caraher, M. Finlay, E., Leeson, P., McFarlane, G. & Taylor, A. 2020, *Food Insecurity and COVID-19 Report to Department for Communities, Northern Ireland.* Unpublished report to Department for Communities.

Furey, S., McLaughlin, C., Beacom, E., Quinn, U. & Surgenor, D. 2019, "What predicts food insecurity? An online survey", *Lancet,* vol. 394, S41, p. 41. https://doi.org/10.1016/S0140-6736(19)32838-7

Gallegos, D., Ramsey, R. & Ong, K.W. 2014, "Food insecurity: is it an issue among tertiary students?" *Higher Education,* vol. 67, no. 5, pp. 497–510. https://doi.org/10.1007/s10734-013-9656-2

Garner Gruber, T. 2006, "'Fixing' hunger in the 21st century: how food sovereignty might turn agriculture 'Right-side Up'", *Appetite,* vol. 47, p. 390. https://doi.org/10.1016/j.appet.2006.08.023

Garthwaite, K. 2016, *Hunger Pains: Life Inside Foodbank Britain,* Policy Press, Bristol.

Godfray, H. & Charles, J. 2010, "Food security: the challenge of feeding 9 billion people", *Science,* vol. 327, no. 5967, pp. 812–818. https://doi.org/10.1126/science.1185383

Godrich, S., Lo, J., Davies, C., Darby, J. & Devine, A. 2017, "Prevalence and socio-demographic predictors of food insecurity among regional and remote Western Australian children", *Australian and New Zealand Journal of Public Health,* vol. 41, no. 6, pp. 585–590. https://doi.org/10.1111/1753-6405.12716

Gundersen, C. & Ziliak, J.P. 2015, "Food insecurity and health outcomes", *Health Affairs,* vol. 34, no. 11, pp. 1830–1839. https://doi.org/10.1377/hlthaff.2015.0645

Güney Işıkara, B. 2021, "The weight of essentials in economic activity", *Review of Radical Political Economics,* vol. 53, no. 1, pp. 95–115. https://doi.org/10.1177/0486613420906900

Houthakker, H.S. 1992, "Are there laws of consumption?" in *Aggregation, Consumption and Trade*, eds. L. Philips & L.D. Taylor, Springer, Dordrecht, pp. 219–223.

Houthakker, H.S. 1957, "An international comparison of household expenditure patterns, commemorating the centenary of Engel's law", *Econometrica*, vol. 25, no. 4, pp. 532–551.

IFAN 2021, *Using Shopping Vouchers Instead of or Alongside Food Parcel Provision*. www.foodaidnetwork.org.uk/cash-first

Irani, Z. & Sharif, A.M. 2018, "Food security across the enterprise: a puzzle, problem or mess for a circular economy?" *Journal of Enterprise Information Management*, vol. 31, no. 1, pp. 2–9. https://doi.org/10.1108/JEIM-03-2017-0045

Joseph Rowntree Foundation 2021, *Universal credit – the impact of cutting the £20-a-week*. Available from https://www.jrf.org.uk/universal-credit-cut-impact-constituency.

Kantor, L., Lipton, K., Manchester, A. & Oliveira, V. 1997, "Estimating and addressing America's food losses", *Food Review*, vol. 20, no. 1, pp. 2–12.

Kisby, B. 2010, "The Big Society: power to the people?", *The Political Quarterly*, vol. 81, pp. 484–491. https://doi.org/10.1111/j.1467-923X.2010.02133.x

Kneafsey, M., Dowler, E., Lambie-Mumford, H., Inman, A. & Collier, R. 2013, "Consumers and food security: uncertain or empowered", *Journal of Rural Studies*, vol. 29, pp. 101–112. https://doi.org/10.1016/j.jrurstud.2012.05.005

Knight, A., O'Connell, R. & Brannen, J. 2018, "Eating with friends, family or not at all: young people's experiences of food poverty in the UK", *Children & Society*, vol. 32, no. 3, pp. 185–194. https://doi.org/10.1111/chso.12264

Lambie-Mumford, H. 2013, "'Every town should have one': emergency food banking in the UK". *Journal of Social Policy*, vol. 42, no. 1, pp. 73–89. https://doi.org/10.1017/S004727941200075X

Lambie-Mumford, H. & Dowler, E. 2014, "Rising use of 'food aid' in the United Kingdom", *British Food Journal*, vol. 116, no. 9, pp. 1418–1425. https://doi.org/10.1108/BFJ-06-2014-0207

Lambie-Mumford, H. & Green, M.A. 2017, "Austerity, welfare reform and the rising use of food banks by children in England and Wales", *Area*, vol. 49, no. 3, pp. 273–279. https://doi.org/10.1111/area.12233

Lambie-Mumford, H. & Sims, L. 2018, "'Feeding hungry children': the growth of charitable breakfast clubs and holiday hunger projects in the UK", *Children & Society*, vol. 32, no. 3, pp. 244–254. https://doi.org/10.1111/chso.12272

Lanchester, J. 2014, *There's poverty in the UK but we are better off calling it inequality*. Available from: https://www.theguardian.com/society/2014/sep/05/poverty-uk-better-calling-it-inequality.

Leather, S. 1996, *The Making of Modern Malnutrition: An Overview of Food Poverty in the UK*, Caroline Walker Trust, London.

Lindberg, R., Lawrence, M., Gold, L. & Friel, S. 2014, "Food rescue – an Australian example", *British Food Journal*, vol. 116, no. 9, pp. 1478–1489. https://doi.org/10.1108/BFJ-01-2014-0053

Living Wage Foundation 2021, *If businesses are serious about ending food poverty, they must pay their own staff a real living wage*. Available from: https://www.livingwage.org.uk/news/if-businesses-are-serious-about-ending-food-poverty-they-must-pay-their-own-staff-real-living.

Loopstra, R. 2020, *Vulnerability to food insecurity since the COVID-19 lockdown Preliminary report*. London: Food Foundation. Available from: https://foodfoundation.org.uk/sites/default/files/2021-10/Report_COVID19FoodInsecurity-final.pdf.

Maxwell, S. & Smith, M. 1992, "Household Food Security: A Conceptual Review" in *Household Food Security: Concepts, Indicators, and Measurements: A Technical Review*, eds. S. Maxwell & T. Frankenberger, UNICEF and IFAD, New York and Rome.

Mayhew, M. 1988, "The 1930s nutrition controversy", *Journal of Contemporary History*, vol. 23, pp. 445–464. https://doi.org/10.1177/002200948802300307

Meybeck, A. & Gitz, V. 2017, "Conference on sustainable food consumption: sustainable diets within sustainable food systems", *Proceedings of the Nutrition Society*, vol. 76, pp. 1–11. https://doi.org/10.1017/S0029665116000653

Michelini, L., Grieco, C., Ciulli, F. & Di Leo, A. 2019, "Uncovering the impact of food sharing platform business models: a theory of change approach", *British Food Journal*, vol. 122, no. 5, pp. 1437–1462. https://doi.org/10.1108/BFJ-06-2019-0422

Mihoreanu, L., Cismas, M.L. & Dănilă, L.M. 2019, "Application of the food security index at European Union regions", *Journal of Economic Development, Environment and People*, vol. 8, no. 1, pp. 38–51.

Mott, R., Keller, K., Britt-Rankin, J. & Ball, A. 2018, "'Out of place around other people': experiences of young people who live with food insecurity", *Children & Society*, vol. 32, no. 3, pp. 207–218. https://doi.org/10.1111/chso.12270

Norman, J. 2010, *The Big Society: the Anatomy of the New Politics*, The University of Buckingham Press, Buckingham.

O'Connor, N., Farag, K. & Baines, R. 2016, "What is food poverty? A conceptual framework", *British Food Journal*, vol. 118, no. 2, pp. 429–449. https://doi.org/10.1108/BFJ-06-2015-0222

O'Connell, R., Owen, C., Padley, M., Simon, A. & Brannen, J. 2019, "Which types of family are at risk of food poverty in the UK? A relative deprivation approach", *Social Policy and Society*, vol. 18, no. 1, pp. 1–18. https://doi.org/10.1017/S1474746418000015

Office for National Statistics 2018, *Indicator 2.2.2*. Available from: https://sdgdata.gov.uk/2-2-2/.

O'Hagan, E. 2013, "Taking action against poverty: unite community", *Community Practitioner*, vol. 86, no. 2, pp. 36–37.

Olson, C.M., Anderson, K., Kiss, E., Lawrence, F.C. & Seiling, S.B. 2004, "Factors protecting against and contributing to food insecurity among rural families", *Family Economics and Nutrition Review*, vol. 16, no. 1, pp. 12–20.

Orr JB. Food, 1936 Health and Income: Report on a Survey of Adequacy of Diet in Relation to Income, Macmillan & Co., London.

Papargyropoulou, E., Lozano, R., Steinberger, J.K., Wright, N. & bin Ujang, Z. 2014, "The food waste hierarchy as a framework for the management of food surplus and food waste", *Journal of Cleaner Production*, vol. 76, pp. 106–115. https://doi.org/10.1016/j.jclepro.2014.04.020

Peña, M. & Bacallao, J. 2000, *Obesity and Poverty: A New Public Health Challenge*, Scientific Publication no 576, Pan American Health Organization, Washington, DC.

Pollard, T., Arnold, S., Caddick, D. & Stirling, A. 2022, *Social Security for All Universal Credit Auto-Enrolment and a Weekly National Allowance*, New Economics Foundation, London. Available from: https://neweconomics.org/uploads/files/NEF_SOCIAL-SECURITY-FOR-ALL.pdf.

Poppendieck, J. 1998, *Sweet Charity? Emergency Food and the End of Entitlement*, Penguin Group, New York.

Porter, M.E. & Kramer, M.R. 2002, "The competitive advantage of corporate philanthropy", *Harvard Business Review*, vol. 80, no. 12, pp. 56–68.

Power, M., Doherty, M.B., Small, N., Teasdale, S. & Pickette, K.E. 2017, "All in it together? Community food aid in a multi-ethnic context", *Journal of Social Policy*, vol. 46, no. 3, pp. 447–471. https://doi.org/10.1017/S0047279417000010

Purdy, J., McFarlane, G., Harvey, H., Rugkasa, J. and Willis, K. 2007, "Food poverty: fact or fiction?". Available from: https://www.safefood.eu/SafeFood/media/SafeFoodLibrary/Documents/Professional/Food%20Poverty/PHA2007_FoodPovertyFactorFiction.pdf.

Riches, G. 2018, *Food Bank Nations: Poverty, Corporate Charity and the Right to Food*, Routledge, Oxon.

Robson, W.A. 1963, "New Introduction" in: *English Poor Law History*, eds. S. Webb and B. Webb, Longmans, Green and Company, Edinburgh, pp. v–xx.

Rombach, M. & Bitsch, V. 2015, "Food movements in Germany: slow food, food sharing, and dumpster diving", *International Food and Agribusiness Management Review*, vol. 18, no. 3, pp. 1–24.

Rose, M.E. 1971, *The English Poor Law 1780–1930*, David & Charles, Newton Abbot.

Rowntree, S. 1941, *Poverty and Progress: A Second Social Survey of York*, Longmans, Green, London.

Saab, A. 2018, "An international law approach to food regime theory", *Leiden Journal of International Law*, vol. 31 no. 2, pp. 251–265. https://doi.org/10.1017/S0922156518000122

Saiia, D.H., Carroll, A.B. & Buchholtz, A.K. 2003, "Philanthropy as strategy: when corporate charity 'begins at home'", *Business & Society*, vol. 42, no. 2, pp. 169–201. https://doi.org/10.1177/0007650303042002002

Safefood, Consumer Council for Northern Ireland, Food Standards Agency in Northern Ireland 2021, *What is the cost of a healthy food basket in NI in 2020?* Available from: https://www.safefood.net/getattachment/dcaa7b5f-354b-41a0-bf57-80cc7387ac9e/Cost_of_a_healthy_food_basket_NI_Report.pdf?lang=en-IE.

Sage, C. 2012, *Environment and Food*, Routledge, Oxon, UK.

Scottish Government 2021a, *Good Food Nation Bill introduced.* Available from: https://www.gov.scot/news/good-food-nation-bill-introduced/.

Scottish Government 2021b, *Ending the need for food banks: consultation on a draft national plan.* Available from: https://www.gov.scot/isbn/9781802015119.

Scottish Government 2016, *Dignity: ending hunger together in Scotland. The report of the independent working group on food poverty*, The Scottish Government, Edinburgh.

Sen, A. 1981, *Poverty and Famines: An Essay on Entitlement and Deprivation*, Clarendon Press, Oxford.

Sen, A. & Drèze, J. 1999, *The Amartya Sen and Jean Drèze Omnibus: (Comprising) Poverty and Famines; Hunger and Public Action; and India: Economic Development and Social Opportunity*, Oxford University Press, India.

Sert, S., Garrone, P. Melacini, M. & Perego, A. 2018, "Corporate food donations: altruism, strategy or cost saving?", *British Food Journal*, vol. 120, no. 7, pp. 1628–1642. https://doi.org/10.1108/BFJ-08-2017-0435

Shannon, D. 2016, "Food justice, direct action and the human rights enterprise", *Critical Sociology*, vol. 42, no. 6, pp. 799–814. https://doi.org/10.1177/0896920515608924

Shaw, B. & Post, F.R. 1993, "A moral basis for corporate philanthropy", *Journal of Business Ethics*, vol. 12, no. 10, pp. 745–751. https://doi.org/10.1007/BF00881305

Siddique, H. 2020, Marcus Rashford forces Boris Johnson into second u-turn on child food poverty, *The Guardian*, https://www.theguardian.com/education/2020/nov/08/marcus-rashford-forces-boris-johnson-into-second-u-turn-on-child-food-poverty.

Silvasti, T. & Riches, G. 2014, "Hunger and Food Charity in Rich Societies: What Hope for the Right to Food?" in: *First World Hunger Revisited*, eds. G. Riches & T. Silvasti. Palgrave Macmillan, London, pp. 191–208.

Statista 2022, *The UK economy - statistics & facts.* Available from: https://www.statista.com/topics/6500/the-british-economy/.

Tarasuk, V., Fafard St-Germain, A.A. & Loopstra, R. 2019, "The relationship between food banks and food insecurity: insights from Canada", *Voluntas*, pp. 1–12. https://doi.org/10.1007/s11266-019-00092-w

Taylor, A. & Loopstra, R. 2016, *Too Poor to Eat: Food Insecurity in the UK*, Food Foundation, London.

Taylor-Robinson, D., Rougeaux, E., Harrison, D., Whitehead, M., Barr, B. & Pearce, A. 2013, "Letters: malnutrition and economic crisis – the rise of food poverty in the UK", *British Medical Journal*, vol. 347, p. f7157. https://doi.org/10.1136/bmj.f7157.

Thane, P. 2018, *Divided Kingdom: A History of Britain, 1900 to the Present*, Cambridge University Press, Cambridge.

Thompson, C., Smith, D. & Cummins, S. 2018, "Understanding the health and wellbeing challenges of the food banking system: a qualitative study of food bank users, providers and referrers in London", *Social Science and Medicine*, vol. 211, pp. 95–101. https://doi.org/10.1016/j.socscimed.2018.05.030

Townsend, P. 1979, *Poverty in the United Kingdom: A Survey of Household Resources and Standards of Living*, Penguin, Harmondsworth.

Trussell Trust 2022, *Almost 1.3 million emergency parcels provided in last 6 months.* Available from: https://www.trusselltrust.org/2022/11/10/almost-1-3-million-emergency-parcels-provided-to-people-across-uk-experiencing-hunger-over-past-six-months-as-cost-of-living-emergency-drives-tsunami-of-need-to-food-banks/?utm_source=sfmc&utm_medium=email&utm_campaign=Budget+Reaction+Nov+2022+-+Campaigners&utm_term=devastating+statistics&utm_id=310055&sfmc_id=96309004.

Trussell Trust 2021, *End of year stats.* Available from: https://www.trusselltrust.org/news-and-blog/latest-stats/end-year-stats/.

Trussell Trust 2019, *The Trussell Trust responds to the spring statement*, 13th March. Available from: https://www.trusselltrust.org/2019/03/13/trussell-trust-responds-spring-statement/.

UK Government 2018, Gove appoints food waste champion. Available from: https://www.gov.uk/government/news/gove-appoints-food-waste-champion.

UKSSD 2018, *Measuring up: how the UK is performing on the UN Sustainable Development Goals*. Available from: https://sdgtoolkit.org/tool/measuring-up-how-the-uk-is-performing-on-the-un-sustainable-development-goals/.

Ungoed-Thomas, J. 2022, Buy now, pay later grocery schemes are a 'debt trap' for struggling families, *The Guardian*. Available from: https://www.theguardian.com/money/2022/jan/29/buy-now-pay-later-grocery-schemes-are-a-debt-trap-for-struggling-families.

United Nations 1989, *Convention on the rights of the child*. Available from: https://www.ohchr.org/en/professionalinterest/pages/crc.aspx.

United Nations 1966, *International covenant on economic, social and cultural rights*. Available from: https://www.ohchr.org/en/professionalinterest/pages/cescr.aspx.

United Nations 1948, *The Universal Declaration of Human Rights*, The United Nations, New York.

UN-OCHR 2018, *Statement on visit to the United Kingdom, by Professor Philip Alston, United Nations Special Rapporteur on extreme poverty and human rights*. Available from: https://www.ohchr.org/en/NewsEvents/Pages/DisplayNews.aspx?NewsID=23881.

Webb, B. 1910, "The Minority Report in its relation to public health and the medical profession", *Public Health*, vol. 23, pp. 153–164.

Weber, M. 1976 [1930], *The Protestant Ethic and the Spirit of Capitalism*, 15th impression edn, Allen and Unwin, Channel Islands.

Welsh Government 2021a, *ATISN 15267 - food strategy*. Available from: https://gov.wales/sites/default/files/publications/2021-07/atisn15267.pdf.

Welsh Government 2021b, *Explanatory memorandum: The Food (Wales) Bill*. Available from: food-wales-bill-em-october-2021-final-e.pdf (senedd.wales).

Welsh Government 2021c, *Welsh Government programme for government: update*. Available from: https://gov.wales/programme-for-government-2021-to-2026-html.

Welsh Government 2015, *Well-being of Future Generations (Wales) Act 2015: essentials guide*. Available from: https://gov.wales/sites/default/files/publications/2021-10/well-being-future-generations-wales-act-2015-the-essentials-2021.pdf.

Wills, W.J., Danesi, G., Kapetanaki, A.B. & Hamilton, L.K. 2018, "The socio-economic boundaries shaping young people's lunchtime food practices on a school day", *Children & Society*, vol. 32, no. 3, pp. 195–206. https://doi.org/10.1111/chso.12261

5 Sustainable diets

Linking nutrition and environment

Introduction

As documented in previous chapters, concerns about the global impact of the food system are growing, with frequent reports linking both food production and consumption to planetary ill health in complex and multifaceted ways (Willett et al., 2019, FAO et al., 2021). While world-wide the food production system has been refined and developed to feed billions of people, consumption of the food this system produces impacts billions who are affected by the so-called "triple burden" of malnutrition (see Chapter 2): overweight and obesity, insufficient nutrients and hunger (Labadarios, 2005, Pinstrup-Andersen, 2007). In 2016, more than 1.9 billion adults aged 18 years and older were overweight. Of these, over 650 million adults were obese. Thirteen per cent of the world's adults and 124 million children and adolescents (6% girls and 8% boys) were obese in 2016 (WHO, 2021a). Most recent data (Global Nutrition Report, 2021) show that globally, 149.2 million children under five years of age are stunted, 45.4 million are wasted and 38.9 million are overweight. Over 40% of all men and women (2.2 billion people) are now over-weight or obese. This "triple burden" of malnutrition has been exacerbated by the COVID-19 pandemic (FAO et al., 2021), which has increased food insecurity worldwide. At the same time, 30% of all food produced is lost or wasted, and the food system contributes to approximately one-third of all greenhouse gases (GHGs) emitted, as well as biodiversity loss, pollution and soil degradation (Ingram et al., 2020). Academics and actors in the food policy sphere have argued that both healthier and more environmentally sustainable diets are not only possible but compat-ible, arguing that, for example, a largely plant-based diet is better for both human and planetary health (Willett et al., 2019).

The origins of the concept of sustainable diets are credited to Gussow and Clancy (1986), and the literature in this area has grown since the late twentieth century. More recent work links healthy diets with a wider vision of sustainability, encompassing more than environmen-tal concerns. Mason and Lang proposed a multi-criteria six-pronged approach to sustainable diets, giving equal weight to nutrition and public health, the environment, sociocultural issues, food quality, economics and governance (Mason & Lang, 2017); see Chapters 2 and 3 for fur-ther discussions. This echoes the work of other academics in the UK and globally working to develop the concept of "food systems" and a "food systems approach", which strives to connect the food system and all its actors, processes and actions to its drivers and outcomes, including environmental, health, social, political and economic drivers and outcomes (Ericksen et al., 2012, van Berkum et al., 2018, Parsons et al., 2019). Food policy, as an academic subject, is the study of the relationship between all these areas of concern and how policies are formed or not developed despite the weight of the evidence (see also Chapter 2). Parsons et al. (2019) depicted this in a map of the food system designed to aid analysis of the drivers and outcomes of food

DOI: 10.4324/9781003260301-5

policy interventions for food systems change (see Chapter 2, Figure 2.1). In relation to policy formulation, this requires an understanding of the interconnections between policy areas which directly relate to the food supply chain, such as food safety standards, as well as those that have an indirect but interconnected impact, such as migration policy.

Despite this work on food systems and a more holistic view of the drivers and outputs of the food system as a whole, many of the existing and historic food policies can be divided into two groups: the first are those that have nutritional health as their focus and the second are agricultural/processing policies (Bronner, 1997, Milo & Helsing, 1998); see also Chapter 2. Egger and Swinburn make the link between the nutrition implications and the planetary ones in the subtitle of their book *How we're eating ourselves and the planet to death* (Egger & Swinburn, 2010), echoing the earlier work of popular US writer Frances Moore Lappe in 1971, with her *Diet for a Small Planet* (Lappe, 1971) followed by others in the UK, including Colin Tudge (1980) with *Future Cook: A Taste of Things to Come*. There are two important arguments in this arena. One, that policies relating to food, whether its consumption or production, should be integrated and coherent (Parsons, 2019). The second, that food policy should not become a distinct area of endeavour, seeking instead to become part of, and embedded in, other policies. Like the concept of health in all policies (see Chapter 2), food should be in all policies (Parsons & Hawkes, 2019). This in reality is difficult to achieve, and the fallback position is to develop a separate food policy. This usually takes the form of a nutrition-based policy and/or a separate agricultural one (Milo & Helsing, 1998, Caraher & Coveney, 2004), despite recommendations from WHO for the development of joint policies following the 1992 International Conference on Nutrition. Public concerns with fair trade and sustainability, which emerged in the 1960s, have found new nuances in current movements such as Extinction Rebellion in the UK. The confluence of Brexit and concerns with both diet-related chronic diseases and environmental concerns with food production offer an opportunity to reform the food system. However, there are still few food policies that attempt to define or implement both healthy and sustainable diets (Fanzo & Davis, 2021).

Concerns over climate change and livelihoods connected with the food system and their impacts have given rise to new concerns with food policymaking. This chapter explores the development of UK food policy in this area through five examples of approaches to sustainable diets: Eco-Nutrition; the One Health approach; the United Nations Sustainable Development Goals (SDGs); Food Citizenship; and finally, industry initiatives such as Voluntary Sustainability Standards (VSSs).

Eco-nutrition

The term "Eco-Nutrition" or "ecological nutrition" has been developed by Lang and others (Lang, 2007, Lang et al., 2009, Rayner & Lang, 2012, Lang & Heaseman, 2015, Mason & Lang, 2017) as a feature of the Ecological Public Health concept, first credited in the academic literature to Kickbusch (1989). Both Ecological Public Health and Eco-Nutrition have their roots in the Brundtland Report of 1987, produced for the World Commission on Environment Development chaired by Dr Gro Harlem Brundtland, the former Norwegian Prime Minister and public health doctor. The Brundtland Report argued for sustainable development as a central focus of economic policy (World Commission on Environment and Development, 1987), with an integrated approach extending beyond an individual focus on nutrition or public health:

> These health, nutrition, environment, and development links imply that health policy cannot be conceived of purely in terms of curative or preventive medicine, or even in terms of

greater attention to public health. Integrated approaches are needed that reflect key health objectives in areas such as food production; water supply and sanitation: industrial policy, particularly with regard to safety and pollution; and the planning of human settlements. Beyond this, it is necessary to identify vulnerable groups and their health risks and to ensure that the socio-economic factors that underlie these risks are taken into account in other areas of development policy.

(World Commission on Environment and Development, 1987, p. 94)

Rayner and Lang (2012) situate Ecological Public Health as one of five models of public health (see Table 5.1). Chronologically developed, Ecological Public Health is positioned as central to policy responses required in the twenty-first century, due to increasing and multiple impacts of climate change and a need to find a model for public health that acknowledges and deals with complexity and system dynamics. The central idea of Ecological Public Health is that "health depends on the successful co-existence of the natural world and social relationships" (Rayner & Lang, 2012, p. 101).

Ecological nutrition or Eco-Nutrition builds on this Ecological Public Health notion of successful co-existence between the natural world and society, but with an obvious tighter focus on human nutrition. Earlier models of the Eco-Nutrition approach define the "eco" of Eco-Nutrition in narrow terms, interpreting this approach as a call to eat within planetary limits (Lang et al., 2009). This was updated with an increased emphasis on ecological nutrition in the 2019 EAT-Lancet Commission report (Willett et al., 2019). The EAT-Lancet Commission was made up of 37 international experts who worked together to define a healthy diet from a sustainable food system. The EAT-Lancet "Global Planetary Health Diet" was devised from peer-reviewed academic literature and is high in fruits and vegetables, legumes, whole grains, nuts and unsaturated fats and low in seafood, dairy and poultry. It contains very little red or processed meat, refined grains or added sugar.

The report and the reference diet it promoted were high profile and among the first attempts in the world to define a sustainable diet, although notable exceptions can be found in a handful of countries, for example, Sweden and Brazil, where governments have developed national food-based dietary guidelines that include sustainability (Fischer & Garnett, 2016). The EAT-Lancet Report was welcomed by many in the nutrition, environment and public health arenas and received widespread media coverage and public debate. However, it was not without its critics, some of whom particularly pointed to unintended consequences and negative implications for the livestock sector; others noted a "one-size-fits-all" diet may not be appropriate for populations across high-, middle- and low-income countries (Fanzo & Davis, 2021) and

Table 5.1 Five models of public health

Model	Core idea
Sanitary-environmental.	The environment is a threat to health.
Biomedical.	Health improvement requires understanding of biological causation.
Social-behavioural.	Health is a function of knowledge and behaviour patterns.
Techno-economic.	Economic and knowledge growth is prime elevator of health.
Ecological public health.	Health depends on successful co-existence of the natural world and social relationships.

Source: Adapted from Rayner and Lang (2012, p. 101).

that the diet itself may not be accessible or affordable for all. Hirvonen et al. (2020) estimated that the cost of food on the EAT-Lancet diet represents a small fraction of the average income in high-income countries, but exceeds household per capita income for at least 1.58 billion people in the world. An EAT-Lancet Commission 2.0 has been announced, again co-chaired by Professor Walter Willett with Professor Johan Rockström and Dr. Shakuntala Thilsted. Working with 24 Commissioners from 19 countries and a range of disciplines, EAT-Lancet 2.0 will build on the work of the first Commission and include new elements. These seem to address some of the criticisms of the first report and include "a greater focus on diversity and the adaptation of regional and local diets, strengthened diversity in the composition of the Commission and a new focus on food justice and social food system goals" (EAT Forum, 2022). EAT-Lancet 2.0 is due to report in 2024.

Other approaches to ecological nutrition broaden its framework in order to encapsulate a wider range of domains than just health and environment. Mason and Lang's (2017) version of Eco-Nutrition gives equal weight to nutrition and public health, the environment, sociocultural issues, food quality, economics and governance. This attempts to bring order and rationality to policy from what is either seen as too complex to handle or is addressed simplistically and ineffectually. This is in line with the Food Systems Approach outlined earlier in this chapter and global attempts to organise food policy. For example, the FAO's Biodiversity and Sustainable Diets Symposium (Food and Agriculture Organization, 2010) defined sustainable diets more broadly than nutrition plus environment (or calories plus carbon):

> Sustainable Diets are those diets with low environmental impacts which contribute to food and nutrition security and to healthy life for present and future generations. Sustainable diets are protective and respectful of biodiversity and ecosystems, culturally acceptable, accessible, economically fair and affordable; nutritionally adequate, safe and healthy; while optimizing natural and human resources.
>
> (Food and Agriculture Organization, 2010)

Allied to this are issues of livelihoods in the food system such as modern slavery, animal welfare, farm gate prices and migrant worker rights.

In terms of food policymaking in the UK, the Eco-Nutrition approach towards sustainable diets has gained traction across the four devolved administrations (see Table 5.2). Each nation, to some extent, acknowledges the importance of sustainable diets. For example, the National Food Strategy (NFS) for England (Dimbleby, 2021) argued that diets need to change to meet health, climate and nature commitments. In Northern Ireland, the Draft Environment Strategy includes a sustainable agri-food industry which promotes health and well-being through locally sourced nutrition. In Scotland, the food standards agency Food Standards Scotland (FSS), has produced a Strategy for 2021–2026 which argues for "Healthy Safe and Sustainable Food" (Food Standards Scotland, 2021), and in Wales, their recently proposed Food (Wales) Bill (Welsh Parliament, 2022), which although only in the first of four stages of its passage through the Senedd at the time of writing, is an indication of the appetite for policy change. The proposal is for "a Bill that would establish a more sustainable food system in Wales to strengthen food security, improve Wales' socioeconomic well-being, and enhance consumer choice" (Welsh Parliament, 2022).

Sustainable diets have successfully been put on the policy agenda and proposed across the UK. It remains to be seen whether policy implementation follows.

Table 5.2 Policy examples of sustainable diet approaches

	Food policy example (England)	*Food policy example (Northern Ireland)*	*Food policy example (Scotland)*	*Food policy example (Wales)*
Ecological Nutrition.	National Food Strategy (Dimbleby, 2021).	Northern Ireland Draft Environment Strategy (DAERA, 2022).	Food Standards Scotland Strategy for 2021–2026 (Food Standards Scotland, 2021).	Food (Wales) Bill (Welsh Parliament, 2022).
OneHealth.	HM Government (2019b). Tackling Antimicrobial Resistance 2019–2024: The UK's Five-Year National Action Plan.	Changing the Culture 2019–2024 – One Health (DAERA, 2019).	Health Protection Scotland, 2017. Scottish One Health Antimicrobial Use and Antimicrobial Resistance Report in 2016.	Wales Animal Health and Welfare Framework Implementation Plan 2022–2024 – One Health One Welfare One Wales (Welsh Government, 2022).
SDGs.	UK's Voluntary National Review of the Sustainable Development Goals (HM Government 2019a). Implementing the Sustainable Development Goals (HM Government, 2021a).	Sustainability for the Future "DAERA's Plan to 2050" (DAERA, 2021b).	Scotland and the sustainable development goals: a national review to drive action (Scottish Government, 2020).	Wales and the Sustainable Development Goals (Welsh Government, 2019).
Food Citizenship.	Liverpool "Good Food Plan" (Liverpool Express, 2021).	Northern Ireland Food Strategy Framework (Public Consultation Document) (DAERA, 2021a).	Aberdeen as a Sustainable Food Place (Aberdeen City Council, 2022).	Welsh Food Partnerships Funding (Sustainable Food Places, 2022).
Industry Initiatives.	Tesco Food Waste Initiatives (Tesco, n.d.).	Veg NI "Parful Produce" (Veg NI, 2021).	Scottish Salmon Sustainability Charter (Salmon Scotland, 2022).	Food and Drink Wales: a Vision for the Food and Drink industry from 2021 Building on our Success (Food and Drink Wales, 2021).

One Health

The term One Health derives from the early part of the twenty-first century and emerged in response to a series of global health crises created by zoonotic viruses that had the potential to create pandemics (Gibbs, 2005, Gibbs, 2014). The term "zoonosis" had been coined in the nineteenth century by Rudolf Virchow, a German doctor, interested in the links between human and animal diseases. Zoonoses are diseases which spread from animals to humans and vice versa, and Virchow's understanding paved the way for important links between human and veterinary medicine to be made. Links between animal and human health have long been recognised, dating back to Hippocrates and Aristotle who wrote about the links between human health and the environment. However, the motivating factor for interest in these connections tended to be an overriding desire to protect human health rather than a more holistic consideration of planetary health (Evans & Leighton, 2014). The One Health concept arose from a desire to recognise not only the importance but the interconnectedness of human, animal and plant health, and later on in its development, air, water and soil health into one overall planetary health.

In 2009, the One World – One Health: Brazil 2009 Meeting called for a "unity of approach achievable only through a consilience of human, domestic animal and wildlife health – One Health" (OWOH, 2009, Destoumieux-Garzón et al., 2018). Later definitions identified a broader range of interlinked priorities consistent with developing work on ecosystems and planetary health, including human, animals and plants as well as the wider ecosystem. One of the drivers behind the development of this integrated approach was the spread of anti-microbial resistance (AMR). The overuse of antibiotic medicines, both in human and animal treatments, has led to bacterial resistance to antibiotics, so that they are becoming less and less effective at treating common illnesses. The World Health Organization (WHO) views AMR as one of the greatest threats to global health, development and food security (Hutchinson, 2017, WHO, 2020). Many countries have acknowledged the importance of the One Health approach as a way to tackle this threat, implementing AMR National Action Plans (see, e.g., Government of Canada, 2017, HM Government, 2019b, Ministere des Solidarit*è*s et de Sant*é*, 2021, or, for a full library of AMR National Action Plans, see WHO, 2022). However, despite general agreement that the One Health approach is effective in tackling AMR, the concept is still more commonly embraced by veterinarians than medics (Järhult, 2015), and the pathways to interdisciplinary work and practical collaboration between general medical practitioners and veterinarians remain unclear (Steele et al., 2019).

More recently, the COVID-19 pandemic has shone a new spotlight on the concept and importance of the One Health approach. Most emerging infectious diseases originate in animals (CDC, 2022) and along with Ebola and avian influenza as well as bovine tuberculosis, COVID-19 has been designated as a zoonosis (Haider et al., 2020). Why is this important for food policy? It is the closer interactions between humans, animals and the environment due to globalised and industrial food systems, and climate change and the loss of natural habitats that can increase the likelihood of new diseases and a further global pandemic emerging (Benton, 2020, Rivera-Ferre et al., 2021). It has been argued that systems approaches and collaborations beyond the normal siloes such as One Health are required to prepare for this eventuality (Aarestrup et al., 2021), although exactly what this would look like in practice is not always clear. The so-called Tripartite of FAO, OIE and WHO (the Food and Agriculture Organization of the UN; the World Organisation for Animal Health, formerly the Office International des Epizooties and the World Health Organization) was set up in the wake of the avian influenza pandemic of 2009. Its mission to promote and endorse the One Health approach at a global level, working with UNEP (the United Nations Environment Programme) to "mainstream" One Health in order to be able to prepare, predict, detect and respond to future global health threats. Since COVID-19, the Tripartite expert group has announced a new definition of One Health:

> One Health is an integrated, unifying approach that aims to sustainably balance and optimize the health of people, animals and ecosystems. It recognizes the health of humans, domestic and wild animals, plants, and the wider environment (including ecosystems) are closely linked and inter-dependent. The approach mobilizes multiple sectors, disciplines and communities at varying levels of society to work together to foster well-being and tackle threats to health and ecosystems, while addressing the collective need for clean water, energy and air, safe and nutritious food, taking action on climate change, and contributing to sustainable development.
>
> (WHO, 2021b)

In 2023 UNEP (United Nations Environment Programme) joined the Tripartite to form a Quadripartite (UNEP, 2023). At this global level, there are calls for a pandemic treaty along One Health lines, which would allow increased international surveillance across disciplines and sectors alongside communication and co-ordination of the results. All this would require greater funding and structured implementation through a new global body (Carabin, 2021). At the time of writing, the political focus, certainly in the UK, has moved away from pandemic preparedness towards geopolitics with the invasion of Ukraine, and global political tensions may drive policy and funding in the short term.

In terms of food policymaking across the UK, a number of policies across the devolved administrations have taken a One Health approach, and these often reference the COVID-19 pandemic as relevant for their development or continuation of the policy (see Table 5.2). In the UK as a whole, the government has implemented a National Action Plan using One Health principles to tackle AMR (HM Government, 2019b). In Northern Ireland, "Changing the Culture 2019–2024 – One Health" supplements the UK's national strategy with a particular focus on Northern Ireland, where the strategy acknowledges the "current antibiotic prescribing rate is significantly higher than in the rest of the UK" (Department of Health, 2019). In Scotland, a One Health approach to AMR was taken from 2016 and National Services Scotland produces an annual Antimicrobial Resistance Report which provides data from human and animal healthcare settings for monitoring purposes (e.g. see National Services Scotland, 2021). In Wales, a new Animal Health and Welfare Framework was published in 2022 with a key "One Health, One Welfare and Biosecurity" message, acknowledging the interdependency of human, animal and environmental health, particularly in the wake of the pandemic and Brexit (Welsh Government, 2022).

Global governance of sustainable diets: SDGs

As noted in Chapters 1 and 8, while this book focuses on food policy in the UK, this is not made in a vacuum and global food governance sets the overall context in which our food policies are developed and made. Since food production and consumption are both impacted by and have an impact on sustainability, which knows no national boundaries, the work of global governance organisations such as the WHO or the FAO are particularly important in the Sustainable Diets space.

The SDGs were unveiled by the UN in 2015 as part of the 2030 Agenda for Sustainable Development. These 17 Goals are an attempt to galvanise action among all countries. They ask nations to work together to tackle climate change and at the same time end poverty and reduce inequalities – all while improving health and education and fostering economic growth (UN, 2015). This ambitious programme was a call to action which had, at its heart, the notion of coherence, aiming for the positive outcomes outlined above to be achieved without negative trade-offs or compromises. The UN described how strategies to achieve an end to poverty and inequality must go hand in hand with strategies to improve health and education. This notion of co-benefits or synergies echoes the holistic food systems approach, described earlier in this chapter, and is laudable as an aim, but as outlined above, difficult to achieve in practice. The UN described the decades of work that preceded the SDGs (UN, n.d.) – see Table 5.3, and below we describe how these meetings moved towards an integrated approach to sustainable development.

As with the other approaches already outlined in this chapter (Eco-Nutrition and One Health), the SDGs were developed from previous, less comprehensive conceptions of sustainability. The early UN environment conference of 1972 had focussed on what was called the "Human Environment", and the 26 principles in the declaration did not discuss "sustainability" or "sustainable development", instead concentrating on ecological issues such as water, earth and air pollution. Social and economic prosperity were discussed, but the focus here was on the gap between "developing countries" and "industrialized countries" (UN, 1973). As noted above, the Brundtland Report following the 1987 World Commission on Environment and Development (1987) developed this thinking and promoted the term "sustainable development", which became popular worldwide, although a clear definition has remained elusive. The Earth Summit of 1992 extended the concept with an action plan for sustainable development ("Agenda 21") that took a more multilateral and integrative approach, taking into account horizontal collaboration as well as vertical involvement across different levels: local as well as national and international (Tokuç, 2013).

The concept of "Goals" was introduced at the Millennium Summit in 2000, with the introduction of the eight Millennium Development Goals (MDGs) (UN, 2000). These focussed on

Table 5.3 UN progress towards the Sustainable Development Goals

Date	Meeting	Outcome
June 1972.	UN Conference on the Human Environment, Stockholm, Sweden.	Stockholm Declaration and Plan of Action (UN, 1973). Creation of UNEP (United Nations Environment Programme).
June 1992.	Earth Summit, Rio de Janeiro, Brazil.	Agenda 21 (UNSD, 1992) Rio Declaration (UN, n.d.).
September 2000.	Millennium Summit, UNHQ, New York	UN Millennium Declaration (UN, 2000). Millennium Development Goals (MDGs) (UN 2015).
September 2002.	World Summit on Sustainable Development, Johannesburg, South Africa.	Johannesburg Declaration on Sustainable Development and Plan of Implementation (UN, n.d.).
June 2012.	UN Conference on Sustainable Development (Rio+20), Rio de Janeiro, Brazil.	The Future We Want (UN, n.d.).
September 2015.	UN Sustainable Development Summit.	2030 Agenda for Sustainable Development and 17 Sustainable Development Goals (UN, 2015).

Source: Adapted from UN (n.d.).

the eradication of poverty with interlinked goals designed to meet the needs of the poorest on the planet. Two years later, the Johannesburg Summit of 2002 defined sustainable development across three pillars, broadening the definition from environmental sustainability to also include economic and social sustainability. Again, broad participation in policy at local, regional and national level was emphasised. The Rio+20 conference of 2012 reaffirmed the principles of the Rio 1992 conference and previous action plans while agreeing to work towards a new set of SDGs which would build on the MDGs. Unlike the MDGs, which concentrated on alleviating poverty and the sustainable development of low-income countries, SDGs are intended to be universal; that is, they apply to all countries and this has consequences for their implementation. In the same way that the EAT-Lancet Diet (2019) could not be applied to all contexts, neither can the SDGs, and this poses ethical questions of equality, diversity and inclusion that policymakers must tackle (Fanzo, 2019).

What does all this mean for food policy? Of the 17 SDGs (see Table 5.4), more than half directly rely to some extent on food policy for their delivery, including SDG2 "Zero Hunger"; SDG3 "Good Health and Well-Being"; SDG6 "Clean Water and Sanitation"; SDG8 "Decent Work and Economic Growth"; SDG10 "Reduced Inequalities"; SDG11 "Sustainable Cities and

Table 5.4 The Sustainable Development Goals

SDG1	No poverty: end poverty in all its forms, everywhere.
SDG2	Zero hunger: end hunger, achieve food security and improved nutrition and promote sustainable agriculture.
SDG3	Good health and well-being: ensure healthy lives and promote well-being for all at all ages.
SDG4	Quality education: ensure inclusive and equitable quality education and promote lifelong learning opportunities for all.
SDG5	Gender equality: achieve gender equality and empower all women and girls.
SDG6	Clean water and sanitation: ensure availability and sustainable management of water and sanitation for all.
SDG7	Affordable and clean energy: ensure access to affordable, reliable, sustainable and modern energy for all.
SDG8	Decent work and economic growth: promote sustained, inclusive and sustainable economic growth, full and productive employment and decent work for all.
SDG9	Industry, innovation and infrastructure: build resilient infrastructure, promote inclusive and sustainable industrialization and foster innovation.
SDG10	Reduced inequalities: reduce inequality within and among countries.
SDG11	Sustainable cities and communities: make cities and human settlements inclusive, safe, resilient and sustainable.
SDG12	Responsible consumption and production: ensure sustainable consumption and production patterns.
SDG13	Climate action: take urgent action to combat climate change and its impacts.
SDG14	Life below water: conserve and sustainably use the oceans, seas and marine resources for sustainable development.
SDG15	Life on land: protect, restore and promote sustainable use of terrestrial ecosystems, sustainably manage forests, combat desertification and halt and reverse land degradation and halt biodiversity loss.
SDG16	Peace, justice and strong institutions: promote peaceful and inclusive societies for sustainable development, provide access to justice for all and build effective, accountable and inclusive institutions at all levels.
SDG17	Partnerships for the goals: strengthen the means of implementations and revitalise the Global Partnership for Sustainable Development.

Source: Author using UN data (UN, 2015).

Communities"; SDG12 "Responsible Consumption and Production"; SDG13 "Climate Action"; SDG14 "Life Below Water"; and SDG15 "Life on Land". Many, if not all, of the other goals also relate to food policy, but less directly; for example, SDG5 "Gender Equality", since enhancing women's ability to produce and procure food, for example, through leadership opportunities and land rights could help to achieve food security for many households around the world.

Each goal has targets. The goal most relevant to food policy is SDG2, which has eight targets. These focus on ending hunger and malnutrition, increasing sustainable food production and safeguarding biodiversity. With many of the targets set to be achieved by 2030, this is ambitious and pressing, and the UN admits progress to date is slow. The most recent SDG report and progress chart (UN, 2022a, 2022b) clearly shows a deterioration in progress towards many of the goals, including SDG2 and food security. This is attributed to climate change, the pandemic and conflicts, with the UN asking for urgent co-ordinated responses to reverse the change. Why these co-ordinated responses are so hard for global governance to muster is perhaps well illustrated by the UN Food Systems Summit of 2021.

The use of the term "food systems", particularly in the context of "food systems transformation", has become commonplace, both in national UK food policymaking and in global governance. This was put front and centre by the UN through their Food Systems Summit of 2021 (UN, 2021), which set out a bold vision to harness food systems post-pandemic for a transformed and brighter future. The Summit argued that while food systems were fragile and vulnerable, particularly for marginalised communities, we "know what we need to do to get back on track". Key to this was working together and the summit was set to involve "key players from the worlds of science, business, policy, healthcare and academia, as well as farmers, indigenous people, youth organizations, consumer groups, environmental activists and other key stakeholders" (UN, 2021). However, as outlined in Chapters 2 and 6, there are many competing solutions to fragile and collapsing food systems; these compete for policy space, and these tensions are a key issue in food policy. In the lead up to the Summit and afterwards, critics voiced concern over the lack of attention to corporate power in the food system (Clapp, 2021) and a lack of involvement for civil society groups in setting the agenda for the Summit. Some civil society groups boycotted events (Anderson et al., 2022). Academics reflected on issues of equity and participation in the Summit, noting a lack of indigenous knowledge and representation (Nisbett et al., 2021). Exactly *how* we work together across competing sectors, disciplines and country contexts to transform food systems and overcome challenges such as climate change and malnutrition is itself a wicked problem that needs to be addressed.

In terms of food policymaking across the UK, the SDGs provide a framework against which other policy priorities are set in context (see Table 5.2). In London, the then Department for International Development co-ordinated and produced the UK's comprehensive Voluntary National Review of Progress towards the SDGs in 2019 (DfID, 2019). This was produced in collaboration with the devolved administrations. In 2021, the UK government's Cabinet Office, Department for International Development and the Foreign, Commonwealth and Development Office, produced a "corporate report" outlining the implementation process by which they would deliver the SDGs: implementing the SDGs (HM Government, 2021a). Plans to achieve SDG2 "End Hunger" in this report do mention sustainability but in relation to a productive and resilient agriculture, fishing and food and drink sector as well as supporting sustainable development abroad rather than considering wider social sustainability concerns, for example, food insecurity at home.

In Northern Ireland, the Department for Agriculture, Environment and Rural Affairs (DAERA) announced that an exercise to map progress against the SDGs had taken place;

however, there is no specific mention of the SDGs in the "Sustainability for the Future – DAERA's Plan to 2050" document (DAERA, 2021b).

In Scotland, the government produced a national review to report how SDGs were being met in Scotland to feed into the UKs Voluntary National Review of Progress. This provides specific evidence regarding all the goals; for example, for SDG2, they review data on food security and healthy eating as well as agriculture and environmental protection (Scottish Government, 2020) and relate this specifically to Scottish examples for each SDG. Similarly in Wales, the government produced a comprehensive report to contribute to the UK's Voluntary National Review of Progress for the SDGs, and this reports on initiatives in Wales to support progress towards all 17 SDGs in the context of the Well-being of Future Generations (Wales) Act of 2015. This specifically tries to integrate four dimensions of sustainable development, economy, society, environment and culture into one policy in a more coherent way (Welsh Government, 2019). However, Wales's SDG report shows a tendency to rely on local projects to deliver, for example, on issues of food poverty.

Food citizenship

Food Citizenship is defined by Wilkins (2005, p. 269) as "the practice of engaging in food-related behaviours that support, rather than threaten, the development of a democratic, socially and economically just, and environmentally sustainable food system". The development of the food citizen concept began in the early 1990s and is linked to "food democracy" and "food sovereignty". Despite the long trajectory, the concept is still described as "emerging" (Migliorini et al., 2020). The argument for food citizens rather than consumers is that individuals should play an active role in shaping the food system and should demand greater benefits from and access to it. The term "consumer" rather narrowly defines and places individuals in a passive setting rather than allowing them agency and control to impact, affect and improve the food system (Welsh & MacRae, 1998; Lang, 1999). Proponents of a move towards the use of the term food citizen or food citizenship argue that eating is a political act and citizens have democratic power and should be encouraged to use that power to change the food system. Aligned to the food citizenship movement are writers such as Michael Pollan, to whom the phrase "Eating is a Political Act" is often attributed, and the American agriculturalist, writer and poet Wendell Berry, who wrote:

> There is, then, a politics of food that, like any politics, involves our freedom. We still (sometimes) remember that we cannot be free if our minds and voices are controlled by someone else. But we have neglected to understand that we cannot be free if our food and its sources are controlled by someone else. The condition of the passive consumer of food is not a democratic condition. One reason to eat responsibly is to live free.
>
> (Berry, 1990)

Arguments for greater awareness of food citizenship as a concept came from explorations of the notion of food democracy, and key to this are not only individual agency but the concepts of rights and responsibilities, and a recognition that since eating is a political act, each individual has the responsibility or duty to produce, choose and consume food for the greater good of society rather than simply as a result of their own tastes or preferences. This is easier said than done, and while eating can be political and eating habits can influence food production and markets, this assumes individuals have freedom of choice, access to and the money with which to make informed food choices. We know that in times of deprivation, such as the current cost of living crisis, food is considered an "elastic" item in the shopping basket and ethical and environmental considerations are often foregone in favour of lower prices (Lloyd et al., 2011, Caraher & Furey, 2018).

One way to encourage greater food citizenship has been explored through the theory of "Education for Sustainable Development" (Advance HE, n.d.). The assumption here is that teaching and learning programmes informing students about the global impacts of food production and consumption can change their behaviour. This could lead to greater Food Citizenship where individuals make food choices aligned to concerns not only of personal taste but also about environmental protection, social justice, workers' rights and animal rights (Migliorini et al., 2020). While individual action is important and changes in demand can lead to changes in supply, this focuses attention on the individual and downstream intervention. Leaving food policy to consumer demand can neglect a focus on policy or societal solutions (Tedstone et al., 2022). Some critics of the food citizenship or responsible citizen concept argue that a more pragmatic approach is needed that also employs other strategies such as the development of alternative proteins and broader cultural change to support consumers on the sustainability journey (de Bakker & Dagevos, 2012).

Food Citizenship has manifested itself in UK food policy largely through downstream initiatives and the work of civil society organisations. Particularly relevant in this area are the Food Ethics Council and the Sustainable Food Places organisation which is a partnership led by the Soil Association, Food Matters and the Sustain alliance (see Chapter 11). While the Food Ethics Council is an independent not-for-profit organisation which operates as a think tank and as experts in food ethics and sustainability, Sustainable Food Places is an umbrella organisation that encourages and supports the development of local food councils and partnerships. This can be seen as part of a food policy landscape where policy development is devolved to local organisations. One benefit of the Sustainable Food Places movement has been the renewed focus on local food governance with a proliferation of local food partnerships (see Table 5.2 for examples). At the same time, we see national food policy floundering and the challenge for food systems governance is to harness and integrate the local into the national.

Industry initiatives and sustainability standards

So far in this chapter, there has been little mention of the food industry's role in sustainable diets. While industry commentators may see sustainability as a "trend", the food industry is not only driven by corporate social responsibility agendas to improve the environmental, social and economic sustainability of their products. Motivation for more sustainable food businesses as for food citizens comes from a range of sources. These include organisational or personal value systems; consumer demand; higher income (e.g. from certified higher welfare products); organisational reputation; and government regulation or legislation. See Table 5.2 for examples of industry sustainability initiatives linked to approaches outlined above, including sustainable diets and the SDGs.

Stakeholder partnerships and voluntary agreements can support sustainable food systems transformation. An example is the Courtauld Commitment, a series of voluntary agreements funded by UK governments and the food sector and delivered by food waste organisation WRAP (Waste and Resources Action Programme) (WRAP n.d.). Started in 2005 with a focus on food and primary packaging, the latest iteration of the scheme, the Courtauld Commitment 2030, has almost 200 signatories agreeing to take action across the food chain to reduce food waste, GHG emissions and water stress. These actions often include food redistribution schemes and these may have unintended consequences regarding food insecurity and poverty (UNEP, 2023) –

see Chapter 4 for more in-depth discussion on this. Another stakeholder partnership initiative is the Food Foundation's Peas Please campaign, which brings together businesses, farmers and citizen advocates to grow serve and sell more vegetables. A stimulus for joining such schemes is the promise of support towards "net zero", in line with the UK government's stated aim for GHG emissions across the economy to reach net zero by 2050 (HM Government, 2021b). One of the ways food processing companies can try to achieve the net zero target is through product development such as moves towards plant-based meat substitutes in processed foods. This, in turn, could see a change in land management in the UK.

Another way the food industry aims to contribute to sustainable diets is through Sustainability Standards. These are common in the contemporary food system and are a feature of complex and long supply chains. Sustainability standards and certification schemes such as Fairtrade or organic are intended to improve production processes by addressing social or environmental issues, for example, the use of pesticides or poor working conditions. Such schemes are often collaborations between industry actors and non-governmental organisations (NGOs) with compliance by the industry partner, which is usually voluntary. Regular monitoring to receive continued verification of standards via certification schemes takes place and the cost of the scheme is often paid for by the higher prices charged for goods carrying the certification mark (Rousset et al., 2015, Lambin & Thorlakson, 2018, Wijen & Chiroleu-Assouline, 2019, Meemken et al., 2021).

Consumer demand for products, which are a part of the sustainability certification scheme, has driven the introduction of different schemes, and while such schemes are more important for some crops such as coffee and cocoa, the overall amount of land under certification scheme is very small. NGOs and multinational corporations most often play a part in standard setting, and NGOs have played an important role in persuading companies to take part in such schemes (Meemken et al., 2021) with collaboration required among many actors along the supply chain (Wijen & Chiroleu-Assouline, 2019). Lack of government standards in the country of production can provide impetus for the introduction of voluntary environmental standards. The proliferation of different schemes and standards has led to competition, and one role of the government and policy in this area is to support proper schemes and help distinguish between greenwash or worse, fraudulent claims and sustainable practices for consumer verification (Rousset et al., 2015, Wijen & Chiroleu-Assouline, 2019). From a policy perspective, Rousset et al. (2015) argue that governments can use the existing sustainability standards to develop and implement public policies.

Policy responses

The focus on food policy in the UK towards healthy eating and sustainability dating from the late twentieth century was marked by an approach in government circles focused on choice and consumerism and encouraging the formation of standards in the private sector (Panjwani & Caraher, 2018). This was true of both Labour and Conservative administrations. Food was seen as plentiful and cheap, with a Labour government report praising supermarkets for their plentiful supply of "cheap" food.

During the 1990s and early 2000s, we saw the rise of local community enterprises and of the consumer citizen or Food Citizenship concept. Scotland led on the former while the latter was mostly driven by NGOs and issues such as fair trade and transition towns. Local food growing and distribution projects and their work in local communities became the norm and the government failed to invest in upstream work (see Chapter 2). Most of this local work was funded by local public health budgets (Caraher & Cowburn, 2004). The full potential of these local community projects was never realised; there was no effective lobbying force to unite them and no forum to give them a voice. By the middle of the teens of the twenty-first century, the funding for local community food projects had all but dried up and many local projects were struggling to survive.

Similar moves have been documented where a curious mix of the alternative health ("don't trust the man") and local food movements morphed over time to become the new entrepreneurs. Hines grouped these moves under the term "localism", which was a corrective to globalisation (Hines, 2000). This resulted in a mix of voluntary and non-governmental approaches alongside industry initiatives, the latter often under the banner of corporate responsibility. This status quo has also been attributed to lock-in theory (Mason & Lang, 2017), where the political and economic power that food manufacturers and retailers hold over food governance results in feedback loops that reinforce models of production and consumption. This lock-in can prevent food policy change, for example, the lack of food systems discourse following the 2007–2008 food price crisis and even now the entrenchment of food policy responses to COVID-19 in an industrial agricultural model of sustainable intensification.

Causes of food policy challenges such as climate change and malnutrition are complex and require systemic approaches to develop solutions. Despite this, food policy continues to be made across many different government departments with at least 16 different departments and public bodies in England responsible for making policy that affects the food system in 2019 (Parsons, 2020). The potential for policymaking to be disjointed is great, with fragmentation potentially leading to policies that are incoherent or undermining (Parsons, Sharpe & Hawkes, 2020). Cross-departmental approaches are possible, as shown by the approach taken by DAERA in Northern Ireland to develop their Food Strategy Framework. DAERA led with input from other departments and external stakeholders.

Although more recent UK policy developments, for example, the NFS in England, acknowledge the links between human nutrition and the environment, we have seen political events interfere with the implementation of policy recommendations and stall progress of planned legislation. One of the current food policy debates in England relates to land management. This hinges around the extent to which UK-based policy replacing the EUs Common Agricultural Policy post-Brexit should reward farmers for sustainable farming and the so-called "public goods". Policies in development under the new environmental land management schemes (ELMS) focus on making agricultural activities more environmentally sustainable, for example, to increase biodiversity and reduce inputs such as inorganic fertilisers and pesticides. Changing land use could have an impact on diet, but there is less focus on this within the policy documents, and the extent to which nutrition is a consideration is unclear (e.g. see HM Government, 2022). In addition, the break from the EU has seen devolved UK nations develop their own food policy, and these rarely give equal weight to interactions between diet and other dimensions such as the economic or social. For example, Scotland's Good Food Nation policy (Scottish Parliament, 2022) and the Food (Wales) Bill (Welsh Parliament, 2022) as well as the proposed Northern Ireland Food Strategy Framework (DAERA, 2021a) – while a systems approach may have been taken on paper, in practice balancing priorities across dimensions will be difficult.

Despite this, the examples we have outlined in this chapter have all gained some traction in food policymaking in the UK. See Table 5.2, which provides examples to be explored as responses to an increasing policy interest in holistic or food systems approaches to sustainable diets.

Conclusion

Both researchers and food policymakers have argued that healthier and more environmentally sustainable diets are not only possible but compatible. In this context, food systems approaches have become popular as a way of finding "joined-up" solutions to food policy problems that can tackle more than one policy aim. Despite the widespread focus on food systems and a more holistic view of the drivers and outputs of the food system as a whole, food policies can still generally be divided into two groups: those that have nutritional health as their focus and those that are agricultural or production-related. Current linked global crises, including environmental degradation, food insecurity and geopolitical instability, offer a strong stimulus to reform the food system. However, there are still few food policies that attempt to define or implement both healthy and sustainable diets. Approaches towards sustainable food systems have been explored in this chapter, including Eco Nutrition; One Health; SDGs; Food Citizenship; and industry initiatives. These have tended to expand over time from single criteria (ecological sustainability) towards multi-criteria models of sustainability that include social, health and environmental components. Many of these approaches have made their way into food policies in the UK across all nations, but recent progress has stalled or deteriorated as a result of political, environmental and economic permacrisis.

References

Aarestrup, F.M., Bonten, M. & Koopmans, M. 2021, "Pandemics– One Health preparedness for the next", *The Lancet Regional Health – Europe*, vol. 9, p. 100210. https://doi.org/10.1016/j.lanepe.2021.100210

Aberdeen City Council 2022, Aberdeen as a sustainable food place, https://www.aberdeencity.gov.uk/services/environment/sustainable-food

Advance HE n.d., Education for sustainable development in higher education, https://www.advance-he.ac.uk/teaching-and-learning/education-sustainable-development-higher-education.

Anderson, M., Hoey, L., Hurst, P., Miller, M. & De Wit, M.M. 2022, "Debrief on the United Nations Food Systems Summit (UNFSS)", *Journal of Agriculture, Food Systems, and Community Development*, vol. 11, no. 2, pp. 13–17.

Benton, T.G. 2020, "COVID-19 and disruptions to food systems", *Agriculture and Human Values*, vol. 37, no. 3, pp. 577–578.

Berry, W. 1990, "The Pleasures of Eating" in *What Are People For? Essays*, North Point Press, San Francisco, CA, pp. 145–152.

Bronner, F. 1997, *Nutrition Policy in Public Health*, Springer Pub., New York.

Carabin, H. 2021, "One Health: a crucial approach to preventing and preparing for future pandemics", *The Conversation*, 23rd December, https://theconversation.com/one-health-a-crucial-approach-to-preventing-and-preparing-for-future-pandemics-173637.

Caraher, M. & Furey, S. 2018, *The Economics of Emergency Food Aid Provision*, Palgrave Macmillan, London. https://doi.org/10.1007/978-3-319-78506-6

Caraher, M. & Coveney, J. 2004, "Public health nutrition and food policy", *Public Health Nutrition*, vol. 7, no. 5, pp. 591–598.

Caraher, M. & Cowburn, G. 2004, "A survey of food projects in the English NHS regions and Health Action Zones in 2001", *Health Education Journal*, vol. 63, no. 3, pp. 197–219 https://doi.org/10.1177/001789690406300302

CDC, 2022. Centers for Disease Control and Prevention: zoonotic diseases, https://www.cdc.gov/one-health/basics/zoonotic-diseases.html.

Clapp, J. 2021, "The problem with growing corporate concentration and power in the global food system", *Nature Food*, vol. 2, no. 6, pp. 404–408. https://doi.org/10.1038/s43016-021-00297-7

DAERA 2022, Draft environment strategy, https://www.daera-ni.gov.uk/sites/default/files/consultations/daera/Draft%20Environment%20Strategy.PDF.

DAERA 2021a, Northern Ireland food strategy framework, https://consultations2.nidirect.gov.uk/daera/food-at-the-heart-of-our-society-a-prospectus/supporting_documents/21.22.076%20NI%20Food%20Strategy%20Framework%20Consultation.PDF.

DAERA 2021b, Sustainability for the future – DAERA's plan to 2050, https://www.daera-ni.gov.uk/publications/sustainability-future-daeras-plan-2050.

DAERA 2019, *Changing the culture 2019–2024 – one health*, https://www.daera-ni.gov.uk/publications/changing-culture-2019-2024-one-health.

De Bakker, E. & Dagevos, H., 2012, "Reducing meat consumption in today's consumer society: questioning the citizen-consumer gap", *Journal of Agricultural and Environmental Ethics*, vol. 25, no. 6, pp. 877–894.

Department of Health 2019, *Changing the Culture 2019–2024: One Health. In Tackling Antimicrobial Resistance in Northern Ireland: A Five-Year Action Plan*, Department of Agriculture, Environment and Rural Affairs, London. https://www.daera-ni.gov.uk/publications/changing-culture-2019-2024-one-health.

Destoumieux-Garzón, D., Mavingui, P., Boetsch, G., Boissier, J., Darriet, F., Duboz, P., Fritsch, C., Giraudoux, P., Le Roux, F., Morand, S. & Paillard, C. 2018, "The one health concept: 10 years old and a long road ahead", *Frontiers in Veterinary Science*, vol. 5, p. 14.

Dimbleby, H. 2021, National food strategy, independent review: the plan, https://www.nationalfoodstrategy.org.

EAT Forum 2022, About EAT-Lancet 2.0, https://eatforum.org/eat-lancet-commission/eat-lancet-commission-2-0/about-eat-lancet-commission-2-0/.

Egger, G. & Swinburn, B. 2010, *Planet Obesity: How We're Eating Ourselves and the Planet to Death*, Allen and Unwin, Crows Nest, NSW.

Ericksen, P., Stewart, B., Dixon, J., Barling, D., Loring, P., Anderson, M. & Ingram, J. 2012, "The Value of a Food System Approach" in *Food Security and Global Environmental Change*, Earthscan, Abingdon, pp. 45–65.

Evans, B.R. & Leighton, F.A. 2014, "A history of One Health", *Revue Scientifique et Technique*, vol. 33, no. 2, pp. 413–420.

Fanzo, J. 2019, "Healthy and sustainable diets and food systems: the key to achieving sustainable development goal 2?", *Food Ethics*, vol. 4, no. 2, pp. 159–174. https://doi.org/10.1007/s41055-019-00052-6

Fanzo, J. & Davis, C. 2021, *Global Food Systems, Diets, and Nutrition*, Palgrave Macmillan, Cham.

FAO, IFAD, UNICEF, WFP & WHO 2021, *The State of Food Security and Nutrition in the World 2021. Transforming Food Systems for Food Security, Improved Nutrition and Affordable Healthy Diets for All*, Rome, FAO.

Fischer, C.G. & Garnett, T. 2016, *Plates, Pyramids, and Planets: Developments in National Healthy and Sustainable Dietary Guidelines: A State of Play Assessment*, Food and Agriculture Organization of the United Nations.

Food and Agriculture Organization 2010, International scientific symposium. Biodiversity and sustainable diets-united against hunger, https://www.fao.org/ag/humannutrition/23781-0e8d8dc364ee46865d5841c48976e9980.pdf.

Food and Drink Wales 2021, A vision for the food and drink industry from 2021, https://www.gov.wales/sites/default/files/publications/2021-11/vision-food-drink-industry-2021_1.pdf.

Food Standards Scotland 2021, Healthy, safe, sustainable: driving Scotland's food future. Food standards Scotland strategy for 2021–2026, https://www.foodstandards.gov.scot/downloads/FSS_Strategy_2021-2026.pdf.

Gibbs, E.P.J. 2014, "The evolution of one health: a decade of progress and challenges for the future", *Veterinary Record*, vol. 174, no. 4, pp. 85–91.

Gibbs, E.P.J. 2005, "Emerging zoonotic epidemics in the interconnected global community", *Veterinary Record*, vol. 157, pp. 673–679.

Global Nutrition Report 2021, *Global Nutrition Report: The State of Global Nutrition*, Development Initiatives, Bristol, https://globalnutritionreport.org/reports/2021-global-nutrition-report/.

Government of Canada 2017, Tackling antimicrobial resistance and antimicrobial use: a Pan-Canadian framework for action, https://www.canada.ca/en/health-canada/services/publications/drugs-health-products/tackling-antimicrobial-resistance-use-pan-canadian-framework-action.html.

Gussow, J.D. & Clancy, K.L. 1986, "Dietary guidelines for sustainability", *Journal of Nutrition Education*, vol. 18, pp. 1–5.

Haider, N., Rothman-Ostrow, P., Osman, A.Y., Arruda, L.B., Macfarlane-Berry, L., Elton, L., Thomason, M.J., Yeboah-Manu, D., Ansumana, R., Kapata, N. & Mboera, L. 2020, "COVID-19—Zoonosis or emerging infectious disease?", *Frontiers in Public Health*, vol. 8, p. 763.

Health Protection Scotland 2017, Scottish One Health antimicrobial use and antimicrobial resistance report in 2016, https://hps.scot.nhs.uk/web-resources-container/scottish-one-health-antimicrobial-use-and-antimicrobial-resistance-report-2016/.

Hines, C. 2000, *Localization: A Global Manifesto*, Earthscan, Abingdon.

Hirvonen, K., Bai, Y., Headey, D. & Masters, W.A. 2020, "Affordability of the EAT–Lancet reference diet: a global analysis", *The Lancet Global Health*, vol. 8, no. 1, pp. e59–e66. https://doi.org/10.1016/S2214-109X(19)30447-4

HM Government 2022, Environmental land management schemes: outcomes, https://www.gov.uk/government/publications/environmental-land-management-schemes-outcomes.

HM Government 2021a, Implementing the sustainable development goals. Corporate Report, https://www.gov.uk/government/publications/implementing-the-sustainable-development-goals/implementing-the-sustainable-development-goals--2.

HM Government 2021b, Net zero strategy: build back greener, https://assets.publishing.service.gov.uk/government/uploads/system/uploads/attachment_data/file/1033990/net-zero-strategy-beis.pdf.

HM Government 2019a, UK's voluntary national review of the sustainable development goals, https://www.gov.uk/government/publications/uks-voluntary-national-review-of-the-sustainable-development-goals.

HM Government 2019b, *Tackling Antimicrobial Resistance 2019–2024: The UK's Five-Year National Action Plan,* Department of Health and Social Care, London, https://www.gov.uk/government/publications/uk-5-year-action-plan-forantimicrobial-resistance-2019-to-2024.

Hutchinson, E. 2017, *Governing Antimicrobial Resistance*, The Graduate Institute of International and Development Studies, Global Health Centre.

Ingram, J., Ajates, R., Arnall, A., Blake, L., Borrelli, R., Collier, R., de Frece, A., Häsler, B., Lang, T., Pope, H. & Reed, K. 2020, "A future workforce of food-system analysts", *Nature Food*, vol. 1, no. 1, pp. 9–10. https://doi.org/10.1038/s43016-019-0003-3

Järhult, J.D. 2015, "One Health: a doctor's perspective", *Veterinary Record*, vol. 176, no. 14, pp. 351–353.

Kickbusch, I. 1989, "Approaches to an ecological base for public health", *Health Promotion International*, vol. 4, pp. 265–268.

Labadarios, D. 2005, "Malnutrition in the developing world: the triple burden", *South African Journal of Clinical Nutrition*, vol. 18, no. 2, pp. 119–121.

Lambin, E.F. & Thorlakson, T. 2018, "Sustainability standards: interactions between private actors, civil society, and governments", *Annual Review of Environment and Resources*, vol. 43, no. 1, pp. 369–393.

Lang, T. 2007, "Choice, power and food: nutrition in an ecological public health era", paper to the Australian Public Health Nutrition Academic Collaboration (APHNAC) Conference 'Public Health Nutrition in Australia: New Directions, New Priorities', held at Emmanuel College, University of Queensland, Brisbane.

Lang, T. 1999, "Food policy for the 21st century: can it be both radical and reasonable?", International Development Research Centre *for Hunger-Proof Cities: Sustainable Urban Food Systems*, p. 216.

Lang, T., Barling, D. & Caraher, M. 2009, *Food Policy: Integrating Health, Environment and Society*, OUP, Oxford.

Lang, T. & Heasman, M. 2015, *Food Wars: The Global Battle for Mouths, Minds and Markets*, Routledge, London.

Lappe, F.M. 1971, *Diet for a Small Planet*, Random House, New York.

Liverpool Express 2021, Liverpool launches 'Good Food Plan', 4th October, https://liverpoolexpress.co.uk/liverpool-launches-good-food-plan/.

Lloyd, S., Lawton, J., Caraher, M., Singh, G., Horsley, K. & Mussa, F. 2011, "A tale of two localities: healthy eating on a restricted income", *Health Education Journal*, vol. 70, no. 1, pp. 48–56.

Mason, P. & Lang, T. 2017, *Sustainable Diets: How Ecological Nutrition Can Transform Consumption and the Food System*, Routledge, Abingdon.

Meemken, E.M., Barrett, C.B., Michelson, H.C., et al. 2021, "Sustainability standards in global agrifood supply chains", *Nature Food*, vol. 2, pp. 758–765. https://doi.org/10.1038/s43016-021-00360-3

Migliorini, P., Wezel, A., Veromann, E., Strassner, C., Średnicka-Tober, D., Kahl, J., Bügel, S., Briz, T., Kazimierczak, R., Brives, H., Ploeger, A., Gilles, U., Lüder, V., Schleicher-Deis, O., Rastorgueva, N., Tuccillo, F., Talgre, L., Kaart, T., Ismael, D. & Rembiałkowska, E. 2020 "Students' knowledge and expectations about sustainable food systems in higher education", *International Journal of Sustainability in Higher Education*, vol. 21, no. 6, pp. 1087–1110. https://doi.org/10.1108/IJSHE-12-2019-0356

Milo, N. & Helsing, E. (eds) 1998, *European Food and Nutrition Policies*, World Health Organization Europe, Copenhagen.

Ministere des Solidarites et de la Sante 2021, French national action plan on antimicrobial resistance: innovative measures, https://solidarites-sante.gouv.fr/IMG/pdf/8_pages_antibioresistance-final-en.pdf.

National Services Scotland 2021, Scottish One Health antimicrobial use and antimicrobial resistance in 2020, https://www.nss.nhs.scot/publications/scottish-one-health-antimicrobial-use-and-antimicrobial-resistance-in-2020/

Nisbett, N., Friel, S., Aryeetey, R., da Silva Gomes, F., Harris, J., Backholer, K., Baker, P., Jernigan, V.B.B. & Phulkerd, S. 2021, "Equity and expertise in the UN Food Systems Summit", *BMJ Global Health*, vol. 6, no. 7, p. e006569. https://doi.org/10.1136/bmjgh-2021-006569

OWOH 2009, One world – One Health: Brazil 2009 meeting, 22 October, 2009, http://www.oneworldonehealth.org/.

Panjwani, C. & Caraher, M. 2018, "CASE 11 Voluntary Agreements and the Power of the Food Industry: The Public Health Responsibility Deal in England" in *Public Health and the Food and Drinks Industry: The Governance and Ethics of Interaction. Lessons from Research, Policy and Practice*, ed. M. Mwatsama, UK Health Forum, London, pp. 110–120.

Parsons, K. 2019, *Brief 3: Integrated Food Policy – What is it and How Can It Help Connect Food Systems*, Centre for Food Policy, City, University of London, London.

Parsons, K. 2020, *Who Makes Food Policy in England?*, Food Research Collaboration, London.

Parsons, K. & Hawkes, C. 2019, *Brief 4: Embedding Food in All Policies*, Centre for Food Policy, City, University of London, London.

Parsons, K., Hawkes, C. & Wells, R. 2019, *Brief 2: What is The Food System? A Food Policy Perspective*, Centre for Food Policy, City University of London, London.

Parsons, K., Sharpe, R. & Hawkes, C. 2020, *Who Is Making Food Policy in England*, Centre for Food Policy, City, University of London, London.

Pinstrup-Andersen, P. 2007, "Agricultural Research and Policy to Achieve Nutritional Goals" in *Poverty, Inequality and Development: Essays in Honor of Erik Thorbecke*, eds. A. de Janvry, R. Kanbur, Kluwer, Amsterdam, pp. 353–370.

Rayner, G. & Lang, T. 2012, *Ecological Public Health: Reshaping Conditions for Good Health*, Routledge/Taylor and Francis Group, London.

Rivera-Ferre, M.G., López-i-Gelats, F., Ravera, F., Oteros-Rozas, E., di Masso, M., Binimelis, R. & El Bilali, H. 2021, "The two-way relationship between food systems and the COVID-19 pandemic: causes and consequences", *Agricultural Systems*, vol. 191, p. 103134.

Rousset, S., et al. 2015, "Voluntary Environmental and Organic Standards in Agriculture: Policy Implications", *OECD Food, Agriculture and Fisheries Papers*, No. 86, OECD Publishing, Paris. https://doi.org/10.1787/5jrw8fg0rr8x-en

Salmon Scotland 2022, Scottish Salmon sustainability charter: a better future for all, https://www.salmon-scotland.co.uk/facts/sustainability/scottish-salmon-sustainability-charter-a-better-future-for-all.

Scottish Government 2020, Scotland and the sustainable development goals: a national review to drive action, https://www.gov.scot/publications/scotland-sustainable-development-goals-national-review-drive-action/pages/5/.

Scottish Parliament 2022, Good Food Nation (Scotland) Act, https://www.legislation.gov.uk/asp/2022/5/contents/enacted.

Steele, S.G., Toribio, J.A., Booy, R. & Mor, S.M. 2019, "What makes an effective One Health clinical practitioner? Opinions of Australian One Health experts", *One Health*, vol. 8, p. 100108.

Tedstone, A.E., Sabry-Grant, C., Hung, E. & Levy, L.B. 2022, "Five years of national policies: progress towards tackling obesity in England", *Proceedings of the Nutrition Society*, vol. 81, no. 2, pp. 1–20.

Tesco n.d. Food Waste https://www.tescoplc.com/sustainability/planet/food-waste/

Tokuç, A. 2013, "Johannesburg Declaration, 2002" in *Encyclopedia of Corporate Social Responsibility*, eds. S.O. Idowu, N. Capaldi, L. Zu, A.D. Gupta, Springer, Berlin, Heidelberg. https://doi.org/10.1007/978-3-642-28036-8_18

Tudge, C. 1980, *Future Cook*, Littlehampton Book Services Ltd., Worthing, UK.

UN n.d., Conferences: environment and sustainable development, https://www.un.org/en/conferences/environment.

UN 2022a, The sustainable development goals report 2022, https://unstats.un.org/sdgs/report/2022/The-Sustainable-Development-Goals-Report-2022.pdf.

UN 2022b, The sustainable development goals progress chart 2022, https://unstats.un.org/sdgs/report/2022/Progress-Chart-2022.pdf.

UN 2021, Food systems summit 2021: about the summit, https://www.un.org/en/food-systems-summit/about.

UN 2015, Resolution adopted by the General Assembly on 25 September 2015, https://documents-dds-ny.un.org/doc/UNDOC/GEN/N15/291/89/PDF/N1529189.pdf?OpenElement.

UN 2000, Millennium declaration, https://documents-dds-ny.un.org/doc/UNDOC/GEN/N00/559/51/PDF/N0055951.pdf?OpenElement.

UN, 1973 Report of the United Nations Conference on the Human Environment, United Nations, New York, https://documents-dds-ny.un.org/doc/UNDOC/GEN/NL7/300/05/IMG/NL730005.pdf?OpenElement

UNEP (United Nations Environment Programme) 2023, Quadripartite call to action for One Health for a safer world https://www.unep.org/news-and-stories/statements/quadripartite-call-action-one-health-safer-world.

UNSD 1992, *AGENDA 21,*https://sdgs.un.org/sites/default/files/publications/Agenda21.pdf.

van Berkum, S., Dengerink, J. & Ruben, R. 2018, "The food systems approach: sustainable solutions for a sufficient supply of healthy food", *Wageningen, Wageningen Economic Research, Memorandum 2018–064.*

Veg NI 2021, *Parful Produce*, https://www.vegni.co.uk/.

Welsh, J. & MacRae, R. 1998, "Food citizenship and community food security: lessons from Toronto, Canada", *Canadian Journal of Development Studies/Revue canadienne d'études du développement*, vol. 19, no. 4, pp. 237–255.

Welsh Government 2022, Animal health and welfare plan key to Wales' future – Rural Affairs Minister. Press release, 4th January, https://www.gov.wales/animal-health-and-welfare-plan-key-wales-future-rural-affairs-minister.

Welsh Government 2019, Wales and the sustainable development goals, https://www.gov.wales/sites/default/files/publications/2019-07/supplementary-report-to-the-uk-review-of-progress-towards-the-sustainable-development-goals-2030_0.pdf.

Welsh Parliament 2022, Food (Wales) Bill,https://business.senedd.wales/mgIssueHistoryHome.aspx?IId=40509

WHO 2022, *Library of AMR national action plans*, https://www.who.int/teams/surveillance-prevention-control-AMR/national-action-plan-monitoring-evaluation/library-of-national-action-plans.

WHO 2021a, Obesity and overweight: key facts, 9th June, https://www.who.int/news-room/fact-sheets/detail/obesity-and-overweight.

WHO 2021b, *Tripartite and UNEP support OHHLEP's definition of "One Health". Joint Tripartite (FAO, OIE, WHO) and UNEP Statement*, World Health Organisation News, https://www.who.int/news/item/01-12-2021-tripartite-and-unep-support-ohhlep-s-definition-of-one-health Accessed 08/03/2022.

WHO 2020, Antibiotic resistance: key facts, 31st July, https://www.who.int/news-room/fact-sheets/detail/antibiotic-resistance.

Wijen, F. & Chiroleu-Assouline, M. 2019, "Controversy over voluntary environmental standards: a socio-economic analysis of the Marine Stewardship Council", *Organization & Environment*, vol. 32, no. 2, pp. 98–124. https://doi.org/10.1177/1086026619831449

Wilkins, J.L. 2005, "Eating right here: moving from consumer to food citizen", *Agriculture and Human Values*, vol. 22, no. 3, pp. 269–273. https://doi.org/10.1007/s10460-005-6042-4

Willett, W., Rockström, J., Loken, B., Springmann, M., Lang, T., Vermeulen, S., Garnett, T., Tilman, D., DeClerck, F., Wood, A. & Jonell, M. 2019, "Food in the anthropocene: the EAT–Lancet Commission on healthy diets from sustainable food systems", *The Lancet*, vol. 393, no. 10170, pp. 447–492.

World Commission on Environment and Development 1987, *Our common future*, Oxford University Press, Oxford.

WRAP n.d. The Courtauld Commitment https://wrap.org.uk/taking-action/food-drink/initiatives/courtauld-commitment

6   Food media, marketing and advertising

Introduction

The media is often said to have an important influence on individual and societal food production and food choices as well as playing an important role in setting the policy agenda. In the last 20 years, social media, in addition to traditional mass media outlets on television, on radio, online and in print, has been cited as having a significant impact on food trends. This chapter describes media coverage of food issues, influences on media outputs as well as underlying theories underpinning the literature in this area. Taking particular account of the UK food policy context, it traces food policy recommendations and regulations regarding media and marketing content.

The post-war period saw the rise of food media in the UK concurrent with technological developments in broadcasting with television ownership increasing as well as a proliferation of food magazines, and later, websites, blogs and vlogs (Rousseau, 2012). Much food media coverage in the UK has been concerned with food preparation and recipes, with television cookery programmes first pioneered by home economists such as Marguerite Patten, soon involving celebrity chefs, of which more later in this chapter. Food media in the UK does not tend to take a systems approach that takes into account the five domains of the food system, as described by Parsons et al. (2019) and discussed in Chapters 2 and 5. Some celebrity chefs in the UK have straddled the domains of the political, health and the sociocultural, having been also involved in food campaigns and activism; see also the section in Chapter 11 on celebrity influencers. The overall approach to food media has been and still is one of entertainment with a rise in reality shows and competitions involving "ordinary people" such as the long-running *MasterChef* series and the hugely successful *The Great British Bake Off*. Successful television formats such as these are not only developed with spin-off series such as *MasterChef: The Professionals* in which professional chefs compete or *The Great Celebrity Bake Off* pitting celebrities against one another. They are also syndicated and the formats sold worldwide, for example, *MasterChef* Australia, Canada, India, Italia and The Great Irish, South African and Australian *Bake Offs*.

Food issues are also covered by the news media. Media coverage of scientific advances, for example, in nutrition, tend to be covered by science or medical correspondents. Political issues tend to be covered by political correspondents. Notable exceptions are the long-running *The Food Programme* on BBC Radio 4 and its sister programme *Farming Today* which strive to explore the food system, holistically taking into account several of the political, environmental, economic, social and health aspects of the food system and their interlocking nature.

With this rise in food media, the academic literature on media coverage of food and food issues has grown, and now includes but is not limited to topics such as the production processes of food media (Phillipov, 2017); the rise of the celebrity chef (Caraher et al., 2000, Rousseau,

DOI: 10.4324/9781003260301-6

2013, Johnston & Goodman, 2015, Matta, 2019); gendered representations of food production and consumption in the media (Parasecoli, 2005, Naccarato & LeBesco, 2013); food on digital devices (Lewis, 2020) and digital platforms such as blogs and vlogs (Lupton & Feldman, 2020); and food and social media (Rousseau, 2012, Mann, 2018, McLennan et al., 2018).

A smaller body of research and academic literature and interest exists on the interaction between food policy and media in the UK. This represents a gap in available literature, which has been partially filled by work on food policy and food scares in the media (e.g. Reilly, 1998, Henderson et al., 2014); the UK Soft Drinks Industry Levy (SDIL) or "sugar tax" in the media (e.g. Hilton et al., 2017, Thomas-Meyer et al., 2017); obesity policy in the media (e.g. Inthorn & Boyce, 2010, Ries et al., 2011, Hilton et al., 2012, Eli & Ulijaszek, 2016); and food banks and the media (e.g. Wells & Caraher, 2014). One of the areas of greater growth in research and food policy activity is in marketing and advertising of food, especially as it affects children. Here, there is a large raft of literature (e.g. see Hastings et al., 2003, Russell et al., 2019, Thompson et al., 2021, Boyland et al., 2022). Indeed, work done in the UK underpins some of the international food systems governance strategies on this topic (Boyland & McGale, 2022). The development of UK policy in this area is discussed later in this chapter.

An area of debate is not whether the media have an effect but how these effects can be measured and a causal link established to show evidence for specific influences of media or marketing outputs on health or environmental outcomes (McDonald, 2004, McQuail, 2010, Williams, 2010). Essentially, it is difficult to isolate the effects of media coverage without further research, and this is a problem of measurement and evidence. Researchers can analyse media output and show trends in reporting such as numbers of articles over time, actors interviewed for media coverage, stakeholder opinion and framing of issues. However, media reporting per se should not be mistaken for impact on audiences or indeed policymakers.

Research in this area has tended to focus on mass media and measurement of outputs as these have, up until recently, been manageable research objectives. This is because of researcher access to texts, as well as the methodologies used to collect and analyse data. Social media posts can be harder to capture and analyse and research on these tends to be quantitative in nature, analysing large datasets. Media coverage can be hard to analyse without digitally searchable copies of, for example, podcast transcripts or advertisements. A growth area for research is engagement on platforms like YouTube, Instagram and more recently TikTok (such as Brooks et al., 2022). However little research has to date been carried out on the policy presence on these newer social media platforms, for example, international food systems governance organisations such as FAO. These organisations are active on this increasingly popular platform. They are, however, dwarfed by TikTok "influencers" – individuals with very high numbers of followers on social media platforms with the potential to influence behaviour, such as purchases of goods or services. There are arguments for greater public health presence on this rapidly growing platform (Zenone et al., 2021).

Food policy agenda-setting

Cairney (2012) sums up agenda-setting with two key statements:

> 1: There is an almost unlimited amount of policy problems that could reach the top of the policy agenda. Yet, very few issues do, while most others do not.
>
> 2: There is an almost unlimited number of solutions to those policy problems. Yet, few policy solutions will be considered while most others will not.
>
> (Cairney, 2012, p. 183)

Agenda-setting theories are used in food policy research alongside other policy concepts, theories and models, such as punctuated equilibrium or multiple streams theory (see Chapter 2, Table 2.2). Used here by Cairney in a public policy context, they are also important in the fields of journalism and media studies and as such are part of the research into "media effects". Media effects, as described above, examine whether and how the media has an effect on, for example, its audience, societal norms or policymaking. Analysing media effects can help to identify the Overton Window (see Chapter 2). To do this, media researchers collect, measure and analyse media coverage. Such research might search for particular discourses in reporting, or identify and quantify mentions of actors, for example, from particular stakeholder groups, analysing when and how they appear in media coverage. Researchers undertake sentiment analysis, both qualitatively and quantitatively, to understand reported attitudes towards food policies. Others qualitatively analyse texts to understand discourses and arguments and debates that are played out in media coverage. So, media coverage can be measured and analysed both quantitatively and qualitatively. However, it is very difficult to prove a causal interaction between media out-puts and audience behaviours. This is because measurement of media reporting is not designed to measure the effects of the media, but to better understand and track what is being reported and how it is being reported, for example, the media framing of obesity over time (Kim & Willis, 2007, Hilton et al., 2012) or the reported policy responses to shortages of migrant horticultural workers (Carnibella & Wells, 2022). Further and different research is needed to understand both the context in which the reporting takes place and the effect of that reporting on audiences and food policy, for example, the use of qualitative interviews with journalists or surveys with members of the public (e.g. see Simmonds & Vallgårda, 2021). Also identified within media reporting are "frame contests", where journalists or interviewees favour one policy option over another or argue one particular stance over another. For example, the portrayal of meat as healthy or unhealthy or the solution to food waste as food banks. This echoes the "war of ideas" where competing narratives vie for policy space (Smith, 2013, Caraher & Perry, 2017) in order to impact the Overton Window (as discussed in Chapter 2).

Even when the impacts or outcomes of media are measured, there is debate as to the extent of the effects. Media research theorists, such as McQuail (2010), doubt the ability of the mass media to influence any measurable change in policy or public opinion – or, at least, the ability of scholars to assess the effect on public actions or political opinion. This is due to the large number of confounding variables which can affect research findings; it is very difficult to isolate media messages from other influences in society such as formal education, cultural background or other advertising. One area where media effects have been convincingly proved is the area of marketing and advertising of food to children and this has led to policy change and is discussed further later in this chapter.

The development of agenda-setting research as it relates to media is generally said to stem from Bernard Cohen's 1963 book *The Press and Foreign Policy* in which he interviewed American journalists and policymakers to examine the relationship between press and govern-ment. This gave rise to his famous quote that the press "may not be successful much of the time in telling people what to think, but it is stunningly successful in telling its readers what to think about" (Cohen, 1963, p. 13).

Early agenda-setting work tended to suggest that this was a simple one-way relationship, with the influence moving from media to audience. Later work, for example, by McCombs and Shaw (1972) and Dearing and Rogers (1996), refined this view to take into account a reciprocal relationship between the public, the media and policymakers. Baumgartner and Jones's (2009) Punctuated Equilibrium theory places agenda-setting and the media's role within a much bigger group of policy concepts, such as bounded rationality and policy monopolies (see Table 2.2,

Chapter 2). This suggests that most policies stay the same for long periods of time, but can suddenly encounter or be punctuated by periods of change, with the media and other influencers playing a part in this change (see Chapter 11). In food policy, this can be seen in the development of obesity policy, and public health advocates have called for further media attention in this area as one way to drive policy change. Huang et al. (2015) argue for a move away from policy driven by collaboration between public health researchers and policymakers towards the mobilisation of popular support for policy action. Media coverage, they argue, could play a part in strategies to achieve this.

Journalism's economic model and churnalism

In terms of mass media or what is sometimes called "legacy media", there are large players within the UK such as the BBC, ITV and Channel 4 as well as newspapers such as tabloids, for example, *The Sun*; mid-market newspapers such as *The Daily Mail*; and broadsheets such as *The Guardian*, *The Times* and *The Telegraph*. All of these include food media in their coverage and still have impact, despite a changing economic landscape and economic model for journalism. Newspapers and broadcasters that once dominated the market are now navigating a landscape where much of their coverage is freely available online. This may be via the original source or shared via a third party. With so much freely available, fewer people are willing to pay for reporting, and this puts pressure on the news production process with less money available to pay for journalism and journalists being expected to provide more copy for less money (Davies, 2009). Despite this, the big media players are still powerful in the media space; in the UK, this includes media organisations previously producing newspaper in hard copy and now providing content online across a wide variety of platforms and media, including the printed word but also video and audio, separately or in combination.

Linked to the funding model for journalism is the concept of *churnalism* (Davies, 2009) that relates to practices used by time-pressed journalists to quickly generate copy from the many press releases they receive, copying and pasting sections from these and this can be repeated across media outlets, sometimes generated by press release distribution services or news agencies. This can have the effect of creating gatekeepers; for example, the same quotations from the same individual or organisation being reproduced multiple times in multiple outlets, making particular views or perspectives more prevalent, for example, in reporting on food banks (Wells & Caraher, 2014). This also has an impact on the way that news is produced, with journalists less likely to find and interview contributors for stories themselves, relying on news wires or press releases in order to find interviewees, for example, in science coverage of climate change (Davies et al., 2021). This, in turn, impacts the framing of stories on food and the coverage of food policies, with press release framing commonly being reproduced in subsequent reporting (Wells, 2017).

Framing

Framing in media coverage (Goffman, 1974) examines how problems are defined in the media and this can play a part in agenda-setting. Some research has noted that in nutrition reporting, diet is often framed as an individual's responsibility rather than a societal responsibility (Clarke & van Amerom, 2008, Kim & Willis, 2007, Wells, 2017) and this can hamper food policy development. Hilton et al. (2012) have analysed the media discourse around obesity in the UK, mapping a gradual change from obesity being portrayed in the media as a problem for the individual to address towards a societal problem caused by the "obesogenic environment".

There is a suggestion that for public policy to change, there needs to be a change in discourse and a move away from placing responsibility for obesity on the individual towards societal responsibility. The argument goes that if media coverage rarely explores societal responses to food policy challenges, then these are not on offer for the voting public to consider, a matter of informed consent.

Framing can also be driven by journalists at an individual level, as explored by Shoemaker and Reese (2014), where individual views, values, perspective and experience can have an impact on reporting. That said, complex social processes combine in the production of food media and this has been explored by several authors, notably Phillipov (2017). How does coverage of food policies and food issues get made? What are the production processes and power relationships that might impact the resulting programmes or reporting? An explanation of the tensions within food media is that media coverage of food issues can be seen to happen within a contested space or food policy triangle (Lang, 2005). Here, there are tensions between three main actors: the state, the food supply chain and civil society. Different actors or stakeholders try to exert influence over the coverage or the framing of the coverage, and this can play a part in the agenda-setting function of the media for food policy.

Kitzinger (2000) introduced the concept of media templates as another form of media framing, and this can be applied to food scares in the media. These can be used by journalists as shorthand, for example, to inform the framing and structure of their work. For example, interviewees can be categorised in terms of experts, victims and perpetrators. The expert may be a scientist or an academic researcher. The victim may be someone who has been or is potentially impacted by food poisoning or food fraud. The perpetrator, the person or organisation is seen to be responsible for the food scare. Some of these different areas may overlap, with, for example, the government potentially framed as both the expert and the organisation with responsibility for the problem. An example relating to food policy is seen with the 2013 horsemeat scandal, when horsemeat was found as an undeclared ingredient in processed foods such as beef burgers and ready meals (for more on this see Chapter 10). Journalists quickly identified this as a newsworthy food scare story with a potential cast of characters fitting a food scare template (Henderson et al., 2014).

News values and food media

We know from agenda-setting theories outlined above that there are many food policy issues that could rise up the news agenda, but only a few make it into news coverage. Less clear is what gets attention and what does not and why. Since there are many stories or "news items" to cover, why do some appear in reporting and others do not?

Another concept linked to food policy media agenda-setting that helps to explain this phenomenon is news values. The media have been shown to filter information through the use of "news values" which determine what is newsworthy, that is, what characteristics merit inclusion in the news (Galtung & Ruge, 1965, Harcup & O'Neill, 2001). Galtung and Ruge's (1965) study into foreign news identified 12 News Factors, which, if satisfied, would increase the likelihood of an event becoming news. These included unexpectedness, negativity, concerning elite nations or elite people. Many have revisited and updated this list, including Harcup and O'Neill (2001, 2017), and have suggested additions to the list. These include scientific advances or something brand new, for example, the discovery of a new or rare ingredient. Division within government and arguments within government or government suppression have also been suggested as key news values – and these have contributed to the huge press response to the BSE outbreak and food scare around beef and the associated vCJD cases of the mid-1990s (see Chapter 10).

Harcup and O'Neill (2001) suggested that "celebrity" was an obsession within modern media and should be included as a news value (see some examples in Chapter 11). This is particularly relevant for food policy due to the popularity and prevalence of celebrity chefs in our media.

The celebrity chef is a concept largely developed through television exposure but now also applicable to social media and online presence. The influence of celebrity chefs has been well documented (Caraher et al., 2000, Rousseau, 2013, Johnston & Goodman, 2015), with a feature of their more recent incarnations being their involvement in food policy advocacy (Matta, 2019, Hollows, 2022). Celebrity chefs are part of the food entertainment industry to such a large extent that they have influence over the food landscape of the UK, from the ingredients that are produced and how they are produced to what is eaten and how it is eaten (Hollows, 2022). One of the most cited examples of this is the chef Jamie Oliver, who started campaigning on school meals in the UK in 2005 (see Chapters 9 and 11) and who has also played a part in campaigning on the "sugar tax", and more recently, on free school meals in the UK. Another example is the TV cook and author Hugh Fearnley-Whittingstall, who has undertaken campaigns on food waste and fishing policy. These campaigns are sometimes linked to media outputs such as cookery books or television series. They can also be linked to advocacy groups who use celebrities to front campaigns due to their draw for the media and their ability to push issues up the media agenda.

Advocacy groups know that one of the things that might help them to get media coverage for their issue is a well-known figure who is in demand by the press. For their part, public figures also recognise that their profile helps them to raise awareness of particular issues that are important to them or that may have a social impact. The case of Marcus Rashford is instructive in this area. Rashford is a high-profile professional footballer who, at the time of writing, is a player for the England men's football team. He has talked about his own experience of free school meals as a schoolboy (see Chapters 9 and 11) and has taken part in campaigns notably to provide free school meals during the summer holidays of 2020 (Keith, 2020).

Press officers are aware of the way news values work. They know that a public figure such as Marcus Rashford, who is well known to an audience as well as journalists, and who is already in demand as a celebrity due to their work in another field or area, is more likely to garner attention. This helps increase reading, listening, viewing and sharing figures, which, for both traditional and modern media platforms, is how much reporting is monetised. Thus, celebrity chefs and other public figures not necessarily related directly to the food sector have acted as "policy entrepreneurs" (Kingdon, 2011) (see also Chapter 11). These are individuals motivated to invest their time, energy and reputation in a cause that they believe in. Kingdon suggests such policy entrepreneurs are seeking reward, for example, policy change, but also potentially personal satisfaction or reputational reward. Such figures have played a part in positive policy change (Lalli, 2021), including reviews of school meals policy (see Chapter 9). However, there are also concerns raised about their role as authority figures and their accountability in this role as well as debate as to the value of their "interference" which can blur the boundaries of education and entertainment (Rousseau, 2013).

In summary, the media's relationship with food policy is complex and draws on historic food scares as well as the scientific, moral and social underpinnings of nutrition's history. Mass and social media operate within a complex structure of forces, and these exert influence on the articles that appear and the way they are framed. In many areas of food and health reporting, coverage does not reflect social or environmental determinants of health but relies heavily on individualised messaging. The extent to which this influences food policy and policymakers is unclear; however, it is understood that media have an agenda-setting role in terms of drawing attention towards or away from particular policy issues or framing of issues.

Marketing and advertising

It should be noted that media reporting, whether mass media or social media, is only one of several information sources available to consumers: advertising and promotion activities can also affect consumers' choices. The following section discusses the promotion of food, particularly in reference to children and young people.

The issues of childhood obesity and promotion of unhealthy foods to children are huge issues for the UK where more than one in four children aged 4–5 years (27.7%) and four in ten aged 10–11 years (40.9%) are overweight or obese (Office for Health Improvement and Disparities, 2022). It is claimed that these children represent the first generation that will die before their parents if the problem is not tackled urgently (Olshansky et al., 2005). Although there may be a number of factors contributing to this, undoubtedly irresponsible food promotion plays a part. In 2021, more than £600 million was spent by brands on all online and television food advertising annually, and the government's 2020 consultation on restricting promotions of products high in fat, sugar and salt by location and by price estimated that children under 16 were exposed to 15 billion junk food advertisements online in 2019 compared with 700 million two years earlier (Sweney, 2021). Researchers have shown that there was a significant difference with those children who watched a high percentage of commercial television consuming an average of 520 additional unhealthy food products each year (Burki, 2018). In addition, children from minoritised and socio-economically disadvantaged backgrounds are disproportionately exposed to unhealthy food advertising (Backholer et al., 2021), pointing to health inequalities in this area. To date, the voluntary approach to responsible food promotion by the industry has largely failed and this policy area is an example of where action has occurred to reduce children's exposure to HFSS (High Fat, Salt, Sugar) foods. Action by Ofcom (Office of Communications) in 2007 has strengthened regulations around children's television viewing times, whereby HFSS food promotions are not permitted while the Obesity Strategy 2019 planned to extend restrictions on advertising of HFSS products on broadcast, TV and online media, with a 9 pm watershed on television for all adverts for HFSS products. However, in December 2022, the government announced that the introduction of a 9 pm watershed and online ban on paid for advertising for HFSS foods and drinks would be delayed until October 2025 (UK Parliament, 2022).

Additionally, an amendment to the Food (Promotion and Placement) Regulations was introduced in October 2022 (DHSC, 2022b). This allowed for the restriction of the promotion of unhealthy foods in stores or online marketplaces. Larger stores can no longer place HFSS foods in prominent places such as checkouts or end of aisles and this hopes to combat incidental purchases of unhealthy foods or so-called 'pester power' from young children. The UK government is the first country to introduce such legislation and despite concerns about enforcement this move has been welcomed (Muir et al., 2023).

While it is encouraging to see examples of food policy success and their focus and relevance, particularly to children and young people, we note here and elsewhere a recent and concerning stalling of food policy, which we discuss below.

Food advertising and marketing: history

The terms marketing and advertising are often used interchangeably, but there are differences between the two ideas, even though these are not always clearly defined or consistently agreed upon. Generally, advertising is usually part of a wider marketing strategy, which can include the development of a brand identity for use in product and/or in or on store labelling as well as product labelling and associated merchandise.

Tedlow (1990) breaks up the history of marketing and advertising into a four-stage sequence. First, Fragmentation, where local products were separately manufactured and promoted before foods and drinks were mass-produced and distributed pre-industrial revolution. This was followed by Unification (1880s–1920s) involving mass production and advances in preservation techniques which inspired big single brands with national distribution. At the same time, the rise of the mass media, for example, newspapers, made national advertising of big brands possible. This was the age of the big manufacturers, e.g. Nestlé, Unilever. The third stage is Segmentation (1920s–1980s), which, in the mid- to late twentieth century, saw the rise of a new Public Relations industry and advertising agencies. They used product differentiation to appeal to different market segments and demographics. For example, in the 1970s chocolate Yorkie Bars used male lorry drivers as leading characters in their advertising commercials and these were portrayed as macho men who needed "chunky" milk chocolate bars. This product even had a strap line "It's Not for Girls" during the early 2000s in a marketing campaign that was dubbed "tongue in cheek" by the marketing department of Nestlé (Day, 2002). At the same time, this period saw the growth of the advertising industry as a separate entity not located within product companies. Last, the fourth phase of the sequence is Hyper-Segmentation (post-1980s and beyond) where computerised or digital and micro-marketing is used so that individuals' personal preferences or buying habits can be collected. They can then be targeted through their personal electronic devices with adverts for specific products. This also involves micro-promotions of products through billing mechanisms such as loyalty cards or loyalty points. More recently, we have seen multi-platform selling and advergaming as marketing techniques. Also common is the use of algorithms to suggest advertising to consumers via online platforms using previously bought or searched for items. This is now a staple of marketing.

This latest stage of hyper-segmentation and individualised marketing has developed further in recent years with the rise of virtual assistant software or VAPA (Voice Activated Personal Assistant) such as Google Assistant, Apple's Siri or Amazon's Alexa. These assistants listen to questions and search the internet for answers or listen to commands to activate other devices such as lights or music. Concerns around privacy and surveillance as well as discrimination have been raised by researchers as to the use of "eavesmining" where personal data are being collected, stored and analysed (Neville & Coulter, 2022). For food policymakers, these new technological advancements add to the problem of policy keeping up with changing media devices and media consumption habits – in many senses, the medium is still the message (McLuhan & Fiore, 1967).

Modern marketers use a combination of tried-and-tested strategies and new techniques and technologies to promote products. The classic or traditional strategy used by companies to market products was called the Marketing Mix. The "Four Ps" – Product, Price, Place and Promotion – are used to consider marketing approaches. In the digital age, marketers consider different ways of placing advertising across different platforms and using these to encourage user engagement. For example, influencers such as celebrities or popular vloggers or bloggers on social media are used for target audiences to promote products in paid promotions (e.g. see Cadbury's Adopt a Cow campaign from 2017 [Talking Retail, 2017]). Food companies make use of dedicated stores or "worlds" where branded merchandise can be bought (M&M, 2023). Commercial relationships with online worlds or immersive interactive environments used by the gaming industry are beneficial for food companies as there is a pre-existing online community to invest in.

Today, ultra-recognisable brands are familiar simply from colour choices or elements of their logos. Think of McDonald's "golden arches" or the Cadbury shade of purple. Marketing and advertising can now be more sophisticated using small indicators or colours to suggest the brand. Toys given with purchase and the use of cartoon characters to promote fast food is still prevalent as is product placement in gaming or films and television programmes, a tactic with a long history (Newell et al., 2006).

Companies build "full service" relationships with customers, so connecting with them on multiple platforms, for example in-store, via an online shop, or app, to collect data and watch behaviour. In these environments, advergaming may be used, for example, by winning points in an online game for buying more of a particular product, and this can help collect data on purchasing behaviours.

All this marketing activity is matched by big budgets, which have been steadily growing but have also been negatively impacted by the COVID-19 pandemic. Food and beverages in 2016 were the fifth largest worldwide advertising spending category, spending USD 23.2 billion. The automotive industry was the top spender with personal care and household products at number two, entertainment and media at number three and retail at number four (Johnson, 2017). In the same year, Nestlé food and drink category had the third highest worldwide advertising spend after Proctor and Gamble in the personal care category and Samsung in the electronics category (Johnson, 2017). By 2020, Amazon was the world's largest advertiser with other internet companies such as Netflix also appearing as fast-growing advertisers in the market (Johnson, 2020). This reflected both the general rise of digital platforms, but also the rise in demand for home-based entertainment and delivery services during the worldwide lockdowns of 2020 and 2021. Overall, however, advertising spend shrank considerably during the pandemic, with the market expected to recover in 2022/2023.

Social marketing

The rise and rise of food marketing and advertising and the associated concerns about its link with diet-related disease have led to the development of so-called "social marketing" for food (Hastings, 2007, Hastings et al., 2011). Social marketing aims to harness techniques used by private companies in order to promote healthier diets or positive social change rather than economic gain. Those promoting social marketing argue that it transcends mere advertising campaigns or one-dimensional promotion activity, rather encompassing social change that can promote good health and nutrition.

An example of social marketing is the UK government's Change4Life campaign, which was introduced in 2009 and updated to "Better Health" in 2022. The relaunch came after the 2020/2021 COVID-19 pandemic and referenced rises in childhood obesity since the start of the pandemic, with:

> latest data highlighting that one in 4 (27.7%) children of reception school age are overweight or obese; this rises to 4 in 10 (40.9%) in Year 6 (ages 10 to 11). Evidence shows that families purchased food more during lockdowns and this remained above normal levels even once lockdowns ended.
>
> (DHSC, 2022b)

The current campaign borrows some of the marketing techniques used by commercial companies outlined above to support users to reduce unhealthy eating behaviours. These include a "Food Scanner App" to promote healthier alternatives; use of a celebrity to promote the programme; a national multi-platform advertising campaign and school resources linked to the app for primary school teachers (DHSC, 2022b). The app is designed to engage children with the programme.

Criticisms of such government campaigns are that they are not as sophisticated or engaging as those developed by big businesses and do not have the associated budgets. However, similar campaigns to promote fruit and vegetable intake among children have shown some signs of success. The "Eat Them to Defeat Them" campaign is run by the television channel ITV in collaboration with VegPower, an alliance of commercial partners across the horticulture sector. With a sizable campaign budget and a wide range of marketing techniques, an analysis showed an average 2.3% weekly uplift of vegetable sales during the weeks that the campaign ran in 2019 (Folkvord et al., 2021). This shows potential for further reach and impact. Such collaborations between advertisers, industry and public health advocates have been rare and the continuing success of the campaign may encourage other similar endeavours.

Similar industry initiatives include the Nectar fruit and veg challenge which uses "gamification" techniques to challenge customers to buy more fruit and vegetables. This earns them points that can be spent in partner stores (Sainsbury's, 2022). Other supermarkets are similarly involved with projects to promote better marketing, for example, Tesco, alongside other retailers joined the charity BiteBack 2030 to call for action to limit marketing of HFSS products to young children (Quinn, 2022) BiteBack 2030 is a charity supporting young people to work together to advocate for change. Campaigns include exposés of subliminal food marketing techniques and their impacts as well as "Don't Hide What's Inside" about advertising claims on products. All these are examples of voluntary initiatives by industry to try to work to promote change, and while these changes are welcome they can sometimes be problematic for several reasons outlined below (see also Chapters 2, 3, 7, 8 and 10.

Policy responses

How can we use policy to try to manage advertising and marketing and concern over advertising that is targeting children and negatively impacting their health? Concerns about advertising to children have been well voiced for a number of years and policy action has taken place not only in the UK but around the world (for a list of examples, see the WCRF Nourishing Framework, WCRF, 2023). This has been largely welcomed by public health experts. Policy development and implementation have, however, not been without their challenges. Many countries have introduced restrictions, particularly for adolescents and children, and lessons learnt from this include:

- Advertising restrictions or "bans" tend to encourage advertisers to move to other areas, for example, television advertisements move to cinema or online platforms.
- There is variation in defining children or adolescents in terms of age and this has hampered consistent policy development. Consumption of media is different among different age groups and therefore differentiated policy solutions could be needed.
- With restrictions come a need to define healthy or unhealthy foods. Policymakers have, up until now, relied on HFSS as a definition, but this could overlook research pinpointing ultra-processed food consumption as an indicator of health.

Many countries rely on voluntary agreements between industry and government, and some of the UK social marketing initiatives listed above are testament to this popular approach.

In the UK, the development of policy in this area has looked particularly at putting in restrictions and legislation to restrict advertising of unhealthy food defined as HFSS foods. In 2007, advertisements for HFSS products were prohibited from appearing during children's TV programmes, on dedicated children's broadcast channels and in programmes appealing to children under 16 (Ofcom, 2007, Conway, 2023). Since 2007, further policy developments have been called for by public health advocates. The government and the regulators ASA (Advertising Standards Authority) and Ofcom have agreed that advertising has impact, but have tended to argue that the evidence for the impact is small, contending that they are caught in the middle of "competing and equally fervent viewpoints" from campaigning groups and companies and are trying to take a balanced and evidence-based approach (Conway, 2023).

One impetus for further policy change is the speed at which advertising technology and capability as well as media habits among the very young change. Public health officials have been wary of how policy can keep pace with changing media practices and audience consumption. In July 2017, the ASA banned HFSS food adverts in children's online media, in line with the standards already in place for television. This new rule stated that:

> HFSS product advertisements must not be directed at people under 16 through the selection of media or the context in which they appear. No medium should be used to advertise HFSS products if more than 25% of its audience is under 16 years of age.
>
> (Conway, 2023)

In June 2018, the government published "Childhood Obesity: a plan for action" (DHSC, 2018), the second part of its plan to tackle childhood obesity. This included plans for a consultation on the introduction of a 9 pm TV watershed for HFSS products – 9 pm traditionally considered a time after which fewer children are watching television. Two consultations on this proposal took place in 2019 and 2020.

Meanwhile, health professionals wanted policy to go further, and in 2019, the then UK Chief Medical Officer Professor Dame Sally Davies commented:

> With more children going online, government policy needs to protect children, by adapting to the algorithms that target children with embedded adverts appealing to their age, location and preferences. The government will rightly look at how new rules for TV could be mirrored not just on streaming sites but on social media and YouTube too.
>
> (Donnelly, 2019)

At the same time, a notable regional policy development was a ban on the advertising of HFSS foods by Transport for London, in place since February 2019. This included advertising on the underground or tube network, bus stops and at train stations. Preliminary research has linked this to lower purchases of unhealthy food and drink (Yau et al., 2022).

In July 2020, after two rounds of consultation, the government announced they were intending to ban junk food advertising on TV prior to 9 pm in the evening, the so-called "watershed", after which it is considered that children will no longer be watching television. Marketing Week reported:

> Number 10 cites research published by Cancer Research UK in September 2019 that suggests almost half of all food adverts (47.6%) shown on ITV, Channel 4, Channel 5 and Sky One were for HFSS products. That rises to almost 60% between 6pm and 9pm – the peak viewing period for children.

However, they also raised concerns that such a policy change could cost broadcasters more than £200 million in lost revenue (Rogers, 2020). The government launched a consultation in November of the same year (DHSC and DMCS, 2020) about what they called a "total online advertising restriction for HFSS products to reduce the amount of HFSS advertising children are exposed to online".

The journey of this potential policy change highlights the tensions outlined by the ASA and reported above in the debate on this issue (Conway, 2023). Health advocacy campaigners, on the one hand, were complaining that there were already too many exemptions in the proposals and that they were not going far enough given the scale of the obesity problem. On the other hand, the food industry as well as the broadcasters and advertising industry were also complaining that the policy proposal was going to disproportionately affect their sales, at a time when they had already been facing financial difficulty during the pandemic. Despite this, in April 2022, the proposals were written into law as part of the Health and Care Act, and this received royal assent and was due to come into effect in January 2023. However, in May 2022, this legislation was delayed for 12 months, with a further delay announced in December 2022. At the time of writing, the changes are not due until October 2025 (UK Parliament, 2022).

This delay coincides with a chaotic period in the UK government with changing ministers as the Prime Minister Boris Johnson struggled to keep his job. This stalling of policies restricting advertising of unhealthy food in the UK is in line with other current sluggish food policy implementation. Other examples include the recommendations of the National Food Strategy, discussed further in other chapters.

Conclusions

There is a worldwide concern over the influence of advertising and marketing of unhealthy food on food behaviours. HFSS foods have been particularly targeted by health advocates, and restrictions and regulations have been put in place in a number of different countries. There is a particular concern about protecting children and adolescents who are seen as vulnerable groups less able to understand and process commercial messages. Young children are regarded as less able to critically assess advertising claims (Boyland & McGale 2022, WCRF, 2023).

Within this context, health experts have used evidence from extensive research into advertising content to successfully argue that children are particularly susceptible to advertising messages. These can affect their diet and long-term health. This has led to regulation and legislation around the world, including in the UK; however, the implementation of advertising restrictions and policy banning adverts has not been smooth. There are ongoing tensions between interested stakeholders. These include health and food campaigners, food industry representatives and media organisations as well as advertising companies. The latter stand to lose revenue from these policies in a climate of ongoing economic uncertainty and reduced revenues for some media organisations (Rogers, 2020).

Academic literature in this area is unbalanced in favour of research looking at the impact of food advertising on children's health and food choices. Up until recently, print media and television have been the main focus of research, due to easier access with searchable databases and replacing hard copies or microfiches. Research is now moving towards digital media, social media and the internet. Popular online platforms are inviting interest due to the speed with which they develop and attract followers from among younger audiences. Academic research, along with policy, lags behind technological developments due to the time it takes to fund, undertake and publish research. Policy processes can be long and difficult to navigate, characterised by political pragmatism as well as the separate timetable of election cycles. Policy windows of opportunity are few and far between, with tensions between stakeholders hampering development and implementation. Advertising innovation and fast-changing media consumption, particularly among younger audiences, contribute to the need for policy development.

There are a lot of tensions in this space and polarised perspectives as well as few examples of partnerships. The marketing, food industry and public health organisations rarely work together for change, social marketing initiatives notwithstanding. While there have been some policy successes, development of policy in this area at the time of writing is slow, despite strong evidence for policy change.

References

Backholer, K., Gupta, A., Zorbas, C., Bennett, R., Huse, O., Chung, A., Isaacs, A., Golds, G., Kelly, B. & Peeters, A. 2021, "Differential exposure to, and potential impact of, unhealthy advertising to children by socio-economic and ethnic groups: a systematic review of the evidence", *Obesity Reviews*, vol. 22, no. 3, p. e13144. https://doi.org/10.1111/obr.13144

Baumgartner, F.R. & Jones, B.D. 2009, *Agendas and Instability in American Politics*, The University of Chicago Press, Chicago; London.

Boyland, E. & McGale, L. 2022, *Food Marketing Exposure and Power and Their Associations with Food-Related Attitudes, Beliefs and Behaviours: A Narrative Review*, World Health Organization, Geneva. Licence: CC BY-NC-SA 3.0 IGO.

Boyland, E., McGale, L., Maden, M., Hounsome, J., Boland, A. & Jones, A. 2022, "Systematic review of the effect of policies to restrict the marketing of foods and non-alcoholic beverages to which children are exposed", *Obesity Reviews*, p. e13447. https://doi.org/10.1111/obr.13447.

Brooks, R., Christidis, R., Carah, N., Kelly, B., Martino, F. & Backholer, K. 2022, "Turning users into 'Unofficial Brand Ambassadors': marketing of unhealthy food and non-alcoholic beverages on TikTok", *BMJ Global Health*, vol. 7, no. 6, p. e009112. https://doi.org/10.1136/bmjgh-2022-009112

Burki, T.K. 2018, "TV advertising and childhood obesity in the UK", *The Lancet Diabetes & Endocrinology*, vol. 6, no. 8, p. 604. https://doi.org/10.1016/S2213-8587(18)30179-7

Cairney, P. 2012, *Understanding Public Policy: Theories and Issues*, Palgrave Macmillan, Basingstoke.

Caraher, M., Lang, T. & Dixon, P. 2000, "The influence of TV and celebrity chefs on public attitudes and behavior among the English public", *Journal for the Study of Food and Society*, vol. 4, no. 1, pp. 27–46. https://doi.org/10.2752/152897900786690805

Caraher, M. & Perry, I. 2017, "Sugar, salt, and the limits of self regulation in the food industry", *BMJ*, vol. 357. https://doi.org/10.1136/bmj.j1709

Carnibella, F. & Wells, R. 2022, "Framing of policy responses to migrant horticultural labour shortages during Covid-19 in the Italian print media', *Journal of Rural Studies*, vol. 95, pp. 278–293. https://doi.org/10.1016/j.jrurstud.2022.09.007

Clarke, J. & Van Amerom, G. 2008, "Mass print media depictions of cancer and heart disease: community versus individualistic perspectives?", *Health & Social Care in the Community*, vol. 16, no. 1, pp. 96–103.

Cohen, B.C. 1963, *The Press and Foreign Policy*, Princeton University Press, Princeton, NJ.

Conway, L. 2023, *Advertising to Children*, House of Commons Library. https://commonslibrary.parliament.uk/research-briefings/cbp-8198/.

Davies, N. 2009, *Flat earth News: An Award-Winning Reporter Exposes Falsehood, Distortion and Propaganda in the Global Media*, Vintage, London.

Davies, S.R., Franks, S., Roche, J., Schmidt, A.L., Wells, R. & Zollo, F. 2021, "The landscape of European science communication", *Journal of Science Communication*, vol. 20, no. 3. https://doi.org/10.22323/2.20030201

Day, J. 2002, "Nestle bans women from Yorkie bars", *The Guardian*, 27th March, https://www.theguardian.com/media/2002/mar/27/advertising.marketingandpr.

Dearing, J.W. & Rogers, E.M. 1996, *Agenda-Setting* (Communications Concepts Vol. 6), Sage, Thousand Oaks, CA.

DHSC 2022a, Guidance: Restricting promotions of products high in fat, sugar or salt by location and by volume price: implementation guidance, https://www.gov.uk/government/publications/

restricting-promotions-of-products-high-in-fat-sugar-or-salt-by-location-and-by-volume-price/
restricting-promotions-of-products-high-in-fat-sugar-or-salt-by-location-and-by-volume-price-
implementation-guidance.

DHSC 2022b, *New Campaign Launched to Help Parents Improve Children's Diet*, 10th January, https://
www.gov.uk/government/news/new-campaign-launched-to-help-parents-improve-childrens-diet.

DHSC 2018, "Childhood Obesity: A Plan for Action, Chapter 2", 25th June, https://www.gov.uk/
government/publications/childhood-obesity-a-plan-for-action-chapter-2.

DHSC & DMCS 2020, "Consultation outcome: total restriction of online advertising for products
high in fat, sugar and salt (HFSS)", 10th November, https://www.gov.uk/government/consultations/
total-restriction-of-online-advertising-for-products-high-in-fat-sugar-and-salt-hfss.

Donnelly, L. 2019, "Crackdown on junk food ads as Chief Medical Officer warns of impact of social
media promotions", *Sunday Telegraph*, 17th March, https://www.telegraph.co.uk/news/2019/03/17/
crackdown-junk-food-ads-chief-medical-officer-warns-impact-social/.

Eli, K. & Ulijaszek, S. 2016, *Obesity, Eating Disorders and the Media*. Routledge, Abingdon.

Folkvord, F., Naderer, B., Coates, A. & Boyland, E. 2021, "Promoting fruit and vegetable consumption
for childhood obesity prevention", *Nutrients*, vol. 14, no. 1, p. 157. https://doi.org/10.3390/nu14010157

Galtung, J. & Ruge, M.H. 1965, "The structure of foreign news", *Journal of Peace Research,* vol. 2, no.
1, pp. 64–91.

Goffman, E. 1974, *Frame Analysis: An Essay on the Organization of Experience*, Penguin, Harmondsworth.

Harcup, T. & O'Neill, D. 2017, "What is news? News values revisited (again)", *Journalism Studies*,
vol. 18, no. 12, pp. 1470–1488.

Harcup, T. & O'Neill, D. 2001, "What is news? Galtung and ruge revisited", *Journalism Studies*, vol. 2,
no. 2, pp. 261–280.

Hastings, G. 2007, *Social Marketing: Why Should the Devil Have all the Best Tunes?*, Elsevier, Oxford.

Hastings, G., Angus, K. & Bryant, C.A. 2011, *The SAGE Handbook of Social Marketing*, Sage Publications,
London.

Hastings, G., Stead, M., McDermott, L., Forsyth, A., MacKintosh, A.M., Rayner, M., Godfrey, C., Caraher,
M. & Angus, K. 2003, *Review of Research on the Effects of Food Promotion to Children*, Food Standards
Agency, London.

Henderson, J., Wilson, A., Meyer, S.B., Coveney, J., Calnan, M., McCullum, D., Lloyd, S. & Ward, P.R.
2014, "The role of the media in construction and presentation of food risks", *Health, Risk & Society*,
vol. 16, no. 7–8, pp. 615–630. https://doi.org/10.1080/13698575.2014.966806

Hilton, S., Buckton, C.H., Katikireddi, S.V., Lloyd-Williams, F., Patterson, C., Hyseni, L., Elliot-Green, A.
& Capewell, S. 2017, "Who says what about sugar-sweetened beverage tax? Stakeholders' framing of
evidence: a newspaper analysis", *The Lancet*, vol. 390, p. S44.

Hilton, S., Patterson, C. & Teyhan, A. 2012, "Escalating coverage of obesity in UK newspapers:
the evolution and framing of the 'obesity epidemic' from 1996 to 2010", *Obesity*, vol. 20, no. 8,
pp. 1688–1695.

HM Revenue and Customs 2016, *Policy Paper: Soft Drinks Industry Levy*, https://www.gov.uk/government/
publications/soft-drinks-industry-levy/soft-drinks-industry-levy.

Hollows, J. 2022, *Celebrity Chefs, Food Media and the Politics of Eating*, Bloomsbury Publishing, London.

Huang, T.T., Cawley, J.H., Ashe, M., Costa, S.A., Frerichs, L.M., Zwicker, L., Rivera, J.A., Levy, D.,
Hammond, R.A., Lambert, E.V. & Kumanyika, S.K. 2015, "Mobilisation of public support for policy
actions to prevent obesity", *The Lancet*, vol. 385, no. 9985, pp. 2422–2431. https://doi.org/10.1016/
S0140-6736(14)61743-8

Inthorn, S. & Boyce, T. 2010, "'It's disgusting how much salt you eat!' Television discourses of obesity,
health and morality", *International Journal of Cultural Studies*, vol. 13, no. 1, pp. 83–100. https://doi.
org/10.1177/1367877909348540

Johnson, B. 2020, "World's largest advertisers 2020, prime time: Amazon vaults into top spot, displacing
procter & gamble", *Advertising Age*, 7th December.

Johnson, B. 2017, "World's largest advertisers", *Advertising Age*, 5th December, https://adage.com/article/
cmo-strategy/world-s-largest-advertisers-2017/311484.

Johnston, J. & Goodman, M.K. 2015, "Spectacular foodscapes: food celebrities and the politics of lifestyle mediation in an age of inequality", *Food, Culture & Society*, vol. 18, no. 2, pp. 205–222.

Keith, R. 2020, "Marcus Rashford: a brief history of free school meals in the UK", *The Conversation*, https://theconversation.com/marcus-rashford-a-brief-history-of-free-school-meals-in-the-uk-140896.

Kim, S.H. & Anne Willis, L. 2007, "Talking about obesity: news framing of who is responsible for causing and fixing the problem", *Journal of Health Communication*, vol. 12, no. 4, pp. 359–376.

Kingdon, J.W. 2011, *Agendas, Alternatives, and Public Policies*, Longman Pub Group, London.

Kitzinger, J. 2000, "Media templates: patterns f association and the (re)construction of meaning over time", *Media, Culture & Society*, vol. 22, no. 1, pp. 61–84.

Lalli, G.S. 2021, "A review of the english school meal: 'progress or a recipe for disaster'?", *Cambridge Journal of Education*, https://doi.org/10.1080/0305764X.2021.1893658

Lang, T. 2005, "Food control or food democracy? Re-engaging nutrition with society and the environment", *Public Health Nutrition*, vol. 8, no. 6a, pp. 730–737.

Lewis, T. 2020, *Digital Food: From Paddock to Platform*, Bloomsbury Publishing, London.

Lupton, D. & Feldman, Z. (Eds.). 2020, *Digital Food Cultures*, Routledge, London.

Mann, A. 2018, "Hashtag Activism and the Right to Food in Australia" in *Digital Food Activism*, eds. T. Schneider, K. Eli, C. Dolan & S. Ulijaszek, Routledge, London, pp. 168–184.

Matta, R. 2019, "Celebrity Chefs and the Limits of Playing Politics from the Kitchen", in *Globalized Eating Cultures*, eds. J. Dürrschmidt & Y. Kautt, Palgrave Macmillan, Cham, pp. 183–201.

McCombs, M.E. & Shaw, D.L. 1972, "The agenda-setting function of mass media", *The Public Opinion Quarterly*, vol. 36, no. 2, pp. 176–187.

McDonald, D. 2004, "Twentieth-Century Media Effects Research", in *The Sage Handbook of Media Studies*, eds. J.D. Downing, D. McQuail, P. Schlesinger & E. Wartella, Sage Publications, Inc., Thousand Oaks, CA, pp. 183–200. https://doi.org/10.4135/9781412976077.n10

McLennan, A.K., Ulijaszek, S. & Beguerisse-Díaz, M. 2018, "Diabetes on Twitter: Influence, Activism and What We Can Learn from all the Food Jokes", in in *Digital Food Activism*, eds. T. Schneider, K. Eli, C. Dolan & S. Ulijaszek, Routledge, London pp. 43–69.

McLuhan, M. & Fiore, Q. 1967, *The Medium Is the Massage: An Inventory of Effects*, Bantam Books, New York.

McQuail, D. 2010, *McQuail's Mass Communication Theory*, Sage Publications Limited, London.

M&M 2023, *M&Ms London*, https://www.mms.com/en-gb/mms-world-store-london.

Muir, S., Dhuria, P., Roe, E., Lawrence, W., Baird, J. & Vogel, C. 2023. "UK government's new placement legislation is a 'good first step': a rapid qualitative analysis of consumer, business, enforcement and health stakeholder perspectives". *BMC medicine*, vol. 21, no. 1, pp. 1–14.

Naccarato, P. & LeBesco, K. 2013, *Culinary Capital*, Bloomsbury Publishing, London.

Neville, S.J. & Coulter, N. 2022, "'Hey Siri': virtual assistants are listening to children and then using the data", *The Conversation*, 14th July. Available from: https://theconversation.com/hey-siri-virtual-assistants-are-listening-to-children-and-then-using-the-data-186874.

Newell, J., Salmon, C.T. & Chang, S. 2006, "The hidden history of product placement", *Journal of Broadcasting & Electronic Media*, vol. 50, no. 4, pp. 575–594.

Ofcom 2007, *Television Advertising of Food and Drink Products to Children: Final Statement*, 22nd February, https://www.ofcom.org.uk/__data/assets/pdf_file/0028/47746/Television-Advertising-of-Food-and-Drink-Products-to-Children-Final-statement-.pdf.

Office for Health Improvement and Disparities 2022, *National Child Measurement Programme: Information for Schools*, https://www.gov.uk/government/publications/national-child-measurement-programme-operational-guidance/national-child-measurement-programme-2022-information-for-schools.

Olshansky, S.J., Oassaro, D.J., Hershow, R.C., Layden, J., Carnes, B.A., Brody, J., Hayflick, L., Butler, R.N., Allison, D.B. & Ludwig, D.S. 2005, "A potential decline in life expectancy in the United States in the 21st century", *New England Journal of Medicine*, vol. 352, pp. 1138–1145. https://doi.org/10.1056/NEJMsr043743

Parasecoli, F., 2005, "Feeding hard bodies: food and masculinities in men's fitness magazines", *Food and Foodways*, vol. 13, no. 1–2, pp. 17–37. https://doi.org/10.1080/07409710590915355

Parsons, K., Hawkes, C. & Wells, R. 2019, *Brief 2: Understanding the Food System: Why It Matters for Food Policy* (Rethinking Food Policy), Centre for Food Policy, City University, London.

Phillipov, M. 2017, *Media and Food Industries: The New Politics of Food*, Springer, Cham.

Quinn, I. 2022, "Tesco leads call for government action on obesity after junk food ads backtrack", The Grocer, 14 December. https://www.thegrocer.co.uk/health/tesco-leads-call-for-government-action-on-obesity-after-junk-food-ads-backtrack/674546.article

Reilly, J. 1998, "'Just another food scare?' Public understanding and the BSE crisis", in *Message Received: Glasgow Media Group Research, 1993–1998*, eds. G. Philo & Glasgow Media Group, Longman, Harlow, pp. 128–145. https://doi.org/10.1057/jphp.2010.39

Ries, N.M., Rachul, C. & Caulfield, T. 2011, "Newspaper reporting on legislative and policy interventions to address obesity: United States, Canada, and the United Kingdom", *Journal of Public Health Policy*, vol. 32, no. 1, pp. 73–90.

Rogers, C. 2020, "Government rolls out junk food ad ban", *Marketing Week*, 27th July, https://www.marketingweek.com/government-junk-food-ad-ban-coronavirus.

Rousseau, S. 2013, *Food Media: Celebrity Chefs and the Politics of Everyday Interference*, Berg, London.

Rousseau, S., 2012, *Food and Social Media: You Are What You Tweet*, Rowman Altamira, Plymouth.

Russell, S.J., Croker, H. & Viner, R.M. 2019, "The effect of screen advertising on children's dietary intake: a systematic review and meta-analysis", *Obesity Reviews*, vol. 20, no. 4, pp. 554–568. https://doi.org/10.1111/obr.12812

Sainsbury's 2022, *Grape News: Sainsbury's Rewards Shoppers with Bonus Nectar Points as the 'Great Fruit & Veg Challenge' Returns*, 18th July, https://www.about.sainsburys.co.uk/news/latest-news/2022/18-07-2022-nectar-great-fruit-and-veg-challenge-returns.

Shoemaker, P.J. & Reese, S.D. 2014, *Mediating the Message in the 21st Century: A Media Sociology Perspective,* Routledge, New York; London.

Simmonds, P. & Vallgårda, S. 2021, "'It's not as simple as something like sugar': values and conflict in the UK meat tax debate', *International Journal of Health Governance*. vol. 26, no. 3, pp. 307–322. https://doi.org/10.1108/IJHG-03-2021-0026

Smith, K. 2013, *Beyond Evidence-Based Policy in Public Health: The Interplay of Ideas,* Palgrave Macmillan, London.

Sweney, M. 2021, "UK to ban junk food advertising online and before 9pm on TV from 2023", *The Guardian*, https://www.theguardian.com/media/2021/jun/23/uk-to-ban-junk-food-advertising-online-and-before-9pm-on-tv-from-2023.

Talking Retail 2017, *Cadbury Unveils 'Adopt a Cow' Promotion. Product News/Confectionery,* 5th May, https://www.talkingretail.com/products-news/confectionery/cadbury-unveils-adopt-cow-promotion-15-05-2017/.

Tedlow, R. 1990, *New and Improved: The Story of Mass Marketing in America*, Basic Books, New York.

Thomas-Meyer, M., Mytton, O. & Adams, J. 2017, "Public responses to proposals for a tax on sugar-sweetened beverages: a thematic analysis of online reader comments posted on major UK news websites", *PLoS One*, vol. 12, no. 11. https://doi.org/10.1371/journal.pone.0186750

Thompson, C., Clary, C., Er, V., Adams, J., Boyland, E., Burgoine, T., Cornelsen, L., De Vocht, F., Egan, M., Lake, A.A. & Lock, K. 2021, "Media representations of opposition to the 'junk food advertising ban' on the transport for London (TfL) network: a thematic content analysis of UK news and trade press", *SSM-Population Health*, vol. 15, p. 100828. https://doi.org/10.1016/j.ssmph.2021.100828

UK Parliament, 2022, *Health Update: Statement Made on 9 December 2022*, https://questions-statements.parliament.uk/written-statements/detail/2022-12-09/hcws433.

WCRF 2023, *NOURISHING and MOVING Policy Databases*, https://policydatabase.wcrf.org./

Wells, R. 2017, "Mediating the spaces of diet and health: a critical analysis of reporting on nutrition and colorectal cancer in the UK", *Geoforum*, vol. 84, pp. 228–238.

Wells, R. & Caraher, M. 2014, "UK Print Media coverage of the food bank phenomenon: from food welfare to food charity?", *British Food Journal*, vol. 116, no. 9, pp. 1426–1445. https://doi.org/10.1108/bfj-03-2014-0123

Williams, K. 2010, *Understanding Media Theory*, Arnold, London.

Yau, A., Berger, N., Law, C., Cornelsen, L., Greener, R., Adams, J., Boyland, E.J., Burgoine, T., de Vocht, F., Egan, M. & Er, V. 2022, "Changes in household food and drink purchases following restrictions on the advertisement of high fat, salt, and sugar products across the transport for London network: a controlled interrupted time series analysis", *PLoS Medicine*, vol. 19, no. 2, p. e1003915. https://doi.org/10.1371/journal.pmed.1003915

Zenone, M., Ow, N. & Barbic, S. 2021, "TikTok and public health: a proposed research agenda", *BMJ Global Health*, vol. 6, no. 11, p. e007648. https://doi.org/10.1136/bmjgh-2021-007648

7 The UK food industry

Introduction

In previous chapters, there have been references to the food system and how it supplies food to the consumer (Chapters 1–3). One way of conceptualising the way food gets from farm to fork is via the concept of the food industry or the food chain. Tracing food from growing to consumption and disposal is variously referred to as farm to fork, paddock to plate, soil to society and, more colloquially, as field to fart. This is a complex, often global network of diverse businesses that supply much of the food consumed by the world's population. The term "food industries" encompasses a series of large-scale industrialised activities directed at the production, distribution, processing, conversion, preparation, storage, preservation, transport, certification and packaging of foodstuffs. The words industry and industrial provide clues to the focus which is large-scale, mechanised and mass-produced levels of farming, food processing and retail provision. While there is a concern with "closed loop" systems of food production and the need to provide an eco-nutrition food system, the reality is that it is highly complex and often dependent on global supply networks (Ellen MacArthur Foundation, 2021, van Zanten et al., 2022).

This complexity has become even more evident in the wake of the COVID-19 lockdown and the war in Ukraine – the latter of which has wider ramifications for the global supply system. Ukraine, along with Russia, was a major exporter of wheat on the global market, accounting for nearly 30% of global wheat supplies and 80% of sunflower seeds. Due to the war, existing stocks cannot be shipped (at least 15 million tonnes of grains were in storage in mid-2022) and farmers are facing problems harvesting and planting, triggering major concerns on global trading markets. The drive for national self-sufficiency in China triggered by the invasion of Ukraine has resulted in less exports of urea (Lau, 2022). Diesel additive (AdBlue) is manufactured from urea mostly imported into Australia from China. So, food deliveries in Australia are under threat due to a lack of AdBlue. The lack of urea in Europe has resulted in food prices rising because of a lack of fertiliser (of which urea is an important part: urea contains phosphate necessary for fertiliser production). The global food system is complex and many of its adherents point to its efficiency and inter-relationships with other industries such as steel production where the use of high temperatures and energy has been used to produce ammonia as a by-product. As an example, take what is generally referred to as the "Haber-Bosch" process, already referred to in the introduction.[1] This involves making ammonia which goes towards the making of fertilisers; the by-products of the process then are used in other fertiliser production as well as disinfectant, diesel exhaust fluid (AdBlue), carbon dioxide used in the food industry for stunning pigs and chickens, for fizzy drinks as well as a preservative in some bagged food products. So, a shortage of CO_2 has resulted in a shortage of some goods on supermarket shelves such as packed salads, meat and bread products. The rise in energy prices, linked to the war in Ukraine, has resulted in

DOI: 10.4324/9781003260301-7

many factories using the process of shutting down or cutting back production. Thus, fertiliser is in short supply, prices rise, farmers use less resulting in smaller yields, all contributing to food price increases, all showing the global reach and interconnectedness of the food system.

So, here is a circular loop system but one dependent on global, not local, regional or country based, supply chains. In the UK, organic food production was reported as under threat as imports of organic feedstuff were in short supply and had tripled in price, especially organic soy from Southeast Asia. Yet most people assume that the UK organic food chain is locally based (Levitt, 2022).

The span of the food industry today has become highly diversified, with manufacturing ranging from small, traditional, family-run activities that are highly labour-intensive producing artesian food, to large, capital-intensive and highly mechanised industrial processes (see Table 7.1). All of these cater to different market segments of the population: cheap food for the masses and organic pesticide-free for those who can afford it – a two-tier food system prevails (Caraher, 2011).

Only subsistence farmers, hunter-gatherers and those who have consciously opted out of the dominant food system and who survive on what they grow can be considered outside the reach of the modern food industry. Within modern developed economies, there are some who opt out of the dominant system of supply, but these often require resources to do so. Even the organic sector, long a mainstay and symbolic of alternative lifestyles, has been commercialised and industrialised and may rely, as we saw above, on organic imports to complete the cycle (Levitt, 2022). A major alternative organic producer, Whole Foods, begun in Austin, Texas, in 1980, expanded worldwide to become a major player using the modes of operation of major retailers (Conaway et al., 2018). In 2017, Whole Foods was bought by Amazon who incorporated it into their online ordering. It also gave them access to food supply chains which are as important as the physical retail outlets included in the purchase. Much of the concentrations and developments in the food industry are through mergers and acquisitions (M&As) of existing companies, not the emergence of new companies started from scratch. Examples of this will be provided in the section on supermarkets.

The National Food Strategy (NFS) said: "Supermarkets and chain restaurants sell us the majority of the meat we eat. They will therefore have a vital role to play in tempting us to eat more plants and a bit less meat" (Dimbleby, 2021, p. 126). This is true not only of meat but of food in general. The top ten UK retailers account for eight out of every ten pounds spent on food. And Tesco is the third largest retailer in the world after Walmart and Carrefour with global sales of £70 billion. So, there is a policy conundrum as to how you regulate or make policy for

Table 7.1 The range of the food industry

Agriculture.
Food processing and packaging.
Retail grocery, farmers markets, public markets and other retailing.
Hospitality, both public (schools, hospitals etc.) and private.
Marketing and promotion of food products.
Regulation at local, regional, national and international levels of hygiene, consumer rights and pricing.
Education: academic research, consultancy and vocational training for those working in the food industry.
Research and development: food science, food microbiology, food technology, food chemistry and food engineering.
Financial services: credit, insurance (see Chapter 8).

such a complex and diverse system and tackle the power relationships which favour the large retailers.

The irony, as can be seen in Chapters 2 and 3 (see also Chapter 8 on financialisation for a global perspective), is that we have a food system that is controlled at the middle and consumer distribution ends by a small number of companies while relying on a large number of small-scale producers to grow the raw materials. The UK food system is not any different with the retail end being controlled by a small number of companies who can demand standards and control prices from suppliers. Figure 7.1 sets out the food chain with £200 billion plus of sales for the UK. Using this, this chapter is set out under the three main headings of agriculture, food retail and food catering. The case for agriculture as an industry is made as the majority of farms are large scale and rely on mechanised labour.

The importance of the link between agriculture and food retail and catering or hospitality lies in the fact that raw food is processed and sold to the public in forms that often barely resemble the raw products. As we saw in Chapter 3, the UK consumes the highest proportion of ultra-processed foods (UPFs) in Europe, and this contributes to the triple burden of disease (Monteiro et al., 2018a, 2018b), hence the importance of examining the food chain. The NFS made a plea for more of the food industry to produce, stock and encourage consumption of fresh foods along with a strategy to break what it calls the "junk food cycle" (Dimbleby, 2021). The junk food cycle can be seen as a consequence of the total food system. This latter category includes UPFs which are generally high in fat, salt and sugar, referred to as HFSS foods.

The focus of this chapter is the dominant mainstream commercial food chain or system, not the alternative or off-the-grid systems (e.g. self-sufficiency, freeganism), which, while illustrative of protest or rebellion against the dominant food system, are in the minority (Sharzer, 2012, Thompson, 2015, Kauffman, 2018). The paradox can be seen in the trends where those on low incomes are eating cheap (and often unhealthy) processed foods which has travelled many miles, while the rich are paying more to eat healthier and less food which is often local in nature. While there is this range of supply, the power and control in the food chain remains highly concentrated and some say it is concentrating more and more.

Agriculture in the UK

Lang says that the UK is self-sufficient in approximately 60% of its food supply with notable gaps in production of fresh fruit and vegetables (Lang, 2020). These figures are based on current usage, food production and consumption patterns and do not allow for changes necessary to meet a healthy and sustainable diet. In Figure 7.1, the gross added value of farming is estimated at £10.3 billion with a total labour force of 447,000. In the UK, agriculture – like other sections of the food chain – is dominated by large farms; half of all make a significant loss on their agricultural activities – the price they sell their produce for (known as farm gate) is not covered by the costs of growing or raising it, and this was before the current crisis where the cost of fertiliser and oil skyrocketed. Twenty-five per cent accrue a tiny profit, with the majority of income coming from support payments, which have traditionally been based on the amount of land. So, the larger the farm, the larger the grant, irrespective of what was produced. The top 25% of farms can make a profit, with scale of production and efficiency being key. The largest farms make up only 8% of the total, but occupy 30% of farmland and produce 57% of farming output. Work on the farm has become more and more mechanised and the use of technology means fewer are employed on the land. At the start of the twentieth century, 11% of the population worked in agriculture; by the end of the twentieth century, just 2% worked in agriculture

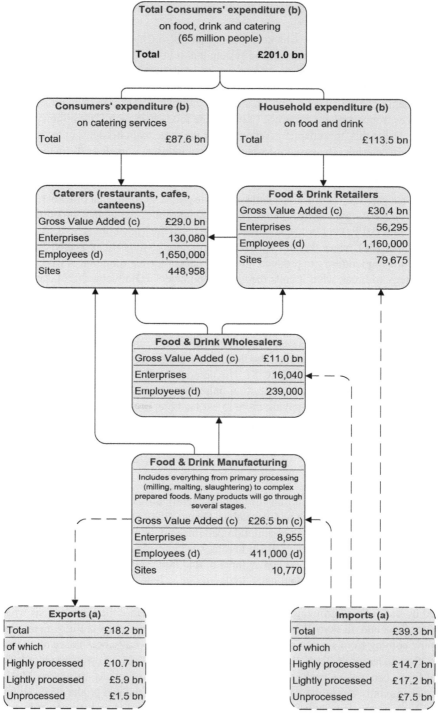

Figure 7.1 The UK food chain.

Source: Department for Environment, Food and Rural Affairs (DEFRA) (2017).

(Collingham, 2017, Lang, 2020). Approximately 70% of English farms are small or very small, taking up 28% of total land in and producing 13% of all agricultural output.

The supply base of the UK food system and food industry is in danger UK agriculture in a precarious situation with 85% of the farmland in the UK and abroad used to graze animals or to produce crops to feed the animals as opposed to crops going directly to feed humans. The NFS reported that:

> Agriculture currently takes up 70% of UK landmass. Yet golf courses occupy five times as much of our land as orchards. And all the UK's built-up areas combined are only two-thirds the size of our peat bogs. But what is most striking is how much land we use to rear lamb, beef and dairy cattle.
>
> (Dimbleby, 2021)

The conversion ratios are high for meat production; it takes 2.5 pounds of grain to produce 1 pound of beef and a broiler chicken has a conversion ratio of between 1.5 and 1.9. Technological developments, selective breeding and gene technology are being harnessed to make these production systems more efficient. Also, a growing trend and threat to traditional farming are developments in lab-produced meat and plant-based alternatives (Stewart et al., 2021).

UK farming has undergone a series of crisis from the clearances, the loss of common land and the Corn Laws to more modern shocks such as foot and mouth disease, BSE (mad cow disease), avian flu, swine fever, Brexit and now the global crisis triggered by war in Ukraine (Devine, 1994, Lang, 1998, Ratzan, 1998, Curry et al., 2002, van Zwanenberg & Millstone, 2005, Vivero-Pol et al., 2020).

The contribution of agriculture to greenhouse gas (GHG) emersions is considerable (Mason & Lang, 2017). Food is responsible for approximately 26% of all global GHG emissions within the food chain. The contribution of agriculture is as follows:

- Livestock and fisheries count for 31% of emissions.
- Crop production accounts for 27% of emissions.
- Land use accounts for 24% of emissions and includes elements such as the release of nitrous oxide from the application of fertilisers and manure; methane emissions from rice production; and carbon dioxide from agricultural machinery (Fanzo & Davis, 2021, United States Department of Agriculture, Economic Research Service, 2022).

A further challenge to faming is the issue of GHG emissions and the area of land devoted to animal production. The contribution of UK farming to the environmental damage is significant. When compared to total emissions from all sectors, agriculture was the source of 10% of total GHG emissions in the UK and 35% of GHG are accounted for by the total food system. Double the emissions result from land use for livestock (16%) as for crops for human consumption (8%), the supply chains account for 18% of food emissions (United States Department of Agriculture, Economic Research Service, 2022). There is detail in Chapters 2, 3 and 5 on the issue of eco or sustainable diets and how food growing would have to change to meet these criteria. The NFS recommended that the government should take action to reduce meat production and consumption to avoid climate breakdown.

The social appetite for meat and dairy products puts a particular strain on the UK's resources (Rogers, 2004, Stewart et al., 2021). The combined weight of animals bred for food is now ten times the combined weight of all wild mammals and birds put together (Lang, 2020). The calls for a sustainable food system that delivers healthy food is far from being realised (see Chapter 2 for more detail).

Yet the NFS did not set a target for self-sufficiency or for self-reliance in a changing global political economy (Lang & McKee, 2022). The invasion of Ukraine in 2022 has resulted in global shortages of grain, sunflower oil and rising energy prices – issues which could and should be dealt with by a food policy. A national UK food policy, by setting targets for food to be grown and produced in the UK, could help guard against shocks in the global food system such as were seen in the COVID-19 lockdown and with the global situation in 2022 related to trade wars and the Russian/Ukrainian crisis (Lang & McKee, 2022). The UK Agricultural Bill, which is meant as a replacement for the EU Common Agricultural Policy (commonly referred to as the CAP) does not address the issue of the amounts or types of crops grown or animals reared in terms of the needs of the UK population. Instead, it opts for an approach to replace CAP subsidies with rewards for conservation and land set aside to encourage biodiversity. At the very time the EU CAP is addressing issues of food production, the issue is not being addressed by the UK food policy to deliver national food security and self-sufficiency. Chapter 1 showed that UK agriculture accounts for less than 1% of GDP and that many politicians and policymakers are of the opinion that we should open the borders to imports from abroad, based on the provision of cheap food. The future policy direction is not clear at the time of writing. After much toing and froing, the government in November 2022 committed to continuation of the Environmental Land Management Scheme (ELMS) for England, this is being designed to replace the Basic Payment Scheme which, in turn, replaced payments under the CAP when the UK left the EU. ELMS is designed to promote:

- Sustainable Farming Incentive
- Local Nature Recovery
- Landscape Recovery

For more detail on the ELMs scheme see www.gov.uk/government/publications/environmental-land-management-schemes-overview/environmental-land-management-scheme-overview.   The scheme was criticised by the National Farmers Union (NFU) for not having enough emphasis on farming and being too much focussed on environmental issues. After pressure from its own members, the NFU reversed its stance. ELMS is for England as agriculture is one of the devolved functions to Northern Ireland, Scotland and Wales. What the devolved nations plan for agricultural support was not clear at the time of writing in early 2023.

The future of farming remains under debate and new developments such as lab-based meat, plant-based protein and new technologies such as "smart farming" will influence the future direction and shape of UK agriculture. When analysed by income, half of UK farms make a significant loss on their agricultural activities – that is, the price they sell their produce for doesn't even cover the costs of growing or raising it. A further quarter makes a tiny profit, with the bulk of their income coming from support payments. However, the top 25% of farms make a living income from agriculture.

Despite its low value as a contributor to national wealth in the form of GDP, farming is still considered as an industry to be regulated and controlled. More recent developments have, as seen above, been linked to ecological sustainability, but little attention has been given to overall production in terms of national food security or how what is produced relates to health outcomes (Mason & Lang, 2017). The Trade and Agriculture Commission published its final report in March 2021 with a vision that:

> The UK has an ambitious trade policy which contributes to a global farming and food system that is fair and trusted by all its participants, including farmers, businesses and citizens, from source to consumption. Our food is safe, healthy, affordable, produced in a

way which does not harm the planet, respects the dignity of animals and provides proper reward for those involved.

(Trade and Agriculture Commission, 2021, p. 48)

The Commission aligns action principles; chief among these is the promotion of "liberalisation of trade, to positively influence innovation and productivity, and price and choice for consumers" (p. 49), whereby the UK pursues free trade agreements that reduce and remove tariffs and quotas, provided that a set of nationally and globally important standards are met. At least, the report does not refer to "cheap" food or support the acquisition of "lower food standards". It focuses on three key areas: affordable food, protecting the environment and helping those who want to lead healthier lives in a system which is fair for all involved while simultaneously promising to not undermine decades of solid, hard-won progress, nor "off-shore" the impacts of food consumption in the UK. However, the report stops short of using trade policy to ameliorate food insecurity, deferring to domestic policy to address structurally food poverty:

> There is concern expressed in public debate, amplified by the current COVID-19 situation, that rising food insecurity will lead the UK government to lower trade barriers, opening up the UK market to more food produced to lower standards. However, UK consumers do not view this as a sensible solution to the problem, because it could lead to the poorest in society only having access to food which may not meet domestic standards. Given that UK shoppers pay comparatively less for food than shoppers in some other countries, trade policy may have limited incremental impact on food insecurity and poverty, and it is for domestic policy to address the core issue of food insecurity.
>
> (p. 37)

The scope of food security within the above quote is focused on adequate supplies for national food security, so adequate stocks or fully functioning supply chains and less concern with from where the food comes. It is not about food security or food poverty at the community or household level – again showing a gap in joined-up thinking. It also seems to be located in a pre-pandemic and pre-invasion of Ukraine world where global trade was dominant. So, when supplies were short in one area due to a poor harvest, the global traders simply sourced from elsewhere in the globe. The invasion of Ukraine, along with China's declaration to achieve self-sufficiency and climate emergencies, shows that these options are less available in the new world. The new normal has been described by some as a "permacrisis" where the old certainties no longer operate.

The food insecurity and more general poverty referred to above are issues for rural communities engaged in the growing of food. The proposed Food Strategy for England, the Agricultural Bill and the views of the devolved administrations in Holyrood, Cardiff and Stormont could help shape the nature of these agreements and the food system and supply chain. However, what is becoming clear is that the links and consensus between these various aspects are not consistent or joined-up. So, for example:

- The Agricultural Bill does not protect British farmers against the importation of lower standard and lower priced foods that may be imported.
- Nor does the Bill address the issue of carbon emissions in domestic or international food chains.
- The Food Strategy Plan for England was not clear on what is an adequate or safe level of domestic production to ensure national food security.

Concerns about any decline in UK food self-sufficiency post-Brexit are not reassured by the rejection of a series of amendments added to the Agriculture Bill in the Lords. The line taken by the government places some UK farm sectors, like beef, lamb and horticulture, highly vulnerable to post-Brexit trade deals. Proposed but rejected amendments sought to guarantee that no food could be imported at lower environmental, food safety and animal welfare standards than those required of British farmers. The Farm Minister said the imposition of quality standards to protect British farmers did not influence the negotiations in securing new trade deals, thus putting British framing at risk from low-quality imported food.

In the twenty-first century, technology and digital technologies for community-supported agriculture have enabled farmers to directly sell produce and engage with consumers. So while there are now ways to connect directly with the consumer, overall control and dominance at the retail level is still highly concentrated. For the most part, the majority of food grown in the agricultural sector goes to the dominant food supply chain through the supermarkets and hospitality outlets, with speciality produce such as Welsh lamb and Scottish beef commanding premium markets abroad. Agriculture currently accounts for 70% of UK landmass, yet golf courses occupy five times as much land as orchards. But it is how much land is used to rear lamb, beef and dairy cattle that is worrying in light of the contribution to GHG emissions. The NFS reported that the total area of land, given over to rearing lamb, beef and dairy cattle to feed the UK population here and abroad, is larger than the entire landmass of the UK.

The future for and of farming

There are many debates over the shape of the global agricultural system and how it can be made more ecologically sustainable, contribute to health outcomes, provide enough food and offer a living to those farming the land (Scott, 2017, Dimbleby, 2021, Fanzo & Davis, 2021, Chambers, 2022, McKinsey, 2022). While the UK has entered these debates, the food policy direction remains unclear; in the EU, the policy framework for farming, the CAP, rewarded farmers for set aside and sustainability practices. Currently, the EU is reforming the CAP to be more cognisant of food growing and linking this with ecological concerns; but this no longer applies to the UK. The UK, post-Brexit, followed the old model of rewarding landowners not for growing food but on the basis of the amount of land they owned and for environmental benefits such as re-establishing hedgerows and wild areas. DEFRA (Department for Environment, Food and Rural Affairs) is responsible for the delivery of ELMS and it is not clear what the future direction for food policy related to agriculture holds, as its roll-out is slow and subject to lessons learned from on-going evaluation. The Ukrainian crisis, the cost of fertilisers and other agricultural inputs along with concerns about domestic food security may be bringing about a rethink.

The NFU has argued a position that farmers should be paid for growing food and wild areas creating ecological friendly sites. Others point out that linking food production and environmental concerns have long been a concern of certain branches of farming such as organic production. What is clear is that whichever approach is taken, there is a need to address sustainability issues (Falloon et al., 2022). A number of approaches and debates are set out in Table 7.2 and they are not mutually exclusive. In an interview the chairman of Natural England, Tony Juniper said that "Rewilding should be rebranded 'nature recovery', … warning that the debate over the future of the countryside is becoming increasingly polarised" (Spencer, 2022). George Monbiot, previously an advocate of regenerative farming, has advanced the notion that the future of meat production lies not in agricultural practices but in technology such as cultured meat production (Monbiot, 2022b, 2022a). So, the debates over the future of farming are big, contentious and subject to lobbying by many powerful groups. A summary of the different approaches can be

Table 7.2 Summary of future scenarios for agricultural production

Approach to farming	Aims and key principles
Sustainable intensification (SI) is an approach to agricultural production.	To increase agricultural yields without unfavourable environmental impact and without the conversion of additional non-agricultural land. Critics see it as an extension of the existing dominant production system using technology and smart farming processes to maximise the efficient use of fertilisers (Dicks et al., 2019, Santini et al., 2016).
Regenerative farming.	To combine a conservation and rehabilitation approach to farming. It incorporates four practices: (1) promoting biodiversity; (2) reductions and elimination of tillage; (3) reducing the use of fertiliser and (4) using regenerative grazing management for livestock. Critics see its potential as unproven (Monbiot, 2022b).
Rewilding/nature recovery.	To return landscapes untouched by people and so risk disempowering local communities. Can be combined with regenerative farming (Egoh et al., 2021, Rewilding Britain, 2022).
Technical solutions such as cultured or cultivated meat production and precision fermentation.	To eliminate the need to raise farm animals for food. Plant-based substitutes produced in factory conditions – alternative plant-based proteins. Meat produced in vitro; this involves using starter cells from animal sources in a growth medium in large bioreactors. Critics point to the fact that currently the growth medium and bioreactors are expensive, not available in the quantities necessary to feed the world and that this is currently a First World solution to an impending global crisis.

found in Table 7.2. It is worth reading the following for more detail by Monbiot, Lang and Dicks (Dicks et al., 2019, Lang, 2020, Monbiot, 2022b).

Food retail

Figure 7.1 from DEFRA shows expenditure on catering and retail food of over £200 billion combined in 2016 compared to the gross value of agriculture of £10 billion. There were indications that in the period prior to COVID lockdown, the UK was on track for spending on catering services to equal in value that of the retail spend. The COVID-19 restrictions and lockdowns resulted in many catering establishments shutting down, bringing about an increase in retail ordering as people could not eat out. In the early stages of the lockdown, the catering sector had not come to grips with online ordering and delivery. As we came out of the lockdown and the removal of restrictions in March 2022, there are indications that the hospitality industry was recovering as people returned to eating out, along with online ordering and delivery of fast food, due to restrictions on social gatherings and the shutting down of many restaurants. The Ukrainian crisis along with shortages of food and rising inflation have resulted in the hospitality industry facing another crisis, as the retail sector enters into a price war to keep customers.

Supermarkets

During the twentieth century, supermarkets became the defining retail element of the food industry in the UK (Seth & Randall, 1999, Lescent-Giles, 2005, Seth & Randall, 2005, Murray & Caraher, 2019). The larger format supermarkets can have up to 30,000 food items on display. In 2020, the food retail market was valued at over £200 billion, with supermarkets as the dominant store format; the increases in retail from 2017 (seen in Figure 7.2) can be accounted for by COVID-19 lockdowns when eating out all but disappeared due to restrictions on social mixing. The UK's grocery landscape has been traditionally controlled by the "big four" supermarket chains: Tesco (27% of food sales), Asda (13%), Sainsbury's (14%) and Morrisons (9%). In 2022, Aldi overtook Morrisons for the fourth place. Aldi, considered a discount retailer by analysts, has been expanding its supermarkets and leading on price promotions.

Some of these smaller chains were often remnants of the retail end of big wholesale companies, which were finding it hard to compete against the purchasing power of the major supermarkets. For example, Home and Colonial, which became Allied Suppliers in 1961, was in the 1920s/1930s the largest retail chain in the UK. It had outlets in many small towns. After acquiring other food stores and businesses, it was renamed Allied Suppliers, and in 1982 was acquired by Argyll Food before Argyll was merged with Safeway in 1987. What distinguished companies such as Home and Colonial Stores from the newer supermarkets was that they owned many of the farms and factories that produced food for them, whereas the new entrants eschewed this approach in favour of outsourcing and buying in bulk. Lyons & Co were once at the heart of a major food empire; in fact, they were referred to as "the first food empire" (Bird, 2000). The company was a conglomerate, manufacturing food with factories in Hammersmith and Greenford producing bread, cakes, pies, tea, coffee and ice cream. In the public eye, they were known for Lyons Corner House Cafés. They also owned farms, steak houses and had franchises for Wimpy Bars (1953–1976) and Dunkin' Donuts (Harding, 2019).

Together, the top ten account for two-thirds of the total grocery retail market. The second division of food retailers includes Lidl (6%) and smaller chains such as the Co-Op (5%), Waitrose (4%), followed by Marks & Spencer (3%) and Iceland (2%). This means that for every £10 spend on food, slightly more than £8 is spent in one of the majors or that £2 is spent in the independent sector. As noted earlier, growth and control in food retail have been achieved by M&As. Table 7.3 shows how some of the smaller chains that have been absorbed within larger

Table 7.3 List of some defunct supermarkets (since the 1960s) and who purchased them.

Alldays purchased by the Co-op.	Hintons purchased by Morrison
Allied Suppliers (previously Home and Colonial) taken over by Argyll Foods and converted to Presto or Lo-Cost stores.	Jackson's regional chain in Yorkshire and North Midlands, bought by Sainsbury's in 2004.
Bejam purchased by Iceland.	Laws Stores defunct.
Day & Nite bought by Tesco.	Lipton absorbed by Allied Suppliers, then taken over by Argyll Foods, before being converted to Presto or Lo-Cost stores.
Carrefour UK bought by Somerfield and then sold to ASDA.	Premier Stores (a Booker Cash & Carry plc symbol group), a convenience store group acquired by Tesco.
Fine Fare purchased by Gateway and then integrated into Somerfield (see below).	Safeway (UK) purchased by Morrisons.
Fitch Lovell.	Sainsbury's Freezer Centres.
Frank Dee Supermarkets.	SavaCentre.
FreshXpress.	Somerfield purchased by the Co-op.
Galbraith supermarkets purchased by Allied Suppliers and then sold to Argyll Group before being rebranded.	Stewarts Supermarket Limited included *Crazy Prices* purchased by Tesco.
Gateway purchased by the Co-op.	Ugo bought by Poundstretcher in 2012.
David Greig bought by Somerfield.	Victor Value purchased by Tesco.
Hillards purchased by Tesco.	William Low purchased by Tesco.

conglomerates, rebranded and many, over time, sold on yet again. So, for example, Gateway became Somerfield and this was taken over by the Co-Op in 2011. Hillards was a small chain in the north of England which was acquired by Tesco in 1987. In 2022, the convenience chain McColl's was in danger of going into administration before being taken over by Morrisons, the fourth largest supermarket chain in the UK by market share: in 2021, Asda, owned by Walmart, was purchased by a company with a dominant presence in petrol forecourt petrol shops and is still undergoing change, and in October 2022, confirmed the acquisition of 132 Co-Op grocery retail sites with attached petrol stations. This is part of its strategy to enter the convenience retail space with smaller store formats. This fits the development of new outlets through M&As.

The dominant drivers in the retail sector are increased control with a reduced spread of ownership. The M&As, shown in Table 7.3, are a small selection of all that have occurred. The drive has been competiveness and profits within the retail sector, not the health of the consumer or issues related to food access. These are global trends with regional variations: so, in the UK, Tesco dominates in some areas, Sainsbury's in others; in other countries, such as the US, Walmart dominates (Norman, 1999, Seth & Randall, 2005). A 2022 report from the consumer organisation Which? identified the need for supermarkets in areas of deprivation, showing the dominance of supermarkets of the retail environment (Which?, 2022). A similar trend was reported in the USA in the 1990s referred to as the "Walmart effect" where, due to the dominance of Walmart, a town without one was deemed to be a food desert (Bianco, 2006).

The nature of the scale of supermarkets and the size of operations means that they rely on global food supply chains. They source food where prices are low and build in added value via processing. The UK supermarkets are no exception to this. Processing of foods has two advantages for the retailers: first, processed foods store and travel better than fresh foods; and second, they develop consumer dependence and deskilling (Stitt, Jepson & Paulson-Box, 1995, Lang, Barling & Caraher, 2009, Lang et al., 2009). However, these advantages come at a cost to the health and sustainability of the global food system: the drive towards the consumption of UPFs resulting in longer food chains and issues for sustainability (Monteiro et al., 2018a, 2018b, Popkin & Reardon, 2018). Major retailers claim that the scale of operation results in economies of scale (Popkin & Reardon, 2018), including less damage to the environment (Desrochers & Shimizu, 2012). According to this premise, many small independent shops are more wasteful, relying on many lines of supply and repeating processing at the local level (Seth & Randall, 2005). The counterargument is that the global nature of the food chain, operated by supermarkets, allows costs and damage to the environment and health to be hidden or externalised along the way; so, low wages in growing countries, degradation of local environments and pollution along the food distribution chain can be more easily concealed (Mason & Lang, 2017).

This concentration of power allows the supermarkets and hospitality industry to control the food supply chain at both the farm production and consumer levels (Dixon, 2015). At the level of production, this is done not by owning the land that food is grown on or the factories that it is processed in, but via contract specifications. A consequence of this vertical control by the retailers is that alternative sources of supply such as wholesalers are "written out" of the supply chain. Within this intermediate element, many small retailers struggle to source goods (Table 7.4).

Retail outlets are changing and the consequence of this is an increasing tension between the big supermarket giants versus smaller food stores, food social enterprises, farmers markets, bartering and food hubs (Estrada-Florez and Larsen, 2010). The retail food sector has become a major employer, often with poor employment practices – a lack of security and low wages (Murray & Caraher, 2019). Grower and employee security and income problems run right through the food system, from farm to fork. The UK went through a recession between

Table 7.4 Shifting power in the food value-added chain.

Period	Farming	Manufacture	Wholesale	Retail	Food service
Before 1900	**Dominant**	Minor	Major	Very Minor	Minor
1900–1950	Declining (but WWII saw farming gain in importance)	**Dominant**	Major.	Minor	Declining.
1960–1970	Rebuilding in Europe, the Common Agricultural policy	**Dominant**	**Dominant**	Emerging	Latent
1980–2000s	Declining	Declining	Rapidly Declining	**Dominant**	Emerging/ challenging retail
2000s	Returning	Uncertain	Minor	**Dominant**	Dominant

Source: Adapted from Von Schirach-Szmigiel (2005).

2007 and 2012 and witnessed changes in shopping behaviours driven by the twin influences of increases in food prices (30% increases) and greater awareness of sustainability and food waste issues. The monthly shop was replaced by top-up-shopping and the retreat of the supermarkets back to town centres, after abandoning them in the 1990s and early 2000s. The "food deserts" were filled with smaller size supermarket stores offering a limited range of essential goods at prices often up to 15% higher than they sell for at their "big bins" or online. The growth in small supermarket format on the high street is being led by the major supermarkets and does not reflect a growth in independent ownership. All this is possible because of technology and changes in supply chains. Supermarkets do not keep stocks of food on site, new systems such as just in time (JIT) retailing, allow goods to be shipped as they are bought and move off the shelves. From a health and sustainability perspective, there are now moves to using electric vehicles and carbon neutral approaches for transport, with some of the major supermarkets and their suppliers now using the rail networks ("roll-on/roll-off" container systems) to transport food from outside the UK to central hubs in the UK, a move away from using road transport for the total journey (Behrends, 2012). The COVID-19 crisis and the 2022 global crisis driven by the invasion of Ukraine and rising fuel and food prices are again changing food purchasing practices.

For health policy the control of food provided by the supermarkets tends to focus behavioural and information approaches such as labelling and healthy food promotions along with some voluntary restrictions on unhealthy promotions. Legislation to control the content of food and reformulation are less in favour (Caraher & Perry, 2017). The Obesity Strategy for England has placed limits on the promotion of foods that is HFSS by restricting volume promotions such as buy one get one free and the prominent locational placement of these foods that can encourage purchasing, both online and in physical stores in England (Department of Health and Social Care, 2021). With specific reference to children, the Strategy sought to ban television and online advertising of HFSS products before 9 pm. The intended HFSS promotional plans have been delayed until October 2023. Speculation exists that the backtrack in removing volume-based promotions is due to the cost-of-living crisis, while the online/broadcast media restrictions have been delayed until 2025 (Dimbleby & Lewis, 2023).

Recent developments include not just online ordering of groceries but quick (20/30 minutes) delivery of snacks and top-up foods. One of the biggest companies in this area is GETIR (https://getir.uk/), who has its own warehouses and promise delivery within 20/30 minutes. Initial data show that these services are mostly used for drinks and snacks, especially at the weekends. Other companies such as Deliveroo will deliver from established premises and shops, but are also establishing their own "dark kitchens" and supermarkets, so Deliveroo opened a supermarket in Bristol supplied by Morrisons. The distinction between retail and hospitality is being blurred by these new developments. The main users of these quick delivery services seem to be a younger generation who order "snack food and drinks". Amazon, the online ordering system, is now delivering to the home or own physical food stores for collection as well as delivering food from the Co-Op and Morrisons. These are developments that will expand in the future and may change the face of retail along with online ordering and fast home delivery. The other development which is impacting both retail and hospitality ordering is what are called buy now pay later (BNPL) apps. These are a form of credit or micro instalment loans that allow you to buy items or services now and repay the balance in instalments over time.

Hospitality

The food service industry offers prepared food, either as finished products or as partially prepared components for final "assembly". Restaurants, cafes, bakeries and mobile food trucks provide opportunities for consumers to purchase food.

In the UK, the average person eats one in every six meals outside the home, and we consume up to a quarter of our calories when eating out, according to the Food Standards Agency (FSA). The 2022 wave of Food and You 2, a biannual survey commissioned by the FSA to measure consumers' self-reported knowledge, attitudes and behaviours related to food safety and other food issues amongst adults in England, Wales and Northern Ireland, reported that eating habits had changed for most respondents in the period of COVID lockdowns, with only 19% of respondents indicating that there had been no change in their eating habits. Eating out less (reported by 57% of respondents) and eating fewer takeaways (39%) are the most prevalent behavioural changes which must be understood in the context of the COVID-19 global pandemic and subsequent impact on our catering industries (Food Standards Agency, 2022).

The same survey reported that more than half (52%) of respondents had ordered food or drink via on online ordering and delivery company (e.g. Just Eat, Deliveroo, Uber Eats) and 30% had ordered via an online marketplace (e.g. Deliveroo, Amazon, Gumtree, Etsy). This consumer behaviour has been enabled by the digitalisation of food ordering and plays to consumers' appetite for ease and convenience and the preceding narrative that the general public is cooking less and participating more in meal assembly and eating out.

In Northern Ireland, local catering businesses (pubs and restaurants) started providing food support such as delivering hot meals to elderly people and people registered as being in vulnerable circumstances. Two websites were created to provide dynamic information on local food businesses continuing to operate throughout the lockdown. "InYourArea" is a website which allowed people to search for businesses that were open for takeaway and delivery by postcode and there was a Facebook Page *Who is Delivering?* with an interactive searchable map that shares information on businesses across the country delivering fresh food, groceries and pre-made meals (Walker, 2020).

Changes which respondents had made in the previous 12 months

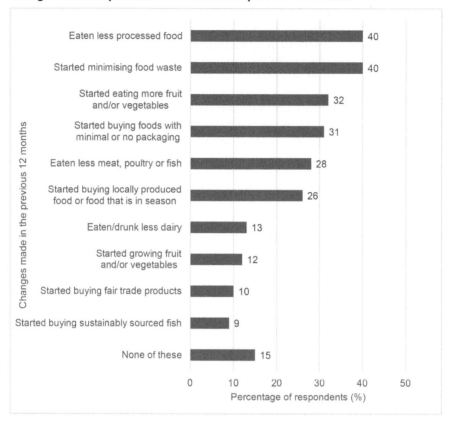

Figure 7.2 Ten most common changes in eating habits in the last 12 months.

Source: FSA Food and You 2 (2022, p. 80).

Chapter 9 deals with public sector catering and procurement; here, the focus is on the commercial sector. To set this in context, the 1970s saw the formal provision of meals at work being run down. Despite this, the public sector, through hospitals, schools and prisons, remains a major provider of meals accounting for 29% of all meals outside the home, but only 6% of sales. Another reason was the loss of government subsidies (Cabinet Office, 2008, Caraher, et al., 2020). The less than positive memories of the 1940s and 1950s and institutional catering with the lack of choice are cited as contributory reasons for the growth in popularity of commercial out-of-the-home eating. Health and food policy concerns with the sector will continue for two reasons. The first is that in eating food not prepared by you, you cede control of the content of your food and the second and related issue is that such foods are generally HFSS.

Over time, work habits were changing, with fewer and fewer taking an hour-long lunch break and the need for social feeding originating from WWII (World War II) was no longer being seen as a necessity. Alan Sugar, the entrepreneur was reported as follows in 1987: "At Amstrad the staff start early and finish late. Nobody takes lunches – they may get a sandwich slung on their desk" (Knight, 2017). Snacking at the desk became a feature of work and sandwiches remained the biggest seller (up to the COVID-19 crisis). Other foods began to be introduced, alongside developments in delivery and ordering such as delivery to the workplace and internet ordering. Increased travel time to work and work pressures have all contributed to desk top eating while at work. A survey carried out by the Mindful Chef (a British meal kit retailer) on 2,000 adults in Britain reported that more than half expressed the desire to achieve a healthy diet but are hindered by their hectic work life and two-thirds reported they often eat "badly" because they don't have the time to prepare nutritious food, while 75% revealed they skip meals entirely for the same reason. Mindful Chef's research found of those who have tried a recipe box, eight in ten said it made eating healthily easier (Knight, 2017).

Long working hours result in workers turning to quick and convenient methods of lunch – namely convenience and fast foods. In 2019, the value of the industry was £97 billion. Following the pandemic, consumer spending on hospitality started to increase in May 2021, but remains at less than 70% of pre-pandemic levels; a similar picture is seen in turnover – in May, this remained one-quarter lower than the 2019 levels but is rapidly increasing as customers return to eating out. The crisis, triggered by the war in Ukraine and the rise in oil prices has prompted concerns over rising food prices, falls in the real value of incomes and welfare are likely to impact on recovery in the hospitality sector. Some predict a rise in home ordering and a decline in fine dining while others are more pessimistic and see the whole sector as suffering.

Fast food developments

The 1970s saw further changes in food delivery and habits of the population. The 1970s saw the changes, which had become apparent in the late-1960s, bedding down across the population. Oddy refers to the 1970s as the "global phase of fast food" and further terms it as "eating without effort", while others refer to the period as that of the "global village" where food from all over the world was available on your plate (Oddy, 2003b). Eating out continued to increase, reliance on processed foods continued to grow and concerns about the impacts of diets on health and the environment began to grow. These developments were aided by changes in technology, food price drops and increasing wages. These changes were accompanied by consolidation in the hospitality sector with the entrance of large multinationals to the UK such as McDonald's, KFC and Domino's Pizza (Warde & Martens, 2000, Jacobs & Scholliers, 2003, Oddy, 2003b, 2003a). New technologies and central food processing ensured continuity of supply, convenience and predictability; so the burger in a McDonald's in Glasgow was same as the one bought in London.

The second stage of the nutrition transition change is rooted in the food system becoming more industrial and concentrated so that processed foods and fast food become more affordable to all. Fast food is "fast" thanks to modern technology and blends with modern lifestyles (Schlosser, 2002) and in many instances is a viable option for those on low incomes (the Big Mac index is an indicator of how much time you have to work to afford a Big Mac). Fast food was fast in terms of preparation and also in terms of service; this was seen by many as an advantage where time became a precious commodity (Gershuny, 1989, Gershuny & Sullivan, 2020). Cooking became for many a chore and competed for time against leisure activities and family life. Fieldhouse's quote – "if prepared food is so easily accessible, why bother to learn to cook"? – has an element of truth in it when you are battling leisure time and work commitments (Fieldhouse, 1995). The downside is that you lose control over the content of the food and much of the food and drink from fast food outlets tends to be HFSS foods.

The use of takeaway and fast food (sometimes referred to as street food) often becomes an important money- and labour-saving mechanism for many who are engaged in piecemeal or fee per item work. Fast has become a key fact of food consumption as we live busy lives. Oddy

(2003a) sees this trend as being related to less eating in institutional settings such as workplaces and workplace canteens, including school meals. From 1975 to 1984, the average number of meals eaten outside the home fell at a rate of 1.5% per year, while meals purchased in commercial venues such as restaurants, public houses, fast food outlets, ethnic food outlets and fish and chips shops increased. In the same period, takeaway meals grew from 14% to 27% of all meals eaten, with one in three in low-income groups purchasing a takeaway meal and eating it at home at least once a week (Heald, 1987, Pascoe, Dockerty & Ryley, 1987).

Fast food can give rise to snacking and the loss of time spent together over food. The new online ordering discussed earlier may increase this likelihood (Cummins et al., 2020, Devereux, Béné & Hoddinott, 2020). The growth of a "snacking culture" in the last quarter of the twentieth century was aided by the rapid development of new products in confectionery and packaged drinks. Snack foods became widely available in Britain in the 1990s, being sold in over 150,000 retail outlets and offered the ability for workers to "transport" the food back to their desks. The ubiquitous sandwich became a multimillion-pound industry and the largest providers were not sandwich shops but supermarkets offering meal deals, which often included crisps and a soda or sugary drink. By 2017, the sandwich industry was £8 billion/year with a large level of concentration in the industry, with a small number of factory sandwich makers making pre-packed sandwiches for the supermarkets alongside sandwich specialists such as Greggs and Subway (Knight, 2017).

Contrast this with France where, until 2021, eating at the desk was not permitted under legislation. Additionally, the retreat from institutional catering, where food was offered as a perk, has contributed to these trends and unhealthy eating in the workplace (Caraher et al., 2017). In the immediate aftermath of WWII, UK companies providing food were offered a tax deduction. When this ended, there was little incentive to continue the practice (Wanjek, 2005). Here, we see another move away from food control and setting structural agendas to an approach to policy which is based on the behaviour of individuals and free choice and companies deciding what was best for them and their employees.

The late 1950s and 1960s saw a rise in immigration from the former British colonies. And with them came different dishes and flavours. Although the first Chinese restaurant was opened in 1908 in London and there were a number of Indian restaurants to cater for the Raj (Basu, 1999), the true spread of "foreign" restaurants began in the late 1950s and 1960s with the arrival of migrants from Hong Kong and India.

Eating outside the home continued to grow in popularity in the 1950s and 1960s. In the 1950s, every small town had its fish and chips shop. By the 1960s, this was changing with new groups of migrants arriving in Britain and the increase in foreign holidays resulting in a demand for more than fish and chips (Allegra Food Strategy Forum, 2009). Another reason for the increase in eating out was the shutting down of many work canteens which had been run and subsidised by the Ministry of Food during the war. Disposable income increased towards the end of the 1960s allowing people to spend on eating outside the home.

Food swamps

As noted above, there is a plethora of food businesses on the high street aiming to tempt us with meals and snacks intended to be eaten out of the home as we seek solutions to our quest for satiety in often time-poor periods of hunger. "Food swamp" is a term that has been used to characterise retail landscapes which are populated with frequent fast food restaurants, supermarkets and convenience stores selling typically HFSS foods via a corporate, industrial and increasingly global food system. Living where there is a greater prevalence of less healthy food options has an area effect on food choice and consumption and is significantly associated with a higher incident rate of diabetes (Adams et al., 2015, Webster, 2016, Caraher, 2019). North American research concluded the presence of a food swamp is a stronger predictor of obesity rates than the absence of full-service grocery stores (Cooksey-Stowers, Schwartz & Brownell, 2017, Elton, 2019). The term is purposely deleterious to articulate candidly the injurious nature of the food offer available, which is in stark contrast to "food deserts" where healthy and fresh food is conspicuously absent or inaccessible. However, a contrasting school of thought asks us to reconsider our language framing since the term "food swamp" does not help to identify the underlying health and sustainability issues in the food system (Caraher et al., 2013). Sustainability and eco-diets were addressed in Chapters 2, 3 and 5.

It is an interesting observation that the food swamp effect was significantly stronger in counties with greater income inequality and where residents are less mobile. Much has been written in the UK about the need for zoning laws simultaneously restricting access to unhealthy food outlets and incentivising healthy food retailers to locate in underserved neighbourhoods to solve, at least in part, the food system failures of an obesogenic environment, health inequity and healthy food accessibility. For example, Caraher et al. (2013) considered how health promotion can use planning and citizen engagement as tools to enhance healthy eating choices, drawing on research in relation to the availability and concentration of fast food outlets in a London borough (Caraher et al., 2013, Caraher, Lloyd & Madelin, 2014). They called for a social determinant-based health promotion strategy involving local people in shaping their local food environment as well as its function in pursuit of healthy outcomes as being consistent with a national regulatory infrastructure supporting planning, fast food outlets and/or drive-through outlets. Recommendations included specifying quotas, density or distances for fast food outlets from schools and hospitals, restricting opening hours and menu labelling in fast food outlets to effect place-based solutions to inform both public health and local authority planning.

Public health responsibility deal: salt and sugar reduction targets and the national food strategy

The NFS set out as one of its primary recommendations the introduction of a £3/kilogramme tax on sugar and a £6/kilogramme tax on salt sold for use in processed foods or in restaurants and catering businesses to break the "junk food cycle". There were concerns from the Strategy's author that the landmark plan to introduce the world's first salt and sugar reformulation tax is unlikely to be in the anticipated White Paper this year (2022) as it is considered to be "politically very difficult because of the cost of living" (Hill, 2022).

We know that as a population we eat too much sugar We now know that the government rejected these proposals in the formal response (Dimbleby & Lewis, 2023). (50 grams/day instead of the recommended 30 grams/day) and salt (8.4 grams/day compared to the recommended 6 grams/day) (Dimbleby, 2021). Previous voluntary schemes such as the Public Health Responsibility Deal's (PHRD) salt and sugar reduction targets had made some initial progress, and we have discussed elsewhere (Chapters 2 and 3) the ineffectiveness of voluntary schemes on population-level nutrition goals. This is reinforced by the knowledge that some partners withdrew their support for the PHRD because of allegations of the government prioritising industry over public health while the Health Select Committee remained unconvinced that the "nudging" approach would be effective (Panjwani & Caraher, 2014, Knai et al., 2015, Douglas et al., 2018).

The PHRD was launched in March 2011 with the meritorious aim to encourage a partnership approach with businesses and other organisations to improve public health and tackle health inequalities through their influence over food and other related lifestyle factors. Signatories to the various pledges committed to take action to improve public health in England. Meanwhile, the UK government worked in parallel with other health policies and messaging. The pledges related, for our purposes here, to out-of-home calorie labelling, salt reduction, artificial trans-fat removal calorie reduction, salt in catering and fruits and vegetables (Panjwani & Caraher, 2018).

With specific reference to salt, targets were developed for salt reduction for 80 specific food groups that contribute most to people's salt intakes through food retail and a specific pledge for salt reduction in catering through staff training and kitchen practice, procurement and reformulation by 2012. The NFS stated how the voluntary salt reduction programme was successful in its early phase, with salt intakes reducing from an average of 9.5 grams/day in 2000 to 8.1 grams/day in 2011. However, progress has since stalled. Only half of the targets for 2017 were met, in part because reporting requirements were weakened and enforcement was minimal (Burt et al., 2022). A similar voluntary sugar reduction programme challenged food manufacturers to cut sugar in their products by 20% before 2020, but only achieved a reduction of 3%. Yet, despite these compelling arguments, the government decided not to pursue the issue of a sugar or salt tax (Department for Environment Food & Rural Affairs, 2022, Food Ethics Council, 2022).

Calorie labelling on menus (MenuCal) and calorie labelling (out-of-home sector) (England) regulations

The energy balance is important in human nutrition and public health because it refers to the relationship between energy input (calories consumed through food and drinks) and energy output (calories expended by the body for our energy requirements). Where these are in or out of balance dictates whether we lose or gain weight or if our weight remains constant. The population energy intake goals are 2,000 kilocalories/day for woman and 2,500/day for men. However, 2018 data from the Office for National Statistics suggest that in the UK, one-third of us underestimate our daily caloric intake, with men regularly eating more than 3,000 kilocalories/day while claiming to eat 2,000, while women self-report eating about 1,500/day while actually consuming nearly 2,500. The issue is complicated by us eating one in six meals outside of the home, where we may perceive we have less control over our dietary choices and contributing 20% of energy intake for adult women and 25% for men. Once again, the PHRD included a pledge for participating food businesses to provide calorie information for food and non-alcoholic drink for customers in out-of-home settings from 1 September 2011 in accordance with the principles for calorie labelling (Douglas et al., 2018). The main body of evidence on the effects of calorie labelling schemes on consumers comes from the US, where studies have shown mixed results in terms of calorie purchasing behaviour and awareness/use of calorie labelling initiatives. The idea was introduced into the UK to support businesses in offering healthier choices and encourage customers to make healthier, more informed choices. Food service signatories were asked to provide clear calorie labelling prominently at the point of choice. Since the implementation in September 2011, there is now increased visibility of calorie labelling on the high street.

The FSA piloted Caloriewise in Northern Ireland in 2012, where nine participating businesses committed to providing information for customers on the calories contained in the food items on their menus. Businesses displayed calorie information clearly and prominently at the point of choice (e.g. on menus) and showed the calories per portion, item or meal, so that customers could easily use the information when making their food choices, alongside reference information pertaining to guideline daily amounts for energy for men and women. The pilot was well received (Ray et al., 2013) and resulted in the launch of Caloriewise as a free and voluntary scheme across local councils in Northern Ireland, supported by MenuCal – a free online tool[2] which helps food businesses put allergen and calorie information on menus across participating businesses in Northern Ireland and Scotland.[3]

Calorie labelling on menus became compulsory in England in 2021; outlets must display calorie counts "clearly and prominently" at the point of choice – typically a menu (HM Government, 2021). The regulations apply to businesses with over 250 employees and the following types of outlets:

- Restaurants, fast food outlets, cafes, pubs and supermarkets;
- Home delivery services and third party apps (such as Deliveroo or Uber) selling food that is in scope of the legislation;
- Cafes and takeaways within larger shops and venues, such as supermarkets, department stores and entertainment venues such as cinemas;
- Specialist food stores, delicatessens, sweet shops and bakeries;
- Contract catering, for example, for events and canteens; and
- Domestic transport businesses.

There are exclusions to the labelling requirement: items on a menu for less than 30 days (e.g. seasonal menus); foods that require preparation before consumption (e.g. uncooked meat, fish and eggs); drinks with over 1.2% alcohol by volume; loose fruits or vegetables; and condiments where they are added by the consumer.

Soft Drinks Industry Levy

Another UK food policy initiative was the 2018 introduction of a Soft Drinks Industry Levy (SDIL) or sugar tax with the laudable aim to reduce sugar in soft drinks and tackle childhood obesity (Bandy et al., 2021, 2020). Soft drink manufacturers are expected to reformulate their products to reduce their sugar content. Those that do not meet the reformulation thresholds (<5 grams of sugar per 100 millilitres) will have to pay 18p per litre of drink if it contains between 5 and 8 grams of sugar per 100 millilitres and 24p per litre of drink if it contains 8 grams of sugar per 100 millilitres. The levy was announced in 2016, and in the two years preceding its introduction, 50% of soft drinks manufacturers had already reformulated their beverages to avoid incurring the levy. The Treasury announced that all revenues raised through the levy would directly fund new sports facilities in schools as well as healthy breakfast clubs, ensuring children lead healthier lives. While this is true for England, it is less clear for Northern Ireland, where any revenue obtained from the levy, certainly originally, could not be used to target health issues due to the lack of Northern Ireland ministers to sign-off on proposals. Instead, it was simply being divided up proportionally between Stormont departments rather than being ring-fenced for obesity combatting measures as originally envisaged for the rest of the UK. By 2022, this commitment to use the levy to fund children's health programmes had further derailed on a UK-wide basis, and a 2022 Freedom of Information query uncovered that the money is understood to no longer be directly linked to specific health programmes and has been subsumed into the general tax funding pot (Bissett, 2021).

It will be important that, if in the future, a junk food tax as recommended in the NFS is implemented that the revenue from an extended sugar tax be spent on public health actions in order to remove as many empty calories as possible from the population's diet and impede the public health time bomb.

The evidence of impact for labelling on food prepared out of the home is weak; however they should be seen as part of a wider raft of public health measures which may, in this instance, include reformulation by restaurants and takeaways (Shangguan et al., 2019, Kaur et al., 2022).

Impact of Russia/Ukraine war on catering supplies (wheat, sunflower oil etc.)

The Russian invasion of Ukraine in 2022 has had far-reaching sociopolitical and logistical implications globally. The impact on both nations' citizens must not be underplayed but is outside the scope of this chapter (for an international perspective, refer to Chapter 8). Instead, we focus on the impact on commodity prices serving to devastate further the hospitality sector which is already on its knees as a consequence of COVID-19. The food supply chain is dependent on global suppliers, and the current geopolitical situation places additional pressure where the sector is already witnessing unprecedented levels of food and drink inflation, caused by spikes in commodity prices, increased transportation and import costs and higher labour costs. The commodities involved include feed, fuel and fertiliser:

- Cereals and Grain: The conflict poses a risk to global food prices as Ukraine and Russia dominate the grain trade as they are among the top five international exporters for wheat, sunflower and corn.
- Feed: Costs are expected to increase substantially, which is concerning for milk and meat production in the UK.
- Poultry: As a result of increasing feed costs due to loss of grain from both Ukraine and Russia into the supply chain having a significant impact on prices and loss of chicken processing from Ukraine and other neighbouring countries, for example, Poland facing disruption due to the invasion.
- Vegetable Oil: Global weather challenges compounded by disrupted supply from Ukraine which supplies 60% of the world's sunflower oil will inevitably lead to cost increases.
- Fertiliser: Russia is an important producer of fertilisers; sanctions will limit the supply of fertiliser with consequences for prices, application. Some forecasters predict that yields could reduce by 50% and market forces will dictate final product prices.
- Utilities and fuel: Higher fuel costs driven by oil price rises significantly increase production and distribution costs, which will have to be passed on to caterers (Lang & McKee, 2022, Linsell, Ramnarayan & Goodman, 2022, Price, 2022, Veloso & Hirtzer, 2022).

The industry cannot absorb this basket of increasing costs and it must surely be borne by the consumer who is simultaneously experiencing high inflation on the essentials of daily living alongside incomes that do not hold pace with the rising cost of living. This signals the need for our food system to be sustainable by importing only what is needed and encouraging the consumption of local and seasonal foods where possible. It further illuminates the need for effective policy solutions that put sufficient income in people's hands in a dignified way to guarantee our citizens right to food.

Conclusions: opportunities for food retail and distribution in contributing to a healthy and sustainable food system

The food industry has a large influence on consumer trends through the promotion, placement and pricing of unhealthy foods but also the control that the supermarkets and the hospitality sector exercise over supply chains and prices. Recommendation number two of the NFS set out a case for mandatory reporting for large companies in their actions to tackle health and sustainability. This is akin to the eco-nutrition or sustainable diet approach discussed in chapters 2 and 5, and some have suggested that the SDGs are a way of measuring this progress. This is based on the premise that "voluntary action will not be enough" (Dimbleby, 2021, p. 147). Such an annual report could include figures (both value in sterling and volume in tonnes) for:

- Sales of food and drink HFSS, excluding alcohol.
- Sales of protein by type (of meat, dairy, fish, plant or alternative protein) and origin.
- Sales of vegetables.
- Sales of fruit.
- Sales of major nutrients: fibre, saturated fat, sugar and salt.
- Food waste.
- Total food and drink sales.

All this is a good idea, but what will be done with this information, how and who will monitor the situation and how any sanctions might be applied are not clear. The response seems to be based on further consultation, not implementation:

> The strategy launches our Food Data Transparency Partnership. This provides a unique opportunity to leverage the collective energy and enthusiasm found across the food system and drive a real transformation in health, animal welfare and environmental outcomes through our food. We will consult on implementing mandatory public reporting against a set of health metrics and explore a similar approach to sustainability and animal welfare. We will also provide consumers with the information they need to make more sustainable, ethical, and healthier food choices and incentivise industry to produce healthier and more ethical and sustainable food. The partnership will ensure we have a robust framework for tackling some of the fundamental questions for our food system, raising transparency and responsibility.
>
> (Department for Environment Food & Rural Affairs, 2022)

The NFS called for the introduction of sugar and salt tax to tackle the problem of obesity and diet-related non-communicable diseases such as heart disease and raised blood pressure; this received no support in the response from government (Dimbleby and Lewis, 2023). The Food Strategy (NFS) offered the potential to link the various elements of the food system. Dimbleby (2021) also pointed out the fact that "governance of food and health falls under the aegis of the devolved administrations. Scotland, Wales and Northern Ireland each have their own food strategies" but suggests little about how to achieve coherence. Brexit is presented as an opportunity for food sovereignty, but unlike say the reports of the 1930s and 1940s from Le Gros Clark and Titmuss as well as Orr, there is little detail linking national food security to household food security and inequality (Le Gros Clark & Titmuss, 1939, Orr & Lubbock, 1940, Stitt & Prisk, 1997, Lang, 2020).

The past 30 years have seen a policy focus on voluntary agreements with the industry, not regulation of food content or controlling the power of the industry and the current response to the NFS proposals seems to follow this path (see Chapter 2) (Mwatsama, 2018). Rising concerns with obesity and other diet-related diseases saw a search for more effective interventions (Mwatsama, 2018, Theis & White, 2021). There were and are a number of successful policy initiatives, perhaps the most significant was the introduction of a sugary drinks tax in 2018; this has proved to be a success in addressing consumption of sugar-sweetened beverages and reformulation by the industry (Bandy et al., 2020).

There were many promises in the NFS consultations and reports which never materialised, including the publication of data on how industry was responding to fat, salt and sugar reductions (Caraher & Perry, 2017, Caraher & Hughes, 2019, Dimbleby, 2021, Dimbleby, 2020). The prevention strategy for England released in July 2020 contained "promises" and ideas to deliver but contains few tangible plans (Department of Health and Social Care, 2018). There were plans announced in December 2020 for a total advertising ban on foods high in fat, salt and sugar aimed at children, but a lesser approach with restrictions but not total ban was outlined by the government. However, the post COVID-19 and global geopolitical situation in 2022 resulted in this being postponed on the basis that these would place undue restrictions on industry and the banning of two for one offers would not help cash-strapped families. In late 2022, the government's position is unclear on a number of food policy issues, complicated by changes in prime ministers. Boris Johnson when prime minister decided to postpone some of the initiatives due to the pressures on business; Liz Truss, in her short period as prime minister, threated not to implement any and to rescind a number of previous initiatives such as the soda tax; she resigned before any of this could be realised. In the early months of 2023, Prime Minister Rishi Sunak has not made public the position of his government on the various food policy proposals. The overall emphasis still seems to be on individual behaviour and how to help individuals and families make the correct decisions and a distrust of what are seen as "nanny state" interventions (White, 2022). This downstream approach is equivalent to "pulling people out of the river" instead of the more proactive philosophy to "change the weather, don't just hand out wellies".

The suggested way forward on this is in the first NFS report (Dimbleby, 2020) in a section called "Empowering everyone with the right information to make healthier choices". This section details via labelling systems both in retail and out-of-home eating situations with, for example, hospitality businesses with more than 250 employees (cafés, restaurants, pubs, takeaways) having to provide energy content in kilocalories on the majority of the food they sell; this has been implemented. However, the commitment to upstream legislative reform is hedged in statements such as "We will continue to work with business and industry through the government's reduction and reformulation programmes on sugar, calories and salt and remain committed to further action if results are not seen", and as we now know, the proposal for a sugar and salt tax received no government support (Dimbleby, 2020, White, 2022). There is little to address the structural power of the food industry at the retail and catering levels to make healthier choices the easier choices (Which?, 2022). The danger of seeing the current dominant providers (retail and hospitality) as the only solution runs the danger of a US "Walmart effect", discussed earlier. Nor is there any reference to planning and local or regional monopolies of supermarkets or areas where there is a lack of adequate provision. So there are some minor successes along with the soda tax announced in 2016, but these do not add up to a comprehensive policy or population approach (Adams, 2021, Bandy et al., 2021). The overall approach to preventing obesity suffers from similar limitations (Theis & White, 2021).

It is likely that the future trends shaping grocery and supermarket expansion will come in the virtual world of internet ordering and delivery, as will be the case with catering and hospitality. Although currently small in overall terms, such developments are set to grow. The expansion of Amazon into home food delivery and its acquisition of Wholefoods are indicative of this trend; its opening of physical outlets also indicates a new trend. The food offer in these Amazon outlets is not that different from what already exists, but what is different is the technology: scanning or need to present payment is all done automatically once you scan a barcode on entering the shop. Regulation of such initiatives will present new challenges to both nutrition and eco-sustainability. It is likely that initial policy will be consumer as opposed to health-focussed and may concentrate, for example, on BNPL apps. For food policy advocates, these wider policy initiatives need to have a close eye trained on them.

What is to be done about supermarkets and hospitality comes with their power and role as the "shock troops" of economic neoliberalism. The challenge for existing supermarkets and hospitality food distribution systems is to transport goods between producers and customers with the lowest possible impact on the environment, improving health, while rewarding growers and employees with fair wages and incomes. Estrada-Flores and Larsen in Australia investigated best practice food distribution systems, and their report shows that farm and consumer-led initiatives do exactly this (Estrada-Florez & Larsen, 2010). These types of systems – including farmers markets; marketing cooperatives; community supported agriculture; and direct and online sales hubs – will promote shorter distances between producers and consumers. Such "last mile" distribution solutions provide further opportunities for sustainable development in the food industry, making food more easily accessible by reconnecting consumers with food producers.

Can supermarkets/hospitality deliver more healthy and sustainable food? We believe they can; however, a paradigm shift is needed. Even hard-line "productionists" are recognising the increasing need to transition to ecologically integrated thinking and practice in response to food system challenges in the coming decades. The benefits to the supermarkets and hospitality sectors are at both ends of the food chain; the production and processing element results in fewer costs in transport and processing, and at the retail end of the chain, it appeals to customers' concerns about health and the environment. It's now difficult to find many companies or governments who doubt food's impact on health and the environment and the role of food within sustainability.

Notes

1 This involves the extraction of ammonia from the air of which nitrogen is a key component. Carbon dioxide (CO_2) is a by-product of this process. The process uses large amounts of energy and the increase in energy prices linked to the war in Ukraine has increased costs significantly.
2 www.food.gov.uk/business-guidance/menucal-calorie-and-allergen-tool.
3 https://menucal.fss.scot/Account/LogOn?ReturnUrl=%2f.

References

Adams, J. 2021, "National food strategy: what's in it for population health?", *BMJ*, vol. 374, p. n1865. https://doi.org/10.1136/bmj.n1865

Adams, J., Goffe, L., Brown, T., Lake, A.A., Summerbell, C., White, M., Wrieden, W. & Adamson, A.J. 2015, "Frequency and socio-demographic correlates of eating meals out and take-away meals at home: cross-sectional analysis of the UK national diet and nutrition survey, waves 1‚Äì4 (2008‚Äì12)", *International Journal of Behavioral Nutrition and Physical Activity*, vol. 12, no. 1, p. 51. https://doi.org/10.1186/s12966-015-0210-8

Allegra Food Strategy Forum 2009, *Eating Out in the UK: A comprehensive Analysis of the Informal Eating Out Market*, Allegra Strategies, London.

Bandy, L.K., Hollowell, S., Harrington, R., Scarborough, P., Jebb, S. & Rayner, M. 2021, "Assessing the healthiness of UK food companies' product portfolios using food sales and nutrient composition data", *PLoS ONE*, vol. 16, no. 8, p. e0254833. https://doi.org/10.1371/journal.pone.0254833

Bandy, L.K., Scarborough, P., Harrington, R.A., Rayner, M. & Jebb, S.A. 2020, "Reductions in sugar sales from soft drinks in the UK from 2015 to 2018", *BMC Medicine*, vol. 18, no. 1, p. 20. https://doi.org/10.1186/s12916-019-1477-4

Basu, S. 1999, *Curry in the Crown: The Story of Britain's Favourite Dish*, Harper Collins, India.

Behrends, S. 2012, "The urban context of intermodal road-rail transport – threat or opportunity for modal shift?", *Procedia – Social and Behavioral Sciences*, vol. 39, pp. 463–475. https://doi.org/10.1016/j.sbspro.2012.03.122

Bianco, A. 2006, *The Bully of Betonville: How the high cost of Wal-Mart's everyday low prices is hurting America*, Double Day, New York.

Bird, P. 2000, *The First Food Empire: A History of J. Lyions & Co*, Phillimore and Co Ltd, West Sussex.

Bissett, G. 2021, *Government scraps pledge to use sugar tax revenue to fight obesity*, Dentistry.co.uk, https://dentistry.co.uk/2022/01/04/government-scraps-pledge-to-use-sugar-tax-revenue-to-fight-obesity/.

Burt, H.E., Brown, M.K., He, F.J. & MacGregor, G.A. 2022, "Salt: the forgotten foe in UK public health policy", *BMJ*, vol. 377, p. e070686. https://doi.org/10.1136/bmj-2022-070686

Cabinet Office 2008, *Food Matters Towards a Strategy for the 21st Century*, Cabinet Office, HM Government, London.

Caraher, M. 2019, "High Cost Cheap Food" in *The Blackwell Encyclopedia of Sociology*, ed. G. Ritzer, Blackwell, pp. 1–3. https://doi.org/10.1002/9781405165518.wbeos1494

Caraher, M. 2011, "Food Austerity: a lifestyle choice for whom", *Journal of Home Economics Institute of Australia*, vol. 18, no. 2, pp. 17–25.

Caraher, M. & Hughes, N. 2019, "Tackling salt consumption outside the home", *BMJ*, vol. 364, p. l1087. https://doi.org/10.1136/bmj.l1087

Caraher, M., Jakšic, D., Dolciami, F., Stiglianim, A., Wynne, R., Stracci, F. & Masanotti, G.M. 2017, "Promoting healthy eating habits in the working population: the FOOD program", *MOJ Public Health*, vol. 6, no. 4, pp. 394–399. https://doi.org/10.15406/mojph.2017.06.00181

Caraher, M., Lloyd, S. & Madelin, T. 2014, "The 'School Foodshed': schools and fast-food outlets in a London borough", *British Food Journal*, vol. 116, no. 3, pp. 472–493. https://doi.org/10.1108/BFJ-02-2012-0042

Caraher, M., Masanotti, G.M., Bertrand, N., Léauté, R., Lloyd, S. & Tavakoly, B. 2020, "Healthy eating promotion for the workplace: the European FOOD (Fighting Obesity through Offer and Demand) Programme Promozione di un'alimentazione sana sul posto di lavoro: il programma europeo FOOD (Combattere l'obesità attraverso l'offerta e la domanda)", *Sistema Salute*, vol. 64, no. 2, pp. 241–253.

Caraher, M., O'Keefe, E., Lloyd, S. & Madelin, T. 2013, "The planning system and fast food outlets in London: lessons for health promotion practice", *Revista Portuguesa de Saude Publica*, vol. 31, no. 1, pp. 49 57. https://doi.org/10.1016/j.rpsp.2013.01.001

Caraher, M. & Perry, I. 2017, "Sugar, salt, and the limits of self regulation in the food industry", *BMJ*, vol. 357. https://doi.org/10.1136/bmj.j1709

Chambers, S. 2022, How will we put food on the table?, 13th March, *The Sunday Times*, London.

Collingham, L. 2017, *The Hungry Empire: How Britain's Quest for Food Shaped the Modern World*, The Bodley Head, London.

Conaway, R.N., Regester, K., Martin, S., Nixon, C. & Senior, B. 2018, "Amazon whole foods: when e-commerce met brick-and-mortar and saved the brand of conscientious capitalism", *Journal of Marketing Development & Competitiveness*, vol. 12, no. 3.

Cooksey-Stowers, K., Schwartz, M.B. & Brownell, K.D. 2017, "Food swamps predict obesity rates better than food deserts in the United States", *International Journal of Environmental Research and Public Health*, vol. 14, no. 11. https://doi.org/10.3390/ijerph14111366

Cummins, S., Berger, N., Cornelsen, L., Eling, J., Er, V., Greener, R., Kalbus, A., Karapici, A., Law, C., Ndlovu, D. & Yau, A. 2020, "COVID-19: impact on the urban food retail system and dietary inequalities in the UK", *Cities & Health*, pp. 1–4. https://doi.org/10.1080/23748834.2020.1785167

Curry, D., Browning, H., Davis, P., Ferguson, I., Hutton, D., Julius, D., Reynolds, F., Tinsley, M., Varney, D. & Wynne, G. 2002, *Farming and Food: A Sustainable Future: Report of the Policy Commission on the Future of Farming and Food*, Policy Commission on the Future of Farming and Food, Crown Copyright, London.

Department for Environment Food & Rural Affairs (DEFRA) 2022, *Government Food Strategy*, DEFRA, https://www.gov.uk/government/publications/governmentfood-strategy/government-food-strategy.

Department for Environment, Food and Rural Affairs (DEFRA) 2017, *Food Statistics Pocketbook 2016*, DEFRA, London.

Department of Health and Social Care 2021, *The Food (Promotion and Placement) (England) Regulations 2021*, STATUTORY INSTRUMENTS No. 1368 edn, England, London.

Department of Health and Social Care 2018, *Prevention Is Better Than Cure: Our Vision to Help You Live Well for Longer*, https://assets.publishing.service.gov.uk/government/uploads/ system/uploads/ attachment_data/file/753688/Prevention_is_better_than_cure_5–11.pdf.

Desrochers, P. & Shimizu, H. 2012, *The Locavore's Dilemma: In praise of the 10,000-Mile Diet*, PublicAffairs, USA.

Devereux, S., Béné, C. & Hoddinott, J. 2020, "Conceptualising COVID-19's impacts on household food security", *Food Security*, vol. 12, pp. 769–772. https://doi.org/10.1007/s12571-020-01085-0

Devine, T.M. 1994, *Clanship to Crofters' War: The Social Transformation of the Scottish Highlands*, Manchester University Press, Manchester.

Dicks, L.V., Rose, D.C., Ang, F., Aston, S., Birch, A.N.E., Boatman, N., Bowles, E.L., Chadwick, D., Dinsdale, A. & Durham, S. 2019, "What agricultural practices are most likely to deliver 'sustainable intensification' in the UK?", *Food and Energy Security*, vol. 8, no. 1, p. e00148. https://doi.org/10.1002/ fes3.148

Dimbleby, H. 2021, *National Food Strategy, Independent Review: The Plan*, https://www.nationalfood-strategy.org.

Dimbleby, H. 2020, *The National Food Strategy: Part One – July 2020*, DEFRA, London.

Dimbleby, H. & Lewis, J. 2023, *Ravenous: How to get ourselves and our planet into shape*, Profile Books, London.

Dixon, J. 2015, *IUHPE Position Paper: Advancing Health Promoting Food Systems*, International Union for Health Promotion and Education, Saint-Denis, France.

Douglas, N., Knai, C., Petticrew, M., Eastmure, E., Durand, M.A. & Mays, N. 2018, "How the food, beverage and alcohol industries presented the Public Health Responsibility Deal in UK print and online media reports", *Critical Public Health*, vol. 28, no. 4, pp. 377–387. https://doi.org/10.1080/09581596. 2018.1467001

Egoh, B.N., Nyelele, C., Holl, K.D., Bullock, J.M., Carver, S. & Sandom, C.J. 2021, "Rewilding and restoring nature in a changing world", *PLoS One*, vol. 6, no. 7, p. p.e0254249. https://doi.org/10.1371/ journal.pone.0254249

Ellen MacArthur Foundation 2021, *The Big Food Redesign: Regenerarting Nature with the Circular Economy*, Ellen MacArthur Foundation, London.

Elton, S. 2019, "Reconsidering the retail foodscape from a posthumanist and ecological determinants of health perspective: wading out of the food swamp", *Critical Public Health*, vol 29, pp. 370–378. https:// doi.org/10.1080/09581596.2018.1468870

Estrada-Florez, S. & Larsen, K. 2010, *Best Practice Food Distribution Systems*, Victorian Eco-Innovation Lab, Melbourne.

Falloon, P., Bebber, D.P., Dalin, C., Ingram, J., Mitchell, D., Hartley, T.N., Johnes, P.J., Newbold, T., Challinor, A.J., Finch, J., Galdos, M.V., Petty, C., Cornforth, R., Bhunnoo, R., Pope, E., Enow, A., Borrion, A., Waterson, A., MacNeill, K. & Houldcroft, A. 2022, "What do changing weather and climate shocks and stresses mean for the UK food system?", *Environmental Research Letters*, vol. 17, no. 5, p. 051001. DOI 10.1088/1748–9326/ac68f9

Fanzo, J. & Davis, C. 2021, *Global Food Systems, Diets, and Nutrition*, Palgrave Macmillan, Cham.

Fieldhouse, P. 1995, *Food and Nutrition: Customs and Culture,* Chapman and Hall, London.

Food Ethics Council 2022, *Responding to the Government Food Strategy*, Food Ethics Council, https:// www.foodethicscouncil.org/resource/government-food-strategy-response/.

Food Standards Agency (FSA) 2022, *Food and You 2*, FSA, London.

Gershuny, J. 1989, "Technical Change and the Work-Leisure Balance" in *Technology and Economic Progress*, ed. A. Silberston, Macmillan, London, pp. 181–215.

Gershuny, J. & Sullivan, O. 2020, *What We Really Do All Day: Insights from the Centre for Time Use Research*, Pelican, London.

H.M. Government 2021, *Calorie Labelling (Out of Home Sector) (England) Regulations 2021*, Department of Health and Social Care, https://www.legislation.gov.uk/uksi/2021/909/made.

Harding, T. 2019, *Legacy: One Family, a Cup of Tea and the Company that Took on the World*, Penguin Random House UK, London.

Heald, G. 1987, "Trends in Eating Out" in *Proceedings of the Seventh British Nutrition Foundation Annual Conference*, ed. R. Cottrell, British Nutrition Foundation, London, p. 75.

Hill, J. 2022, *Fears food strategy white paper will be delayed*, 23rd March, Local Government Chronicle, https://www.lgcplus.com/services/health-and-care/fears-food-strategy-white-paper-will-be-delayed-23-03-2022/.

Jacobs, M. & Scholliers, P. 2003, *Eating out in Europe: Picnics, Gourmet Dining and Snacks since the Late Eighteenth Century*, Berg, Oxford.

Kauffman, J. 2018, *Hippie Food: How Back-to- the-Landers, Longhairs and Revolutionaries Changed the Way We Eat*, William Morrow, New York.

Kaur, A., Briggs, A., Adams, J. & Rayner, M. 2022, "New calorie labelling regulations in England", *BMJ*, vol. 377, p. o1079. https://doi.org/10.1136/bmj.o1079

Knai, C., Petticrew, M., Durand, M.A., Eastmure, E., James, L., Mehrotra, A., Scott, C. & Mays, N. 2015, "Has a public–private partnership resulted in action on healthier diets in England? An analysis of the Public Health Responsibility Deal food pledges", *Food Policy*, vol. 54, pp. 1–10. https://doi.org/10.1016/j.foodpol.2015.04.002

Knight, S. 2017, How the sandwich consumed Britain, 24th November, *The Guardian*, https://www.theguardian.com/news/2017/nov/24/how-the-sandwich-consumed-britain.

Lang, T. 2020, *Feeding Britain: Our Food Problems and How to Fix Them*, Pelican, London.

Lang, T. 1998, "BSE and CJD: Recent Developments" in *The Mad Cow Crises: Health and the Public Good*, ed. S.C. Ratzan, UCL Press, London, pp. 65–85.

Lang, T., Barling, D. & Caraher, M. 2009, *Food Policy: Integrating Health, Environment and Society*, Oxford University Press, Oxford.

Lang, T. & McKee, M. 2022, "The reinvasion of Ukraine threatens global food supplies", *BMJ*, vol. 376, p. o676. https://doi.org/10.1136/bmj.o676

Lau, M. 2022, China can't count on global markets for food security, Xi Jinping says, 7th March, *South China Morning Post*, https://www.scmp.com/news/china/politics/article/3169467/china-cant-count-global-markets-food-security-xi-jinping-says.

Le Gros Clark, F. & Titmuss, R. 1939, *Our Food Problem: A Study of National Security*, Penguin Books, Harmondsworth.

Lescent-Giles, I. 2005, "The Rise of Supermakets in Twentieth-Century Britain and France" in *Land, Shops and Kitchens: Technology and the Food Chain in Twentieth-Century Europe*, eds. C. Sarsúa, P. Scholliers & L. Van Molle, BREPOLS, Turnhout, Belgium, pp. 188–211.

Levitt, T. 2022, UK organic dairy farmers fear for futures as food prices soar, 16th April, *The Guardian*, https://www.theguardian.com/environment/2022/apr/16/uk-organic-dairy-farmers-fear-futures-food-prices-soar.

Linsell, K., Ramnarayan, A. & Goodman, D. 2022, Cheap food in Britain is about to become a thing of the past, 13th May, *Bloomberg UK*, https://www.bloomberg.com/news/articles/2022-05-13/supermarket-food-prices-increase-above-uk-inflation-in-cost-of-living-crisis?utm_campaign=news&utm_medium=bd&utm_source=applenews.

Mason, P. & Lang, T. 2017, *Sustainable Diets: How Ecological Nutrition Can Transform Consumption and the Food System*, Routledge, London.

McKinsey 2022, *The net-zero transition: What it would cost, what it could bring?*, McKinsey Global Institute, https://www.mckinsey.com/business-functions/sustainability/our-insights/the-net-zero-transition-what-it-would-cost-what-it-could-bring.

Monbiot, G. 2022a, Farm Peril: where sheep safely graze- and destroy the planet, 17th August, *The Guardian*, London.

Monbiot, G. 2022b, *Regenesis: Feeding the World without Devouring the Planet*, Allen Lane, London.

Monteiro, C.A., Cannon, G., Moubarac, J., Levy, R.B., Louzada, M.L.C. & Jaime, P.C. 2018a, "The UN Decade of Nutrition, the NOVA food classification and the trouble with ultra-processing", *Public Health Nutrition*, vol. 21, no. 1, pp. 5–17. https://doi.org/10.1017/S1368980017000234

Monteiro, C.A., Moubarac, J.C., Levy, R.B., Canella, D.S., Louzada, M.L.D.C. & Cannon, G. 2018b, "Household availability of ultra-processed foods and obesity in nineteen European countries", *Public Health Nutrition*, vol. 21, no. 1, pp. 18–26. https://doi.org/10.1017/S1368980017001379

Murray, S. & Caraher, M. 2019, "Food Retail and Distribution: A Focus on Supermarkets" in *Healthy and Sustainable Food Systems*, eds. M. Lawrence & S. Friel, Routledge, Abingdon, Oxon, pp. 93–100.

Mwatsama, M. (ed) 2018, *Public Health and the Food and Drinks Industry: The Governance and Ethics of Interaction. Lessons from Research, Policy and Practice*, UK Health Forum, London.

Norman, A. 1999, *Slam-Dunking Wal-Mart: How You Can Stop Superstore Sprawl in your Hometown*, Raphael Publishing, Atlantic City, NJ.

Oddy, D.J. 2003a, "Eating Without Effort: The Rise of the Fast-food Industry in Twentieth-Century Britain" in *Eating out in Europe: Picnics, Gourmet Dining and Snacks since the Late Eighteenth Century*, eds. M. Jacobs & P. Scholliers, Berg, Oxford, pp. 301–316.

Oddy, D.J. 2003b, *From Plain Fare to Fusion Food; British Diet from the 1890s to the 1990s*, The Boydell Press, Suffolk.

Orr, J.B. & Lubbock, D. 1940, *Feeding the People in War-Time*, MacMillan and Co, London.

Panjwani, C. & Caraher, M. 2018, "CASE 11 Voluntary Agreements and the Power of the Food Industry: The Public Health Responsibility Deal in England" in *Public Health and the Food and Drinks Industry: The Governance and Ethics of Interaction. Lessons from Research, Policy and Practice*, ed. M. Mwatsama, UK Health Forum, London, pp. 110–120.

Panjwani, C. & Caraher, M. 2014, "The public health responsibility deal: brokering a deal for public health, but on whose terms?", *Health Policy*, vol. 114, no. 2, pp. 163–173. https://doi.org/10.1016/j.healthpol.2013.11.002

Pascoe, J.M., Dockerty, J. & Ryley, J. 1987, "Fast Foods" in *Nutrition in Catering: Proceedings of the Seventh British Nutrition Foundation Annual Conference*, ed. P. Cotttrell, British Nutrition Foundation, London, p. 97.

Popkin, B. & Reardon, T. 2018, "Obesity and the food system transformation in Latin America", *Obesity Reviews*, vol. 19, no. 8, pp. 1028–1064. https://doi.org/10.1111/obr.12694

Price, K. 2022, Ukraine invasion could impact UK food and drink prices, 7th March, *The Caterer*, https://www.thecaterer.com/news/ukraine-invasion-impact-uk-food-drink-prices.

Ratzan, S.C. (ed) 1998, *The Mad Cow Crises: Health and the Public Good*, UCL Press, London.

Ray, K., Clegg, S., Davidson, R. & Vegeris, S. 2013, *Evaluation of Caloriewise: A Northern Ireland Pilot of the Display of Calorie Information in Food Catering Businesses*, Policy Studies Institute, University of Westminster, London.

Rewilding Britain 2022, *What Is Rewilding?* [Homepage of Rewilding Britain], [Online]. Available from: https://www.rewildingbritain.org.uk/explore-rewilding/what-is-rewilding [2022, 10/5].

Rogers, B. 2004, *Beef and Liberty: Roast Beef, John Bull and the English Nation*, Vintage Books, London.

Santini, C., Marinelli, E., Boden, M., Cavicchi, A. & Haegeman, K. 2016, "Reducing the distance between thinkers and doers in the entrepreneurial discovery process: An exploratory study", *Journal of Business Research*, vol. 69, no. 5, pp. 1840–1844. https://doi.org/10.1016/j.jbusres.2015.10.066

Schlosser, E. 2002, *Fast Food Nation: What the All-American Meal Is Doing to the World*, Penguin, London.

Scott, P. 2017, "Global panel on agriculture and food systems for nutrition: food systems and diets: facing the challenges of the 21st century", *Food Security*, vol. 9, no. 3, pp. 653–654. https://doi.org/10.1007/s12571-017-0678-y

Seth, A. & Randall, G. 2005, *Supermarket Wars: Global Strategies for Food Retailers*, Palgrave, London.

Seth, A. & Randall, G. 1999, *The Grocers: The Rise and Rise of the Supermarket Chains*, Kogan Page, London.

Shangguan, S., Afshin, A., Shulkin, M., Ma, W., Marsden, D., Smith, J., Saheb-Kashaf, M., Shi, P., Micha, R., Imamura, F. & Mozaffarian, D. 2019, *A Meta-Analysis of Food Labeling Effects on Consumer Diet Behaviors and Industry Practices*, vol. 56, no. 2, pp. 300–314. https://doi.org/10.1016/j.amepre.2018.09.024

Sharzer, G. 2012, *No Local: Why Small-Scale Alternatives Won't Change the World*, Zero Books, Winchester.

Spencer, B. 2022, Rewilding is bogging us down. Let's call it 'nature recovery', 21st August, *The Sunday Times*, London.

Stewart, C., Piernas, C., Cook, B. & Jebb, S.A. 2021, "Trends in UK meat consumption: analysis of data from years 1–11 (2008–09 to 2018–19) of the National Diet and Nutrition Survey rolling programme", *The Lancet Planetary Health*, vol. 5, no. 10, pp. e699–e708. https://doi.org/10.1016/S2542-5196(21)00228-X

Stitt, S., Jepson, M. & Paulson-Box, E. 1995, "Taking the cooking out of food: nutrition & the national curriculum", *Nutrition Health*, vol. 10, no. 2, pp. 155–164. https://doi.org/10.1177/026010609501000205

Stitt, S. & Prisk, E. 1997, "A Ministry of Food for Britain for 21st century?", *Nutrition Health*, vol. 12, no. 1, pp. 1–15. https://doi.org/10.1177/026010609701200101

Theis, D.R.Z. & White, M. 2021, "Is obesity policy in England fit for purpose? Analysis of government strategies and policies, 1992–2020", *The Milbank Quarterly*, vol. 99, no. 1, pp. 126–170. https://doi.org/10.1111/1468-0009.12498

Thompson, P.B. 2015, *From Field to Fork: Food Ethics for Everyone*, Oxford University Press, Oxford.

Trade and Agriculture Commission. 2021, *Final Report*, Crown Copyright, https://www.gov.uk/government/publications/trade-and-agriculture-commission-tac.

United States Department of Agriculture, Economic Research Service 2022, February 04, 2022-last update, *Ag and Food Stats* [Homepage of USDA Economic Research Service], [Online]. Available from: https://www.ers.usda.gov/data-products/ag-and-food-statistics-charting-the-essentials/farming-and-farm-income/ [2022, 05/05].

van Zanten, H.H.E., Groot, J.C.J., Brouwer, I.D. & Huppertz, T. 2022, *Healthy foods produced in circular food systems*, 2022-03-11 edn, Wageningen University, https://library.wur.nl/ojs/index.php/CircularWUR2022/article/view/18314.

van Zwanenberg, P. & Millstone, E. 2005, *BSE: Risk, Science and Governance*, Oxford University Press, King's Lynn.

Veloso, T. & Hirtzer, M. 2022, Crop trading giant ADM sees years of tight markets fueled by war, 26th April, *Yahoo! Finance*, https://finance.yahoo.com/news/crop-trading-giant-adm-sees-144310441.html.

Vivero-Pol, J.L., Ferrando, T., De Schutter, O. & Mattei, U. 2020, *Routledge Handbook of Food as a Commons*, Routledge, London.

Von Schirach-Szmigiel, C. 2005, "'Who is in power today and tomorrow in the food system', keynote speech" in *Policy and Competitiveness in a Changing Global Food Industry conference, USDA Economic Research Service*, USDA Economic Research Service, Washington DC, 28th April.

Walker, E. 2020, How In Your Area is helping restaurants turning to takeaway during the coronavirus pandemic, 28th March, *In Your Area*, https://www.inyourarea.co.uk/news/how-inyourarea-is-helping-restaurants-turning-to-takeaway-during-the-coronavirus-pandemic/?_ga=2.159214457.212464629.1613473163-196384144.1609758220.

Wanjek, C. 2005, *Food at Work: Workplace Solutions for Malnutrition, Obesity and Chronic Disease*, International Labour Office, Geneva.

Warde, A. & Martens, L. 2000, *Eating Out: Social Differentiation, Consumption and Pleasure*, Cambridge University Press, Cambridge.

Webster, K. 2016, *Too many takeaways? How the food environment affects the health and wellbeing of communities: Policy Briefing 39/2016*, The University of Bristol, https://www.bristol.ac.uk/media-library/sites/policybristol/briefings-and-reports-pdfs/pre-2017-briefings--reports-pdfs/PolicyBristol_Briefing_39_2016_fast_food.pdf.

Which? 2022, *Affordable Food for All: How Supermarkets Can Help in the Cost of Food Crisis*, Which?, London.

White, M. 2022, "Half hearted and half baked: the government's new food strategy", *BMJ*, vol. 377, p. o1520. https://doi.org/10.1136/bmj.o1520

8   Global food trade and commodities

The financialisation of food

Introduction

A 2020 report highlighted three aspects of the dominant food system which expose its vulnerabilities. They are:

- First, a food system based on industrial agriculture and food processing is driving habitat loss and creating the conditions for viruses to emerge and spread human and animal disease across national borders following trade routes.
- Second, a range of disruptions which test the resilience of food supply chains and reveal underlying vulnerabilities at both the grower/producer and consumer ends of the food system.
- Third, linked to number two is the greater economic vulnerability whereby hundreds of millions of people are living permanently on the cusp of hunger, malnutrition and extreme poverty, and are therefore highly vulnerable to the effects of a global recession and/or disruptions in the supply chain (The International Panel of Experts on Sustainable Food Systems, 2020).

We add a fourth which is the current lack of regulation of the global food system and the trade in agricultural and food commodities and the dominance of policy by "Big Food" and commercial interests (Canfield, Anderson & McMichael, 2021). Nowhere is this more evident than in the globalisation of the food system accompanied by what Clapp and colleagues have termed the financialisation of food (Clapp & Isakson, 2018). Others talk about the commercial determinants of food policy as an influence (Kickbusch, Allen & Franz, 2016, Swinburn et al., 2011). An Oxfam report pointed out that the COVID-19 crises and the cost of living crisis triggered by the war in Ukraine has resulted in the biggest increase in extreme poverty in over 20 years while the profits of large food corporations increase (Oxfam, 2022). The report shows that "billionaires and corporations in the food, energy, pharmaceutical, and technology sectors are reaping huge rewards at the same time as the soaring cost of living is hurting so many worldwide". The report goes on to say that the pandemic has resulted in a new billionaire every 30 hours while a million people "fall into extreme poverty". This points to two problems: first, the growth of extreme wealth among a small group of individuals and corporations; and second, the control and influence of the food chain by a small number of corporations.

As the public sector and governments scale down their food policy involvement and allow those who control the global commercial food system to influence public policy decisions, this is variously referred to as "state capture" or "corporate capture of public health" (Mindell et al., 2012). With reference to Chapter 2, it is important to remember that food policy avoidance

DOI: 10.4324/9781003260301-8

and voluntary agreements can also be classified as forms of food policy. The fallout from these developments is a growing philanthropy sector (at national and international levels), which supposedly addresses food poverty and nutrition but is dependent on industry support and philosophy for its continuance (Haydon, Jung & Russell, 2021, Rieff, 2016). The financialisation of food has resulted in food speculation on global commodity markets.[1] Despite global concerns with obesity, there is a failure to recognise in governance frameworks that the food system is a major contributor to rising obesity levels in relationship to the food system and the triple burden of diet-related non-communicable diseases, dealt with in more detail in Chapter 3 (Deconinck et al., 2022). This development has become known as philanthrocapitalism,[2] which is where the operating principles of capitalism are applied to the charity sector with funds from charity and business (Haydon, Jung & Russell, 2021). For food policy practitioners, much of this action happens at a level which is not visible to them. The consequences of these policy decisions are another matter, with public food policy often left to pick up the pieces.

Global food trade

The current global trading food system is spread across many land borders and includes many players from growers to financial speculators operating as a free market economy. The equilibrium price (this is the intersection where the cost of a product and the demand for that product intersect) will be determined by the demand and supply of the goods. So, the more demand and the smaller the supply, the higher the price, whereas when there is ample supply and less demand, prices will typically fall. Price volatility (the range of price movements over a particular period of time) has been at its highest level in the past 50 years. There are organisations set up to overview the global food system, for example, Food and Agriculture Organization (FAO) of the UN, and while producing analysis and monitoring, they are often without policy and regulatory bite.

Food policy has not been successful in gaining a foothold or even voice in the regulation of global food commodities, except in the area of phytosanitary concerns (Carolan, 2011, 2013). This is important from two perspectives for UK food policy: first, the reliance of the UK on imports of key foodstuffs and basic materials required for fertiliser production, and second, the UK financial sector is a site of speculation for trade in certain foodstuffs such as coffee, cocoa, sugar and cereals (Caraher, 2022, Lang, 2020, Lang & McKee, 2022, Mason & Lang, 2017). As was seen in Chapter 1, food policy often has to compete for space against financial interests. José Bové and Françous Dufour wrote a book *The World is not for Sale* (2001); in fact, the world and food commodities are being sold across borders every day with little regulation as the title of another book *The World for Sale* suggests (Blas & Farchy, 2021). The UN Special Rapporteur on the Right to Food said this trend began before 2008:

> Beginning in 2001, food commodities derivatives markets and commodities indexes began to see an influx of non-traditional investors, such as pension funds, hedge funds, sovereign wealth funds, and large banks … Strong similarities can be seen between the price behaviour of food commodities and other refuge values, such as gold.
>
> (De Schutter, 2010, p. 6)

Food has always been traded and the early origins of food and what is called futures trading can be traced back to as early as the 1690s in Japan, where traders were buying and selling rice futures (Kingsman, 2017). Early state and church intervention in food trading often possessed a food control element, setting aside food for a time of shortage for the population. This continued in muted forms up until the mid-twentieth century when capitalist economics markets were seen as the way forward. A more modern example is The Chicago Mercantile Exchange (CME), a global derivatives marketplace. The CME was founded in 1898 as the Chicago Butter and Egg Board, an agricultural commodities exchange to facilitate buying in the mid-west of the USA (Kingsman, 2017, 2019). There are now financial trading markets across the globe, with New York and London remaining key players. For the UK, control of food was most marked in World War II (WWII), with the government engaging in trade and the building of stocks of food, price controls and rationing (Hammond, 1954).

Trading food on a global market

Food is now a global commodity, traded on global markets, often travelling long distances from farm to fork and controlled by a small number of global companies (Clapp, 2018). The fallout from concentrations of power in the food system has resulted in new developments in food policy governance by the private sector, driven by the intrusion of speculators in food commodities since 2008. Like other elements of the food chain, there are concentrations in global market trading. Table 8.1 shows some examples of concentration of trading in the food chain. Note how many of these are not household or brand names known to the consumer. To some

Table 8.1 Some examples of concentration in global trade

Commodity	Main players	Significance
Cereals.	What are known as the big seven ABCD+ (Archer Daniels Midland [ADM], Bunge, Cargill, Dreyfus, Glencore, COFCO International[a] and Wilmar).	Seven companies control over 50% of global trade in cereals.
Coffee.	The two big players are ED&F Man Volcafe and ECOM. Roasters with their own in-house trading sections include Neumann Kaffee Gruppe, Nestlè, Kraft, Sara Lee, Smucker's (P&G), Dalmayr, Starbucks, Tchibo, Aldi, Melitta, Lavazza and Segafredo.	These control between 30% and 40% of the global market in coffee futures. A large proportion of the remaining 60% is controlled by roasters who have their own in-house trading sections.[b]
Soya.	Dupont, Archer Daniels Midland (ADM), Cargill, Kerry, Now Foods, Burcon, Sotexpro, Farbest, Wilmar and CHS Inc.	These ten control 60% of trade in soya; note the overlap with cereals.[b]
Sugar[c] (there are three major areas for sugar production: Brazil, India and the EU).	Associated British Foods Plc (UK), Cosan (Brazil), Biosev (Brazil), Mitr Phol Sugar Corporation, Ltd. (Thailand), Nordzucker AG (Germany), Sudzucker (Germany), Tereos (France), Thai Roong Ruang Group (Thailand), Wilmar International Limited (Singapore) and Cargill (US).	These nine control 65% of trade in sugar.

[a]This is a state-owned Chinese company.
[b]Within these, there will be differing value markets for non-GM and organic produce which will command higher prices.
[c]Sugar also has uses in the pharmaceutical industry and in the production of biofuels.

extent, this volatility had calmed down once food prices had levelled off and speculation turned to other products; but in 2022, the Ukrainian invasion along with a number of other global factors (climate crisis, COVID, trade wars) have resulted in food futures for wheat rising by 20% and then 70%.

The impacts within global commodity chains are direct and indirect. An indirect example comes from Australia, where shortages of food on supermarket shelves are due to a lack of a diesel additive (AdBlue) which is manufactured from urea mostly imported from China. China has restricted exports due to fertiliser prices in China rising steeply and to protect its own supply system and to build self-sufficiency. Such protectionist trade policies and panic hoarding are preventing food from reaching markets in other countries, contributing to potentially deadly food shortages. The lack of urea from China has resulted in food prices rising in Europe because of a lack of fertiliser and rising prices, as urea contains phosphate necessary for fertiliser production leading to less fertiliser being purchased and applied to crops and a reduction in crop yield. Cornering or controlling the market is not just a feature of private capital and companies. The "Great Russian Grain Robbery" in the 1970s was a result of the then USSR purchasing massive amounts of grain on the world market; there was also the Australian oil-for-wheat scandal known as the "AWB scandal" (Australian Wheat Board), where bribes were paid to the regime of Saddam Hussein in contravention of UN Sanctions (Bartos, 2006). In 2022, facing global food shortages, China is attempting to build up its short- and long-term self-sufficiency and hence why the export of key goods is controlled and limited (Lau, 2022). Here can be seen the global effects of national policy and the impact on global markets, including the UK, with increases in production costs leading to food price increases.

The base of the food system

For context, in areas such as Sub-Saharan Africa agriculture accounts for 53% of total global employment and food security and poverty reduction is correlated to the overall developments in agriculture (Giller et al., 2021). Small farms (i.e. those of less than two hectares) are critical to ensuring regional and local food security, as they produce approximately one-third of the world's food and supply chains are more likely to be locally based (Lowder, Sánchez & Bertini, 2021). Despite this, control and power in the food system are not embedded in the producing countries but with global traders and "Big Food" companies (see Table 8.1). There is pressure on farming to reduce its carbon emissions and to become more sustainable, yet the scope of small-scale farming makes it difficult for them to build this in as a factor leading to more and more industrial farming where scale allows the cost of eco-sustainability to be factored in (Madre & Devuyst, 2016, McKinsey, 2022). The difference with the US can be seen from the example of cereals, where industrial-scale farming now means that 55% of all grain storage occurs on farms, allowing these farmers to hold back grain in times of over-supply and low prices. Previously, in spot markets, merchants used to buy grain at harvest time and store it. New technologies have helped small producers manage the financial system with more up-to-date information; so, many small-scale coffee producers in Colombia now use mobile phones to monitor buying prices of their product before selling it to traders. But unlike the USA grain producers, they do not have the capacity to store it themselves; the average size of a coffee holding in Colombia is 4.4 hectares.

Why is this all a problem when products such as soya, wheat, corn, high fructose corn syrup (HFCS) or palm oil are not foods that the average consumer buys in any bulk? The reason is related to our food system and the consumption of processed foods (see the more detailed discussion on ultra-processed foods in Chapter 2); for example, in the UK on supermarket shelves, there are between 33,000 and 40,000 items of which:

- Forty per cent contain corn.
- Fifty per cent contain palm oil.
- Wheat is a major component of bread, confectionery and pasta.
- HFCS is a filler for many soft drinks and sweetened foods.
- Soya is an important part of animal feedstuff for beef, chicken and pork (Kingsman, 2017).

So, commodity prices influence the price of the foods that a consumer places in their basket.

Types of trading markets

There are two sorts of global financial markets: spot markets and derivatives markets. Spot markets are physical or cash markets where commodities are bought for delivery. There is in addition a distinction between traders in food commodities and speculators. Speculation is about trying to make a profit from a price change (i.e. buying low, selling high), whereas hedging attempts to reduce the amount of risk, or volatility, associated with a security's price change. Derivative markets deal in futures and options to buy/sell. More recent developments in futures markets include an ability to hedge against water and climate changes:

> Beginning in 2001, food commodities derivatives markets and commodities indexes began to see an influx of non-traditional investors, such as pension funds, hedge funds, sovereign wealth funds, and large banks … Strong similarities can be seen between the price behaviour of food commodities and other refuge values, such as gold.
>
> (De Schutter, 2010)

The US financial investor Warren Buffett is quoted as saying that "Derivatives are financial weapons of mass destruction".

In this chapter, the focus is on the speculation that occurs in food-based derivative markets and not spot trade in foods. Food policy often has to compete for space against commercial interests, and few food companies are addressing the Sustainable Development Goals (SDGs). Only 0.2% of companies were strongly aligned to meeting the UN SDGs (Neufeld, 2021). However, there was some evidence of action under the targets for "Responsible Production and Consumption" (SDG12) which fell under a corporate social responsibility (CSR) agenda.

Financialisation of food

Clapp shows how financial actors have increasingly interweaved themselves into various aspects of food and agricultural supply chains, from the top to the bottom (Clapp & Scott, 2018, Hudson & Donovan, 2014). From a policy perspective, these processes of financialisation are hidden and remain largely out of sight in the global political regulation scenario. This is partly due to the ways in which global finance works and also because few, including food scholars, have an understanding of financial markets, equities, derivatives, assets, index funds and so forth (Clapp, 2020, Kingsman, 2017). In business schools and government finance departments, there is knowledge of such approaches, suggesting a link that food policy advocates could make. Clapp argues financialisation, financial processes and the activities of financial actors have a significant impact on the shape of the food system and the ways in which food is produced, distributed, priced and consumed. Furthermore, of concern is the fact that these activities are driven by the drive for profits rather than for the greater good (Clapp, 2020, Clapp & Isakson, 2018).

The intensification of financialisation

While, as noted, food has always been the subject of trade, the global recession of 2008 and the rising price of food increasingly made food an object of speculation on global markets in much the same way that precious metals are traded (Blas & Farchy, 2021, Field, 2016). A complex interplay of events, food shortages, food price rises, increases in oil prices and the subsequent use/diversion of food commodities to produce ethanol produced the perfect condition for speculation by hedge funds.[3] Before this time, there, of course, had always been some speculation around food, but in the main, it was confined to specialist, high-value products like coffee, spices or exotic foods (e.g. mangoes) that could only be grown in limited geographical areas. This is of relevance for the UK, as the City of London remains a key centre for futures and speculative trading.

The Great Recession of 2008 resulted in rises in oil prices, civil unrest, diverting already limited food crops to ethanol production and speculation by hedge funds on food commodities (Field, 2016, Hudson & Donovan, 2014). The impact on the UK was a rise in food prices between 2008 and 2012 of between 25% and 30% (Department for Environment, Food and Rural Affairs, 2012). So the hedging or betting, as some have termed it, on food prices rising or falling had direct consequences for UK domestic consumers. Regulation of speculation on the London Stock Exchange is minimal and not subject to many regulatory standards (Newell, Taylor & Touni, 2018). Clapp and Scott have described how, since 2008, food speculation has increased and food has become a commodity like any other; and for many producers, this has resulted in a loss of income as the markets and speculators gain (Clapp & Scott, 2018).

The period of increasing speculation linked to new technologies also saw the rise of algorithmic speculators: those who relied on technology and computer modelling to predict price rises and falls. These speculators often did not possess knowledge of the commodity chain, the product itself and in most cases, never intended to take delivery of the goods but to buy and sell as prices fluctuate on global commodity markets to make a profit from the trading (speculation) of the right to the contract. These speculators rarely take the product and store it, but sell on the right to that food commodity. The basis of this speculation is buying when prices are low and selling when prices are high. This is not speculation to ensure a final product for selling or manufacture but to profit from rises or falls in price.

Although Clapp and others make some distinctions between trading and speculation, there is an argument that commodity traders and the use of futures contribute to addressing food insecurity by providing upfront payments to farmers and producers (Kingsman, 2017). So while a critique of speculative trading is offered here, there is some case to be made for futures trading and derivatives. The problem is a lack of regulation of both forms of trading, especially with respect to contributions to the greater good and global health as contained in the SDGs. Arguments in support of futures markets include the rationale that traders facilitate the movement of goods on the world market connecting growers with manufacturers, while speculators gamble on moves in the price of commodities and sell on the rights to those commodities. Currently, however, the power and influence lie with the "Big Food" and trading companies (Canfield, Anderson & McMichael, 2021).

A textbook example comes from 2010 and cocoa. In 2010, London-based Amajaro hedge fund built up a billion-dollar position in the cocoa futures market, which amounted to 7% of the then world supply or the whole of Europe's cocoa. This triggered extreme instability in the markets. The move was so unexpected that traders and big consumers, like Cadbury and Nestlé, were surprised and in the language of the markets "caught short". This happens when traders borrow stock and sell it on the market hoping to buy it back at a later stage when prices drop, so making a profit (Kingsman, 2017). Civil society NGOs criticised the actions taken by Amajaro as it caused problems for farmers and plunged many into poverty.

Control and regulation

The "Trump era" of politics saw the US withdraw from many UN agencies and incentives such as the WHO (World Health Organization) and the Paris Climate Agreements. While this was a travesty in terms of global governance, it diverted attention away from a bigger trend, which is philanthropy replacing and overtaking the funding of UN agencies (Valley, 2020). The Bill and Melinda Gates Foundation was the single biggest funder of global initiatives on poverty in 2016 (Rieff, 2016). Concerns were raised over this dependence and the origins of the Foundation's funds in a 2017 Open Letter to the Executive Board of the WHO headed "Conflict of interest safeguards far too weak to protect WHO from influence of regulated industries (the case of the Bill and Melinda Gates Foundation)" (Various Public Interest, Health, and Citizens' Groups, 2017). The letter claimed that the Foundation invested its monies "in many of the food, alcohol, and physical inactivity-related consumer products that cause or treat the current crisis of preventable heart disease, stroke, cancer, and diabetes". They called for greater investigation of such donations and a great conflict of interest scrutiny.

The problem with unregulated markets and the lack of control over global trade and donations to global regulatory organisations has many implications for those at the start of the food supply chain (Clapp, 2020, Newell, Taylor & Touni, 2018). One of the key facts that traditional food policymakers and influencers seem unaware of is the power of global traders. The 2008 Great Recession, like the OPEC (Organization of the Petroleum Exporting Countries) oil crisis of a previous era, gave more power to global traders and eclipsed the already waning power of large transnational companies (Blas & Farchy, 2021, Clapp & Isakson, 2018). There are parallels between oil and food: oil forms the base of the current food system (oil for transport, oil for processing, oil derivatives for fertilisers etc.) and the supply system of oil in the OPEC days was reflected in a concentration among seven global companies (called the "7 sisters"). The oil companies lost power when the oil-producing countries took power and so the "7 sisters" lost their hold in these countries. The producing countries (Venezuela, Saudi Arabia etc.) still needed to "shift" the product and turned to the global trading houses to enable this. A similar set of circumstances occurred post-2008; with many countries facing bankruptcy and lacking the resources to move goods, they turned to global trading houses (Hunter, 2022).

There have been many discussions about ways to control and regulate these global commodity markets to address food insecurity and global supply issues. One such proposal is a "Robin Hood" tax called the "Tobin Tax". This is a proposal for a simple sales tax on currency trades across borders. The idea originated with James Tobin, a Nobel laureate economist. Tobin Taxes could be enacted by national legislatures but require multilateral co-operation to be effectively enforced. The proposal is that each trade would be taxed at 0.1%–0.25% of volume (about 10–25 cents per USD 100). The idea is that a Tobin tax would help fund UN agencies and global welfare programmes such as the World Food Programme (WFP) and the FAO.

Such a tax would discourage frequent short-term speculative currency trades but leave long-term productive investments mostly unaffected. This would raise sufficient funds to meet urgent global health and environmental concerns including disease and poverty. A side effect would be the strengthening of national economies and more money flows at this level providing the fiscal capacity to increase public spending to increase agri-food productivity.

What can policy do about financialisation?

The COVID-19 crisis followed by the war in Ukraine has exposed flaws in the global food system and made more visible what was known from the 2008 Great Recession. The current crises are extensive and more far-reaching than that of 2008; the extreme of food insecurity and famine is threatened because of the breakdown in global food supplies. Following the crisis in 2008, there were major impacts on global food poverty levels and political unrest; the Arab Spring was triggered by concerns, riots and deaths over rising food prices. Food policy has again become a topic of both political and public concern, driven by factors such as rising food prices, food crises such as that in Yemen and Afghanistan, the UK leaving the EU (Brexit), China/US trade wars, the COVID-19 crisis, outbreaks of swine flu fever in Germany and China, the possible global relaxing of food standards in support of further trade liberalisation regimes and global disruption caused by the Russian invasion of Ukraine (Deconinck et al., 2022, Lang & McKee, 2022, Oxfam, 2022). The threat of famine in Afghanistan and Yemen with Northern parts of Nigeria and Somalia on the brink is linked to these disruptions in the global food chain. In mid-2022, it was estimated that 30 million people are facing alarming levels of hunger and malnutrition, with ten million of them facing famine conditions. Famine is the most serious level of food insecurity. The reasons for famine in these areas are complex and reflect a mix of geopolitical food chain disruptions, poor harvests and climate events. The situation in 2022 in these areas was exacerbated by the global politics of power with food being "weaponised" or perhaps hunger being "weaponised" as a tool of war (Hunter, 2022, World Economic Forum, 2023). It is not just scarcity of supply but the lack of control and uncertainty over supply chains. Ukraine is a major exporter of wheat on the global market accounting for 13% of global wheat supplies and 80% of sunflower seeds, and due to the war, farmers cannot plant or harvest existing crops, triggering major concerns on global trading markets. For Russia, due to financial sanctions and trade embargos, they will need to feed their own population in the light of food inflation, and shortages therefore have seriously curtailed their exports. In the early months of 2022, on global markets the future predicted price of wheat increased by 73% compared to prices from April 2021; this has been generated by the invasion of Ukraine. In a "normal" year, traders would compensate for a shortage of supply from the Black Sea region by turning to the US or Canada. The problem now is that there is nothing "normal" about the situation from the scale of shortages to the rise in prices. So simply diverting supplies to areas of need runs the risk of being out of the reach of many living in poverty in these countries; without government price subsidies, access may well be determined by a financial right, in essence the right of the consumer as opposed to a citizen (O'Donovan, 2022, Sen, 1992, The World Bank, 2021). We are entering an era of what has been called the "permacrises".

An indirect consequence of this global disturbance has been the focus on food policy in China on national self-sufficiency, with the Chinese President reported as saying, "The rice bowls of the Chinese people must be filled with Chinese grain" (Lau, 2022). This, as already discussed, has had implications for fertiliser production in Europe and the UK as well as the production of AdBlue for use in Australia.

The USD 5.1 trillion traded each day across national borders does not always involve the movement of goods, but currency. It is important to remember that with food speculation, it is not the commodity that is traded on the world markets but money flows based on speculation on rises or falls in the price of the food commodity. Also, much of trading occurs outside of national boundaries and is therefore unregulated (Newell, Taylor & Touni, 2018). Profit is made on speculating in rises or falls in the price of food commodities. Many of the current responses to the various crises have not been based on state policy but on ceding more control to the food sector and global food markets, often without safeguards or external monitoring or guarantees of long-term support (Berners-Lee et al., 2018, Biermann, Kanie & Kim, 2017). There are many who argue that food policy is now as much about the influence of the food industry/"Big Food" as state policy (Carolan, 2013, Hudson & Donovan, 2014). Neoliberal trade environments with low taxes and low regulation of labour safeguards form the context for food policy and conditions in food chains (Navarro, 2020). There is an argument that much food policy is influenced by neoliberal economic concepts (Ngqangashe et al., 2022) resulting in a bias towards industry perspectives, including global trade. Within the frame of financialisation, food is reduced to a commodity which is traded and to which safeguards around national food security are often left to market forces. Another growing area of concern is the influence of China in emerging economies through the funding of infrastructural projects by foreign direct investment (FDI) and land grabs. The Chinese government is now focussing on self-sufficiency and self-reliance. This does not mean that all the food it requires will be produced in China; some of it will be offshored but controlled (Adisu, Sharkey & Okoroafo, 2010, McMichael, 2020).

For the reasons above, food trade requires regulation to ensure that the growers and producers receive a fair price and that environments are protected, both domestically within the UK and internationally (Paarlberg, 2010). Food policy is not just a UK domestic issue, as set out in the opening chapters of this book, but one subject to international influences and the hidden influences of major players in the areas of trade in food commodities and speculation. The decisions the UK makes about its food supply are not just concerned with protecting borders and ensuring an adequate supply of food for its population, but also about broader commitments to the global community and how UK sourcing and consumption patterns influence these agendas, including the livelihoods of many in developing and emerging economies (Chambers, 2022, Linsell, Ramnarayan & Goodman, 2022, Price, 2022). Political turmoil and conflict have disrupted normal agriculture by displacing families and separating them from their primary food sources. One of the major cereal trading companies ADM (Archer Daniels Midland), referred to in Table 8.1, reported record profits in the first months of 2022; this was aided by growth in its nutrition segment using alternative oilseeds such as soybeans into vegetable oils and reduced global crop supplies which resulted in boosting its profit margins. So, at a time of shortage and rising levels of global food insecurity, including the UK, trade is continuing with little reference to global needs or inequities, as pointed out in the SDGs. The importance of food as a necessity for life is missing in activities where food is financialised.

The plight of growers/producers in developing and emerging economies is also being impacted by decisions to cut aid budgets. In the UK, the cut is from 0.7% to 0.5% of gross national income (Kobayashi, Heinrich & Bryant, 2021). As countries such as the UK and the US roll back on foreign aid budgets, their role is being replaced by private companies, who under the heading of CSR are providing support to growers in Africa and Asia (Cullather, 2010). The belief is that food aid as epitomized by the US foreign policy, where food was weaponised as a means of control (Barrett & Maxwell, 2005), is no longer appropriate and the focus should be on trade and creating economically self-reliant economies (US Government Accountability Office, 2020). In times of economic crises, aid is reduced as citizens place a lower priority on aid during economic downturns and politicians respond by cutting aid (Heinrich, Kobayashi & Bryant, 2016). Many companies see funding CSR and welfare programmes as investments in their futures by supporting training for farmers and supporting capital investment projects. As a policy, this represents a shift in governmentality from the state to the private sector. There are some positives to such moves. Often, corporations have resources bigger than many nation states and can move faster than state institutions. The downside is the unregulated nature of such policy developments, with the food industry investing where they can gain most. Another danger is the lack of investment in large infrastructures, such as transport and education. The move away from traditional public policy by national governments which involved providing food welfare, whether direct (provision of food) or indirect (cash transfers), has created a space which "Big Food" has stepped in to fill, often reluctantly (Richards, Kjærnes & Vik, 2016). Entitlements under such schemes are not universal but selective, in that they can apply to growers/producers and even to the communities where the food is grown, but not to the wider population.

The lack of global governance and the drive to low-tax, low-regulation economies have contributed to a diminution of the power and influence of global agencies such as the UN, WHO, FAO and the UNICEF (UN Children's Fund); such developments have aided the move to philanthrocapitalism and given voice to resolutions which are based on high-tech solutions to producing more food, but often do not address the right to food. The aid aspect is epitomised by the Gates Foundation, but many companies now operate their own internal polices generally under the guise of CSR commitments (Rieff, 2016, 2015). In many ways, the gap between welfare capitalism and philanthrocapitalism is shrinking or the overlap is growing bigger. The finances from philanthrocapitalism now outweigh the contributions from national governments to global health agendas.

Conclusion

If all this global trade and speculation seem remote from the UK and everyday lives, there are two things to bear in mind. The first is that London as a financial sector plays a large part in the activities described above. The second is that this influences our everyday lives without us knowing it: on any given day Cargill accounts for 20% of all food traded on global markets; the world's largest meat producing company, JBS, made more in futures trading than it did on meat sales in 2014 (Freitas Jr, 2015). Cargill in 2021 made USD 5 billion in net income, the biggest profit in its history; in 2020, it paid out dividends of USD 1.13 billion, most of which went to members of the extended family. During the COVID-19 pandemic, the value of Cargill grew by USD 20 million per day. This was driven by rising food prices, especially for grains. This resulted in four more members of the extended Cargill family joining the list of the richest 500 people, adding to eight Cargill family members already listed on it. Oxfam estimates that for every new billionaire created during the pandemic – one every 30 hours – nearly a million people could be pushed into extreme poverty in 2022 at nearly the same rate (Oxfam, 2022).

Being aware of these influences on the food system is the first step in bringing about changes; the second is lobbying for change and policy regulation of these practices. At a global level, there should continue to be state-funded investment in food production (food exceptionalism) to compensate for the consistent underinvestment in agriculture over the past decades. In 2011, for the first time, the agriculture ministers of the G20 countries[4] met and agreed to work together to tackle food price volatility and food insecurity. It is important that global food security remains an international priority in terms of global policy attention and resource allocation, that is, food security is paramount. In doing so, all players should adopt an integrated approach to food policy, linking sustainability, food security and health while paying due diligence to CSR commitments that consider health alongside profit. Any financialisation of food trading should be scrutinised to avoid greenwashing and ensure equity. Global markets need to allow lower-income countries to focus on producing their own food, for which they should be paid a fair price so that they may strive to become self-reliant and not become overly dependent on international markets with the precariousness that can result in both food prices and food security. Notwithstanding this, major grain-producing countries, such as India and China, should be encouraged to release grain stocks during critical times to reduce volatility in international markets, with the caveat that indigenous farmers be protected from cheap imports by advancing sustainable agricultural development in regions currently dependent on food imports. No major commodity-producing country should hoard their outputs to drive up prices and depress food security.

Notes

1 Financialisation refers to the role played by financial markets within a specific sector, in this case, the agri-food sector. It is used to describe the surge in commodity derivatives trading by financial traders that followed the 2000 deregulation of commodity markets.
2 Philanthrocapitalism is where donations come from the private sector and promotes a way of doing philanthropy, which mirrors the way that business is done in the for-profit world.
3 Typically a private limited partnership, which engages in speculation using credit or borrowed capital and engages in leveraging or trading in non-traditional assets to earn above-average returns.
4 This is an intergovernmental focus which includes 19 countries and the EU. The 19 countries are Argentina, Australia, Brazil, Canada, China, France, Germany, India, Indonesia, Italy, Japan, Republic of Korea, Mexico, Russia, Saudi Arabia, South Africa, Turkey, the UK and the US.

References

Adisu, K., Sharkey, T. & Okoroafo, S.C. 2010, "The impact of Chinese investment in Africa", *International Journal of Business and Management*, vol. 5, no. 9, p. 3.
Barrett, C.B. & Maxwell, D.G. 2005, *Food Aid After Fifty Years: Recasting Its Role*, Routledge, London.
Bartos, S. 2006, *Against the Grain the AWB Scandal and Why It Happened*, UNSW Press, Canberra.
Berners-Lee, M., Kennelly, C., Watson, R. & Hewitt, C.N. 2018, "Current global food production is sufficient to meet human nutritional needs in 2050 provided there is radical societal adaptation", *Elementa Science of the Anthropocene*, vol. 6, no. 1, p. 52. https://doi.org/10.1525/elementa.310
Biermann, F., Kanie, N. & Kim, R.E. 2017, "Global governance by goal-setting: the novel approach of the UN Sustainable Development Goals", *Current Opinion in Environmental Sustainability*, vol. 26–27, pp. 26–31. https://doi.org/10.1016/j.cosust.2017.01.010
Blas, J. & Farchy, J. 2021, *The World for Sale: Money, Power and the Traders Who Barter the Earth's Resources*, Random House Business, London.
Bové, J. & Dufour, F. 2001, *The World Is Not for Sale: Farmers against Junk Food*, Verso, London.
Canfield, M., Anderson, M.D. & McMichael, P. 2021, "UN food systems summit 2021: dismantling democracy and resetting corporate control of food systems", *Frontiers in Sustainable Food Systems*, vol. 5, p. 103. https://doi.org/10.3389/fsufs.2021.661552
Caraher, M. 2022, "Food Systems and Food Poverty" in *A Research Agenda for Food Systems*, ed. C.L. Sage, Elgar, Cheltenham, pp. 111–128.
Carolan, M.S. 2013, *Reclaiming Food Security*, Routledge, London.
Carolan, M.S. 2011, *Embodied Food Politics*, Ashgate, Farnham, Surrey.
Chambers, S. 2022, How will we put food on the table?, 13th March, *The Sunday Times*, London.
Clapp, J. 2020, *Food*, 3rd edn, Policy, Cambridge.

Clapp, J. 2018, "Mega-mergers on the menu: corporate concentration and the politics of sustainability in the global food system", *Global Environmental Politics,* vol. 18, no. 2, pp. 12–33. https://doi.org/10.1162/glep_a_00454.

Clapp, J. & Isakson, S.R. 2018, "Risky returns: the implications of financialization in the food system", *Development and Change,* vol. 49, no. 2, pp. 437–460. https://doi.org/10.1111/dech.12376Clapp, J. & Scott, C. 2018, "The global environmental politics of food", *Global Environmental Politics,* vol. 18, no. 2, pp. 1–11.

Cullather, N. 2010, *The Hungry World: America's Cold War Battle against Poverty in Asia,* Harvard University Press, Cambridge, MA.

Deconinck, K., Giner, C., Jackson, L.A. & Toyama, L. 2022, "Making better policies for food systems will require reducing evidence gaps", *Global Food Security,* vol. 33, p. 100621. https://doi.org/10.1016/j.gfs.2022.100621

Department for Environment, Food and Rural Affairs (DEFRA) 2012, *Food Statistics Pocketbook 2012,* DEFRA, London.

De Schutter, O. 2010, *Countries Tackling Hunger with a Right to Food Approach: Significant Progress in Implementing the Right to Food at National Scale in Africa, Latin America and South Asia,* Office of the UN Special Rapporteur on the Right to Food, Geneva.

Field, S. 2016, "The financialization of food and the 2008–2011 food price spikes", *Environment and Planning A: Economy and Space,* vol. 48, no. 11, pp. 2272–2290. https://doi.org/10.1177/0308518X16658476

Freitas Jr, G. 2015, *One Company Is Making a Killing on Brazil's Sinking Real,* Bloomberg.com. https://archive.ph/zidDi#selection-3011.0-3011.56.

Giller, K.E., Delaune, T., Silva, J.V., Descheemaeker, K., van de Ven, G., Schut, A.G.T., van Wijk, M., Hammond, J., Hochman, Z., Taulya, G., Chikowo, R., Narayanan, S., Kishore, A., Bresciani, F., Teixeira, H.M., Andersson, J.A. & van Ittersum, M.K. 2021, "The future of farming: who will produce our food?", *Food Security,* vol. 13, no. 5, pp. 1073–1099. https://doi.org/10.1007/s12571-021-01184-6

Hammond, R.J. 1954, *Food and Agriculture in Britain 1939–45: Aspects of Wartime Control,* Stanford University Press, Stanford, CA.

Haydon, S., Jung, T. & Russell, S. 2021, "'You've Been Framed': a critical review of academic discourse on philanthrocapitalism", *International Journal of Management Reviews,* vol. 23, no. 3, pp. 353–375. https://doi.org/10.1111/ijmr.12255

Heinrich, T., Kobayashi, Y. & Bryant, K.A. 2016, "Public opinion and foreign aid cuts in economic crises", *World Development,* vol. 77, pp. 66–79. https://doi.org/10.1016/j.worlddev.2015.08.005

Hudson, J. & Donovan, P. 2014, *Food Policy and the Environmental Credit Crunch: From Soup to Nuts,* Routledge, Oxford.

Hunter, A. 2022, Commodity traders thrust into the spotlight as war exposes risks, 26th April 26, *Financial Post,* https://financialpost.com/pmn/business-pmn/commodity-trading-thrust-into-the-spotlight-as-war-exposes-risks.

Kickbusch, I., Allen, L. & Franz, C. 2016, "The commercial determinants of health", *The Lancet Global Health,* vol. 4, no. 12, pp. e895–e896. https://doi.org/10.1016/S2214-109X(16)30217-0

Kingsman, J. 2019, *The New Merchants of Grain: Out of the Shadows,* Jonathan Kingsman, Great Britain.

Kingsman, J. 2017, *Commodity Conversations: An Introduction to Trading in Agricultural Commodities,* Jonathan Kingsman, Great Britain.

Kobayashi, Y., Heinrich, T. & Bryant, K.A. 2021, "Public support for development aid during the COVID-19 pandemic", *World Development,* no. 138, p. 105248. https://doi.org/10.1016/j.worlddev.2020.105248

Lang, T. 2020, *Feeding Britain: Our Food Problems and How to Fix Them,* Pelican, London.

Lang, T. & McKee, M. 2022, "The reinvasion of Ukraine threatens global food supplies", *BMJ,* vol. 376, p. o676. doi: https://doi.org/10.1136/bmj.o676

Lau, M. 2022, China can't count on global markets for food security, Xi Jinping says, 7th March, *South China Morning Post,* https://www.scmp.com/news/china/politics/article/3169467/china-cant-count-global-markets-food-security-xi-jinping-says.

Linsell, K., Ramnarayan, A. & Goodman, D. 2022, *Cheap Food in Britain Is about to Become a Thing of the Past*, 13 May, Bloomberg UK, https://www.bloomberg.com/news/articles/2022-05-13/supermarket-food-prices-increase-above-uk-inflation-in-cost-of-living-crisis?utm_campaign=news&utm_medium=bd&utm_source=applenews.

Lowder, S.K., Sánchez, M.V. & Bertini, R. 2021, "Which farms feed the world and has farmland become more concentrated?", *World Development*, vol. 142, p. 105455. https://doi.org/10.1016/j.worlddev.2021.105455

Madre, Y. & Devuyst, P. 2016, *How to Tackle Price and Income Volatility for Farmers? An Overview of International Agricultural Policies and Instruments*, Farm Europe, retrieved from www.farm-europe.eu: https://www.farm-europe.eu/travaux/how-to-tackle-price-and-income-volatility-for-farmers-an-overview-of-international-agricultural-policies-and-instruments/.

Mason, P. & Lang, T. 2017, *Sustainable Diets: How Ecological Nutrition Can Transform Consumption and the Food System*, Routledge, London.

McKinsey 2022, *The Net-Zero Transition: What It Would Cost, What It Could Bring?*, McKinsey Global Institute, https://www.mckinsey.com/business-functions/sustainability/our-insights/the-net-zero-transition-what-it-would-cost-what-it-could-bring.

McMichael, P. 2020, "Does China's 'going out' strategy prefigure a new food regime?", *The Journal of Peasant Studies*, vol. 47, no. 1, pp. 116–154. https://doi.org/10.1080/03066150.2019.1693368

Mindell, J.S., Reynolds, L., Cohen, D.L. & McKee, M. 2012, "All in this together: the corporate capture of public health", *BMJ*, vol. 345, p. e8082. https://doi.org/10.1136/bmj.e8082

Navarro, V. 2020, "The consequences of neoliberalism in the current pandemic", *International Journal of Health Services*, vol. 50, no. 3, pp. 271–275. https://doi.org/10.1177/0020731420925449

Neufeld, D. 2021, UN sustainable development goals: how companies stack up, 16th March, *Visual Capitalist*, https://www.visualcapitalist.com/sustainable-development-goals/.

Newell, P., Taylor, O. & Touni, C. 2018, "Governing food and agriculture in a warming world", *Global Environmental Politics*, vol. 18, no. 2, pp. 53–71. https://doi.org/10.1162/glep_a_00456

Ngqangashe, Y., Cullerton, K., Phulkerd, S., Huckel Schneider, C., Thow, A.M. & Friel, S. 2022, "Discursive framing in policies for restricting the marketing of food and non-alcoholic beverages", *Food Policy*, vol. 109, p. 102270. https://doi.org/10.1016/j.foodpol.2022.102270

O'Donovan, D. 2022, Risk of famine with 40pc hike in wheat price after war threatens Ukraine's grain exports, 5th March, *Irish Independnet*, Dublin.

Oxfam 2022, *Profiting from Pain*, Oxfam, https://oi-files-d8-prod.s3.eu-west-2.amazonaws.com/s3fs-public/2022-05/Oxfam%20Media%20Brief%20-%20EN%20-%20Profiting%20From%20Pain%2C%20Davos%202022%20Part%202.pdf.

Paarlberg, R. 2010, *Food Politics: What Everyone Needs to Know*, Oxford University Press, Oxford.

Price, K. 2022, Ukraine invasion could impact UK food and drink prices, 7th March, *The Caterer*, https://www.thecaterer.com/news/ukraine-invasion-impact-uk-food-drink-prices.

Richards, C., Kjærnes, U. & Vik, J. 2016, "Food security in welfare capitalism: comparing social entitlements to food in Australia and Norway", *Journal of Rural Studies*, vol. 43, pp. 61–70. https://doi.org/10.1016/j.jrurstud.2015.11.010

Rieff, D. 2015, "Philanthrocapitalism: A Self-Love Story" in *Why do Super-Rich Activists Mock Their Critics Instead of Listening to Them?*, 1st October edn, The Nation, https://www.thenation.com/article/archive/philanthrocapitalism-a-self-love-story/. Accessed 20/4/2023.

Rieff, D. 2016, *The Reproach of Hunger: Food, Justice and Money in the 21st Century*, Verso, London.

Sen, A. 1992, *Inequality Reexamined*, Oxford University Press, Oxford.

Swinburn, B.A., Sacks, G., Hall, K.D., Mcpherson, K., Finegood, D.T., Moodie, M.L. & Gortmaker, S.L. 2011, "The global obesity pandemic: shaped by global drivers and local environments", *Lancet*, vol. 378, pp. 804–814. https://doi.org/10.1016/S0140-6736(11)60813-1

The International Panel of Experts on Sustainable Food Systems 2020, "Towards a Common Food Policy for the European Union", in *The Policy Reform and Realignment that Is Required to Build Sustainable Food Systems in Europe*, The International Panel of Experts on Sustainable Food Systems, https://www.ipes-food.org/_img/upload/files/CFP_FullReport.pdf.

The World Bank 2021, *Brief: Food Security and COVID-19 (Updated 5th February, 2021)*, The World Bank, https://www.worldbank.org/en/topic/agriculture/brief/food-security-and-covid19#:~:text=In%20 November%202020%2C%20the%20U.N.,insecure%20people%20in%20the%20world.

US Government Accountability Office 2020, *Global Food Security: Information on Spending and Types of Assistance Provided by the United States and Other Donors*, Government Accountability Office, Washington, DC.

Valley, P. 2020, *Philanthropy - From Aristotle to Zuckerberg*, Bloomsbury, London.

Various Public Interest, Health, and Citizens' Groups 2017, *Open Letter to the Executive Board of the World Health Organization: Re: Conflict of Interest Safeguards Far Too Weak to Protect WHO from Influence of Regulated Industries (the Case of the Bill and Melinda Gates Foundation)*, Open Letter, http://healthscienceandlaw.ca/wp-content/uploads/2017/01/Public-Interest-Position.WHO_. FENSAGates.Jan2017.pdf.

World Economic Forum 2023, *The Global Risks Report 2023 18th Edition: INSIGHT REPORT*, World Economic Forum, https://www.weforum.org/reports/globalrisks- report-2023/.

9 Public sector food initiatives

The case of school food and early childhood provision

Introduction

This chapter provides the background to UK school food (with a secondary focus on other public sector food initiatives). In the 1900s the focus was on concerns about the poor health of recruits to the Boer War (1899–1902). In 1904, the Interdepartmental Committee on Physical Deterioration found so many recruits from working-class families to be malnourished and unfit for service. Forty per cent were judged to be unfit due to "physical deterioration". The provision of School Meals was formally recognised in policy by Parliament in 1906 with the passing of the Education (Provision of Meals) Act (HM Government, 1906). This Act was not compulsory and only applied to England and Wales. Scotland was excluded as it was judged that the provision of school meals by charitable bodies was adequate in Scotland.

Through nearly all epochs, it has been easier to argue for policy related to children and schools. Schools offer a captive population where even those who favour the family as the primary caregiver can see the advantages of ensuring that children are fed properly. Le Gros Clark notes in his social history of school meals that in 1906, "there were still in some measure a sense that children ought not to be relieved outside the circle of the family" (Le Gros Clark, 1948, p. 7).

A linking concern in policy development has been the health of our children and young people, and school meals have featured heavily at key time points, responding to changing social, political and economic climates, from not being fit or healthy enough to be recruited to the army in both the Boer and World War I (WWI) to a change in the emphasis of school meals from being focused on the under-nutrition of the early and mid-twentieth century to concerns with issues such as obesity and diet-related non-communicable diseases (DR-NCDs).

Healthy start

In an attempt to ensure children have optimal nutritional status in their early years, the UK government introduced the Healthy Start scheme that provides vouchers to low-income women who are either pregnant or have children under four years old and who are in receipt of other means-tested government benefits. The vouchers can be used to purchase cow's milk, fresh or frozen fruit and vegetables and infant formula. The vouchers are currently £4.25 per week for pregnant women and those with children aged 1–4 years and £8.50 per week for those with infants under one-year-old (NHS, 2023). The scheme has been in operation since 2006, but enrolment has consistently and significantly declined.

An open letter by Sustain and other signatories (Sustain, 2022) concluded that up to 50% of eligible families could not access the Healthy Start scheme in the last year. Given the problems

DOI: 10.4324/9781003260301-9

with the digitisation of the scheme, there have been calls for the government to invest in promoting the scheme, publish uptake data and increase the value of payments in line with inflation with twice-yearly reviews against food prices. However, research has also identified that "the shortcomings of Healthy Start will not be resolved with minor adjustments or more promotion. The policy is based on an inaccurate assessment of the underlying cause for poor nutrition in low-income families" (Egger, 2021, p. 10). Instead, a more fundamental review of Healthy Start has been recommended, extolling the benefits of "making the scheme universal for all pregnant women and children under four years old, of changing the restrictions on purchasable items, and of increasing the voucher amount" (Egger, 2021, p. 10).

Healthy Start is also interesting because it demonstrates how "governmentality" around food has shifted from the state to the charity sector, blurring as it does the responsibility for welfare provision by government, civil society and industry by relying recently on corporate partners to increase the value of the vouchers to recipients (Egger, 2021).

Schools and health

The longer-term health effects from exposure to an unhealthy diet have been proven at different times and for different reasons. This is particularly true, since it has been established that the early years' food choices can determine their diet and subsequent quality of life in later years. Research has indicated that the dietary patterns adopted by children and young people are characterised by a high consumption of fat and/or sugar products and a dislike for healthier alternatives such as fruit and vegetables (Warwick, 1998).

"Every nation has a duty to maintain and protect the health of its children – its next generation of citizens" (Marmot, 2010, p. 7). The much-cited Marmot Review prioritised "giving children the best start" as the most important objective, as it was the one most likely, based on research, to reduce inequalities in society (Marmot, 2010). Of course, obesity and related dietary disorders do not rest solely on children's dietary practices since obesity is a complex public health condition, including physical, social and medical contributors, but it is likewise true that food habits of children are more malleable than those of adults (Oostindjer et al., 2017).

Much has been written about childhood obesity and public health concern regarding the contribution of the nutritional quality and amount of food served in the preschool setting to these problems (Briley & Mcallaster, 2011). Children's food choices and eating patterns are worthy of study because the childcare setting has the potential to be a successful vehicle for health improvement (Gupta et al., 2005) and obesity prevention (Kaphingst & Story, 2008; Story et al., 2009). Schools have an important role providing healthy food to children due to the nature of compulsory education. This facilitates a captive audience to whom to offer nutritious foods five days a week while in school (McNamara, 2004, p. 11), reaching children across socio-economic classes and for 12 years of their lives of compulsory schooling (Oostindjer et al., 2017).

The origins of school food

In 1880, the Education Act made school attendance compulsory between the ages of five and ten; though by the early 1890s, attendance was falling short at 82%. Many children worked outside school hours – in 1901, the figure was put at 300,000 – and truancy was a major problem due to the fact that parents could not afford to give up income earned by their children (Webb & Webb, 1927). Fees were also payable until a change in the law in 1891. Compulsory schooling, despite its shortcomings, offered an ideal opportunity to feed hungry children. Initially, this was mainly provided by charity organisations and not local authorities.

The history of school food in the UK can be traced back to the mid-nineteenth century when charities, such as *The Destitute Children's Dinner Society* and others, took it upon themselves to provide dining rooms to feed children. With the introduction of compulsory education in the 1880s, individual schools provided a midday meal for those children unable to return home. In 1904, with the diagnosis of severe malnutrition in Boer War recruits, attention began to be paid to the population's nutritional health and the Inter-Departmental Committee on Physical Deterioration preceded the Education (Provision of Meals) Act in 1906 (HM Government, 1906). This Act was designed to provide food to children in poverty to support them in benefitting from education.

Before 1906, school meal provision was delivered by charitable bodies in the major cities of the UK. In 1889, in London the School Dinners' Association was formed. By 1905, there were similar bodies in all the English cities. For the Boer War, the health of the male population was judged to be so poor that it compromised recruitment to the armed forces resulting in the establishment of school meals. The Education Act of 1906 allowed councils to provide free meals to children from poor families. The Act also placed limits on the amount that could be drawn from local rates to support the provision of meals.

School meals during the Great War

During WWI, the provision of school meals was still permissive and not obligatory on local authorities. During the Great War years (1914–1918), the expenditure limit for school meals was removed and the introduction of a grant from the Exchequer meant a threefold increase in school meal recipients in the early stages of the War (Caroline Walker Trust, 1992). Despite this, Le Gros Clark reported a drop in the provision of free school meals; with the figure being 156,000 prior to start of the War in 1914, rising to 442,000 in 1915 but thereafter dropping to 118,000 and by 1918 only 43,000 were in receipt of school meals. The reason he suggested was twofold. The first was an impression that children were being fed adequately in the home. Second, the Ministry of Food actively "took measures to discourage its growth" and did not take the school meal service into "the total war time economy" controlled by the Ministry. The reasons for this are not clear but seem to be related to the belief that feeding children was best left to the family, not the state.

In 1914, the 1906 Act was amended and the responsibility for feeding children was given to the newly established school medical services at local level. In the light of the War, a problem arose with the terms of the original Act which only allowed for children to be fed during school times. This excluded weekend and holiday times. A similar situation has arisen in the 2019/2020 COVID-19 crisis, with the feeding of children during holiday periods and the term holiday hunger has emerged to describe this phenomenon (Stretesky et al., 2020).

The interwar years

Any gains were lost unfortunately during the later years of WWI and in post-war years. The subsequent depression witnessed an immediate increase in school meals uptake, but local education authorities' economising efforts impacted negatively on school meals and numbers fell again in 1922–1923. Malnutrition resulted and school meals rallied again in an effort to nourish our school children, but the introduction of an additional qualifying criterion for the eligibility of school meals now required children to be both poor and malnourished to receive a free school meal. In 1934, "needy" children were provided with free milk and by the start of World War II (WWII), the school meals policy was refocused to once again benefit *all* children.

In the years following WWI, school meals came under attack as one way of achieving cost savings. This was not based on any judgement of the contribution to improving the health of children. A report by Sir Eric Geddes, which became known as the "Geddes Axe", recommended cutbacks in expenditure on school food (Higgs, 1922). Geddes justified cuts in school meal provision saying, "We have been accused", he said:

> of starving the minds and, indeed, of endeavouring to starve the bodies also of the children. But is that reasonable. We are passing through a period of extreme difficulty and of great financial stringency. This is not the time for a vast increase in educational expenditure like this, when trade and industry is being strangled by heavy taxation. The only thing that matters in this country is to get down taxation or we die.
>
> (Le Gros Clark, 1948, p. 12)

The number of meals by the late 1920s had fallen by 50%.

WWI and the economic recession of the 1920s and 1930s saw rises in food poverty and poor health. Soup kitchens and charity provision were ways to address these issues. Free school meal provision fell, with cutbacks to key services resulting in only half of all English local authorities providing free meals to the needy. The embryonic welfare state, of the 1920s and 1930s, mainly covered insured men and their dependents. The National Hunger March of 1932 and the well-known 1936 Jarrow March came about because of concerns about incomes, jobs and the inability of families to afford food and the lack of provision of school meals to families in need.

In 1939, facing the coming WWII and looking back to the depression of the 1930s, school food again became a key focus point for reformers as it did in the new welfare state established post-WWII (Le Gros Clark, 1948; Timmins, 2017). This was linked to two concerns: the health of young people and food control; it was seen as more efficient to feed children centrally in schools by cooking in large batches.

School food developments

The history of school feeding shows how the move from philanthropy to state provision occurred as the realisation grew that philanthropic provision was piecemeal and did not deliver population-level improvements in health (Le Gros Clark, 1947).

During WWII, not only was school food controlled, but food was rationed. Allowing for this, the number of school meals served decreased during WWII. The evacuation of children from the cities and other schemes to feed people partially accounted for this drop in numbers. Le Gros Clark points out that there was an initial stigma problem and a need to convince the public that school meals were not a provision under the Poor Laws or Public Assistance but a new provision. The other development in this period was the establishment of central cooking depots that became known as school canteens, although they were often not located in schools and served a broader range of settings other than schools such as hospitals and workplaces. This was done in the interests of efficiency and bulk cooking was one way to achieve this. By 1943, the number of meals served by school canteens had risen from the 1941 figure of 27,000 to 148,000 meals a day. These canteens were not evenly distributed across the country, with the north-west of the country containing more than half the total number, probably reflecting the number of work canteens in the dock areas. By the end of the war, school canteens accounted for 16% of all meals served. The centralisation of kitchens proved problematic post-WWII when local authorities reassumed control and had to establish more local-based services in schools. There was a

Table 9.1 Some key dates for school food policy

Date	Policy initiative
1880s.	Origins of compulsory education and school meals provided by charities.
1904.	Report of the Committee on Physical Deterioration of recruits to the Boer War highlighting the poor health of army recruits linked to poor nutrition.
1906.	The Education (Provision of Meals) Act of 1906 passed, which gave local authorities some powers to provide school meals.
1907.	Medical checks in schools introduced.
1934.	Free milk for "needy" children introduced.
1939/1945.	World War II.
1939/1940.	Rationing introduced and number of school meals fall as children are relocated from towns and cities to the countryside.
1941.	First nutritional standards for school meals established.
1944.	The Education Act (1944) required the provision of a standard meal at a set price.
1955.	First revision to the nutritional standards of school meals.
1980.	The Education Act (1980) reduced the requirement for meal provision by schools only to those children eligible for a free school meal.
1992.	The Caroline Walker Trust expert panel report on nutritional guidelines for school meals published.
2005.	School Food Trust established.
2013.	School Food Plan published.
2021.	NFS comments on lack of progress re school meals.

capital cost involved in building catering kitchens in schools, which undoubtedly slowed down the expansion of services.

Now, in the modern age, school food is seen as key in tackling food poverty and modern malnutrition which includes both hunger and obesity, although the debate has moved from food security and food quality to one of healthy and sustainable food and the continuation of provision beyond the school terms, particularly for those children in receipt of free school meals.

The first nutritional standards are introduced

It was not until 1941 that the first nutritional standards for school meals were established, requiring that a school meal provided a participating child with sufficient calories, quality lean protein and fat to sustain him/her throughout much of the day, due to wartime rationing and the likelihood that meals eaten at home would be nutritionally deficient. The responsibility to provide a school meal by individual schools extended to become the responsibility of the local education authority in 1944, with the implementation of The Education Act (1944) requiring the provision of a standard meal at a set price and the extension of this service to weekends and holidays. In 1945, the school meal was to be available for all pupils who wanted them. In 1946, free school milk was available to all attending children, and by the end of WWII, school meals service had attained its status as a general service for all children. By 1947, the government met the full net cost of school meals (Caroline Walker Trust, 1992).

During WWII, the Milk in Schools scheme was extended to all schoolchildren. School dinners were introduced, providing about 1,000 calories or one-third of children's daily energy needs. By the end of the war in 1945, 40% or 1.5 million children were in receipt of free school meals. Collingham (2011) notes that the circumstances of war removed the stigma that was attached to the charity provision of school meals in the 1930s.

By the 1950s, a standard charge was set for school meals, but this decade witnessed the introduction of alternative (remission) arrangements for those families who would struggle to pay the standard cost.

In 1955, there was the first revision to the nutritional standards of school meals which introduced age-appropriate guidelines for calories, fat and protein. The 1965 report of the Working Party on the Nutritional Standard of the School Dinner recommended maintaining the overall nutritional standard of the school meal and the inclusion of a greater variety of meat as a safeguard for those children for whom the school meal was their principal "one good meal a day" (Caroline Walker Trust, 1992, p. 30).

In 1967, local education authorities assumed financial responsibility for servicing school meals and the pricing policy witnessed successive increases. By 1968, only children in primary and special education schools continued to receive free school milk and by 1971, only children aged between five and seven years were eligible to receive free school milk.

In the 1970s, other nations shifted the focus of their school meals programmes from food security to quality, but it wasn't until the 1990s and 2000s that the UK incorporated this focus (Oostindjer et al., 2017).

By 1980, school meals were deprioritised and identified as one area of public expenditure where significant savings could be made with the least effect on education, essentially undermining the Education (Provision of Meals) Act in 1906 which held sufficient food provision to be important in enabling children to benefit from education provision. The Education Act (1980) reduced the requirement for meal provision by schools only to those children eligible for a free school meal. This Act also removed the standard price of a school meal and the previously established nutritional standards, leaving the local education authorities responsible for determining the cost and nutritional standards of school meals. The Act also made free milk discretionary rather than universal, representing a significant weakening of school meals provision in England, with Scotland following suit via the 1980 Education (Scotland) Act. This should be recognised in the context of the 1983 Department of Health and Social Security survey which found the midday meal at school to be the only substantial meal children from low-income families eat all day deriving 30% of their energy from school meals (Department of Health and Social Security, 1989).

Restrictions continued throughout 1986 when a new Social Security Act was implemented whereby free school milk and meals' eligibility criteria were strengthened, resulting in the loss of this entitlement by some families who were not in receipt of the eligible passport benefits. Families outwith the original eligibility were entitled to a cash substitute nominally included in their benefits for the value of the former school meal. School meals uptake continued to reduce, exacerbating simultaneously child poverty increases (Walker & Walker, 1987). At the same time, the local education authorities also lost the power to remit all/some of the normal charge of the school meal and local authorities became obliged to tender the school meals contracts. The Social Security Act of 1988 also made no provision for external monitoring of mandatory standards of school meals.

The Caroline Walker Trust established an expert panel to develop nutritional guidelines for school meals in an attempt to protect against nutritional problems via school meals provision. The Caroline Walker Trust recommended "a long-term commitment to a healthy school meal service is crucial, at both national and local levels" (Caroline Walker Trust, 1992, p. 79). This may be summarised as school meals that, over a one-week period, contained more bread, cereals and other starchy foods, more fruit and vegetables and which is higher in minerals and vitamins with less fat, sugar and salty foods. The Trust established, for the first time, nutritional recommendations for sugar and fibre. The Caroline Walker Trust report also reported that school meals, while perhaps not nutritionally complete in and of themselves, still represented the best option of all other possible sources of food available to children for their midday meal (e.g. out-of-home food purchases from shops and takeaways). A later review of seven British studies measuring lunchtime nutrient intake among children aged between five and 11 years concluded that the nutritional quality of packed lunches in England to be higher in energy, sugar, satu-rated fat and salt content compared to school lunches (Evans et al., 2010). In 2004, the annual Caroline Walker Trust lecture lauded school meals' catering staff as "health workers in disguise" (Morgan, 2014, p. 13). Morgan (2014, p. 1) speaks powerfully about the benefits of viewing school food beyond a myopic lens, claiming that if school food is truly and broadly valued for its contribution in terms of "public health, social justice and ecological integrity, then school food will be recognised for what it really is – a health and wellbeing service".

The Education and Employment Select Committee later (1999) recommended that quantifi-able nutritional standards, informed by the Caroline Walker Trust, be reintroduced to school meals and evaluated as part of routine school inspections. In the same year, the National Healthy Schools Programme was introduced to bring about reduced health inequalities in schools, with every school aspiring to be a healthy school by 2009.

Throughout the 1990s, the out-of-school provision expanded both before and after school and outside of traditional school term times (Street, 1999). This expansion was not funded by central government monies; initiatives such as breakfast clubs and after school cooking clubs were funded from within existing school budgets and/or supported with charity money or donated food. Breakfast clubs are a particular example of this attention and were expounded for their contribution to meeting children's health needs by providing a balanced meal before the com-mencement of the school day, supporting nutrition for cognition and educational attainment, school attendance and punctuality and also facilitating familial childcare needs by providing a supervised environment before school starts (Street, 1999).

The National Healthy Schools Scheme was a useful underpinning for a whole-school approach to food and nutrition outlined in the 1998 Department for Education and Employment's (DfEE) *Ingredients for Success* consultation, whereby food provision in school was reinforced with food-related lessons. DfEE's consultation of the same year, *Fair Funding – Improving Delegation to Schools*, was a further catalyst to facilitate schools to provide food for the school community using innovative ways, including breakfast clubs (Caroline Walker Trust, 1992).

Sir Donald Acheson's report (Acheson, 1998) highlighted differences in children's diets based on socio-economic status. The Millennium Development Goals (Tanumihardjo et al., 2007), signed in September 2000 by 189 nations, committed world leaders to combat poverty, hunger, disease and illiteracy, among other targets. Yet, school food, considered the litmus test of our commitment to sustainable development and meal providers for a vulnerable subgroup of consumers, seems destined to operate in low-cost food chains. School food can also be seen as a marker of a society's caring ethos where it demonstrates a caring concern for its young citizens, and as many have noted is a right as opposed to some other school initiatives, such as breakfast clubs, which rely on charity and/or donations (De Schutter, 2013).

Commitment to improving the nutritional profile of school food

The turn of the twenty-first century brought more changes to school meals' governance in respect of delegated budgets to schools' governing bodies to provide school meals. The move to competitive tendering in the 1980s introduced a "cheap food" culture into the school meals service; this was replaced, in England and Wales, by a "Best Value" criterion (Morgan, 2004). The *cheap food culture* persisted, placing a duty on local education authorities to deliver services to clear standards of cost and quality but essentially signalling a de-prioritisation of nutritional standards in the awarding criteria. The Department of Health and National Health Service (NHS) secured a government commitment for a National School Fruit Scheme, giving every nursery and infant school child by 2004 a free piece of fruit each school day. However, it should be noted that while it was lauded as one of the government's successes as a means to support learning about healthy eating, school vending machines and corporate sponsorship of school equipment were introduced in the same year (McNamara, 2004) with the potential to undermine the healthy eating message. Scotland largely implemented a similar school fruit scheme, providing a single piece of fruit three times per week for all primary school children in years one and two.

In 2001, the focus was on minimum nutritional standards for school lunches with England's The Education (Nutritional Standards for School Lunches) Regulations, 2000. These standards required caterers to provide foods from at least two nutritional groups (e.g. carbohydrates and dairy) (Riley, 2004). These were reviewed in 2004, with subsequent moves to introduce a greater reliance on organic food, include greater emphasis on teaching nutrition in the curriculum and increase physical activity in school. Equivalent legislation introduced minimum nutritional standards in Wales, and in Northern Ireland, the focus was on food-based nutritional standards requiring the main food groups to be represented (piloted across 100 schools in 2004–2005). In 2004, nutritional standards were introduced in Scottish primary schools, and in 2006, these were extended to post-primary schools.

The Kingston upon Hull experiment

In the early 2000s, the local authority in Hull established an interesting social experiment. *Eat Well Do Well* was a three-year initiative by the Council in 2004 for the city and placed Hull quite firmly at the centre of the "school food movement" – even before Jamie Oliver – occurring up and down the UK. Hull City Council decided to offer free school meals to all children in 2004; the move was so radical that they needed to obtain "Powers to Innovate" from the Department for Education and Skills (DfES) to implement it.

It was a complex initiative, operating on many levels and involving different types of interventions, including free, healthy breakfast, dinner and after-school snack and fruit for approximately 25,000 children up to Key Stage 2. These interventions were rolled out systematically into schools at different times and in different ways. Underpinning the programme was the relationship between healthy eating and academic attainment, with the extension of free school meals compounded by a reinforcing curricular approach to healthy eating.

The study was interesting for many reasons: the evaluation of the experiment concluded that those children originally entitled to receive free school meals, eating habits and questionnaire responses did not differ from those who were not initially eligible, meaning that the two groups are, in fact, homogeneous. This finding informed the recommendation from the study that for nutritional reasons, if one group is eligible for free school meals, then all should be. The study also reported teaching staff noticing differences in all areas of children's behaviour, particularly in relation to children's energy levels and tiredness and academic performance (Colquhoun et al., 2008). From a policy viewpoint, the interesting issue was the lack of central government support and the lack of local government support at the end of the three-year evaluated pilot: a new Liberal Democrat local-controlled council decided not to continue the initiative.

Enabling Acts

The Education Act, 2002, made provision for local authorities to suspend statutory requirements to introduce innovative measures that contribute to raising educational standards serving as the precursor to the introduction of breakfast clubs (Glew, 2004).

The *Choosing Health* (2004) White Paper included a commitment to improving the nutritional profile of school food by reducing the consumption of fat, sugar and salt and increasing the consumption of fruit, vegetables and other nutrients of public health interest. The commitment extended to addressing the healthfulness of foods offered across the school day – breakfast clubs, vending machines, tuck shops and so forth – via a whole-school approach to school food, whereby pupils have ample opportunity to learn about food and nutrition in the school curriculum in ways that are consistent and self-reinforcing (Harvey, 2000) with lunches and other food provision in schools. The follow up paper, *Delivering Choosing Health*, in 2005, provided additional commitment to consider nutrition specification within school food procurement, strengthen the Healthy Schools programme and provide training for catering staff, parents and school governors in respect of school food and healthy eating. The subsequent *Food in Schools* programme in England was introduced to support a whole-school approach to food in school settings.

The School Food Plan

In 2005, British chef Jamie Oliver presented a television series called *Jamie's School Dinners* which sought to improve the nutritional quality of school dinners in one English school. He showcased where improvements could and should be made, and his work led to a broader campaign (*Feed Me Better*) which sought to improve school dinners on a national scale. Subsequently, the Department for Education and Skills established the *School Food Trust* in 2005 as a nondepartmental public body with the aim to provide support and advice to school administrators to improve the standard of school meals.

There was much commentary at the time about how school meals were created for an average ingredient spend. A Soil Association report in 2003 found that, on average, 35p a head was spent on school meals compared with the 60p a head then spent on prison food (Soil Association, 2003), and Jeanette Orrey's[1] declaration in 2004 that at least 70p per pupil per day is the minimum that needs to be spent on the basic food ingredients for a truly nutritious school meal (Morgan, 2004). The School Meals Review Panel in 2005 compared the government's suggested minima of 50p (primary) and 60p (secondary) compared with prisoners' meals with an average food cost of £1.87 per prisoner per day on food (School Meals Review Panel, 2005; National Audit Office, 2006). The expenditure on school meal ingredients is particularly stark when you consider that across the UK, the NHS spent £6.1 billion on overweight and obesity-related ill health in 2014–2015 (projected to reach £9.7 billion by 2050) with the overall cost of obesity to wider society estimated to be £27 billion and projected to reach £49.9 billion per year by 2050 (Public Health England, 2017).

The School Food Plan was published by the Department for Education in July 2013 (Dimbleby & Vincent, 2013). It set out 17 actions for head teachers, industry, the catering service, parents and the government to transform what children eat in schools and how they learn about food. A key problem with the Plan is the lack of expert follow-up and monitoring. The standards are robust but need to be checked in practice. The re-introduction of school food standards in

---

1   Jeanette Orrey is a former dinner lady and children's food campaigner.

the UK has not been centrally coordinated, but by September 2013, they were made compulsory across all four countries in the UK, except in England where academies are now exempt. The 2021 National Food Strategy report pointed out the problems with a lack of monitoring and enforcement of the standards (Dimbleby, 2021).

Despite school meals and the introduction and revision of nutritional standards, at a UN public health meeting in 2011, no UN member states showed major progress in the reduction of obesity (Swinburn et al., 2011). A principal area of concern remains the availability of snacks and drinks sold in schools which contributes to higher total calorie intakes, soft drinks and fat and lower intakes of fruit, vegetables, milk and key nutrients (Story et al., 2009). The matter, of course, is complex as schools are not islands but surrounded by food and food choices. The term "school foodshed" has been used to describe this phenomenon (Caraher et al., 2014, 2016). It raises the point that school policy cannot solve all the problems around healthy eating for young people.

Monitoring nutritional standards

Much of the monitoring of school meals concerns hygiene, health and safety with little consideration of nutrition, reflecting at the time the enforceable requirements of health and safety legislation. By 1992, very few local education authorities had employed a nutritionist to inform food procurement, yet the Caroline Walker Trust stated the cruciality of monitoring the implementation of the school meals nutritional standards to ensure they are being met. However, the inception of the World Health Organization's (WHO) Health Promoting School Model changed this, and school food standards have been monitored variously by school inspectors, Nutritional Associates, school meal advisors, catering staff and the Public Health Agency in Northern Ireland.

The focus is now firmly towards the integration of health and sustainability, since school meals provide the opportunity to strive to achieve nutrition through sustainable diets – a move that has been termed the *Double Dividend* – a later section refers to this in more detail (Pearce et al., 2005).

The importance of the school lunchtime environment

There is a school of thought in the published literature that mealtimes are a social occasion (Husby et al., 2009). Individuals, including children, do not make food choices in a social vacuum; they are likely to be influenced both by those around them and the food environment (Shepherd & Dennison, 1996; Caraher et al., 2016). Therefore, the marketing of foods and the social environment in which school children eat their midday meal will be important in determining their choice of food and whether they consume a healthy meal. It should be noted however that education services should be mindful of commercial sponsorship, and Scotland in particular encouraged schools to de-brand their service (Scottish Executive's Expert Panel, 2003).

A 2001 report by the Child Poverty Action Group (CPAG) investigated how the uptake of free school meals could be improved and provided some stark data on how free school meal recipients were distinguishable from and sat apart from their cash-paying counterparts, and recounted instances when the free school meal ticket did not cover the cost of a basic meal resulting in children returning food they could not afford (Riley, 2004, p. 18).

Previous government-sponsored research has concluded that development of whole-school food policies allows consistent health promotion messages to be generated (School Food Trust, 2012). A school food policy is an essential element of the whole-school approach which should state how schools' food provision (including school lunches and other food in schools provision, including breakfast clubs, vending machines, tuck shops and after-school clubs) are consistent with and reinforce classroom-based lessons continuing food and health messaging. Additional means to inform how to make school meals successful include the merits of establishing a school council or school nutrition action group to facilitate consultation with the children and young people using the school meals service as a key audience of the school community and the ultimate consumers of the decision-making outcome (Townsend et al., 2011; Townsend, 2015; Food Foundation, 2020a).

Other key developments: England

The focus of school meals in England in recent times has emphasised the lack of provision during school holidays. Such "holiday hunger" has been campaigned against throughout the 2000s with commentators calling for food, cash transfers and activities when school is not in session to maintain children's nutrition and learning attainment outside of school (Naik, 2008; Pike & Kelly, 2014).

In the immediate period of lockdown during the COVID-19 pandemic (since 23 March 2020), different stakeholders (e.g. the Food Foundation) called for free school meals to be extended during schools' closures. The Department for Education in England established an electronic voucher system to enable eligible families usually in receipt of free school meals to exchange vouchers for food at selected supermarket chains. The scheme has had its critics because of the delay in introducing the scheme and the difficulty some families have experienced in accessing the electronic system and using their vouchers at their supermarket of choice, including discount supermarkets, which may not participate in the scheme. In addition, the scheme was not anticipated to extend beyond the school term. Meanwhile, devolved education authorities in Scotland, Wales and Northern Ireland instead opted for cash transfers, food parcels and other systems that have "provided poor families with food more quickly, effectively, and in a more dignified manner than the national government's voucher system" (Human Rights Watch UK, 2020).

The Food Foundation's food insecurity and COVID-19 research found that 200,000 children had missed meals during the pandemic (Food Foundation, 2020d). The first tranche of Food Foundation data (7–9 April 2020) reported that 18% of respondents had children entitled to receive free school meals. During early lockdown, 45% of these families expected to receive vouchers to purchase food; 16% reported that food was being prepared for them to collect; and 14% reported that prepared food would be delivered to them. Worryingly, 33% reported receiving no substitute for free school meals during early lockdown. Furthermore, 17% reported that the replacement scheme would not continue over the Easter holidays and 21% did not know. In May 2020, 500,000 children who were having free school meals before lockdown were still not receiving a substitute. However, according to a later Food Foundation report, children's food insecurity has improved since April 2020, suggesting that school food holiday vouchers, additional support to universal credit (UC) and the furlough scheme have helped vulnerable families (Food Foundation, 2020b).

English Premier League footballer Marcus Rashford (see more on him in Chapter 11), who himself had experienced poverty in his childhood, wrote an open letter to Members of Parliament in June 2020 pleading that no child should go to bed hungry. In his letter, he documented his family's reliance on breakfast clubs, free school meals, food banks and similar coping strategies adopted by so many experiencing food insecurity when they turn to their family, friends and neighbours to supplement their food supplies. More than 1.3 million children in England receive free school meals. When this important food source disappears every school holiday, it is estimated that one-quarter of these families are left with the unenviable situation of striving to feed their child from already limited resources. The COVID-19 crisis introduced further school closures, with many more being left vulnerable.

In light of successful campaigning by Rashford and others, in November 2020, the UK government committed to extending free school meals and holiday activities for children from low-income families during Easter, summer and Christmas breaks in England into 2021 (Siddique, 2020). These are short-term U-turns by the government and do not represent permanent changes in policy – something for which Rashford had been campaigning.

Families of children eligible to receive free school meals in England were provided with food parcels following school closures as a result of the Coronavirus pandemic. The Department for Education approved a food parcels first approach to replace free school meals. However, in January 2021, an indignant parent posted images of the school food parcels that were reported to be intended to sustain her child for five days. The nutritional status and quantity of food provided by the contractor fell short of quantitative and qualitative nutritional standards, leading to public outrage and a return to the National Voucher Scheme introduced initially by the Department for Education. For more information on England's School Meals, refer to Bremner and Defeyter (2022).

In late 2022, the Food Standards Agency in partnership with the Department for Education launched a School Food Standards Compliance pilot across 18 participating local authorities in England. Its purpose is to test a new approach in supporting schools' efforts to comply with the existing School Food Standards. Where non-compliances are identified, Local Authorities will work with schools to instigate supportive interventions to help achieve full menu compliance (FSA, 2022a).

Other key developments: Scotland

In 2003, the Scottish Executive accepted the Expert Panel on School Meals' recommendation on the need for nutritional standards and access to free, fresh, chilled drinking water, and the principle of universal free meal provision was accepted with respect to providing free fruit to all pupils in the first two years of their primary education. Additionally, Her Majesty's Inspectorate of Education became responsible for monitoring and evaluating the implementation of the *Hungry for Success* strategy confirmed in amending orders in 2008. In Scotland, school holiday provision was provided up to Easter 2021 to replace free school meals during COVID-19 lockdowns and school closures. For more information on Scotland's School Meals, refer to Brennan et al. (2022).

Other key developments: Northern Ireland

The Department of Education in Northern Ireland specifies that every school should have a food in school policy which adopts the principle of consistency to reinforce healthy eating and healthy lifestyle policies. The Education and Training Inspectorate's 2002 *Health Education Survey* emphasised the merit in involving the whole-school community in food in school policy drafting (Education and Training Inspectorate, 2002), and in 2013, the Department of Education in Northern Ireland published whole-school food policy guidelines.

School meals play an important part in improving the health of children, and as outlined in the Food and Nutrition Strategy for Northern Ireland, "influencing the eating patterns of children and young people offers the potential to improve the health of the population in both the short-term and the long-term" (Health Promotion Agency for Northern Ireland, 1996).

England established compulsory food standards in April 2001, but by 2002 Northern Ireland had no compulsory nutritional standards for school meals – although nutritional guidelines had existed for some time in the primary and special education sectors, while the secondary sector required food to be available that was "adequate in quantity and quality so as to constitute a nutritionally balanced meal" (Department of Education, 2002, p. 2). The Department of Education in Northern Ireland consulted on the creation and implementation of compulsory nutritional standards in 2002, pursuant to the Health Promotion Agency's commissioned research into the eating behaviours of Northern Ireland's children that concluded cause for concern. For example, the healthy eating message was being misinterpreted with a large proportion of adolescent girls admitting to consciously following a weight-restricting diet by decreasing their meat and dairy consumption and simultaneously avoiding advantageous sources of calcium and iron. The same research concluded paradoxically how 40% of children of school age ate savoury snacks at least once a day.

These nutritional standards were realised in the framework *Catering for Healthier Lifestyles* (Department of Education, 2002), wherein the recommendations were based on the categories of the then "Balance of Good Health" (now called the *Eatwell Guide*) (Scarborough et al., 2016). The Standards required that children should have access to a variety of foods from each food group over each week's menu with associated minimum and maximum allowances: bread, potatoes, rice, pasta, noodles and cereals; fruit and vegetables; milk and milk products; meat, fish and alternatives; foods containing fat and foods containing sugar; and access to free, fresh drinking water as a healthy alternative to sugary drinks. The standards were made compulsory from the autumn term of 2005 after a successful pilot in 2003–2004 across 100 schools.

The standards were monitored by the Education and Training Inspectorate which published an evaluation report in 2007, concluding that:

> [W]hilst a majority of schools are making good, or very good, progress towards achieving the food-based nutritional standards, there remain a number of important areas in menu planning where these standards are not being met … relating to the frequency of the availability of fried potato products and garlic bread, and the extent to which menus are balanced nutritionally.
>
> (Education and Training Inspectorate, 2007, pp. 2–4)

Revised nutritional standards for school lunches were introduced in September 2007 for Northern Ireland, while standards for other food and drinks in schools were launched in April 2008 through the *School Food: Top Marks* programme (Department of Education, 2009). These standards formed part of the Department of Education's contribution to the cross-departmental *Investing for Health* and *Fit Futures* initiatives (Department of Health, Social Services and Public Safety, 2002, Department of Health, Social Services and Public Safety, 2006). An evaluation of progress made towards their implementation reported how:

> [W]hilst most schools are making outstanding, or very good, progress towards achieving aspects of the new food-based nutritional standards, there remain a number of important areas in menu planning where these standards are not being met.… These important menu concerns should continue to be addressed, particularly those relating to the: high frequency and availability with which deep-fried foods or other high fat products are served; availability of lower-fat desserts with high fat foods; use of high fat / sugar toppings; and competitive marketing and attractive presentation of healthier options on days when meat products are available.
>
> (Education and Training Inspectorate, 2010)

From 2010, it has been the responsibility of the Education Authority to monitor nutritional standards. In 2014, the Public Health Agency concluded that:

> Schools should ensure that food and drinks sold in vending machines and tuck shops comply with the nutritional standards. ... It is recommended that more regular monitoring of school activity in this area is introduced, considering the role of school catering service and what additional sanction (if any) could be applied to those schools that contravene the standards.
>
> (Gilmore et al., 2010, p. 7)

More recently (during COVID-19 restrictions), the Department of Education in Northern Ireland announced that a cash substitute would be paid directly into parents' bank accounts to replace free school meals entitlement during term-time lockdown and the school summer holidays. The Northern Ireland Executive has pledged to provide free school meals during holidays until March 2023 (BBC News, 2022). Families receive £2.70 per child per day for each day of term the schools are closed, payable on a fortnightly basis. Early reports indicated that the first direct payments were distributed during the week commencing 30 March 2020. This approach has been lauded as progressive with no restrictions on use, as witnessed by the voucher scheme implanted in England during COVID-19. For more information on Northern Ireland's School Meals, refer to Furey and Woodside (2022).

Other key developments: Wales

The Healthy Eating in Schools (Wales) Measure 2009 succeeds the Welsh government's *Appetite for Life* guidelines and makes provision for local authorities and governing bodies to regulate food and drink provided to pupils on school premises and promote healthy eating by pupils in maintained schools. The Measure requires the provision of free drinking water, promotion of free school meals and milk to those eligible to receive them and discretion in the administration of free school meals to ensure that children entitled to receive them are not identifiable. Compliance with the Measure is monitored by governing bodies providing information in their annual report on the action taken to promote healthy eating and drinking by pupils at their schools. The Measure also places a duty on the Chief Inspector of Education and Training in Wales to apprise Ministers about the actions taken to promote healthy eating and drinking at maintained schools by school governing bodies, including consultation with pupils.

The Healthy Eating in Schools (Nutritional Standards and Requirement) Regulations 2013 ("the Healthy Eating Regulations") have been implemented since September 2013 and detail the nutritional guidelines for Welsh school food, including breakfast clubs, lunches, drinking water, and other food and drink provided during the school day (e.g. tuck shops and vending machines).

The School Standards and Organisation (Wales) Act 2013 requires that primary schools provide free breakfast to children who request it. Breakfast foods must be compliant with the Free Breakfast in Primary Schools statutory guidance which states that food choices are selected from the four main food groups: milk-based drinks or yoghurts, cereals, fruit and vegetables and bread and toppings.

Pupils should be given the opportunity to choose from the four main food groups at lunchtime: meat, fish, poultry and vegetarian equivalents, fruit and vegetables, starchy carbohydrates and dairy foods and milk. There are restrictions on the frequency of offering meat products, fried foods, cakes and biscuits, with confectionery and savoury snacks excluded entirely from food options.

Children whose parents claim UC from 1 April 2019 are assessed using an annualised net earned income threshold of £7,400 to assess their free school meals' status. In Scotland and England, all school-aged children in the first three years of education receive a non-means-tested free school meal, irrespective of income. In Northern Ireland, the current earnings threshold for those in receipt of UC is set much higher at £14,000, thereby serving to support more working families (Child Poverty Action Group, 2020). Eligibility for free school meals in Wales is means-tested for children whose parents' annual income does not exceed £16,190. The CPAG has called for the expansion of eligibility of free school meals and estimated that providing a daily lunchtime meal to every child in school, as happens currently in Scotland and England, would cost the Welsh government an additional £130 million per year in addition to the current status quo of means-tested free school meals (Child Poverty Action Group, 2020).

In Wales, the provision of free school meals during holidays has been extended by a year to replace school lunches during the Coronavirus pandemic. Moves are afoot to introduce Universal free school meals in Wales; as of September 2022, universal primary free school meals for all primary school children are being rolled out in a stepwise fashion, starting with the youngest. By 2024, all primary school-aged children will be in receipt of free school meals. For more information on Wales' School Meals, refer to Brophy and Wooley (2022).

Double dividend of health and sustainability

As well as the additional social impacts of the school lunch, there are arguments for the food served being sustainable in terms of supply and reflecting local and seasonal products. The Sustainable Consumption Roundtable's report highlighted parents' call for school meals to set a better example and encourage children to eat a more nutritious diet (Pearce et al., 2005). The devising of new nutritional standards for school meals made reference to the value of seasonality, the inclusion of better quality meat eaten in moderation and avoided recommending an unsustainable level of fish (particularly oily fish) consumption. Researchers refer to this as the "double dividend", contributing to health and sustainability through better nutrition from more sustainable diets. Fortunately, relying on a lower proportion of higher quality meat, reducing reliance on higher priced processed meat and increasing the use of seasonal foods with fewer air miles may offset the additional costs of school caterers cooking from scratch. The preceding Caroline Walker Trust Expert Panel report (Crawley, 2005) recommended a minimum ingredient spend of 70p per primary school meal and 80p per secondary school meal, which accords with Morgan's 2004 estimation regarding required school food investment (Morgan, 2004). Indeed, the *Soil Association's Food for Life Partnership Caterers Circle* estimates that an average take-up levels between 55% and 60% are needed before school meals services can break even and become self-financing (Morgan, 2013). The Sustainable Consumption Roundtable report concurs that this expenditure on ingredients would deliver the double dividend (Pearce et al., 2005). This is particularly true if procurement were extended into hospitals, prisons and wider public sector catering, thereby helping deliver economies of scale and supporting the government in the achievement of its sustainable procurement objectives.

Along with the social impact, it might be considered to be a triple dividend, given how the nourishment of children can encourage their maturing into adults who value a sustainable, balanced diet and all the benefits this can bring in terms of our food culture and future public health and productivity.

The children's future food inquiry

Morgan and Sonnino (2007) pleaded for the consumers' voice (parents and children) to be heard in food in schools' policymaking and implementation. They cited a 2002 industry survey that concluded only 27% of school children had been consulted about school meals in the previous year, rising to 53% where the school had a food group (at a time when only 12% of schools had such a group). This is concerning because non-inclusion of consumer groups in consultations about matters that affect them has repercussions for their ultimate buy-in to any ensuing policy that may be delivered. Parents and children should be actively involved in food in schools matters and be empowered to learn to view and value food differently (Harvey, 2000). The importance of listening to and hearing the voice of children and young people was made clear in the Children's Future Food Inquiry (Food Foundation, 2018). The Inquiry was the first attempt to systematically seek the views of children and young people living in poverty across the UK. The Inquiry's 15 young "Food Ambassadors" (aged between 10 and 18), acting as "courageous human rights defenders" (Food Foundation, 2020a, p. 17), articulated their vision for improving access to nutritious food in the UK. An estimated 3.9 million children are living in poverty in the UK. However, we know little about how many of these children experience food insecurity, how it impacts their lives and what could be done about it. Between 1 April 2022 and 30 September 2022, food banks in the Trussell Trust's UK-wide network distributed 1.3 million food parcels to people facing hardship, representing an increase of 52% compared to the same period in 2019. Half a million of these parcels were distributed to children. Between 1 April 2018 and 31 March 2019, the Trussell Trust's food bank network reported distributing 1.6 million three-day emergency food supplies to people in crisis, a 19% increase from the previous year. More than half a million of these went to children (Trussell Trust, 2022).

Meanwhile, popular media sources report how teachers are using their own money to buy food and clothes for their poverty-stricken pupils. A Scottish media story outlined evidence from the NASUWT teachers' union's submission to Holyrood's Education Committee that increasing numbers of children were given food, clothes and equipment by staff at their own expense (BBC News Scotland, 2016). Seventy-one per cent of teachers had seen pupils coming to school hungry, while 81% noticed youngsters attending classes without the correct equipment. A further 79% were concerned about students lacking in energy and struggling to concentrate because of a poor diet.

With the implementation of UC and associated changes to the eligibility criteria for free school meals entitlement, it is anticipated that up to 2.6 million children whose parents are on benefits could be missing out on free school meals by 2022 (Willcock, 2018). Before the introduction of UC, all children of benefit recipients – who were all unemployed – were eligible for free school meals, but in April 2018 the criteria were tightened based on income. The Children's Society reported that once a family with one child passes the £7,400 threshold allowed under UC, they would need to earn £1,124 a year more (the equivalent of working 2.4 hours more each week at national living wage) to make up for the loss in free school meals (Children's' Society, 2018), so linking benefits such as free school meals and Healthy Start to changes in UC are also important (Caraher & Furey, 2018, p. 68). For example, in Northern Ireland, the net earnings threshold is £16,190 (NI Direct, 2023) and the Food Foundation (2020a) has called for the extension of free school meals to more children in need by applying the income threshold of £14,000 per year used in Northern Ireland to the rest of the UK to allow more children to qualify.

UK statistics suggest that before the introduction of universal infant free school meals in Scotland and England, 1.7 million children were eligible for free school meals on the basis of their family income – fewer than those living in poverty but many more than those receiving food parcels (Royston, 2017, Food Foundation, 2018). Many of the 3.9 million children living in poverty are either not claiming or not eligible for free school meals (Caraher & Furey, 2018). Consequently, it is logical to assume that there are substantial numbers of children who are experiencing or at serious risk of experiencing food insecurity that do not receive any support through the existing mechanisms. Thankfully, the devolved regions of the UK are now at least exploring universal free school meals.

Gilmore et al. reported parental and pupil concerns pertaining to the cost of school food (Gilmore et al., 2010). This issue remains current with the Children's Future Food Inquiry report, including the experience of a working couple on minimum wage who "find the cost of school meals impossible to afford for much of the school year. They prioritise paying for them in the coldest months so that their children have a hot meal instead of a packed lunch" (Food Foundation, 2018, p. 45). Similarly, the Children's Right to Food Campaign included in its Children's Food Charter the policy call to "Increase the free school meal allowance for secondary school children: raise the £2.70 currently allocated per meal per child to £4.00" (Food Foundation, 2020a).

Holiday hunger and educational attainment

The evidence suggests that child food poverty exists and potentially affects millions of children, but that nature, extent and effects of child food insecurity are poorly understood. Poverty and food poverty in children may have implications for educational attendance, engagement, attainment and progression. Children who are hungry in class cannot concentrate or may be disruptive. In addition, the long summer holidays are estimated to result in weeks of learning loss for some children due to the cumulative and compounding effect of social isolation, low levels of stimulation and activity and poor diets. Indeed, research suggests that cognitive functions are more vulnerable in poorly nourished children (Simeon & Grantham-McGregor, 1989).

Nutritious school food provision enabling educational attainment is important because it can determine future trajectories of children's lives, breaking cyclical and intra-generational poverty. It can prevent short-term hunger that impacts negatively on children's memories, attention spans, visual perception, problem-solving skills, creativity, information processing and coding abilities and physical exercise endurance. Healthy school meals can establish healthy dietary practices that pervade throughout life (Simeon & Grantham-McGregor, 1989).

Holiday hunger typically occurs in lower-income households with school-aged children and is characterised by food insecurity during the school holidays (Foster, 2018, Graham et al., 2019, Wall, 2019). The summer school holiday is the single longest school break of the year, where eligible households previously in receipt of a free school meal find themselves going without for concentrated periods of time. Therefore, holiday hunger represents an additional stressor to parents who must find and resource alternative ways to feed their children when not in school (Gooseman et al., 2019).

Schools (typically through government-supported programmes) provide free school meals to children from low-income families to help them meet dietary requirements during the school year and not during the school holidays (this changed during COVID-19). This situation means that food insecurity for such families in the UK is a transitional experience influenced by the seasons.

Shinwell and Defeyter (2017) set out a useful context of existing literature about learning loss outside school terms. Their paper describes how the majority of summer learning loss research has been USA-specific, with research in Europe in its infancy (Verachtert et al., 2009, Paechter et al., 2015). This has fuelled suggestions that summer learning loss is exclusive to the

USA where the school holiday period is longer than that of other countries, and therefore such dramatic losses should not be evident elsewhere in relation to skills and knowledge (Wiseman & Baker, 2012, Shinwell & Defeyter, 2017). However, European studies have demonstrated that although holidays are shorter in Europe, summer learning loss is a phenomenon that is relevant also in the European context (Lindahl, 2001, Verachtert et al., 2009, Paechter et al., 2015). Shinwell and Defeyter's research (2017) concluded in the UK context how, after a summer break of seven weeks, summer learning loss occurred or at least stagnation in learning in relation to spelling in a population of primary school-aged children attending schools in areas of low socio-economic status. However, performance had improved beyond the baseline reported immediately before the summer break after seven weeks of teaching. With the COVID-19 emergency and the shutting of schools for extended periods, adequate nutrition and increases in learning inequalities are both evident.

Hospitals, prisons and wider public sector catering

Public sector catering is a significant player in the food chain, feeding approximately 25% (one in four) of the population accounting for pupils, patients, prisoners, students, care home residents and service personnel in the UK (Public Sector Catering, 2020).

Diet and health are inextricably linked. Food is essential for life, and when people are unwell, food is an important adjunct support to enable them to recover more quickly. Often, patients are admitted to hospital already malnourished. There have been media articles about patient complaints about hospital food and comparisons drawn between the food spent per patient being comparable to that for prisoners stating that "it is difficult to see how the needs of the most unwell in our society can be met at the same cost of £3 per day" (Johnston, 2016). (In respect of prisoners, they are fed three meals per day to include breakfast, lunch and evening meal and drinking water freely available at all times. There is free choice with special diets for cultural and nutritional needs, including religious or health reasons and vegetarian and vegan diets accommodated. The ability to choose is particularly important in locations where the food and meals provided are the sole or primary source of sustenance, particularly over extended periods of detention (Edwards et al., 2007).

The Hospital Food Standards Panel was set up when there were no national mandatory standards for hospital food in England; the food offer was inconsistent across hospitals and diet-related ill health was concerning at the population level. The Panel's remit was to examine existing food standards and advise on how they should be applied, monitored and reported. In 2014, the Panel reported its required standards and recommendations for flavour, taste and presentation so that patients may receive food they can ultimately enjoy. Recommendations focused on the development of a Food and Drink Strategy for patients' nutritional care and the embedding of sustainability as a principle. As of 1 April 2015, the Panel's recommendations have been mandated through the NHS Standard Contract. In terms of monitoring standards, the Soil Association's Food for Life Catering Mark rewards excellence in hospital food (Department of Health, 2014).

In Wales, the *All Wales Nutrition and Catering Standards for Food and Fluid Provision for Hospital Inpatients* apply. They aim to equate the provision of food to the same importance as medication and provide menus that meet the nutritional requirements of the diverse patient population via nutrient- and food-based standards for meals, snacks and fluid that offer patients choice (Welsh Government, 2011). Wales also has Health Promoting Hospital Vending Directions and Guidance to NHS Trusts since 2008 (Welsh Government, 2019). The Guidance was informed by the UK government's nutrient criteria for front-of-pack nutrition labels of pre-packed foods to determine which products may be available. However, a freedom of information request in 2021 uncovered how less healthy foods were still available in Welsh hospitals (Wightwick, 2021).

In Scotland, the ambition is for a person-centred approach where patients receive food that reflects their nutritional needs and meets established nutritional standards. The *Food in Hospitals Catering and Nutrition Specification* "advocates greater use of fresh, seasonal, local and sustainable produce and Procurement Reforms which recognise the purchase of food to improve the health, wellbeing and education of communities in an authority's area, and promote the highest standards of animal welfare" (NHS Scotland, 2016, p. 3).

In Northern Ireland, *Promoting Good Nutrition: A Strategy for Good Nutritional Care for Adults in all Care Settings in Northern Ireland* was launched by the Minister for Health in 2011. This is complemented by *Minimum Nutritional Standards in Catering for Health and Social Care* (Food Standards Agency, Safe Food and the Public Health Agency, 2017). More broadly, again, the Food Standards Agency and local councils are developing nutritional standards, vending standards and procurement guidance for use in council catering establishments. The aim is ultimately to roll out nutritional standards across the wider public sector in Northern Ireland (FSA, 2022b).

As discussed in Chapters 6 and 11, the role of celebrities in food policy has been significant. This is no less true in hospital food where different television chefs, for example, Loyd Grossman's Better Hospital Food Programme (2001), Heston Blumenthal (2010), James Martin's Operation Hospital Food (2012) and Prue Leith (2019), have variously sought to advise government reviews into the quality of hospital food to overhaul the food offer in hospitals.

The most recent NHS hospital food review (published in 2020), headed by Prue Leith, has culminated in a new blueprint for hospital food with recommendations to provide patients with the right food for recovery, including facilitating a 24/7 hospital kitchen service, introducing digital menus and food ordering systems to consider patients' dietary and cultural requirements and nutritional needs; agreeing to national professional standards for NHS chefs with mandatory professional development and allergen training; and increasing the role of (allied) medical staff to ensure that nutritious meals are part of a patient's recovery plan (Department of Health and Social Care, 2020).

As with school food, the public sector generally is striving towards more sustainable procurement policies. The World Summit on Sustainable Development in 2002 called for the promotion of "public procurement policies that encourage development and diffusion of environmentally sound goods and services". The UK government has stated its goal to be a leader on sustainable procurement by 2009 (DEFRA, 2005). This is important because the government can often be the single biggest customer within a country, with the purchasing power to influence the behaviour of private sector organisations (Walker & Brammer, 2009).

Conclusion

There needs to be greater emphasis on the idea of healthy food as a matter of rights and the rights of children to an adequate, appropriate and affordable food supply and there needs to be recognition of food security in the family or household's situation and acknowledgement that families moving to work often end up in employment which is insecure and lacks the guarantee of a regular income, that is, the gig economy (Caraher & Furey, 2018). A simple solution is the extension of free school meals to all on UC and a broader recognition of the existence of food poverty (Royston, 2017). School meals are currently a targeted benefit. There are additional arguments for making school meals free for all or universal on the basis that this addresses stigma and that the costs of provision, if handled correctly, will be outweighed by the long-term health and educational benefits (Morelli & Seaman, 2004, Poppendieck, 2010). Additionally, the role of food in the whole of the school day could be considered, so breakfast and after school clubs could come under the remit of state-supported food provision rather than relying on volunteers, food donations and charity.

From a policy perspective, there is support across political spectrums for school food provision. The devil is in the detail: there needs to be a discussion on the provisions of universal free meals without the focus remaining on extending the entitlement. This is often linked to costs without balancing the short-term costs against long-term savings in health and other social costs (Morelli & Seaman, 2004). It is also important not to elevate school meal provision to being the only solution; it is clearly important and a safety net but the lessons of the past need to be learned. During WWII take-up and provision of school food decreased, yet nutrition increased. Some of this was due to children being moved from urban to rural areas because of the risk of bombing. Other reasons for this improvement can be related to the issues of food control exercised by the Ministry of Food ranging from rationing, food price controls, the development of food canteens and a diet which while austere was healthy. Clearly, while rationing and the restrictions that operated during WWII and up until 1954 would not be socially acceptable today, the lessons are that household income needs to be sufficient to afford a healthy and acceptable diet – a cash first approach. Otherwise, school meal provision will have to be expanded to address these gaps.

What has become clear from this chapter is that school meals receive attention in times of crisis or as ways of tackling problems which are beyond the scope of school meals to solve. The other way of viewing school meals is to see them as a right and an essential bulwark in food welfare provision (De Schutter, 2013). This means moving from viewing them as a way of tackling crises such as obesity or holiday hunger and relocating them within the social fabric of schools where they are as essential as formal education provision. Clearly, adequate nutrition is essential for learning but food, as Morgan notes, is "multifunctional"; it can also address issues of eco-sustainability by the fair and local sourcing of food, as has occurred in other countries through creative food procurement (Morgan, 2014).

A key problem in the provision of school meals is the privatisation and outsourcing of the catering to commercial companies (Gustafsson, 2004). In many ways, this has come about because food (and nutrition) is considered another commodity to be addressed and there is a demand for savings, as was seen during the 1920s, and currently with the outsourcing of school catering services. The point is not that outsourcing *per se* is bad, but if we constantly expect companies to provide healthy meals while reducing budgets this is clearly not a viable option for any of the players. Linking school food to wider sourcing initiatives such as closed loop economies, public procurement drives can help save money through the mechanism of bulk buying, encourage local employment and keeping money flowing in local economies (Morgan, 2014). This problem cannot be solved by simply increasing public procurement services; economies of scale can be achieved by linking the procurement activities of various public bodies (hospitals, prisons, health and social care settings etc.), as this gives them more power in the marketplace. But more money needs to be spent on the area to ensure quality and acceptance of the food served. The Food Matters report from 2008 reported that "education, healthcare and other public services account for 6% of sales of food service and 29% of meals served outside the home" (Cabinet Office, 2008, p. 19). So, public bodies are providing, directly or indirectly through contracted services, one in four meals in the eating outside the home sector, yet only receive 6% of the total spent in the food service sector. The many reports and dissatisfaction with the quality of these meals shows that investment is needed (Morgan & Sonnino, 2008). Such public procurement could also address the double dividend explored above by linking food sourcing with local growers and producers and creating green-based closed loop or circular economics (Gauci et al., 2017, Alhola et al., 2019, Sönnichsen & Clement, 2020).

We agree with Marcus Rashford's call for a longer look at the role of school food and other charitable food provision: we think the past has some indicators and lessons for what we can do. The 2020/2021 COVID-19 crisis has exposed many of the fault-lines in school meal provision and there is a need to revisit the role, functions and provisions of school food to prepare for the next crisis. Learning from the past, it would appear that the area could benefit from more "food control". Key to this, we suggest, is linking school meal provision with local public health services.

References

Acheson, D. 1998, *Independent Inquiry into Inequalities in Health Report*, HMSO, London.

Alhola, K., Ryding, S.O., Salmenperä, H., Busch, N.J. 2019, "Exploiting the potential of public procurement: opportunities for circular economy", *Journal of Industrial Ecology,* vol. 23, pp. 96–109.

BBC News 2022, *School meals: 'Holiday hunger' payments to continue until March 2023.* Available from: https://www.bbc.co.uk/news/uk-northern-ireland-63321546.

BBC News Scotland 2016, *Pupils 'Come to School Hungry', Says Teacher Union.* Available from: https://www.bbc.co.uk/news/education-35873541.

Bremner, M. & Defeyter, M.A. 2022, *School Food Case Study: England*, School Melas Coalition, London. Available from: https://www.docdroid.net/1xZC6hQ/england-school-food-case-study-final-pdf.

Brennan, M., Jones, J. & McKendrick, J.H. 2022, *School Food Case Study: Scotland*, School Meals Coalition, London. Available from: https://www.docdroid.net/u8cS5tj/scotland-school-food-case-study-final-pdf.

Briley, M. & Mcallaster, M. 2011, "Nutrition and the childcare setting", *Journal of American Dietetic Association*, vol. 111, pp. 1298–1300.

Brophy, S. & Wooley, K. 2022, *School Food Case Study: Wales*, School Meals Coalition, London. Available from: https://www.docdroid.net/tczTEHE/wales-school-food-case-study-final-pdf#page=13.

Cabinet Office 2008, *Food Matters Towards a Strategy for the 21st Century*, Cabinet Office, London.

Caraher, M. & Furey, S. 2018, *The Economics of Emergency Food Aid Provision: A Financial, Social and Cultural Perspective*, Palgrave Macmillan, Cham, Switzerland.

Caraher, M., Lloyd, S. & Madelin, T. 2014, "The 'school foodshed': schools and fast-food outlets in a London borough", *BFJ*, vol. 116, pp. 472–493. https://doi.org/10.1108/BFJ-02-2012-0042

Caraher, M., Lloyd, S., Mansfield, M., Alpm C., Breswster, Z. & Gresham, Z. 2016, "Secondary school pupils' food choices around schools in a London borough: fast food and walls of crisps", *Appetite*, vol. 103, pp. 08–20. https://doi.org/10.1016/j.appet.2016.04.016.

Child Poverty Action Group 2020, *Expanding Eligibility for Free School Meals in Wales: Briefing for MSs and MPs in Wales*, Child Poverty Action Group, London.

Children's' Society 2018. *Universal Credit: One Million Children in Poverty to Miss Out on Free School Meals.* Available from: https://www.childrenssociety.org.uk/news-and-blogs/press-releases/universal-credit-one-million-children-in-poverty-to-miss-out-on-free.

Collingham, L. 2011, *The Taste of War: World War Two and the Battle for Hunger*, Allen Lane, London.

Colquhoun, D., Wright, N., Pike, J., Gatenby, L. 2008, *Evaluation of Eat Well Do Well Kingston Upon Hull's School Meal Initiative*, Centre for Educational Studies Institute for Learning, University of Hull.

Crawley, H. 2005, *Eating Well at School: Nutritional and Practical Guidelines*, Caroline Walker Trust, London.

Department of Education 2002, *Catering for Healthier Lifestyles: Compulsory Nutritional Standards for School Meals*, Department of Education, Bangor.

Department of Education and Department of Health, Social Services and Public Safety 2009, *Health Promotion Agency for Northern Ireland. School Food: Top Marks – Nutritional Standards for School Lunches: Guide for Implementation*, Department of Education, Bangor.

Department of Health 2014, *The Hospital Food Standards Panel's Report on Standards for Food and Drink in NHS Hospitals*, Department of Health, London. Available from: https://assets.publishing.service.gov.uk/government/uploads/system/uploads/attachment_data/file/523049/Hospital_Food_Panel_May_2016.pdf.

Department of Health and Social Care 2020, *Report of the Independent Review of NHS Hospital Food*, Department of Health and Social Care, London. Available from: https://www.gov.uk/government/publications/independent-review-of-nhs-hospital-food.

Department of Health and Social Security 1989, *Report on Health and Social Subjects 36: The Diets of British Schoolchildren. Sub-Committee on Nutritional Surveillance. Committee on Medical Aspects of Food Policy*, Her Majesty's Stationery Office, London.

Department of Health, Social Services and Public Safety 2002, *Investing for Health*, Department of Health, Social Services and Public Safety, Belfast.

Department of Health, Social Services and Public Safety 2006, *Fit Futures: Focus on Food, Activity and Young People*, Department of Health, Social Services and Public Safety Belfast.

De Schutter, O. 2013, "The Right to Food in Times of Crisis" in: *Just Fair Freedom from Hunger: Realising the Right to Food in the UK*, ed. Just Fair, Just Fair, London, pp. 7–11.

Dimbleby, H. 2021, *National Food Strategy, Independent Review: The Plan*, https://www.nationalfoodstrategy.org.

Dimbleby, H. & Vincent, J. 2013, *The School Food Plan*, Department of Education, London.

Education and Training Inspectorate 2010, *Evaluation of the Progress Made in the Implementation of the Food-based Nutritional Standards (School Food: Top Marks) and General Approaches to Promoting Healthy Eating in Schools in Northern Ireland*, Department of Education, Bangor.

Education and Training Inspectorate 2007, *Progress Made in the Implementation of Catering for Healthier Lifestyles and General Approaches to Promoting Healthy Eating in Schools in Northern Ireland*, Department of Education, Bangor.

Education and Training Inspectorate 2002, *Health Education Survey*, Department of Education, Bangor.

Edwards, J.S.A., Hartwell, H.J., Reeve, W.G. & Schafheitle, J. 2007, "The diet of prisoners in England", *BFJ*, vol. 109, no. 3, pp. 216–232. https://doi.org/10.1108/00070700710732547

Egger, L. 2021, *From Food Welfare to Healthy Start: A Social and Economic Perspective*. Unpublished Thesis. City University London, London.

Evans, C.E.L., Cleghorn, C.L., Greenwood, D.C. & Cade, J.E. 2010, "A comparison of British school meals and packed lunches from 1990 to 2007: meta-analysis by lunch type", *British Journal of Nutrition*, vol. 104, pp. 474–487.

Food Foundation 2020a, *Children's right 2 Food Charter 2020. A Plan to Tackle Children's Food Insecurity and Inequalities in Obesity and Protect Every Child's Right to Food*, Food Foundation, London.

Food Foundation 2020b, *COVID-19: Latest Impact on Food*, Food Foundation, London.

Food Foundation 2020c, *New Food Foundation Data: Food Insecurity and Debt are the New Reality Under Lockdown*, Food Foundation, London.

Food Foundation 2020d, *The Impact of Coronavirus on Children's Food*, Food Foundation, London.

Food Foundation 2018, *Children's Future Food Inquiry Report*, Food Foundation, London.

Food Standards Agency 2022a, *HSC Nutritional Standards: Executive Summary*, Food Standards Agency, London. https://www.food.gov.uk/business-guidance/hsc-nutritional-standards-executive-summary.

Food Standards Agency 2022b, *School Food Standards Compliance Pilot Underway in 18 Local Authorities across England*, Food Standards Agency, London. https://www.food.gov.uk/news-alerts/news/school-food-standards-compliance-pilot-underway-in-18-local-authorities-across-england.

Food Standards Agency, Safe Food and the Public Health Agency 2017, *Minimum Nutritional Standards in Catering for Health and Social Care*.

Foster, D. 2018, Holiday hunger should be the shame of this government and it isn't, *The Guardian*, https://www.theguardian.com/society/2018/jul/25/holiday-hunger-shame-government-childrens-clubs.

Furey, S. & Woodside, J. 2022, *School Food Case study: Northern Ireland*, School Meals Coalition, London. Available from: https://www.docdroid.net/SdlqeKC/n-ireland-school-food-case-study-final-pdf.

Gauci, C., Calleja, A. & Furtado, A. 2017, *Public Procurement of Food for Health: Technical Report on the School Setting*, Publications Office of the European Union, Brussels.

Gilmore, G., Gossrau-Breen, D., Macdonald, L., Taylor, L. & McGowan, L. 2010, *School Food: Top Marks. A Summary Report on Food on Schools Research in Northern Ireland*, Public Health Agency, Belfast.

Glew, M. 2004, "Free School Meals in Kingston Upon Hull" in: *Recipe for Change: A Good Practice Guide to School Meals*, eds. C. Hurley & A. Riley, Child Poverty Action Group, London, pp. 8–46.

Gooseman, A., Defeyter, M.A. & Graham, P.L. 2019, "Hunger in the primary school setting: evidence, impacts and solutions according to school staff in the North East of England, UK solutions according to school staff in the North East of England, UK", *International Journal of Primary, Elementary and Early Years Education*, vol. 3, pp. 1–13.

Graham, P., Stretesky, P., Long, M., Mann, E. & Defeyter, M.A. 2019, "Holiday Hunger: Feeding Children During the School Holidays" in: *Feeding Children Inside and Outside the Home*, eds. V. Harman, B. Cappellini & C. Faircloth, Routledge, London, pp. 87–106.

Gupta, R.S., Shuman, S., Taveras, E.M., Kulldorff, M. & Finkelstein, J.A. 2005, "Opportunities for health promotion education in childcare", *Paediatrics*, vol. 116, pp. e499–e505. https://doi.org/10.1542/peds.2005-0467

Gustafsson, U. 2004, "The privatisation of risk in school meals policies", *Health, Risk & Society*, vol. 6, pp. 53–65. https://doi.org/10.1080/1369857042000193048

Harvey, J. 2000, *The Chips are Down: A Guide to Food Policy in Schools*, Caroline Walker Trust, London.

Health Promotion Agency for Northern Ireland 1996, *Eating and Health: A Food and Nutrition Strategy for Northern Ireland*, Health Promotion Agency for Northern Ireland, Belfast.

Higgs, H. 1922, "The Geddes reports and the budget", *The Economic Journal*, vol. 32, pp. 251–264. https://doi.org/10.2307/2223277

H.M. Government 1906, *Education (Provision of Meals) Act 1906*, HM Government, London.

Hollows, J. & Jones, S. 2010, "'At least he's doing something': moral entrepreneurship and individual responsibility in Jamie's Ministry of Food", *European Journal of Cultural Studies*, vol. 13, pp. 307–322. https://doi.org/10.1177/1367549410363197

Human Rights Watch UK 2020, *Children in England Going Hungry with Schools Shut - Uneven UK Approach for Covid-19 Doesn't Guarantee Children's Right to Food*, Human Rights Watch UK, London. https://www.hrw.org/news/2020/05/27/uk-children-england-going-hungry-schools-shut#.

Husby, I., Heitmann, B.L. & O'Doherty, J.K. 2009, "Meals and snacks from the child's perspective: the contribution of qualitative methods to the development of dietary interventions", *Public Health Nutrition*, vol. 12, pp. 739–747.

Johnston, C. 2016, Some NI hospital meals cost no more than prison food to make: new thinking needed?, https://sluggerotoole.com/2016/01/26/some-ni-hospital-meals-cost-no-more-than-prison-food-to-make-new-thinking-needed/#comments.

Kaphingst, K.M. & Story, M. 2008, "Child care as an untapped setting for obesity prevention: state child care licensing regulations related to nutrition, physical activity, and media use for preschool-aged children in the United States", *Preventing Chronic Disease*, vol. 6, pp. 5–13.

Keith, R. 2020, Marcus Rashford: A brief history of free school meals in the UK. *The Conversation*, https://theconversation.com/marcus-rashford-a-brief-history-of-free-school-meals-in-the-uk-140896#comment_2255411.

Le Gros Clark, F. 1948, *Social History of the School Meals Service*, London Council of Social Services, London.

Le Gros Clark, F. 1947, "The elements of food education", *Health Education Journal*, vol. 5, pp. 134–137.

Lindahl, M. 2001, *Summer Learning and the Effect of School: Evidence from Sweden IZA Discussion Paper No. 262*, IZA, Bonn, Germany.

Marmot, M.G. 2010, *Fair Society, Healthy Lives: The Marmot Review*, University College London, London.

McNamara, G. 2004, "Poverty and Nutrition" in: *Recipe for Change: A Good Practice Guide to School Meals*, eds. C. Hurley, A. Riley, Child Poverty Action Group, London, pp. 5–12.

Morelli, C.J. & Seaman, P.T. 2004, *Universal versus Targeted Benefits: The Distributional Effects of Free School Meals*. Dundee Discussion Papers in Economics, University of Dundee, Dundee.

Morgan, K. 2014, "The politics of the public plate: school food and sustainability", *The International Journal of Sociology of Agriculture and Food*, vol. 21, pp. 253–260. https://doi.org/10.48416/ijsaf.v21i3.139

Morgan, K. 2013, Is it the end for school dinners?, Wales Online, https://www.walesonline.co.uk/news/health/end-school-dinners-1855800.

Morgan, K. 2004, *School Meals and Sustainable Food Chains: The Role of Creative Public Procurement*, Caroline Walker Trust, London.

Morgan, K. & Sonnino, R. 2008, *The School Food Revolution: Public Food and the Challenge of Sustainable Development*, Routledge, London.

Morgan, K. & Sonnino, R. 2007, "Empowering consumers: the creative procurement of school meals in Italy and the UK", *International Journal of Consumer Studies*, vol. 31, pp. 19–25.

Naik, A. 2008, "Did Jamie Oliver really put school dinners on the agenda? An examination of the role of the media in policy making", *The Political Quarterly*, vol. 79, pp. 426–433. https://doi.org/10.1111/j.1467-923X.2008.00944.x

National Audit Office 2006, *HM Prison Service Serving Time: Prisoner Diet and Exercise*, National Audit Office, London.

NHS 2023, What you'll get and how to shop, https://www.healthystart.nhs.uk/what-youll-get-and-how-to-shop/.

NHS Scotland 2016, Food in hospitals: national catering and nutrition specification for food and fluid provision in hospitals in Scotland, https://www.nss.nhs.scot/media/1097/1479818118-food-in-hospitals-revised-march-2016.pdf.

NI Direct 2023, *Nutrition and School Lunches*, NI Direct, Belfast, https://www.nidirect.gov.uk/articles/nutrition-and-school-lunches.

Oostindjer, M., Aschemann-Witzel, J., Wang, Q., Skuland, S.E., Egelandsdal, B., Amdam, G.V., Schjoll, A., Pachuki, M.C., Rozin, P., Stein, J., Lengard Almli, V. & van Kleef, E. 2017, "Are school meals a viable and sustainable tool to improve the healthiness and sustainability of children´s diet and food consumption? A cross-national comparative perspective", *Critical Reviews in Food Science and Nutrition*, vol. 57, no. 18, pp. 3942–3958.

Paechter, M., Luttenberger, S., Macher, D., Berding, F., Papousek, I., Weiss, E.M. & Fink, A. 2015, "The Effects of nine-week summer vacation: Losses in mathematics and gains in reading", *Eurasia Journal of Mathematics, Science and Technology Education*, vol. 11, pp. 1399–1413.

Pearce, H., Gren, H. & Noble, E. 2005, *Double Dividend? Promoting Good Nutrition and Sustainable Consumption through Healthy School Meals*, Sustainable Development Commission, Bristol.

Pike, J. & Kelly, P. 2014, *The Moral Geographies of Children, Young People and Food: Beyond Jamie's School Dinners*, Palgrave Macmillan, Basingstoke.

Poppendieck, J. 2010, *Free for All: Fixing School Food in America*, University of California Press, Berkeley.

Public Health England 2017, *Health Matters: Obesity and the Food Environment*, Public Health England, London.

Public Sector Catering 2020, Size of the public sector. Available from: https://www.publicsectorcatering.co.uk/in-depth/size-public-sector.

Riley, A. 2004, "The Role of School Meals in Tackling Child Poverty" in: *Recipe for Change: A Good Practice Guide to School Meals*, eds. C. Hurley, A. Riley, Child Poverty Action Group, London, pp. 13–24.

Royston, S. 2017, *Broken Benefits: What's Gone Wrong with Welfare Reform?*, Policy Press, Bristol.

Scarborough, P., Kaur, A., Cobiac, L., Owens, P., Parlesak, A., Sweeney, K. & Rayner, M. 2016, "Eatwell Guide: Modelling the dietary and cost implications of incorporating new sugar and fibre guidelines", *BMJ Open*, vol. 6, p. e013182. https://doi.org/10.1136/bmjopen-2016-013182

Scottish Executive 2002, *Hungry for Success: A Whole School Approach to School Meals in Scotland*, Final Report of the Expert Panel on School Meals, Scottish Executive, Edinburgh.

Scottish Executive's Expert Panel 2003, *Hungry for Success: A Whole-school Approach to School Meals in Scotland*, Scottish Executive, Edinburgh.

School Food Trust 2012, *Eat Better, Start Better: Voluntary Food and Drink Guidelines for Early Years Settings in England – A Practical Guide*, School Food Trust, London.

School Meals Review Panel 2005, *Turning the Tables: Transforming School Food Main Report A Report on the Development and Implementation of Nutritional Standards for School Lunches*, Department for Education and Skills, London.

Scottish Government 2008, *A Guide to Implementing the Nutritional Requirements for Food and Drink in Schools (Scotland) Regulations 2008*, The Scottish Government, Edinburgh.

Shepherd, R. & Dennison, C.M. 1996, "Influences on adolescent food choice", *Proceedings of the Nutrition Society*, vol. 55, pp. 345–357.

Shinwell, J. & Defeyter, M.A. 2017, "Investigation of summer learning loss in the UK-Implications for holiday club provision", *Frontiers in Public Health*, vol. 5, p. 270. https://doi.org/10.3389/fpubh.2017.00270

Siddique, H. 2020, Marcus Rashford Forces Boris Johnson into second U-turn on child food poverty, *The Guardian*, London, https://www.theguardian.com/education/2020/nov/08/marcus-rashford-forces-boris-johnson-into-second-u-turn-on-child-food-poverty.

Simeon, D.T. & Grantham-McGregor, S. 1989, "Effects of missing breakfast on the cognitive functions of school children of differing nutritional status", *American Journal of Clinical Nutrition*, vol. 49, pp. 646–653.

Sönnichsen, S.D. & Clement, J. 2020, "Review of green and sustainable public procurement: towards circular public procurement", *Journal of Cleaner Production*, vol. 245, p. 118901.

Story, M., Nanney, M.S. & Schwartz, M.B. 2009, "Schools and obesity prevention: creating school environments and policies to promote healthy eating and physical activity", *The Milbank Quarterly*, vol. 87, pp. 71–100.

Street, C. 1999, "Introduction", in: *How Breakfast Clubs Meet Heath, Education and Childcare Needs*, eds. N. Donovan, C. Street, New Policy Institute, London, pp. 1–8.

Stretesky, P.B., Defeyter, M.A., Long, M.A., Ritchie, L.A. & Gill, D.A. 2020, "Holiday hunger and parental stress: evidence from North East England", *Sustainability*, vol. 12, no. 10, p. 4141.

Sustain 2022, Urgent improvements are needed to the healthy start scheme, https://www.sustainweb.org/assets/healthy-start-open-letter-dhsc-dwp-nhsbsa-Dec22.pdf.

Swinburn, B.A., Sacks, G., Hall, K.D., McPherson, K., Finegood, D.T., Moodie, M.L. & Gortmaker, S.L. 2011, "The global obesity pandemic: Shaped by global drivers and local environments", *Lancet*, vol. 378, pp. 804–814.

Tanumihardjo, S.A., Anderson, C., Kaufer-Horwitz, M., Bode, L., Emenaker, N.J., Haqq, A.M, Satia, J.A. Silver, H.J. & Stadler, D.D. 2007, "Poverty, obesity, and malnutrition: an international perspective recognizing the paradox", *Journal of the American Dietetic Association*, vol. 107, pp. 1966–1972. https://doi.org/10.1016/j.jada.2007.08.007

The Caroline Walker Trust 1992, *Expert Report Nutritional Guidelines for School Meals*, The Caroline Walker Trust, London.

Timmins, N. 2017, *The Five Giants: A Biography of the Welfare State*, Harper Collins, London.

Townsend, N. 2015, "Shorter lunch breaks lead secondary-school students to make less healthy dietary choices: multilevel analysis of cross-sectional national survey data", *Public Health Nutrition*, vol. 18, pp. 1626–1634. https://doi.org/10.1017/S1368980014001803

Townsend, N., Murphy, S. & Moore, L. 2011, "The more schools do to promote healthy eating, the healthier the dietary choices by students", *Journal of Epidemiology and Community Health*, vol. 65, pp. 889–895. https://doi.org/10.1136/jech.2010.115600

Trussell Trust 2022, *Mid-Year Stats*, Trussell Trust, Wiltshire. Available from: https://www.trusselltrust.org/news-and-blog/latest-stats/mid-year-stats/.

Verachtert, P., Van Damme, J., Onghena, P. & Ghesquiere, P. 2009, "A seasonal perspective on school effectiveness: evidence from a Flemish longitudinal study in kindergarten and first grade", *School Effectiveness and School Improvement*, vol. 20, pp. 215–233.

Walker, H. & Brammer, S. 2009, Sustainable procurement in the United Kingdom public sector, *Supply Chain Management*, vol. 12, no. 2, pp. 128–113. https://doi.org/10.1108/13598540910941993

Walker, A. & Walker, C. 1987, *The Growing Divide: A Social Audit 1979–1987*, Child Poverty Action Group, London.

Wall, T. 2019, Every day we see really hungry kids. They shouldn't be living like this, *The Guardian*, https://www.theguardian.com/society/2019/aug/14/uk-holiday-hunger-schemes-deprived-children-summer. London.

Warwick, J. 1998, *Food Choices of Young People in Northern Ireland – The Influences and Health Implications*, Unpublished Thesis, University of Ulster, Belfast.

Webb, S. & Webb, B. 1927, *English Poor Law History*, Longmans, Green and Company, London.

Welsh Government 2019, *Health Promoting Hospital Vending Guidance*, https://www.gov.wales/sites/default/files/publications/2019-07/directions-to-local-health-boards-in-wales-and-velindre-national-health-service-trust-2012-no-5-guidance.pdf.

Welsh Government 2011, *All Wales Nutrition and Catering Standards for Food and Fluid Provision for Hospital Inpatients*, http://www.hospitalcaterers.org/media/1158/wales-food-fluid.pdf.

Wightwick, A. 2021, *Hospitals are Still Selling Junk Food 13 Years after Welsh Government Ban*, https://www.walesonline.co.uk/news/health/hospitals-still-selling-junk-food-22582787

Willcock, D. 2018, Universal credit changes will bar 2.6 million children from free school meals, warns labour, *The Independent*, London, https://www.independent.co.uk/news/uk/politics/universal-credit-change-free-school-meals-benefits-labour-angela-rayner-a8380921.html.

Wiseman, A.W. & Baker, D.P. 2012, "The American Summer Learning Gap from an International Perspective" in *Summer Learning Research*, eds. G.D. Borman & M. Boulay, Routledge, New York, pp. 1–295.

10   Food scares, food safety and food fraud from chalk in flour to "horsegate"

Introduction

There has been a long history of food contamination in the UK. The medical journal *The Lancet* used newly developed methods of analytical chemistry to campaign against food adulteration in early editions in the 1850s, leading to the first parliamentary inquiry on food adulteration (Collins, 1993, Wilson, 2008). Food contamination and any health effects had been usually local or regional in nature as food chains were limited in their reach. As industrialisation and urbanisation occurred in the nineteenth century, food chains not only lengthened but foodstuffs also passed through many more hands and processes. In addition, the preparation, transport and storage of food were often primitive, lacking cold storage and clean water. Food policy to tackle adulteration was introduced in the late nineteenth century, but the modern global food system means that food often travels very long distances, back and forth across country borders, and is handled at various stages by many people. This means that the possibilities for contamination and adulteration are myriad. While the food system in the UK is highly sophisticated and operates high hygiene standards, there have still been many instances of food contamination resulting in illness and deaths. From a public and environmental health perspective, the issues of contamination have always been of major importance and generally received a quick response due to the dangers to human health. Food contamination has been identified as a risk in the current global political climate as a terrorist intervention or a weapon of war.

In recent years, scholars have categorised different kinds of criminal activity relating to food under an overall classification of "food crime". Lord, Huisman and Paoli (2022) identified Croall (2007) as the first introduction of this broader concept, which includes:

- Food fraud
- Food poisoning involving food handling violations
- Labelling crimes
- Anti-competitive trading
- Illegal pricing
- Exploitation of workers and migrant labourers and trafficking in food production industries
- Food-related financial crime

Food crimes can lead to harms not only to human, animal and environmental health, but also to individuals' cultural and economic integrity; businesses' reputations and economic viability; and trust in governments, both local and national as well as local, national and transnational regulatory systems.

DOI: 10.4324/9781003260301-10

The origins of food contamination and fraud

Through the ages, the addition of foreign material to food has been ever changing and ever justified by adulterers. Burnett (1989) argues that adulteration was a feature of urbanisation and the separation of consumers from the processes of food production. This separation allowed unscrupulous producers the opportunity for commercial fraud, substituting cheaper, lower nutritional quality ingredients for proper ones. Food shortages and high prices in the late eighteenth century due to fluctuations in wheat supply for a population who had become dependent on wheat bread in preference to rye or barley breads led to a period of food riots (Randall, 2006). Price control and weights and measures laws, enforced through local authorities, were often the solution to local unrest, and the controls were often at the level of local markets and fairs. The purpose of such reforms was to control fraud of both the adulteration of foods and underselling of food. One of the consequences of this was that weights and measures often reflected local standards as opposed to national ones (Hoppit, 1993). Weights and measures were not standardised across the UK until the mid-nineteenth century (Velkar, 2012). A practical response was the establishment of the Victorian covered markets by municipal authorities as public health initiatives designed to bring order to the supply of food to the urban poor (Mitchell, 2018, Martin, 2022). These types of policy response are often referred to as midstream policy (as opposed to upstream or downstream policy) as they seek to tackle the outcome of a problem, not the problem itself.

Thus, there is evidence of historic attempts to assuage the concerns of the public through local pricing and control of food fraud, but little evidence of positive or preventive action at a national level. It is worth noting here parallels to the food riots that broke out in 2008 in Africa and were triggered by the world economic crisis and increases in the price of food, which disproportionately affected countries experiencing greater poverty (Berazneva & Lee, 2013).

During the early part of the nineteenth-century, public health campaigners in the UK argued that the government had a role to play in intervening to improve the lives of those on low incomes. This was in contrast to a "laissez faire" attitude by successive previous governments who had believed citizens were largely responsible for their own fate. The "new public health" of the 1840s which had grown in response to concerns about issues, such as overcrowding, poor living and working conditions, pollution and low-quality housing, arising from mass migration to industrialised cities, also had a concern with food purity and contamination. There were two aspects to this: the first was the fraudulent selling of goods which were not what they claimed to be; the second was the danger to health associated with some of these additions used to bulk out food. These two issues, of course, overlapped. The furtive nature of food fraud meant that scrutiny was less likely. During this period, analytical chemistry was in its infancy and weights and measures, along with volumes and density, were used as proxy measures for contamination and were practical for use in the field. For example, bread and its variations were sold by weight with wheaten bread weighing one and half times as much as a white penny loaf and the lowest quality household bread weighing twice as much (Webb & Webb, 1904).

A pioneer was chemist Frederick Accum, who exposed widespread adulteration of food in his Treatise on Adulterations of Food and Culinary Poisons (1820) leading to widespread calls for reform, and further investigations by Arthur Hill Hassall (1855) in the medical journal *The Lancet* and through Select Committees in the House of Commons. This led directly to the first Adulteration of Food and Drink Act of 1860 (The Adulteration of Food and Drink Act, 1860 Willson, 2008), welcomed by reformers but a compromise due to disagreements over the best policy solution to the problem of adulteration. While food manufacturers were in favour of voluntary reform, radical reformers advocated public analysis of food stuffs with strict penalties for adulterators. Subsequent revisions of the Act in 1872 and 1875 resulted in the Sale of Food and Drugs Act, which included provision for heavy fines or imprisonment (Burnett, 1989) for adulteration injurious to health. Common practices exposed by Accum, Hassall and others included the addition of alum to flour, the addition of thorn leaves to tea and the addition of water or chalk to milk. Modern adulteration practices are often similarly concerned with the substitution of a less-valued good for a higher valued one, for example, increasing the amount of rusk in a beef product as a replacement or adding water to frozen chicken to increase its weight. These are examples of fraud or mis-selling. Such practices do not always have health consequences, although there is the associated problem of lack of scrutiny around hygiene measures as it is an illegal activity and therefore less likely to be examined under normal sanitary or phytosanitary arrangements. More serious are those practices which can lead to illness or even death, as in the case of an *E. coli* food poisoning outbreak in Lanarkshire in 1996 (Bradbury, 1997). Very often, the situation emerges after the food has been on the market or people have become ill. This is a problem that is exacerbated when there is inadequate inspection and testing along the food chain and a lack of staff to do the testing. The privatisation of food testing services and the shift in responsibility to the industry to monitor itself were contributors to a lack of early identification of both the BSE (Bovine Spongiform Encephalopathy) outbreak in cattle and the horsemeat scandal – of which more later in this chapter.

Testing and monitoring of food supplies along the food chain can act as early warning systems and as a deterrent to fraud. A driver for fraud is the constant demand for efficiencies and savings in the food system. This can result in processors and manufacturers taking shortcuts and adding cheap bulk to expensive products.

Upton Sinclair's (1906) fictionalised exposé of the Chicago stockyards and processors *The Jungle* showed the human cost as well as the dangers to health from the slaughtering process. Sinclair alleged that the industry was characterised by ruthless capitalism, even claiming that a processing factory failed to halt production when a worker fell into the machinery. *The Jungle* was a novel, but a scandal erupted on publication, and President Theodore Roosevelt, suspicious of Sinclair's radical agenda, ordered a secret inquiry which not only confirmed Sinclair's account but indicated that he had perhaps understated his case. As a result, US Congress passed the Pure Food and Drugs Act (1906) which, up until then, had been effectively blocked by the industry, leading to the creation of new state institutions to deliver change (Kantor, 1976). The BSE crisis in the UK and Europe is perhaps a modern parallel to Sinclair's *The Jungle* (Lang, 1998, Phillips et al., 2000, van Zwanenberg & Millstone, 2005).

There are generally four main types of contaminants: chemical, microbial, physical and allergenic. Examples of dismembered creatures and their excrement are the unfortunate by-product of growing and harvesting food, and the US Food and Drug Administration (FDA), rather than requiring absence of these, now sets acceptable levels of contaminants on the basis of what is reasonable and non-hazardous. For example, a new term has emerged called "food defects" to encompass this. Such standards could become part of the UK system post-Brexit as bilateral trade agreements are signed.

Common examples of physical contaminants in food businesses include:

- Hair
- Fingernails
- Bandages
- Jewellery
- Broken glass, staples
- Plastic wrap/packaging
- Dirt from unwashed fruit and vegetables
- Pests/pest droppings/rodent hair (US Food and Drugs Administration, 2018)

Meat and food scares

The agri-food revolution of the second half of the twentieth century hinged on generating mass production (scale) and lowering prices to consumers. The assumption was that high cost, poor affordability, output and availability were detrimental to health. Economic efficiency and productivity would deliver both health and public good, with meat being seen as key to health (Desrochers & Shimizu, 2012). Technology has certainly helped deliver some economies of cost and the lowering of prices resulted in consumption rising across populations; what was once the preserve of the rich has become accessible to all. In particular, meat has become less of a "feast" item and something that people expect every day in their diet. However, alongside these developments, food scandals have arisen around meat. This is related not just to increases in the production of meat but the ways in which it is now processed and reaches the consumer. While there is potential to pass off cheap cuts of meat at source (e.g. selling pork as lamb), this fraud is made easier if people consume ready-made or processed foods as the deception becomes easier to hide (Stanton & Scrinis, 2005).

The industrialisation of the meat chain has been beset with a number of scandals as the move from the farm/local slaughterhouse to centralised production and CAFOs (Concentrated Animal Feeding Operation) or mega farms has taken place (Lang et al., 2017). There was a major outbreak of foot-and-mouth disease (FMD), a severe viral disease in livestock which affects cattle, sheep, pigs and goats, in 1967. The disease causes fever and blistering, severely impacting production and leaving surviving animals weak (WOAH, 2023). Since the outbreak in 1967, a major development in the UK food system has been the closure of many local abattoirs resulting in animals being transported longer distances.

Demand for more meat as a premium product in emerging economies can be contrasted with calls in high-income countries for less meat consumption alongside tensions for lower prices (Elliott, 2013, 2014, Lawrence, 2014). This identification with meat extends to its perceived place in the everyday diet or daily meal (Holm & Møhl, 2000). Not being able to afford meat in a culture where this is the norm is seen as an indicator of relative poverty. For example, the National Anti-Poverty Strategy in Ireland uses the following indicators along with an income standard: normative expectations of foods and meals (rather than nutrients) as part of its measure of "consistent" poverty; having a meal with meat, fish or chicken every second day; having a roast or its equivalent once a week; and not having gone without a substantial meal in the last two weeks.

Many have written about the place of meat in the British diet as well as its symbolic and cultural power (Fiddes, 1991, Beardsworth & Keil, 1997, Beardsworth & Bryman, 2004, Rogers, 2004, Macdiarmid, Douglas & Campbell, 2016, Lang, 2017, Dagevos, 2021). This forms part of a wider literature on the sociology of food and eating in the UK. Fiddes (1991) outlined how research on the sociology and anthropology of our own eating habits (as opposed to earlier work looking at the eating habits of "others") flourished in the 1960s, 1970s and 1980s. Citing Douglas, Levi Strauss and Barthes, Fiddes notes their realisation that the study of food habits cannot be divorced from the study of their social context. This echoed sociologist Pierre Bourdieu's work on social capital, who understood that food choices were not only linked to price, but also to preferences of taste, which could be influenced by culture or upbringing and body image, also noting gendered differences in food tastes apparent in his data – arguing that biological differences were underlined and symbolically accentuated. In common with Bourdieu and Fiddes, Beardsworth and Keil (1997), Adams (1990) and Sobal (2005) note the traditional association of red meat with men and masculine power. They note some sections of the literature that go further than this and suggest that meat plays a part in the patriarchal domination of men and the subordination of women as they are traditionally the domestic cooks required to prepare and cook food. Fiddes (1991) goes on to address deeper cultural connections with meat – arguing that the high value traditionally placed on meat (and particularly red meat) by Western society reflects the power we have long had over animals and the environment in which we live. This, argues Fiddes, is changing, as environmental concerns suggest that our power over our habitat is damaging our chance for survival. More recent academic work on meat consumption argues for greater reduction in meat and dairy consumption in order to protect environmental sustainability (see Chapter 5; Hedenus, Wirsenius & Johansson, 2014, Springmann et al., 2018). In support of this, increasing acceptance of vegetarianism in society has been documented (Smart, 2004, Cusworth et al., 2021), along with increasing claims made by vegetarian groups establishing a coherent set of arguments and motives in the social discourse. This is balanced by counterclaims from meat industry figures and their supporters, and these echo historical examples of the meat industry championing meat as a healthy food (e.g. see adverts for beef wine; Wellcome Library, 2006).

Meat also has cultural associations with national identity, particularly for England (Beardsworth & Keil, 1997, Rogers, 2004, Lang et al., 2009). Rogers traces the emergence of roast beef as a patriotic emblem for England back to at least the seventeenth century, and notes the early (seventeenth century) nickname of the King's Yeoman of the Guard as "Beefeaters" and the French nickname for the English of "les rosbifs". Rogers (2004) argues that this has penetrated through to modern times, with English farmers marching on the Houses of Parliament with pigs and cows, one even dressed as John Bull (Rogers, 2004, p. 1), an English archetype dating from the eighteenth century commonly depicted as a farmer and often associated with roast beef, bull dogs and anti-French sentiment, expressed in many cartoons and illustrations of the times.

It is within this cultural context that meat in general and red meat in particular has become a hot policy issue, with several high-profile food safety scandals playing an important role in food policy development in the UK, including the Aberdeen food poisoning outbreak, BSE and multiple instances of FMD, as outlined below. As Lang et al. (2009) point out, policies reducing meat production are often seen as politically explosive because of the economic power of meat as an industry and its symbolic power (Bourdieu, 1979, Fiddes, 1991, Rogers, 2004) as well as consumer objections to perceived restrictions on the right to choose one's diet (Lang et al., 2009). Popkin (2004) described the "nutrition transition" model, in which low and middle income countries, as they undergo economic, demographic and epidemiological shifts, move from a traditional diet based on cereals and high fibre towards a more Westernised diet high in sugars, fat and animal-sourced foods (Popkin, 2004). Lang et al. (2009) argue that the dominant political ethos in high-income Western countries is to support the meat industry, since meat consumption has become a proxy for economic, social and cultural progress. Some note that the recent move in these geographical areas towards increasing plant-based diets and decreasing meat and dairy consumption constitutes a "reverse nutrition transition" or "protein transition" (Dagevos, 2021).

Beardsworth and Keil (1997) noted that while meat has traditionally been central to the British diet, and beef is given pre-eminence in terms of status and symbolic value, patterns of meat consumption are not static, fluctuating with supply (e.g. during wartime) and some notable food scares. Long-term figures for per capita meat consumption in the UK show poultry meat rising at the same time as declines in beef, sheep meat and pork (OECD, 2023). Stewart et al. (2021) note that from 2008 to 2019, average meat consumption per capita per day decreased from 103.7 grams to 86.3 grams per day, including an absolute reduction in red meat and processed meat, and an increase of 3.2 grams in white meat consumption. Researchers at the turn of the century, for example, Higgs (2000), relate the reduction in red meat consumption to the "lipid hypothesis" which changed the image of red meat from a highly nutritious food associated with good health and prosperity to one associated with coronary heart disease. Higgs pinpoints the turning point as the UK Government's Committee on Medical Aspects of Food and Nutrition (COMA) report on coronary heart disease of 1984, which identified meat as a major source of saturated fatty acids associated with heart disease. Higgs goes on to argue that coronary heart disease risk is now acknowledged to be multifactorial, but that red meat has retained a "tarnished" image. Therefore, the meat industry has used breeding and feeding techniques and modern butchery to reduce the fat content of red meat, achieving significant results (Higgs & Pratt, 1998, Higgs, 2000). The British meat industry engaged in a large marketing campaign (a "relaunch") during the BSE crisis and the EU British beef ban to restore public confidence in British beef (Baines & Harris, 2000), after a noticeable drop in sales during the BSE crisis in 1996. In more recent years, concerns about climate change and environmental damage caused by rising CO_2 emissions have exacerbated anti-beef sentiment, with work on sustainable diets pointing to beef production as one of the main contributors from the food sector carbon emissions – see the 2019 EAT-Lancet Commission report (Willett et al., 2019), as well as more popular guides (e.g. Bridle, 2020). Sustainable diets and efforts to promote them are discussed in Chapter 5.

Linked to all this for the British consumer are the associations with the eating of other meats such as horsemeat (known as hippography) as something "foreign" and an assault on foods associated with national pride, such as John Bull's British beef. During World War II (WWII), there was an attempt to convince the public that horsemeat (and whale meat) was an acceptable alternative to beef. In the UK in 1938, no horses were slaughtered for domestic consumption, but by 1942, this had risen to 2,000 and a peak of 19,000 in 1947, rationing continued until 1954. Butchers who sold horsemeat were located in low-income areas, and in many instances, horsemeat was sold as higher value beef or veal or used to "flesh-out" meat products (Oddy, 2003, Kynaston, 2007, Roodhouse, 2013), indicating the undesirability and level of social acceptance of horsemeat in the UK. From this time, it appears that the restrictions on meat consumption, introduced through rationing and the promotion of "meals without meat", were highly unpopular among the general public (Oddy, 2003).

Social and cultural influences on food production and choice are often left out of food policy-making, as noted by Douglas (1984) as well as in later research, for example, Napier et al. (2017) and Kapelari et al. (2020, p. 12), who noticed similar tendencies: "food security policies at both the European (e.g., Food 2030) and global level (e.g., SDGs) overlook the cultural dimension of food". The Food Standards Agency (FSA) has tried to address this with its biannual *Food and You* survey which, since 2010, has collected information from a sample of the public on their food safety behaviours, attitudes and knowledge, relating to food purchasing, storage, preparation and consumption. One of the aims of the survey is to allow the FSA to understand whether their advice, for example, on hygienic food preparation is followed by certain sections of the public. Data gathered will help improve and better target their policy communications to, for example, particular age groups or other demographics that might be particularly vulnerable to food-related risks (FSA, 2023). The focus is very much on food safety in the domestic or out-of-home catering environment, over either authenticity or nutrition, and this can contribute or provide evidence for policy but does not measure policy effectiveness. Another focus of the various waves of the survey to date is trust in the food system and the FSA itself, covered later in this chapter.

The Aberdeen food poisoning outbreak

A key incident in British food safety policy was the Aberdeen typhoid outbreak in 1963/1964 (Smith & Phillips, 2000, Pennington, 2003, 2009, Smith, 2005), which resulted from infected corned beef imported from Argentina. There were three deaths and 4,000 cases of typhoid. The cause was contaminated waters used to cool the tins in the factory in Argentina, which probably entered through a defect in the tins. The contaminated meat, in turn, contaminated a meat slicing machine in a shop in Aberdeen, leading to the spread of the disease. The bacteria multiplied further on the meats, as they were placed near a window and exposed to sunlight. So, initial contamination in the factory in Argentina was spread wider by poor hygiene practices in Aberdeen. One of the conclusions about policy implications and implementation of the 1963 was that:

> officials were very willing to take account of the views of industry bodies and to disregard the views of professional bodies such as the Public Health Inspectors' Association, which significantly softened the impact of the Milne Committee's proposals. But there was no evidence of any conflict in this connection between MAFF and the Ministry of Health. As in the decision making over the 1963 typhoid outbreaks, Ministry of Health officials seemed no less willing than their colleagues at MAFF [*Ministry of Agriculture, Fisheries and Food*] to take into account the interests of the food trade, and they were no more willing to substitute voluntary agreements and informal methods of operating with legal regulations.
> (Smith et al., 2005, p. 291).

The conclusion from Smith et al. was that "politicians became involved in the decision making during the Aberdeen typhoid outbreak", but that this involvement included a wider set of influences beyond health and agriculture departments; political and economic decisions were paramount in influencing their decisions and the views of the Foreign Office and the Treasury were important factors in influencing the policy response (Smith et al., 2005). While some food safety measures were introduced, the overall policy trend was to seek out "cheap" food on global markets.

Extended food systems were also one of the reasons for the foot-and-mouth outbreak of 1967, which was focused on Shropshire and the Welsh border. There had been previous major outbreaks in 1922, 1923/1924 and 1953. FMD is a severe, highly contagious, viral disease of livestock that has a significant economic impact. FMD affects cattle, swine, sheep, goats and other cloven-hooved ruminants, but is rarely transmitted to humans. Intensively reared animals are more susceptible to the spread of the disease. FMD has economic as opposed to human health implications. Over the six months of the outbreak, 430,000 animals across 2,300 farms were slaughtered (Department for the Environment Food and Rural Affairs, 2008). On its discovery, a ban was put in place on animal movements for a few days. The 1967 epidemic was mainly a cattle epidemic, and movements then were fewer, both between farms and across the country, and this was different from a later 2001 outbreak, as outlined below. Like the Aberdeen typhoid outbreak, the policy responses were framed by economic concerns and the impact that the loss of carcass meat would have on food prices.

From BSE through food-and-mouth disease (2001)

BSE or "mad cow disease" is a fatal brain disease in cattle, which was first officially identified in the UK in 1986. From the first identified case in 1985, a crisis grew, and at its peak in 1992–1993, there were 100,000 confirmed cases (Sato & Webster, 2022). Exports of British beef, worth hundreds of millions of pounds per year, were banned by the EU as well as other countries around the world (O'Brien, 2000), severely damaging the UK beef farming industry. BSE is part of a family of diseases, some of which can affect humans; the most common of these is Creutzfeldt-Jakob Disease (CJD). Concern about the threat to human health from eating British beef grew, and in 1996, a new variant of CJD (vCJD) was discovered and the government announced in March 1996 that this new variant was likely to be linked to BSE in cattle (National Archives, 2000). Government delays in investigating the crisis; conflicts of interest between farming and trade policy and public health as well as poor communication with the public resulted in a crisis in public trust in science as well as in the UK food system.

The EU ban on imports of British beef lasted until 1999, when 12 of the 14 other EU member states confirmed they had no barrier in place; however, France and Germany held out for longer, and the EU did not approve the lifting of the worldwide ban on British beef exports until 2006. This caused a lot of political controversy and negative publicity for the Labour government coming into power in the UK in 1997 and the previous Conservative government under Prime Minister John Major. Often portrayed (in contrast to his predecessor Margaret Thatcher) as rather weak or grey in character, Major promised in 1996 to fight back in Europe and get the beef ban lifted. When German Chancellor Helmut Kohl visited 10 Downing Street in 1996, he was fed British beef at a specially prepared lunch – to no avail. British politicians were accused of favouring European interests above British interests (Robertson, 1996, see also Bright, 1996).

The BSE crisis highlighted a fundamental disjunction in food policy; the separation in the UK of those parts of government that make food production policy and those parts which control nutrition and consumption policies (Lang et al., 2001, Barling et al., 2002). In addition, key corporate players in the food production system have become important in the market economy and so have been included into government systems of food regulation (Flynn & Marsden, 1992, Panjwani & Caraher, 2014), leading to concern about the marginalisation of public health nutrition in public policy. These authors argue that this has happened in the context of a dominant post-war, neoliberal productionist food policy designed to ensure food security and support the agricultural and food processing industries in both the UK and latterly the EU (Barling et al., 2002). Furthermore, this "productionist paradigm" has failed to address pressing concerns about sustainability in the food chain and mounting public health issues such as obesity, cancer and cardiovascular disease. Steps have been taken to address this lack of integration and lack of joined-up policy in the UK (van Zwanenberg & Millstone, 2005), but these are hampered by the bounded remits or persistent silo mentalities within departments as well as repeated reorganisation in the wake of changing administrations (van Zwanenberg & Millstone, 2005).

When the enormity of BSE or mad cow disease dawned on the UK public, its impact helped shape policy, including the setting up of the FSA in the UK (Ratzan, 1998). The idea was that one body – the FSA – at arm's length would look at food in its broadest sense to link safety, nutrition and processing elements of the food chain. Prior to the Blair government of 1997, responsibility for food and farming was held by MAFF (Ministry of Agriculture, Fisheries and Food) while responsibility for nutrition was held by the Department of Health. After 1997, and in the wake of crises such as BSE in farming and food safety, the new Labour government instituted the FSA in 2000, a non-ministerial departmental body, in an attempt to integrate food policies and put responsibility for them at arm's length from government interference (van Zwanenberg & Millstone, 2005). The FSA had been conceived by Professor Philip James in a report for Tony Blair (James, 1997) and would take responsibility for nutrition away from the Department of Health and off-farm food production and food safety away from MAFF (van Zwanenberg & Millstone, 2005). MAFF was replaced by a new ministry, the Department of the Environment, Food and Rural Affairs (DEFRA). Lang et al. (2001) argue that this hasty policy response in the wake of crises was ill-conceived as it left the central government without core nutrition advice and fragmented further the already disjointed machinery of food policy. After a general election in 2010, the new coalition (Conservative/Liberal Democrat) government broke up the FSA, taking responsibility for nutrition back into the Department of Health and responsibility for nutrition and labelling back to DEFRA, leaving the FSA with responsibility for food safety, hygiene and food law enforcement.

The ongoing process of devolution within the UK as Scotland, Wales and Northern Ireland gain governing powers has further complicated responsibilities. There are some notable differences between devolved nations' policies, for example, the FSA in Northern Ireland still retains responsibility for nutrition. Another example is the Food Hygiene Rating Scheme (FHRS) run by the FSA in partnership with local authorities in England, Wales and Northern Ireland. The FHRS inspects places where food is supplied, sold or consumed (restaurants, shops, hotels, schools and hospitals) and rates their food handling, their premises and their management out of 5, where 5 means that hygiene standards are very good and 0 means urgent improvement is necessary. In England display of the score the premises has received is voluntary, while in Wales and Northern Ireland display of the rating sticker is legally required.

The BSE crisis of the 1990s was followed by a foot-and-mouth outbreak, which is a zoonotic issue, not one of human health (Lang, 1998, van Zwanenberg & Millstone, 2005). The most recent FMD crisis came in 2001 and the first confirmed cases of foot-and-mouth were confirmed at an abattoir in Essex in pigs from Buckinghamshire and the Isle of Wight. The Isle of Wight has no slaughterhouse or abattoirs, with animals being transported to the mainland for slaughter and in many instances the carcasses coming back to butchers on the island. Combined, these two incidents of BSE and FMD contributed to a lack of trust in the meat industry and exposed the intricacies and weaknesses of the meat supply chain, displaying the problems with long food chains.

However, the policy response to BSE and FMD was not about simplifying the supply chain but rather regulating it and creating a central co-ordinating body. The FSA was the co-ordinating body for issues related to food and acted to include a wide range of government departments. In effect an attempt to create a cohesive food strategy by including food in all policies. The powers of the FSA were undermined in 2010 when a new government came into power which redistributed some of FSA functions back to the Departments of Health and Environment and the Department of Food and Rural Affairs. This had implications for how the issue of horsemeat was managed (National Audit Office, 2013).

"Horsegate" or the horsemeat scandal of 2013

In late 2012, when the Food Safety Authority in Ireland discovered traces of horsemeat in samples taken from processing factories, there was initially scepticism of the findings. They used technology which measured traces of DNA, and this was so new that the initial belief was that the equipment was flawed and further tests and samples were taken for assay. This resulted in a delay in communicating the findings of these tests (see Figure 10.1).

Horsemeat in the food chain was not a public health problem but a fraud issue in terms of adulteration, although in the early stages of the scandal there was much uncertainty over the issue. Products of four of the five UK major retailers were affected with traces of horsemeat. The major problem was in the retail chain with the addition of horsemeat to beef-based processed food, with the cheaper horsemeat bulking out beef products and ready meals such as beef burgers and lasagne. The one exception was the retailer Morrisons, which had its own slaughterhouses and was therefore in a better position to control quality. In the processed meat sector, it was easier to add extra ingredients and hide the source of additions. There were no indications of the scandal being about cuts of horsemeat being passed off directly as cuts of beef or lamb. For the British consumer, there were associations with the eating of horsemeat (hippography) as something "foreign" and an assault on national pride, echoing earlier portrayals of English beef and John Bull, discussed above. The 2012/2013 horsemeat scandal was not about the dangers of eating horsemeat *per se* but about crime, fraud and adulteration and the effect on consumer confidence. A review was commissioned, led by Professor Chris Elliott of Queen's University, Belfast. This concluded that the horsemeat scandal was ultimately one of contamination, authenticity, fraud and criminal intent (Elliott, 2013, 2014). The review judged

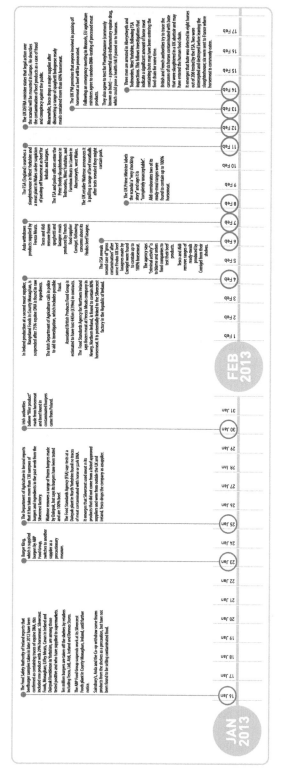

Figure 10.1 Timeline of the emergence of the horsemeat scandal.

Source: Authors' own.

that the crisis may indicate weaknesses in the food chain with obvious implications for future contamination (Elliott 2013, 2014). The complexity of the food chain and the lack of testing and inspection were identified as weak points, which could allow for health concerns in the future.

After the initial identification of undeclared horsemeat in processed beef products, further testing identified pork in products labelled Halal. While this was also not a health issue, it raised issues related to food preferences, whether these are personal or based on faith or religious beliefs, and the right of the consumer to purchase what is indicated on the label. "Horsegate" raised issues of trust in the food chain and of new forms of adulteration, fraud and authenticity. This is also referred to as food integrity or authenticity and assumes that the food you are buying has not been tampered with. From a policy perspective, it showed that testing and sampling safeguards were not in place as early warning systems.

The view taken by many in the food industry and some regulatory actors was that it was not a health crisis, but rather an authenticity issue. This seemed to provide a rationale for viewing it to be not as serious as a health crisis or contamination with toxic substances. From this, the rationales diverged with a number of industry respondents citing the complexity of the food chain as a justification for the contamination. There was a feeling that if only people and journalists understood the complexity, there would be fairer and more balanced reporting. This can be seen as the extreme of the principle of *caveat emptor – let the buyer beware*! Regan et al. found that the public attributed responsibility and blame for "horsegate" under three headings, which were: (1) deliberate and deceitful practices of the food industry; (2) the complexity of the food chain; and (3) the demand from others for cheap food (Regan et al., 2015). The respondents in this survey saw the complexity of the meat chain as contributing to a lack of monitoring and testing. Respondents further saw the reasons as related to cost-cutting by both government(s) and the food industry in the drive to deliver cheap food. This is similar to what van Zwanenberg and Millstone found in relation to the BSE crises and the overall impression of food regulation by Smith and Phillips in the UK (Smith & Phillips, 2000, van Zwanenberg & Millstone, 2005).

Many regulators and media actors saw the "horsegate" issue as a warning sign for the food system (Wilson et al., 2014). If this was wrong, what next? Yet some shared the view of the industry, in that it displayed that the public did not understand the complexity of the food system (Brooks et al., 2017). Many industry players saw this as another blip in the series of UK food scandals and thought the issues were those of managing the media fallout and consumer expectations and that the consumer has a short memory with respect to food scares. For six successive weeks after the first horsemeat reports appeared in the media, sales decreased (Yamoah & Yawson, 2014). Within a year, sales returned to normal levels with only a "small proportion (1%) spontaneously reported horsemeat and halal products as food issues of concern" (DEFRA, 2014, p. 61).

The Comptroller General's report on food safety and authenticity in the food chain identified confusion over the "responsibilities for food policy" and that a consequence of changes "of the Machinery of Government' was that intelligence sharing had been weakened (Comptroller General, 2013). It also emerged that UK authorities had not taken samples to test for horsemeat since 2003. Both the Elliott Review and the Comptroller General's report identified a gap between what the consumer expected for the authenticity of their food and the mechanism in place to ensure this. Both concluded that the public had less confidence in the regulatory bodies and the food industry alike. Both reports saw the complexity of the food chain as a contributor to the fraud but did not view this as an excuse for the fraud.

In all of this, we see the power of the lobby from a highly skilled and lucrative economic sector, with the drivers and the barriers to policy being economic, and trumping human health as a priority issue. The FSA was judged to have acted competently during the horsemeat crisis and its role in informing the public and the industry was judged to show innovative use of social media. Even before the reports from Elliott and the Comptroller General, the then Coalition Government (Conservative and Liberal Democrat) had decided to strip the FSA of some of its responsibilities, essentially making it responsible for food safety but taking away its role in nutrition and food labelling. These were essentially brought back in-house to Whitehall departments such as health and DEFRA and therefore under ministerial control, although the FSA offices in Scotland and Northern Ireland retained their responsibility for nutrition.

A positive outcome was the establishment of a Food Crime Unit within the FSA. The FSA in the UK now views fraud as a food crime and has a unit to deal with incidents, but such an approach assumes regular independent sampling and testing. The unit covers England, Wales and Northern Ireland and works closely with the Scottish Food Crime and Incidents Unit located within Food Standards Scotland (FSS). Another outcome of the Elliott Review was the establishment of the Food Industry Intelligence Network (FIIN) in 2015 by 21 food industry members. FIIN aims to "help ensure the integrity of food supply chains and protect the interests of the consumer" by establishing a so-called safe haven, where information and intelligence can be gathered, analysed and disseminated (FIIN, 2023). The general thrust of both hygiene and food safety policy was to make the food industry responsible while scaling down public sampling and analysis. Thus, early warning systems were in a perilous state in the UK in the 2000s. They continue to be underfunded and resourced with Trading Standards and routine sampling being hit by budget cuts. A particular concern post-Brexit is the divorce of most of the UK from the food safety systems of Europe.

Despite the welcome introduction of the National Food Crime Unit and the FIIN, who do their own testing and sampling, there are still concerns about the lack of border checks on food coming into the country. This has left gaps in monitoring and surveillance as well as a lack of funding for local authorities to fund Trading Standards activity (*Farming Today*, 2023). Devolution, as mentioned above, has led to different policy outcomes in different countries in the UK, with Northern Ireland, Wales and Scotland operating under different policies and regulations. Brexit or EU Exit has caused other complicated differences, as the UK moved away from EU legislation, with a transition period from 2018 to 2020. After this period, a category of Retained EU Law was created consisting of EU-derived legislation that was preserved in our domestic legal framework by the European Union (Withdrawal) Act 2018. Retained EU Law was never intended to sit on the statute book indefinitely, and at the time of writing, the FSA has to go through a process of updating all EU references in its documentations to accurately reflect the law now in force in all new or amended guidance published since the end of 2020. However, in Northern Ireland, EU law will continue to apply in respect to the majority of food and feed hygiene and safety law, as listed in the Northern Ireland Protocol, as long as this continues to exist.

Such a complex and changing policy landscape threatens the UKs highly sophisticated food system, in an example of what Marsden et al. (2022) call "Disruptive Food Governance", which is exacerbated by massive global challenges, such as climate change and biodiversity loss, related to economic and geopolitical shocks such as the war in Ukraine and the ongoing trade tensions. In these conditions, global examples of food fraud thrive. Along with historic examples such as the Spanish olive scandal which resulted from contamination by organophosphates (Johnson, 2009), milk contaminated with melamine in China caused kidney stones and illness for nearly 300,000 children and six infant deaths; overall valuable commodities such as seafood can experience high incidence of food fraud throughout the supply chain (Lawrence et al., 2022).

Labelling, food authenticity and trust

Another potential policy lever to increase authenticity and trust in food is food labelling, and this has seen significant strengthening of informational requirements to increase openness and transparency of food ingredients, provenance and allergens to support and protect further the consumer in making their food choices. In the UK, all pre-packed food must be labelled with certain mandatory information, including a list of ingredients highlighting any of the 14 allergens required to be declared by law; the net quantity and proportion of different ingredients; and a best before or use by date as well as the name and address of the manufacturer and the country of origin. The Food Information Regulations have served to communicate more effectively the true nature of the food product contained within. However, responsibility for policymaking in this area is fragmented across the devolved nations of the UK. In Wales and Northern Ireland, the FSA is responsible for the policy on food labelling and food compositional standards which are safety and non-safety related. In Northern Ireland, this includes nutrition policy and labelling. In Wales, the Welsh government is responsible for nutrition policy and labelling. In England, the FSA is responsible for food safety-related labelling, including allergens. DEFRA is responsible for the policy on food labelling and food compositional standards which are non-safety related only. The Department of Health and Social Care is responsible for nutrition policy and labelling (Food Standards Agency, 2023). This complexity potentially undermines the strength of the FSA to make comprehensive policy decisions. However, in some areas, such as Front of Pack Nutrition Labels (FOPNL), a different approach has been taken. Front of pack labels act as shortcuts to decision-making for consumers who routinely make food choices within seconds of approaching a product. In common with many other countries, these are voluntarily included on products in the UK. These have been informed by nutrient profiling models which have been adopted by food manufacturers and retailers with significant penetration on the market. In the UK, the four nations have worked together to deliver a common "multiple traffic light" or MTL label (Kelly & Jewell, 2018, Food Standards Agency, 2023); this consistent, unified, cross-country approach has been considered a success by the government, replacing the less effective multiple formats of label that had previously existed (Department for Health and Social Care, 2020).

Conclusions: consumer perceptions of food fraud and food crime

The integrity and authenticity of food matters not only for health and economic reasons but because food is an emotive subject and the public should be consulted on decisions that impact ultimately upon them. The FSA, as well as collecting data on food safety behaviours and opinions, regularly surveys the public on their trust in the food system, understanding that trust is a precious commodity, and according to the Square (2013), there's less of it around these days. This is unfortunate because it is easier to maintain trust than regain trust, once lost.

The FSA's Food and You Survey (TNS BMRB et al., 2013) found that respondents were more likely to report being concerned about meat imported from outside the UK (59%) than were concerned about meat produced in the UK (28%). Importantly, this survey was conducted before the "horsegate" scandal. The "horsegate" scandal showed food authenticity can be exacerbated by the long supply chains in the food industry today, and because of the complexity of the food system, the potential for food fraud and food crime is growing.

BSE in the 1990s and the discovery of horsemeat in food products in January 2013 rocked confidence in the entire food system, to the extent that only half of consumers trusted the food industry to provide safe food (Mintel, 2013). For example, one month after the discovery of horsemeat in meat products, three-quarters (73%) of respondents reported being less confident in the safety of processed meat and almost half (49%) reported that they would buy less red meat, processed meat and/or ready meals. Notably, two-thirds (67%) of those intending to buy less reported that this behavioural change was due to lack of trust. Six months later, in August 2013, a repeat FSA Citizens' Forum concluded that consumers continued to buy less red meat, processed meat and ready meals, with associated increases in fish purchases. Lack of trust was still prevalent, with consumers concerned about mislabelling (with the mislabelling issue being of greater concern than eating horse meat itself). Consumers reported feeling less confident about food safety in general in the UK. The recommendations from the consumer research were that consumers want greater transparency of the issue (labelling or public awareness) to help drive up standards in the industry, with associated improvement to food regulation, testing regimes and intelligence gathering.

Post-horsemeat scandal, all the major retailers have tried to move with consumer demand and build shorter supply chains to meet consumer demand for locally sourced, quality produce with clear provenance.

There are two methodologies to build consumer confidence and achieve food safety and quality: (1) management of food supply chains via regulations/standards/certifications; and (2) a food traceability system. Traceability comes at a cost, but the costs of not having it or having inefficient systems in place may be severe for governments, consumers, individual companies and the food industry as a whole (Coveney, 2008, Devaney, 2013, Nath et al., 2013).

It is imperative that we retain our high food standards. From the consumer perspective, there can be no two-tier system for food, whereby only some consumers can afford to buy food of acceptable quality, standards and health, while others cannot afford to eat with food standards uncompromised. It is necessary that we do not let the lowest standards apply – to revert to the lowest common denominator is regressive. Therefore, it is important to understand the consumer perceptions around the importance of consumer trust in food. One thing that emerges from consumption patterns is that threats from contamination and food scares swiftly fade from collective memory and concern among the public. Such scares may thus be good for immediate policy responses but not very effective for longer-term policymaking.

In post-EU Exit times, none of the four nations will be able to enjoy food security without trade agreements. For example, Northern Ireland imports 48% of the food it consumes – any detrimental impact on the food supply chain into Northern Ireland will manifest in consumer food choices being affected, particularly in respect of fresh fruits and vegetables, with the subsequent impacts on dietary choice and public health outcomes. This, coupled with the anticipated impact on costs driving food prices to become unaffordable, presents opportunities for rogue traders to act fraudulently to offer counterfeit food products at prices consumers with constrained budgets are willing to pay.

References

Accum, F.C. 1820, *A Treatise on Adulterations of Food and Culinary Poisons: Exhibiting the Fraudulent Sophistications of Bread, Beer, Wine, Spirituous Liquors, Tea, Coffee, Cream, Confectionery, Vinegar, Mustard, Pepper, Cheese, Olive Oil, Pickles and Other Articles Employed in Domestic Economy; and Methods of Detecting Them*. J. Mallett, Sold by Longman, Hurst, Rees, Orme, and Brown.

Adams, C.J. 1990, *The Sexual Politics of Meat: A Feminist Vegetarian Critique*, Continuum, New York.

Baines, P.R. & Harris, P. 2000, "Kite flying: the role of marketing in the post-BSE British beef export industry", *British Food Journal*, vol. 102, no. 5/6, pp. 454–464. https://doi.org/10.1108/00070700010329362

Barling, D., Lang, T. & Caraher, M. 2002, 'Joined–up food policy? The trials of governance, public policy and the food system', *Social Policy & Administration*, vol. 36, no. 6, pp. 556–574. https://doi.org/10.1111/1467-9515.t01-1-00304

Beardsworth, A. & Bryman, A. 2004, "Meat consumption and meat avoidance among young people: an 11-year longitudinal study", *British Food Journal*, vol. 106, no. 4, pp. 313–327. https://doi.org/10.1108/00070700410529573

Beardsworth, A. & Keil, T. 1997, *Sociology on the Menu: An Invitation to the Study of Food and Society*, Routledge, London.

Berazneva, J. & Lee, D.R. 2013, "Explaining the African food riots of 2007–2008: an empirical analysis", *Food Policy*, vol. 39, pp. 28–39. https://doi.org/10.1016/j.foodpol.2012.12.007

Bourdieu, P. 1979, *La distinction. Critique sociale du jugement*. Paris, éd. de Minuit.

Bradbury, J. 1997 "Report on Scottish E coli O157 outbreak released", *The Lancet*, vol. 349, no. 9058, p.1073.

Bridle, S. 2020, *Food and Climate Change without the Hot Air Change Your Diet: The Easiest Way to Help Save the Planet*, UIT Cambridge Ltd., Cambridge.

Bright, S. 1996, 'I think he's weakening!' [black drawing ink on marker pad], *Brighty's Bloggage.* Available from: http://brightys-bloggage.blogspot.co.uk/2010/07/

Brooks, S., Elliott, C.T., Spence, M., Walsh, C. & Dean, M. 2017, "Four years post-horsegate: an update of measures and actions put in place following the horsemeat incident of 2013", *NPJ Science of Food*, vol. 1, p. 5. https://doi.org/10.1038/s41538-017-0007-z

Burnett, J. 1989, *Plenty and Want: A Social History of Food in England from 1815 to the Present Day*, 3rd edn, Routledge, London.

Collins, E.J. 1993, "Food adulteration and food safety in Britain in the 19th and early 20th centuries", *Food Policy*, vol. 18, no. 2, pp. 95–109. https://doi.org/10.1016/0306-9192(93)90018-7

Committee on Medical Aspects of Food Policy 1984, *Diet in Relation to Cardiovascular Disease*, Department of Health and Social Security, H.M. Stationery Office, London.

Comptroller and Auditor General 2013, *Food Safety and Authenticity in the Processed Meat Supply Chain*, National Audit Office, London.

Coveney, J. 2008, "Food and trust in Australia: building a picture", *Public Health Nutrition*, vol. 11, no. 3, pp. 237–245. https://doi.org/10.1017/S1368980007000250

Croall, H. 2007, "Food Crime" in *Issues in Green Criminology*, eds. P. Beirne & N. South, Routledge, London, pp. 206–229.

Cusworth, G., Garnett, T. & Lorimer, J. 2021, "Legume dreams: the contested futures of sustainable plant-based food systems in Europe", *Global Environmental Change*, vol. 69, p. 102321. https://doi.org/10.1016/j.gloenvcha.2021.102321

Dagevos, H. 2021, "Finding flexitarians: current studies on meat eaters and meat reducers", *Trends in Food Science & Technology*, vol. 114, pp. 530–539. https://doi.org/10.1016/j.tifs.2021.06.021

DEFRA (Department for Environment, Food and Rural Affairs) 2014, *Food Statistics Pocketbook 2014: In-Year Update*, DEFRA, London.

DEFRA (Department for Environment, Food and Rural Affairs) 2008, *FMD: Comparisons with the 1967 FMD Outbreak*, DEFRA, London.

Department of Health and Social Care 2020, *Front-of-Pack Nutrition Labelling in the UK: Building on Success*. Available from: https://www.gov.uk/government/consultations/front-of-pack-nutrition-labelling-in-the-uk-building-on-success.

Devaney, L. 2013, "Spaces of security, surveillance and food safety: interrogating perceptions of the Food Safety Authority of Ireland's governing technologies, power and performance", *The Geographical Journal*. https://doi.org/10.1111/geoj.12001

Desrochers, P. & Shimizu, H. 2012, *The Locavore's Dilemma: In Praise of the 10,000 Mile Diet*, Public Affairs, New York.

Douglas, M. (Ed). 1984, *Food in the Social Order*, Russell Sage Foundation, New York.

Elliott, C. 2013, *Elliott Review into the Integrity and Assurance of Food Supply Networks – Interim Report*, HM Government, London.

Elliott, C. 2014, *Elliott Review into the Integrity and Assurance of Food Supply Networks – Final Report,* HM Government, London.

Farming Today 2023, BBC Radio 4, 11 January 05:45.

Fiddes, N. 1991, *Meat a Natural Symbol*, Routledge, London.

FIIN 2023, *Food Industry Intelligence Network*. Available from: https://www.fiin.co.uk/.

Flynn, A. & Marsden, T. 1992, "Food regulation in a period of agricultural retreat: the British experience", *Geoforum*, vol. 23, no. 1, pp. 85–93. https://doi.org/10.1016/0016-7185(92)90038-6

Food Standards Agency (FSA) 2023, *Labelling and Allergens*. Available from: https://www.food.gov.uk/business-guidanceindustry-specific-advice/allergen-labelling.

Hassall, A.H. 1855, *Food and Its Adulterations*: *Comprising the Reports of the Analytical Sanitary Commission of The Lancet for the Years 1851 to 1854 Inclusive*, Lancet Analytical Sanitary Commission, London.

Hedenus, F., Wirsenius, S. & Johansson, D.J.A. 2014, "The importance of reduced meat and dairy consumption for meeting stringent climate change targets", *Climate Change*, vol. 124, pp. 79–91. https://doi.org/10.1007/s10584-014-1104-5

Higgs, J.D. 2000, "The changing nature of red meat: 20 years of improving nutritional quality", *Trends in Food Science & Technology*, vol. 11, no. 3, pp. 85–95. https://doi.org/10.1016/S0924-2244(00)00055-8

Higgs, J. & Pratt, J. 1998, "Meat, Poultry and Meat Products" in *Encyclopedia of Human Nutrition*, eds. M.J. Sadler, J.J, Strain & B. Caballero, Academic Press, San Diego, CA and London, UK, pp. 1272–1282.

Holm, L. & Møhl, M. 2000, "The role of meat in everyday food culture: an analysis of an interview study in Copenhagen", *Appetite*, vol. 34, pp. 277–283. https://doi.org/10.1006/appe.2000.0324

Hoppit, J. 1993, "Reforming Britain's weights and measures, 1660–1824", *The English Historical Review*, vol. 108, no. 426, pp. 82–104. https://www.jstor.org/stable/573550

James, P. 1997, *Establishment of an Independent Food Standards Agency: Report by Professor Philip James*, Rowett Research Institute (James Report).

Johnson, J.P. 2009, "The Spanish Cooking Oil Scandal: Toxic Oil Syndrome or Cover-Up?" in *Handbook of Frauds, Scams, and Swindles*, eds. S. Matulich & D.M. Currie, Routledge, Abingdon, pp. 205–210.

Kantor, A.F. 1976, "'Upton Sinclair and the Pure Food and Drugs Act of 1906' I aimed at the public's heart and by accident I hit it in the stomach", *American Journal of Public Health*, vol. 66, no. 12, pp. 1202–1205.

Kapelari, S., Alexopoulos, G., Moussouri, T., Sagmeister, K.J. & Stampfer, F. 2020, "Food heritage makes a difference: the importance of cultural knowledge for improving education for sustainable food choices", *Sustainability*, vol. 12, no. 4, p. 1509. https://doi.org/10.3390/su12041509

Kelly, B. & Jewell, J. 2018, *What Is the Evidence on the Policy Specifications, Development Processes and Effectiveness of Existing Front-of-Pack Food Labelling Policies in the WHO European Region?*, WHO Regional Office for Europe, Copenhagen (Health Evidence Network (HEN) synthesis report 61).

Kynaston, D. 2007, *Austerity Britain 1945–51*, Bloomsbury, London.

Lang, T. 2017, "Meat and Policy: Charting a Course through the Complexity" in *The Meat Crisis*, eds. J. D'Silva & J. Webster, Routledge, Abingdon, pp. 317–334.

Lang, T. 1998, "BSE and CJD: Recent Developments" in *The Mad Cow Crises: Health and the Public Good*, ed. S.C. Ratzan, UCL Press, London, pp. 65–85.

Lang, T., Barling, D. & Caraher, M. 2009, *Food Policy: Integrating, Health, Environment and Society*, Oxford University Press, Oxford.

Lang, T., Barling, D. & Caraher, M. 2001, "Food, social policy and the environment: towards a new model", *Social Policy & Administration*, vol. 35, no. 5, pp. 538–558. https://doi.org/10.1111/1467-9515.t01-1-00252

Lang, T., Wu, M. & Caraher, M. 2017, "Meat and Policy: Charting a Course through the Complexity" in *The Meat Crisis*, eds. J. D'Silva & J. Webster, Routledge, Abingdon, pp. 268–288.

Lawrence, F. 2014, Fake-food scandal revealed as tests show third of products mislabeled, *The Guardian*, Saturday, 8th February.

Lawrence, S., Elliott, C., Huisman, W., Dean, M. & van Ruth, S. 2022, "The 11 sins of seafood: assessing a decade of food fraud reports in the global supply chain", *Comprehensive Reviews in Food Science and Food Safety*, vol. 21, no. 4, pp. 3746–3769. https://doi.org/10.1111/1541-4337.12998

Lord, N., Huisman, W. & Paoli, L. 2022. "Food crimes, food harms and the food system", *Crime, Law and Social Change*, vol. 78, pp.455–462.

Macdiarmid, J.I., Douglas, F. & Campbell, J. 2016, "Eating like there's no tomorrow: public awareness of the environmental impact of food and reluctance to eat less meat as part of a sustainable diet", *Appetite*, vol. 96, pp. 487–493. https://doi.org/10.1016/j.appet.2015.10.011

Marsden, T., Lang, T. & Millstone, E. 2022, "Disruptive Governance in the UK Food System and the Case of Wales" in *Agriculture, Environment and Development: International Perspectives on water, land and politics*, eds. A.A.R. Ioris & B.M. Fernandes, Palgrave Macmillan, Cham, pp. 37–61.

Martin, S. 2022, "The pathogenic city: disease, dirt and the planning of Dublin's wholesale fruit and vegetable markets", *Planning Perspectives*, vol. 37, no. 1, pp. 149–168. https://doi.org/10.1080/02665433.2021.2011775

Mintel 2013, Just half of Brits trust the food industry to provide safe food to eat, *Mintel Press Office*, 3rd July. Available from: https://www.mintel.com/press-centre/food-and-drink/food-safety-after-horse-meat-scandal

Mitchell, I. 2018, "Retail markets in northern and midland England, 1870–1914: civic icon, municipal white elephant, or consumer paradise?", *The Economic History Review*, vol. 71, no. 4, pp. 1270–1290. https://doi.org/10.1111/ehr.12653

Napier, A.D., Depledge, M., Knipper, M., Lovell, R., Ponarin, E., et al. 2017, *Culture Matters: Using a Cultural Contexts of Health Approach to Enhance Policy Making*, World Health Organization, Regional Office for Europe.

Nath, J., Henderson, J., Coveney, J. & Ward P.R. 2013, "Consumer faith: an exploration of trust in food and the impact of religious dietary norms and certification", *Food, Culture and Society: An International Journal of Multidisciplinary Research*, vol. 16, pp. 421–436. https://doi.org/10.2752/175174413X13673466711840

National Archives 2000, *Records of the Inquiry into BSE National Archive's Catalogue*. Available from: https://discovery.nationalarchives.gov.uk/details/r/C351

National Audit Office 2013, *Food Safety and Authenticity in the Processed Meat Supply Chain*, NAO, London.

O'Brien, M., 2000, "Have lessons been learned from the UK bovine spongiform encephalopathy (BSE) epidemic?", *International Journal of Epidemiology*, vol. 29, no. 4, pp. 730–733. https://doi.org/10.1093/ije/29.4.730

Oddy, D.J. 2003, *From Plain Fare to Fusion Food: British Diet from the 1890s to the 1990s*, Boydell Press, Woodbridge.

OECD 2023, Meat consumption (indicator), https://doi.org/10.1787/fa290fd0-en

Panjwani, C. & Caraher, M. 2014, "The public health responsibility deal: brokering a deal for public health, but on whose terms?", *Health Policy*, vol. 114, nos. 2–3, pp. 163–173. https://doi.org/10.1016/j.healthpol.2013.11.002

Pennington, T.H. 2003, *When Food Kills*, Oxford University Press, Oxford.

Pennington, T.H. 2009, *The Public Inquiry into the September 2005 Outbreak of e-coli 0157 in South Wales*, Welsh Government, Cardiff.

Phillips, N., Bridgeman, J. & Ferguson-Smith, M. 2000, *The BSE Inquiry: Report: Evidence and Supporting Papers of the Inquiry into the Emergence and identification of Bovine Spongiform Encephalopathy (BSE) and Variant Creutzfeldt-Jakob Disease (vCJD) and the Action Taken in Response to it up to 20 March 1996*, The Stationery Office, London, 16 volumes.

Popkin, B.M. 2004, "The nutrition transition: an overview of world patterns of change", *Nutrition Reviews*, vol. 62, suppl_2, pp. S140–S143. https://doi.org/10.1111/j.1753-4887.2004.tb00084.x

Randall, A. 2006, *Riotous Assemblies: Popular Protest in Hanoverian England*, Oxford University Press, New York; Oxford.

Ratzan, S.C. 1998, *The Mad Cow Crises: Health and the Public Good*, UCL Press, London.

Regan, A., Marcu, A., Shan, L.C., Wall, P., Barnett, J. & McConnon, A. 2015, "Conceptualising responsibility in the aftermath of the horsemeat adulteration incident; an outline study with Irish and UK consumers", *Health Risk & Society*. https://doi.org/10.1080/13698575.2015.1030367

Robertson, G. 1996, "Beef" *Hansard, Oral Answers to Questions*, 1st May, c.1127. Available from: https://www.publications.parliament.uk/pa/cm199596/cmhansrd/vo960501/debtext/60501-15.htm.

Rogers, B. 2004, *Beef and Liberty: Roast Beef, John Bull and the English Nation*, Vintage books, London.

Roodhouse, M. 2013, Break the taboo on horsemeat – or food fraud will continue. Available from: http://www.historyandpolicy.org/opinion-articles/articles/break-the-taboo-on-horsemeat-or-food-fraud-will-continue.

Sato, H. & Webster, A. 2022, "Mixed effects of mass media reports on the social amplification of risk: frequencies and frames of the BSE reports in newspaper media in the UK", *Journal of Risk Research*, vol. 25, no. 1, pp. 48–66. https://doi.org/10.1080/13669877.2021.1905691

Sinclair, U. 1906/1985, *The Jungle*, Penguin, Harmondsworth.

Smart, A. 2004, "Adrift in the mainstream: challenges facing the UK vegetarian movement", *British Food Journal*, vol. 106, no. 2, pp. 79–92. https://doi.org/10.1108/00070700410516775

Smith, D.F. 2005, Lessons for food-safety policy from the Aberdeen typhoid outbreak, 1964, History and Policy. Available from: http://www.historyandpolicy.org/policy-papers/papers/lessons-for-food-safety-policy-from-the-aberdeen-typhoid-outbreak, accessed 9th June, 2015.

Smith, D.F., Diack, H.L., Pennington, T.H. & Russell, E.M. 2005, *Food Poisoning, Policy, and Politics: Corned Beef and Typhoid in Britain in the 1960s*, Boydell & Brewer, Suffolk.

Smith, D.F. & Phillips, J. (eds). 2000, *Food, Science, Policy and Regulation in the Twentieth Century: International and Comparative Perspectives*, Routledge, London.

Sobal, J. 2005, "Men, meat, and marriage: models of masculinity", *Food and Foodways*, vol. 13, nos. 1–2, pp. 135–158. https://doi.org/10.1080/07409710590915409

Springmann, M., Clark, M., Mason-D'Croz, D., Wiebe, K., Bodirsky, B.L., et al. 2018, "Options for keeping the food system within environmental limits", *Nature*, vol. 562, pp. 519–525. https://doi.org/10.1038/s41586-018-0594-0

Square1. (2013) *Retail: Feature: Transparency and Traceability at the IGD Convention*. Available from: https://www.esmmagazine.com/retail/feature-transparency-and-traceability-at-the-igd-convention-2921

Stanton, R. & Scrinis, G. 2005, "Total wellbeing or too much meat?", *Australian Science* October, pp. 37–38.

Stewart, C., Piernas, C., Cook, B. & Jebb, S.A. 2021, "Trends in UK meat consumption: analysis of data from years 1–11 (2008–09 to 2018–19) of the National Diet and Nutrition Survey rolling programme", *The Lancet Planetary Health*, vol. 5, no. 10, pp. e699–e708. https://doi.org/10.1016/S2542-5196(21)00228-X

The Adulteration of Food and Drink Act (1860), *The Lancet*, vol. 76, no. 1933, pp. 272–273. https://doi.org/10.1016/S0140-6736(02)56312-1

TNS BMRB, Policy Studies Institute and University of Westminster. (2013) Exploring food attitudes and behaviours in the UK: Findings from the Food and You Survey 2012. Available from: https://www.food.gov.uk/sites/default/files/media/document/food-and-you-2012-main-report_1.pdf

US Food and Drugs Administration, 2018, Food Defect Levels Handbook. Available from https://www.fda.gov/food/ingredients-additives-gras-packaging-guidance-documents-regulatory-information/food-defect-levels-handbook

van Zwanenberg, P. & Millstone, E. 2005, *BSE: Risk, Science, and Governance*, Oxford University Press, Oxford.

Velkar, A. 2012, *Markets and Measurements in Nineteenth-Century Britain*, Cambridge University Press, Cambridge.

Webb, S., & Webb, B. 1904, "The assize of bread", *The Economic Journal*, vol. 14, no. 54, pp. 196–218.

Wellcome Library 2006, *Advert for Liebig's Beef Wine prepared by S. Stephens, Chemist and Opticians, Milnsbridge*, Wellcome Library, London. Available from: https://wellcomeimages.org/indexplus/image/L0040445.html

Willett, W., Rockström, J., Loken, B., Springmann, M., Lang, T., Vermeulen, S., Garnett, T., Tilman, D., DeClerck, F., Wood, A. & Jonell, M. 2019, "Food in the anthropocene: the EAT–Lancet Commission on healthy diets from sustainable food systems", *The Lancet*, vol. 393, no. 10170, pp. 447–492. https://doi.org/10.1016/S0140-6736(18)31788-4

Wilson, A.M., Henderson, J., Coveney, J, Meyer, S.B., Webb, T, Calnan, M., Caraher, M., Lloyd, S., McCullum, D., Elliott, A. & Ward, P.R. (2014,) "Media actors' perceptions of their roles in reporting food incidents", *BMC Public Health*, vol. 14, p. 1305. https://doi.org/10.1186/1471-2458-14-1305

Wilson, B. 2008, *Swindled: From Poison Sweets to Counterfeit Coffee: The Dark History of the Food Cheats*, John Murray, London

WOAH 2023, *Foot and Mouth Disease*, World Organisation for Animal Health. Available from: https://www.woah.org/en/disease/foot-and-mouth-disease/

Yamoah, F.A. & Yawson, D.E. 2014, "Assessing supermarket food shopper reaction to horsemeat scandal in the UK", *International Review of Management and Marketing*, vol. 4, no. 2, 98–10.

11 Examples of success in UK food policy

Introduction

We have seen in previous chapters examples of food policy endeavours in the UK, many of which are process-driven as opposed to outcome-related and our overall critique verges on the side of "could do better". There are many small-scale successes, but what remains is the lack of an overall food policy strategy. The 2021, "The Food Strategy: The Plan" for England is another example of a policy analysis which, with some gaps in its coverage, was strong on its exploration of the food system and the need to produce a co-ordinated approach across sectors and departments (Dimbleby, 2021). This ultimately failed to gain traction as the government chose to ignore key parts and selectively respond to some recommendations (see Chapters 1–3) (Dimbleby & Lewis, 2023, Eccles, 2023, McGrath, 2023, Department for Environment Food & Rural Affairs, 2022, Food Ethics Council, 2022, White, 2022). This is a case of history repeating itself with reports such as the 2002 "Curry Report" and the 2008 "Food Matters" suffering similar fates, either due to a change of government or lack of a long-term vision or accompanying funding support (Curry et al., 2002, Parsons & Barling, 2022). As noted in Chapters 1–3, food policy is often a reaction to a crisis, so BSE (mad cow disease), foot-and-mouth disease, food poisoning or food fraud fall under the heading of a "whack-a-mole" approach. The actions demanded by food policy are often weighed up against immediate costs as opposed to long-term gains.

Since the end of World War II (WWII), there has not been a comprehensive approach to food policy in the UK. In 1984, the nutritionist Caroline Walker co-authored with Geoffrey Cannon *The Food Scandal: What's Wrong with the British Diet and How to Put it Right* (Cannon, 1989, Walker & Cannon, 1984). It was a bestselling popular book and challenged the Department of Health's official 1981 statement that "nutrition in Britain is generally good". The background to the book was the official National Advisory Committee on Nutrition Education (NACNE) report on the British diet. NACNE was a committee of experts commissioned by the British government to produce a report on food and health in the UK. Walker was the committee's honorary secretary. The report was delayed and suppressed for two and a half years, after lobbying from the food manufacturing industry and its representative organisations. The situation and the report's delay were made public in a front-page lead news story in *The Sunday Times* in June 1983. When the report finally appeared, its message was that the British population would be much healthier if their diet contained less fat and sugar a message repeated in the NFS (Dimbleby, 2021). Although the British diet of the 1950s was restricted, it was healthier (Buss, 1993)[1]; a 1999 study comparing the diets of four-year-olds from the 1950s with those in the 1990s found the 1950s' diet closer to healthy eating guidelines (Prynne et al., 1999). *The Food Scandal* took the findings of the NACNE report and "challenged the unholy trinity of British processed food: saturated fat, commercial sugar, added salt. It was rude about specific branded products".

DOI: 10.4324/9781003260301-11

The Acheson Report of 1998 did have some purchase in the area of health and nutrition (see Chapters 2 and 3) with a newly elected Labour government and resulted in some actions such as the public health strategy for England: "Saving Lives: Our Healthier Nation" (Acheson, 1998). The Acheson Report and the subsequent health strategy that resulted from it strengthened and re-energised initiatives such as the five-a-day fruit and vegetable and school meals campaigns (Sharp, 1996, n.d.). These examples of limited success were all health-focussed, and of course, we are now in a new era where there is a need to link health and environment.

In the chapters so far, we have offered, with an academic lens, critiques of UK-based food policy and hold to an overall position that it is patchy and lacks coherence. Despite this, there are some bright spots and this chapter focuses on successful examples. These are built around a number of approaches. We start with a section on examples from government-based policy that while they may not be comprehensive, they offer something to build on and a way forward. We then turn to policy entrepreneurs/influencers; these are often individuals and groups outside the formal policy area who have identified a gap or need to advocate for change. This is followed by a section with some examples from the devolved administrations of Scotland, Wales and Northern Ireland, which show promise in terms of what can be developed and act as exemplars for policy development. Finally, we offer some examples from the world of academia where individuals have pioneered policy activism via their work; this fits in the classic tradition of public health where the advocacy element of the work is matched and supported by the research. We have chosen the latter two categories to reflect on a range of approaches and how policy gaps can be plugged by campaigning individuals and groups. Our choice of cases is selective, based on what can be shown to be effective in terms of policy development; there are many more groups and individuals out there working hard in the field, delivering services and advocating for change.

Government-based food policy

There are examples of patchy approaches to food policy by UK governments. As noted above, few are comprehensive, but what exists does possess the potential to build on and be the foundations for broader policy initiatives. We have chosen school meals, the soda tax, salt reduction and obesity policy as examples of policy successes and which, with more co-ordination and links, could be improved and act in tandem to deliver more wide-ranging changes. The UK government's own advisor said that the "'response to my review, is not a strategy at all. It is merely a handful of disparate policy ideas........ The government's 'strategy' is far too scant, fragmented and cautious to meet the scale of the problem" (Dimbleby and Lewis, 2023 page 17).

School meals

School meals remain a central plank of frontline services designed to tackle food poverty and unhealthy eating (see Chapter 9 for a fuller discussion). Before 1906, school meal provision was delivered by charitable bodies in the major cities of the UK. In 1889, in London, the School Dinners Association was formed. By 1905, there were similar bodies in all the English cities (Le Gros Clark, 1948). For the Boer War, the health of the male population was judged to be so poor that it compromised recruitment to the armed forces resulting in the establishment of school meals. The Education Act of 1906 allowed councils to provide free meals to children from poor families (H.M. Government, 1906). It is important to note that this was not compulsory but up to each local authority to decide on its provision.

The free school meals (FSMs) provided in the immediate aftermath of WWII was linked with a concern about improving children's diets and was part of the social solidarité that the war had introduced; in effect, a continuation of the spirit of the Beveridge Report of 1942 (Beveridge, 1942). The provision of free milk came to an end in 1970 when the Education Secretary of the time, Margaret Thatcher, ended the scheme, leading to children in playgrounds singing the rhyme "Thatcher the milk snatcher". Nearly 20 years later, in 1989, proposed plans to ban free nursery milk were blocked by Margaret Thatcher in her role as prime minister, still stung by the epitaph "milk snatcher".

In 1992, in recognition of the lost emphasis on nutritional standards of school meals, The Caroline Walker Trust established an expert panel to publish sound nutritional guidelines for school meals (The Caroline Walker Trust, 1992). The Caroline Walker Trust recommended "a long-term commitment to a healthy school meal service is crucial, at both national and local levels" (p. 79).

The focus is now turning towards the integration of health and sustainability concerns into school meal policies, not least because, as Professor Kevin Morgan claimed, school food is the litmus test of a society's commitment to social justice, public health and sustainable development (Morgan, 2004, Morgan & Morley, 2003). So, linking procurement practices with healthy meals refer back to the concept of eco-nutrition/sustainable diets in Chapters 2, 3 and 5.

The Child Poverty Action Group's "Campaign for Free School Meals" was an important part of school meals' history in Scotland. It sought to ensure that in post-devolution Scotland, every school child could have at least one nutritious meal per day (Dickie, 2004). However, despite support from five political parties, the Bill was rejected on the grounds that "money would be better targeted than spent on universal provision" (Dickie, 2004, p. 64).

The arguments for a proper and adequately monitored school food system are that the impacts can be long term and influence home meals. The latest review was in 2013, and since then, we have seen little expansion of the service and in real terms drops in funding and even restrictions at central government level on entitlement (Dimbleby, 2021, Dimbleby & Vincent, 2013). In England, school meals are free to all in reception year 1 or year 2 pupils in state schools; this is regardless of household income. Beyond that, entitlement is based on receipt of one of the following benefits: income support, income-based Job Seeker's Allowance, or income-related Employment and Support Allowance. In Scotland, from January 2022, all children in primary 1 to primary 5 are entitled to FSMs in local authority; the family's financial situation doesn't matter. In Northern Ireland, the Minister for Education has started a review of the eligibility criteria for FSMs, including looking at moving towards a universal approach to some/all year groups as well as raising the income thresholds that apply to the eligibility criteria for applicants in receipt of Universal Credit or Working/Child Tax Credit. A public consultation exercise is expected to take place in 2023 (Northern Ireland Assembly, 2022). Currently, Northern Ireland's eligibility income threshold to £14,000 is almost double that of the rest of the UK, thereby ensuring that more children have access than in other UK contexts using a means-tested FSM system.

The 2020 NFS (National Food Strategy) report highlighted the existence of food poverty and suggested some immediate solutions such as the extension of FSMs, holiday feeding schemes and extension of food welfare schemes (Dimbleby, 2021). The 2021 NFS noted that:

> The Government has not implemented the recommendation to expand the eligibility for the free school meal scheme to include every child (up to the age of 16) from a household where a parent or guardian is in receipt of Universal Credit, or equivalent benefits.
>
> (Dimbleby, 2021)

There were also recommendations about extending holiday time feeding programmes to make up for the loss of school meals and the additional financial burden facing families in poverty. None of these formed part of the government response.

Despite all this, school meals remain important, with some local authorities and devolved administrations choosing to extend the provision of meals beyond what central government recommends as they see them as key to health and learning. The mayor of London has announced the extension of free school meals to all primary school children in the capital.

Salt reduction

In 2004, the Food Standards Agency (FSA) established a salt reduction programme, which reduced average population salt intakes by around 10%. Much of this reduction was achieved through partnership with industry to set voluntary reformulation targets for key categories of processed foods. Policy responsibility for the salt reduction programme was transferred to the Department of Health in 2010 (Wyness, Butriss & Stanner, 2012). The salt reduction strategy was delivered in three strands: a public health campaign, collaboration with industry on reformulation and the development of a single front-of-pack nutrition labelling scheme (Caraher & Hughes, 2019).

The FSA's voluntary salt reduction targets for a range of processed foods were established in collaboration with the food industry. These were published in 2006, and following a review in 2008, the Agency published a revised, more challenging targets for 2010 and 2012, by which time the responsibility had shifted to the Department of Health (He, Brinsden & MacGregor, 2014, MacGregor, He & Pombo-Rodrigues, 2015, Wyness, Butriss & Stanner, 2012).

The initial successful reductions in salt in the population are an example of a successful public-private partnership (PPP) (see Chapter 2 for models of food policy). The focus in the early stages was on reductions in foods which form a big part of the daily intake; so, reductions in salt in bread were responsible for a large part of the success. The transfer of responsibility to the Department of Health in 2010 did not result in many changes to the approaches to salt reformulation which relied on partnerships with the food industry. The rejection of a salt and sugar tax, as set out in the NFS, shows the resistance to formal regulation and the setting of mandatory standards (Burt et al., 2022). The argument from many public health practitioners was that what is now needed are mandatory requirements for the industry (MacGregor, He & Pombo-Rodrigues, 2015). Nonetheless, the initial work of the FSA stands as a mark of success and shows what can be achieved through engagement with the food industry.

Soda tax

The UK soda tax was introduced in the UK in 2018 and consists of a levy of 8p a litre for drinks with 5–8 grams of sugar per 100 millilitres and 24p per litre for those with more than 8 grams of sugar per 100 millilitres. The levy was a hypothecated tax designed to be used for health promotion purposes. The tax was applied to the whole of the UK via a treasury tax and not as a health tax for England. This was envisaged as part of a larger obesity strategy.

Research showed that the volume of soft drinks bought remained the same, but the amount of sugar in those drinks fell by 29.5 grams. UK households bought 10% less sugar through soft drinks in the year after the sugar tax was introduced by the government (Bandy et al., 2021, 2020). The levy resulted in companies reformulating their products to escape the levy. This illustrates the trade-off between calorie reductions on the one hand and raising funds by way of a sugar tax on the other hand, as reformulation to meet the requirements means less revenue for good causes. A tax that prompts large sugar reductions in products will raise less revenue and vice versa. The levy was designated to increase the Primary Physical Exercise and Sports Premium, which goes directly as a supplement to schools, and £360 million has been distributed in this way. However, £760 million of forecasted income generated by the tax on soft drinks has failed to be accounted for by government departments, despite an original promise that all of the tax raised would go towards improving children's health. The tax was a success in terms of reductions in sugar intake through soft drinks, but proposals in the NFS to extend the tax to sugar (and) in foods by setting mandatory standards were not accepted (White, 2022). Recent work by the celebrity chef Jamie Oliver urged the government to use the revenues from the soda tax to provide an extra 800,000 FSMs in England (Evans, 2022).

Obesity strategy

Although it has been long known that obesity was a growing health crisis, it was the publication of a Foresight report in 2007 that spurred policymakers into action (Foresight, 2007, McPherson, Marsh & Brown, 2007). This report set out direct (health care) and indirect costs (loss to the economy and loss of earnings) of obesity that were alarming in their scale. The indirect costs as a loss to the economy at least matched the direct health care costs. This led to a focus on obesity treatment and some prevention and policy interventions. The NHS (National Health Service) spent £6.1 billion on overweight and obesity-related ill health in 2014–2015 (projected to reach £9.7 billion by 2050), with the overall cost of obesity to wider society estimated to be £27 billion and projected to reach £49.9 billion per year by 2050.[39]

We noted in earlier chapters that there was no comprehensive approach to the prevention of obesity (Institute for Government, 2023, Theis & White, 2021); here are, however, some positive individual initiatives which deserve mention. The salt reduction, soda tax and school meals can all be seen as part of a broader approach to obesity policy. The danger to progress is that even those currently implemented may be in danger of being rescinded. This was noted in Chapters 1 and 7 on the food system, where an unstable political environment and three prime ministers with differing views promise different things: one to delay implementation of initiatives due to the unstable financial climate, another who promised to withdraw public health initiatives which threatened individual choice and a third who has not made public his positions on the state of obesity prevention!

So, while the overall obesity strategy is weak and lacks coherence, there are some bright spots which are worthy of note: these include the proposed introduction of a 9.00 pm watershed to limit junk food advertising online and on TV;[2] the introduction of calorie labelling in the out-of-home sector, restrictions on the promotions and placement in retail stores and their online equivalents of certain foods and drinks that are high in fat, salt or sugar (HFSS) or "less healthy"; and the "levelling-up agenda" to address inequalities between the north and south of England. Without a lead agency or minister, the development of comprehensive obesity policy or an approach remain elusive (see Chapters 2, 5 and 7 for a fuller discussion of these issues) including a systems and/or joined up approaches to food policy development. Some of the above initiatives have been kept in the public eye by individual celebrities and pressure groups, which is where we now turn.

Policy entrepreneurs/influencers

We saw above in the introduction to this chapter and chapters 3, 4 and 9 the influence of people like Caroline Walker and Geoffrey Cannon as policy influencers. What marks the modern period of policy development is the influence of some key individuals to sway public and political attitudes through the traditional media channels and new media. Prue Leith (perhaps now better known as a judge on *The Great British Bake Off*) has been concerned with school food, cooking in the school curricula and institutional catering in care homes and hospitals (Leith, 2012, 1998). She championed the case for improvements in all of these areas through chairing a number of committees and personal pronouncements.

There have been similar trends in the US and Australia where "celebrity chefs" have engaged with both implementation and policy formation. Alice Waters in the US and Stephanie Alexander in Australia are documented examples (Rousseau, 2013). The argument for some is that celebrities can bring wider support to campaigns to improve food and can act independently without the shackles with which even the voluntary sectors are saddled. Notwithstanding this, there are concerns over the roles and long-term impacts of such celebrity influence (Kelly & Harrison, 2009, Mentinis, 2017). There is a feeling that little acknowledgement is given to the groundwork done by campaigners and activists and the issues become associated with individual celebrities (Naik, 2008). There is also the possibility of conflict of commercial interests with policy ones (Caraher & Furey, 2022).

Perhaps the best known among these "celebrity" influencers is Jamie Oliver, who waged battles for better school food and the introduction of a soda tax (Naik, 2008).

Jamie Oliver

In 2005, British chef Jamie Oliver presented a television series called *Jamie's School Dinners*, which sought to improve the nutritional quality of school dinners in one English school (Gray et al., 2018, Kelly & Harrison, 2009, Naik, 2008). He showcased where improvements could and should be made and his work led to a broader campaign (*Feed Me Better*) which sought to improve school dinners on a national scale (Hollows & Jones, 2010). Subsequently, the Department for Education and Skills established the *School Food Trust* in 2005 as a non-departmental public body (NDPB) with the aim to provide support and advice to school administrators to improve the standard of school meals.

He has campaigned for the introduction of the soda tax and kept the issue on the agenda at a time when the formal voice of government was not favourable towards such a tax (Gray et al., 2018, Warin, 2011). He continues to campaign for better health through food and his latest work has been to extend school meals using tax revenues from the soda tax (Evans, 2022).

Marcus Rashford

During the COVID-19 lockdowns, there were concerns with the rise in food poverty and how children would access FSMs with schools being shut. A campaign to address this was spearheaded by a Manchester United and England footballer Marcus Rashford (Keith, 2020). He was vocal in his criticism of cutbacks and lack of action to address food poverty among children. He cited his own example of growing up relying on a hard-working mother and benefits such as school meals. In September 2020, he established the Child Poverty task force, a coalition of charities, NGOs and business calling for an end to child poverty (see https://endchildfoodpoverty.org). He has worked with groups such as the Food Foundation as an ambassador to keep issues in the public domain (Bhattacharya & Shepherd, 2020). His celebrity status and personal experience of food poverty enables him to challenge government policy. He wrote an open letter to MPs and along with Henry Dimbleby (the author of the NFS) has written calling for an end to child poverty (Elba, Rashford & Dimbleby, 2020). He succeeded in the shorter term, during the pandemic, in convincing the government to perform U-turns on school feeding during holiday times and on benefit levels (Siddique, 2020).

Jack Monroe

Jack Monroe is an author, cook and food poverty activist who has campaigned ion issues related to food access and affordability (Martin, 2022, Monroe, 2014). She writes from her experience of food insecurity and use of food banks and providing food for herself and young son (Garthwaite, 2016). She has been described by some as an "austerity celebrity" who draws on her own experiences to frame the debate and for some, UK tabloid media has become a controversial figure to attack, with assaults on her personal identify and experiences. She has challenged traditional measures of food insecurity and surveys of food price surveys. She has argued that prices for cheaper food products have soared as availability fell, contributing to rising hunger and poverty and that traditional food cost surveys do not always account for these purchases among low-income households and the disproportionate effect this has on these households. This is what others have called the "poverty premium". Her campaigning work in 2022 persuaded the Office for National Statistics to change its methodology to develop an inflation index to track basic food prices as opposed to a typical basket approach.

Groups plugging gaps

The above forms of policy entrepreneurship do not occur in isolation and there are links to policy groups and charities as well as the groundwork from researchers. There are also examples of NGOs and charity entrepreneurs keeping food policy on the agenda. The Work of Sustain and the Food Foundation stand out in this respect. What is apparent is that they are filling gaps in public sector monitoring and service delivery, often using the data gathered to push for change, thus straddling the activities of monitoring and campaigners.

Like the individual policy entrepreneurs above, there are now a range of groups promoting food policy. These reflect an earlier generation of NGOs such as the Caroline Walker Trust and the Child Poverty Action Group (CPAG) which emerged to tackle food poverty. Following the publication of Brian Abel-Smith and Peter Townsend's work *The Poor and the Poorest*, the CPAG became politically active in the 1970s spurred on by a series of reports on poverty which showed a new face to poverty. Some modern equivalents are provided below: Sustain, The Food Foundation. Nourish Scotland, Nourish Northern Ireland, Food Sense Wales and a range of local food projects.

Sustain

Sustain is an alliance of organisations and communities which work for a better system of food, farming and fishing. The alliance was formed in 1999 from the mergers of The National Food Alliance and the Sustainable Agriculture Food and Environment (SAFE) Alliance, both of which had been established over ten years ago.[3]

Member organisations must have an interest in food or farming issues and support the general aims and work of the alliance. However, support for particular projects or campaigns is on an "opt in" basis; so, membership does not mean that an organisation gives its backing to each Sustain initiative. The alliance fulfils its aims which are through running a multitude of different projects and campaigns to improve food and farming (Reynolds, 2009). They outline seven areas of work:

- Cost of living crisis
- Sustainable farming and fishing
- Climate and nature emergency
- Brexit and trade
- Good food economy
- Good food for all
- Local action

On their website, they list a number of success stories; these include:

- Protecting children's health
- Saving the fish in our seas
- Making our cities healthier
- Improving hospital food
- Helping sustainable farmers
- Saving our antibiotics
- The rise of Real Bread

Details can be found on the website.[4] Working with the members and supporters, Sustain campaigned for a healthy and sustainable food system, which is publicly accountable and socially and environmentally responsible. They also partner with other alliances and campaigning groups as well as linking with high-profile celebrities to get the messages across.

The Food Foundation

The Food Foundation works with individuals such as Marcus Rashford and Jamie Oliver. They describe themselves on their website as:

> policy entrepreneurs … [*who*] use surprising and inventive ideas to catalyse and deliver fundamental change in the food system by building and synthesising strong evidence, shaping powerful coalitions, harnessing citizens' voices and driving progress with impactful communications. We continually identify new opportunities for action, and trial new levers for change.
>
> (The Food Foundation, n.d.)

The Foundation continues to monitor levels of food insecurity and run a number of healthy eating projects.

Nourish Scotland

This is a charity that works with a wide range of stakeholders, including small producers, community groups, NGOs, local authorities and other public bodies to put sustainable, healthy, local food at the heart of Scotland's food system (www.nourishscotland.org). The recent Nourish Scotland promotion of a Good Food Bill through the Scottish Parliament shows what can be achieved.

Food Sense Wales

Food Sense Wales (n.d.) is a charity that developed from initial work in Cardiff. It works with communities, organisations, policymakers and government across Wales. They have adopted "a food in all policies" approach that can be achieved through research, cross sector collaboration and by mobilising citizens and stakeholders as part of a "Wales Good Food Movement" (see Chapter 2 for models of food policy).

Consumer Council for Northern Ireland

This is an example of a non-specialist food organisation which does considerable work on food policy (www.consumercouncil.org.uk). The Consumer Council for Northern Ireland (the

Consumer Council) was established in April 1985 as a NDPB under the General Consumer Council (Northern Ireland) Order 1984 (The Order). It has a degree of operational autonomy from its sponsor, the Department for the Economy (DfE) and the Northern Ireland executive and UK government departments that fund its activities and with which it operates. The Order sets out the Consumer Council's principal statutory duty as promoting and safeguarding the interests of consumers in Northern Ireland by empowering them and providing a strong representative voice to policymakers, regulators and service providers. In addition, the Order gives the Consumer Council powers to research and report on the issues or barriers Northern Ireland consumers might face, in order to access affordable, good, nutritious and enjoyable food of an appropriate quality and quantity to sustain an acceptable standard of living appropriate for all.

The Consumer Council enjoys opportunities to influence food policy at the (pre-) consultation stages; convenes an annual Consumer Week and hosts consumer focus groups for thematic areas; and benefits from a joined-up approach regarding the cost of living, financial inclusion, Brexit and food policy. Given this latter functionality and the Council's statutory duty for financial services/financial inclusion, it acts also as a referral agent to food banks. The Council therefore provides a holistic approach to food policy, given the intelligence it acquires from dedicated food research projects, consumers' complaints, consumer outreach work to priority vulnerable groups, engagement with key stakeholders, consumer resilience work and a statutory food remit focused on food affordability and accessibility.

Nourish NI

Nourish NI is a charity that is working to ensure the availability of good, healthy food to everyone. Its primary purpose is to build and support a sustainable food movement in Northern Ireland and work towards changing the food system dramatically so that healthy and sustainable food becomes a defining characteristic of Northern Ireland, given the region's pride in its food culture.

Nourish NI (formerly known as Belfast Food Network) was initially invited by Sustainable Food Cities (now Sustainable Food Places) to submit a bid to be one of six founding cities of the movement in the UK. It was established in 2013 and set up multi-sectoral working groups across the six core themes: (1) promoting healthy and sustainable food to the public; (2) tackling food poverty, diet-related ill health and access to affordable healthy food; (3) building community food knowledge, skills, resources and project; (4) promoting a vibrant and diverse sustainable food economy; (5) transforming catering and food procurement; and (6) reducing waste and the ecological footprint of the food system). Its work has been informed by citywide scoping of existing food-related activities in Belfast to develop an audit and gap analysis of sustainable food programmes. By 2016, it had secured its Bronze Award status for its work on developing sustainable food systems.

In a move to be less Belfast-centric, Nourish NI is working with many of Northern Ireland's 11 local councils (five at the time of writing, with a further two scheduled to join in 2023) to build a sustainable food movement. It places much emphasis on its co-ordination (linking partners together for the collective benefits of scale) and education roles in terms of sustainable food habits.

Local food projects

There are a vast number of local food projects which deliver on national policy agendas and lobby to influence policy (Caraher & Dowler, 2007, Lang, Dowler & Hunter, 2006). A review

Table 11.1 List of some important websites for local food projects

Description	Examples
The Local Government Association (LGA).	Case studies in Local Authorities at www.local.gov.uk/ our-support/safer-and-more-sustainable-communities/ cost-living-hub/cost-living-food-insecurity-and
(UK) Sustainable Food Places (previously the Sustainable Food Cities).	www.sustainablefoodplaces.org
Food for Cities.	An international group with examples of food in cities - https://dgroups.org/fao/food-for-cities?e=/__e/ vc/1ecbb571-1bb7-4331-b535-a4e41efb7419

of the Scottish Community Diet project highlighted the importance of locally based food initiatives (Lang, Dowler & Hunter, 2006).

Some examples are these are laid out in Table 11.1. These are often a partnership or collaboration between NGOs/charities and local authorities.

Food policy in the devolved administrations

Within the UK, the devolved administrations of Northern Ireland, Scotland and Wales have some separate powers related to food. Policy responsibility for food and health is largely devolved to Scotland, Wales and Northern Ireland. Both Northern Ireland and Wales have their own FSAs. The exceptions to decentralised policy are trade, taxation, food, agriculture and welfare, which apply to all of the UK.

The Northern Ireland development of a food strategy and the consultation "Food at the Heart of Our Society – A Prospectus for Change" shows a willingness to tackle the issues of poverty and the power of the food industry in a cross-departmental way.

Similarly, with regard to school meals and health, Northern Ireland's Food in Schools Forum enables interdepartmental dialogue in Northern Ireland to support a joined-up approach to school food policies and programmes. Furthermore, Northern Ireland policymakers' (Department of Education and Department for Communities) agility in ensuring that the cash equivalent of FSMs was paid into parents' bank accounts during school closures due to COVID-19 to reduce the incidence of holiday hunger was a move that was praised as progressive, with no restrictions on use.

Support for Community Cooking Interventions (CCIs) in Scotland and Wales

A number of national food plans have included cooking and food skills as key components of their strategies. For example, the Brazilian NFS includes cooking and culinary traditions as important factors in achieving healthy diets (Hawkes et al., 2015).

In two of the UK's nations, Scotland and Wales, cooking initiatives are supported from training through to evaluation. In Scotland, the training is supported by NHS Scotland, with classes run by the Royal Environmental Health Institute of Scotland (REHIS). In addition, Community Food and Health Scotland (www.communityfoodandhealth.org.uk) provide extensive guidance and signpost organisations that provide training and run classes. The training offered in Wales also features a quality assurance mechanism to maintain consistent messages across courses. In Wales, the training for practitioners is standardised and provided by nutritionists, accredited by the Welsh awarding organisation, Agored Cymru. The programme's aims are to provide cooking or food literacy skills for life.

Academic policy influencers

Many academics have played important roles in fathering food policy, not just through their research but via their policy advocacy and entrepreneurship. Already mentioned above were Peter Townsend and Caroline Walker. Key among those with strong academic and policy influence are the three listed in Table 11.2. Some of these such as Lang also had experience in the NGO world. There are, of course, many who have contributed to evidence for food policy, but those listed in Table 11.2 have contributed to the evidence base of food policy implementation (see Chapter 2 for a distinction between evidence for and evidence of food policy).

The academics listed in Table 11.2 are part of a larger cadre of those engaged in research and policy practice and might be distinguished from those engaged in "blue sky research" or the distinction that was made in Chapters 2 and 3 of those who design and produce research for food policy. All listed above, Lang, Dowler and Loopstra, produce both research for and of food policy.

Table 11.2 Examples of academic policy influencers

Academic policy influencer	Notable for
Tim Lang.	Campaigner, activist and academic. He ran the London Food Commission (Lang, 2022a, 2022b, 2020, Lang & McKee, 2022).
Elizabeth Dowler.	Responsible for keeping food poverty on the agenda through her academic and civic contributions to communities (Dowler & Calvert, 1995, Dowler & O'Connor, 2012, Dowler, Turner & Dobson, 2001).
Rachel Loopstra.	Has highlighted the modern issue of poverty and food banks (Loopstra & Lalor, 2017, Loopstra et al., 2015, Loopstra & Tarasuk, 2015).

Conclusions

The examples provided above show how many different inputs to food policy there are from the formal policymakers in government (minister and civil servants) through to the groups and individuals who are willing to challenge and promote certain activities.

The success is often noteworthy whether in the area of salt or the soda tax or the introduction of new thinking to food policy, as in the work of Lang on eco-nutrition or sustainable diets (see Chapter 2) (Lang & Mason, 2018, Mason & Lang, 2017) Some initiatives can still lack a comprehensive approach and can rank as individual wins in the bigger war of ideas and implementation of food policy. Theis and White point to the lack of a joined-up approach to food policy (Theis & White, 2021), and as we were writing this chapter, news broke that the promised 9 pm watershed and online ban on paid advertising for food and drink HFSS delayed until 2023 has now been further delayed until October 2025. Food policy actions are often about rearguard action defending existing initiatives while arguing for expansion of a programme or initiative.

This is often so with school meals where exposure of existing limitations or calls for expansion of the programme can lead to some calling for the abandonment of the programme.

An example comes from the programme called Healthy Start which is a food voucher scheme for young children and pregnant women. Egger (2021) says that:

> Despite its popularity with government and charitable organizations, it only reaches half of those eligible, and food insecurity and health inequalities have worsened since its implementation. The significant and steady decline in uptake has focused civil society and the government on increasing uptake and considering modifications to delivery but not on questioning whether the scheme is the best tool to address poor nutrition in young children.

She goes on to make a case for making the scheme universal for all pregnant women and children under four years old, of changing the restrictions on purchasable items and of increasing the voucher amount and perhaps moving to a cash-based system. This would tackle stigma and result in longer-term economic returns via better health and less illness (Egger, 2021).

What emerges from much of the exemplars used in this and other chapters is twofold. First, the push is often because of the lack of formal policy such as regulation or legislation; the proclivity of formal state institutions for informal partnerships such as PPPs and process targets (Knai et al., 2015, Panjwani & Caraher, 2018). There is a place for PPPs in furthering food policy, but they need to be controlled through targets, agreed outcomes and holding companies to account.

With the global crisis in food and energy prices, the need to work with non-food-focussed NGOs becomes even more apparent. We see this in the examples of some of the NGOs such as the Consumer Council for Northern Ireland. We are aware of the need to work with organisations focussed on household debt and income (Caraher & Furey, 2021).

Local food projects can be very powerful in showing the problems and what can be done to ameliorate them (Caraher & Dowler, 2007, Dowler & Caraher, 2003). But they should not be seen as substitutes for state or government action at the local, regional or national levels. Often, such projects end up picking up the pieces from the lack of or as a consequence of government policy. Food banks provide such an example where austerity and changes to welfare have seen the number of food banks increase to meet the needs of the "hungry", but they cannot tackle the underlying issues which result in people requiring help (Caraher, 2014, Caraher & Furey, 2018, Loopstra et al., 2015). What they can do is to continue to provide help to those in need while using their vast resources and networks to lobby for changes in policy.

Among the lessons to be learnt from the examples in this chapter are the importance of perseverance; using media, including social media, to get the case heard and public opinion; using data and case studies to make clear the case for food policy; representing and presenting the voices of those impacted by policy or lack of it; developing and maintaining partnerships; building networks from the ground up; having high-profile ambassadors with public and media credibility; and finally accepting that individual actions are themselves part of a bigger whole policy approach (Page & Caraher, 2020, Wells, 2017).

Notes

1 The last vestiges of rationing did not end until 1954. Sugar in 1953, butter in May 1954, margarine, cooking fats and cheese and finally in June 1954, meat and bacon.
2 Now postponed until November 2025, see Sustain website https://www.sustainweb.org/news/dec22-watershed-delay/?utm_source=Sustain&utm_campaign=ea5460422b-EMAIL_CAMPAIGN_2021_07_07_09_49_COPY_01&utm_medium=email&utm_term=0_d2d28e0c33-ea5460422b-261638093.
3 See https://www.sustainweb.org/about/consultation_document_on_the_creation_of_sustain/.
4 See https://www.sustainweb.org/about/working_together_our_success_stories/.

References

Acheson, D. 1998, *Independent Inquiry into Inequalities in Health Report*, The Stationery Office, London.

Bandy, L.K., Hollowell, S., Harrington, R., Scarborough, P., Jebb, S. & Rayner, M. 2021, "Assessing the healthiness of UK food companies' product portfolios using food sales and nutrient composition data", *PLoS ONE*, vol. 16, no. 8, p. e0254833. https://doi.org/10.1371/journal.pone.0254833

Bandy, L.K., Scarborough, P., Harrington, R.A., Rayner, M. & Jebb, S.A. 2020, "Reductions in sugar sales from soft drinks in the UK from 2015 to 2018", *BMC Medicine*, vol. 18, no. 1, p. 20. https://doi.org/10.1186/s12916-019-1477-4

Beveridge, W.H. 1942, *Social Insurance and Allied Services. Cmd 6404*, His Majesty's Stationery Office, London.

Bhattacharya, A. & Shepherd, J. 2020, *Measuring and Mitigating Child Hunger in the UK*, Social Market Foundation, London.

Burt, H.E., Brown, M.K., He, F.J. & MacGregor, G.A. 2022, "Salt: the forgotten foe in UK public health policy", *BMJ*, vol. 377, p. e070686. https://doi.org/10.1136/bmj-2022-070686

Buss, D.H. 1993, "The British Diet Since the End of Food Rationing" in *Food, Diet and Economic Change Past and Present*, eds. C. Geissler & D.J. Oddy, Leicester University Press, Leicester, pp. 121–132.

Cannon, G. 1989, *The Food Fight: The life and work of Caroline Walker*, Ebury Press, London.

Caraher, M. 2014, *Food Banks as Indicators of the New 'Tory' Style Poor Law* [Homepage of WAKEUPSCOTLAND], [Online]. Available from: https://wakeupscotland.wordpress.com/2014/12/01/martin-caraher-food-banks-as-indicators-of-the-new-tory-style-poor-law/ [2019, 03/06].

Caraher, M. & Dowler, E. 2007, "Food projects in London: lessons for policy and practice – a hidden sector and the need for 'more unhealthy puddings... sometimes'", *Health Education Journal*, vol. 66, no. 2, pp. 188–205. https://doi.org/10.1177/0017896907076762

Caraher, M. & Furey, S. 2022, "The 'Hunger Industrial Complex' and the death of welfare", *Frontiers in Public Health*, vol. 10. https://doi.org/10.3389/fpubh.2022.950955

Caraher, M. & Furey, S. 2021, *Debt and Diet*, 22nd July 2021 edn, Food Research Collaboration, https://foodresearch.org.uk/blogs/debt-and-diet/.

Caraher, M. & Furey, S. 2018, *The Economics of Emergency Food Aid Provision: A Financial, Social and Cultural Perspective*, Palgrave Macmillan, Cham, Switzerland.

Caraher, M. & Hughes, N. 2019, "Tackling salt consumption outside the home", *BMJ*, vol. 364, p. l1087. https://doi.org/10.1136/bmj.l1087

Curry, D., Browning, H., Davis, P., Ferguson, I., Hutton, D., Julius, D., Reynolds, F., Tinsley, M., Varney, D. & Wynne, G. 2002, *Farming and Food: A Sustainable Future: Report of the Policy Commission on the Future of Farming and Food*, Policy Commission on the Future of Farming and Food, Crown Copyright, London.

Department for Environment Food & Rural Affairs (DEFRA) 2022, *Government food strategy*, DEFRA, https://www.gov.uk/government/publications/governmentfood- strategy/government-food-strategy.

Dickie, J. 2004, "The Campaign for Free School Meals in Scotland" in *A Good Practice Guide to School Meals*, eds. C. Hurley & A. Riley, Child Poverty Action Group, London, pp. 63–68.

Dimbleby, H. 2021, *National Food Strategy, Independent Review: The Plan*, https://www.nationalfood-strategy.org.

Dimbleby, H. & Lewis, J. 2023, *Ravenous: How to get ourselves and our planet into shape*, Profile Books, London.

Dimbleby, H. & Vincent, J. 2013, *The School Food Plan*, Department of Education, London.

Dowler, E. & Calvert, C. 1995, *Nutrition and Diet in Lone-Parent Families in London*, Family Policy Studies Centre, London.

Dowler, E. & Caraher, M. 2003, "Local food projects: the new philanthropy?", *Political Quarterly*, vol. 74, no. 1, pp. 57–65. https://doi.org/10.1111/1467-923X.00512

Dowler, E. & O'Connor, D. 2012, "Rights-based approaches to addressing food poverty and food insecurity in Ireland and UK", *Social Science and Medicine*, vol. 74, no. 1, pp. 44–51. https://doi.org/10.1016/j.socscimed.2011.08.036

Dowler, E., Turner, S. & Dobson, B. 2001, *Poverty Bites: Food, Health and Poor Families*, CPAG, London.

Eccles, L. 2023, *Leon founder quits official role over 'insane' failure on obesity*, March 19th, page 11edn, *The Sunday Times*, London.

Egger, L. 2021, *From Food Welfare to Healthy Start: A Social and Economic Perspective*, Ph.D. edn, City, University of London, London.

Elba, I., Rashford, M. & Dimbleby, H. 2020, "We all stand together", *Nature Food*, vol. 1, no. 10, pp. 583–583.

Evans, J. 2022, Jamie Oliver urges UK to use sugar tax to fund free school meals, 27 December, *Financial Times*, https://www.ft.com/content/6229ce34-c59e-4709-9c8a-dd2c500e2584.

Food Ethics Council. 2022, *Responding to the Government Food Strategy*, Food Ethics Council, https://www.foodethicscouncil.org/resource/government-food-strategy-response/.

Food Sense Wales, n.d., *Co-creating a food system for Wales that's good for people and the planet*, www.foodsensewales.org.uk

Foresight 2007, *Foresight. Tackling Obesities: Future Choices – Project Report*, The Stationery Office, London.

Garthwaite, K. 2016, "Foreword by Jack Monroe", in *Hunger Pains: Life Inside Foodbank Britain*, Policy Press, Bristol, pp. ix–xi.

Gray, E.M., Pluim, C., Pike, J. & Leahy, D. 2018, "'Someone has to keep shouting': celebrities as food pedagogues", vol. 9, no. 1, pp. 69–83. https://doi.org/10.1080/19392397.2017.1334566

Hawkes, C., Smith, T.G., Jewell, J., Wardle, J., Hammond, R.A., Friel, S. & Kain, J. 2015, "Smart food policies for obesity prevention", *The Lancet*, vol. 385, no. 9985, pp. 2410–2421. https://doi.org/10.1016/S0140-6736(14)61745-1

He, F.J., Brinsden, H.C. & MacGregor, G.A. 2014, "Salt reduction in the United Kingdom: a successful experiment in public health", *Journal of Human Hypertension*, vol. 28, no. 6, pp. 345–352. https://doi.org/10.1038/jhh.2013.105

H.M. Government 1906, *Education Provision of Meals Act 190. Chapter 57*, Rowland Bailey Esq, London.

Hollows, J. & Jones, S. 2010, "'At least he's doing something': Moral entrepreneurship and individual responsibility in Jamie's Ministry of Food", *European Journal of Cultural Studies*, vol. 13, no. 3, pp. 307–322. https://doi.org/10.1177/1367549410363197

Institute for Government. 2023, *Tackling Obesity: Improving policy making on food and health*, Institute for Government, https://www.instituteforgovernment.org.uk/sites/default/files/2023-04/tackling-obesity.pdf.

Keith, R. 2020, *Marcus Rashford: a brief history of free school meals in the UK*, The Conversation, https://theconversation.com/marcus-rashford-a-brief-history-of-free-school-meals-in-the-uk-140896#comment_2255411.

Kelly, P. & Harrison, L. 2009, *Working in Jamie's Kitchen: salvation, passion and young workers*, Palgrave Macmillan, Chippenham.

Knai, C., Petticrew, M., Durand, M.A., Eastmure, E., James, L., Mehrotra, A., Scott, C. & Mays, N. 2015, "Has a public–private partnership resulted in action on healthier diets in England? An analysis of the Public Health Responsibility Deal food pledges", *Food Policy*, vol. 54, pp. 1–10. https://doi.org/10.1016/j.foodpol.2015.04.002

Lang, T. 2022a, "Boris Johnson's food strategy fails to address food poverty and the cost-of-living crisis", *The New Statesman*, [Online], vol. 13 June, 15th June. Available from: https://www.newstatesman.com/environment/food-farming/2022/06/boris-johnsons-food-strategy-fails-to-address-food-poverty-and-the-cost-of-living-crisis.

Lang, T. 2022b, "Food policy in a changing world: implications for nutritionists", *Proceedings of the Nutrition Society*, vol 81, no 2, pp. 176–189. doi:10.1017/S0029665122000817.

Lang, T. 2020, *Feeding Britain: Our Food Problems and How to Fix Them*, Pelican, London.

Lang, T., Dowler, E. & Hunter, D.J. 2006, *Review of the Scottish Diet Action Plan Progress and Impacts 1996–2005*, NHS Scotland, Edinburgh.

Lang, T. & Mason, P. 2018, "Sustainable diet policy development: implications of multi-criteria and other approaches, 2008–2017", *Proceedings of the Nutrition Society*, vol. 77, no. 3, pp. 331–346.

Lang, T. & McKee, M. 2022, "The reinvasion of Ukraine threatens global food supplies", *BMJ*, vol. 376, p. o676. https://doi.org/10.1136/bmj.o676

Le Gros Clark, F. 1948, *Social History of the School Meals Service*, London Council of Social Services, London.

Leith, P. 2012, *Relish: My life on a Plate*, Quercus, London.

Leith, P. 1998, "Cooking with Kids" in *Consuming Passions: Food in the Age of Anxiety*, eds. S. Griffiths & J. Wallace, Mandolin Press, Manchester, pp. 58–65.

Loopstra, R. & Lalor, D. 2017, *Financial Insecurity, Food Insecurity, and Disability: The Profile of People Receiving Emergency Food Assistance from the Trussell Trust Foodbank Network in Britain Internet*, The Trussell Trust, Salisbury.

Loopstra, R., Reeves, A., Taylor-Robinson, D., Barr, B., McKee, M. & Loopstra, R. 2015, "Austerity, sanctions, and the rise of food banks in the UK", *BMJ*, vol. 350. https://doi.org/10.1136/bmj.h1775

Loopstra, R. & Tarasuk, V. 2015, "Food bank usage is a poor indicator of food insecurity: insights from Canada", *Social Policy and Society*, vol. 14, no. 3, pp. 443–455. https://doi.org/10.1017/S1474746415000184

McGrath, D. 2023, *Food Tsar Blames Conservative Ideology on Obesity Inaction as He Quits*, March 20th edn, Press Association Mediapoint, https://advance.lexis.com/api/document?collection=news&id=urn:contentItem:67TM-JF81-JCBD-Y3NF-00000-00&context=1519360.MacGregor, G.A., He, F.J. & Pombo-Rodrigues, S. 2015, "Food and the responsibility deal: how the salt reduction strategy was derailed", *BMJ*, vol. 350. https://doi.org/10.1136/bmj.h1936

Martin, J. 2022, "Jack Monroe and the cultural politics of the austerity celebrity", *European Journal of Cultural Studies*, vol. 25, no. 4, pp. 1156–1173. https://doi.org/10.1177/13675494211030938

Mason, P. & Lang, T. 2017, *Sustainable Diets: How Ecological Nutrition Can Transform Consumption and the Food System*, Routledge, London.

McPherson, K., Marsh, T. & Brown, M. 2007, "Foresight report on obesity", *The Lancet*, vol. 370, no. 9601, p. 1755. https://doi.org/10.1016/S0140-6736(07)61740-1

Mentinis, M. 2017, "Romanticised chefs and the psychopolitics of gastroporn", *Culture & Psychology*, vol. 23, no. 1, pp. 128–143. https://doi.org/10.1177/1354067X15621477

Monroe, J. 2014, *A Girl Called Jack: 100 Delicious Budget Recipes*, Penguin, Harmonsworth.

Morgan, K. 2004, *School Meals and Sustainable Food Chains: The Role of Creative Public Procurement*, Carloine Walker Trust, London.

Morgan, K. & Morley, A. 2003, *School Meals: Healthy Eating & Sustainable Food Chains*, The Regeneration Institute, Cardiff University, Cardiff.

Naik, A. 2008, "Did Jamie Oliver really put school dinners on the agenda? An examination of the role of the media in policy making", *The Political Quarterly*, vol. 79, no. 3, pp. 426–433. https://doi.org/10.1111/j.1467-923X.2008.00944.x

Northern Ireland Assembly. 2022, *Question results: written questions on the subject free school meals*, Northern Ireland Assembly, http://aims.niassembly.gov.uk/questions/subjectsearchresults.aspx?&t=R5JWGPGj7WT0fSkLN+L7pFQ3czQOeYT1&pn=0&qfv=1&tm=2&ss=R5JWGPGj7WT0fSkLN+L7pFQ3czQOeYT1&sus=1&tc=1.

Page, D. & Caraher, M. 2020, "A novel approach to local level food policy case studies: application of the advocacy coalition framework", *Novel Techniques in Nutrition & Food Science*, vol. 4, no. 5. https://doi.org/10.31031/ntnf.2020.04.000597

Panjwani, C. & Caraher, M. 2018, "CASE 11 Voluntary agreements and the power of the food industry: the Public Health Responsibility Deal in England" in *Public Health and the Food and Drinks Industry: The Governance and Ethics of Interaction. Lessons from Research, Policy and Practice*, ed. M. Mwatsama, UK Health Forum, London, pp. 110–120.

Parsons, K. & Barling, D. 2022, "England's food policy coordination and the Covid-19 response", *Food Security*, vol 14, pp. 1027–1043. https://doi.org/10.1007/s12571-022-01280-1

Prynne, C., Paul, A., Price, G., Day, K., Hilder, W. & Wadsworth, M. 1999, "Food and nutrient intake of a national sample of 4-year-old children in 1950: comparison with the 1990s", *Public Health Nutrition*, vol. 2, no. 4, pp. 537–547. https://doi.org/10.1017/S1368980099000725

Reynolds, B. 2009, "Feeding a world city: the London food strategy", *International Planning Studies*, vol. 14, no. 4, pp. 417–424.

Rousseau, S. 2013, *Food Media: Celebrity Chefs and the Politics of Everyday Interference*, Bloomsbury, London.

Sharp, I. n.d., *Nutritional Guidelines for School Meals: Report of an Expert Working Group*, Caroline Walker Trust, London.

Sharp, I. 1996, *At Least Five a Day Strategies to Increase Vegetable and Fruit Consumption*, National Heart Forum, London.

Siddique, H. 2020, Marcus Rashford forces Boris Johnson into second U-turn on child food poverty, 8 November, *The Guardian*, https://www.theguardian.com/education/2020/nov/08/marcus-rashford-forces-boris-johnson-into-second-u-turn-on-child-food-poverty.

The Caroline Walker Trust. 1992, *Expert Report Nutritional Guidelines for School Meals*, The Caroline Walker Trust, London.

The Food Foundation n.d., Who we are. Accessed 19th March, 2023, https://foodfoundation.org.uk.

Theis, D.R.Z. & White, M. 2021, "Is obesity policy in England fit for purpose? Analysis of government strategies and policies, 1992–2020", *The Milbank Quarterly*, vol. 99, no. 1, pp. 126–170. https://doi.org/10.1111/1468-0009.12498

Walker, C. & Cannon, G. 1984, *The Food Scandal: What's Wrong with the British Diet and How to Put It Right*, Century Publishing, London.

Warin, M. 2011, "Foucault's progeny: Jamie Oliver and the art of governing obesity", *Social Theory & Health*, vol. 9, no. 1, pp. 24–40. https://doi.org/10.1057/sth.2010.2

Wells, R. 2017, "Mediating the spaces of diet and health: a critical analysis of reporting on nutrition and colorectal cancer in the UK", *Geoforum*, vol. 84, pp. 228–238. https://doi.org/10.1016/j.geoforum.2016.05.001

White, M. 2022, "Half hearted and half baked: the government's new food strategy", *BMJ*, vol. 377, p. o1520. https://doi.org/10.1136/bmj.o1520

Wyness, L.A., Butriss, J.L. & Stanner, S.A. 2012, "Reducing the population's sodium intake: the UK Food Standards Agency's salt reduction programme", *Public Health Nutrition*, vol. 15, no. 2, pp. 254–261. https://doi.org/10.1017/S1368980011000966

12 Conclusions, reflections and the future for food policy

Introduction

As has been shown in previous chapters, we are in a state of change where the food system is threatened on a number of fronts: climate, extreme weather events (drought and flooding), energy costs, food production and import cost rises, country tariffs/export duties, lower use of fertilisers and thus reductions in yields, rising prices, and households spending more but buying figure less food. Using wheat as an example, the following is the situation at the beginning of 2023: flooding in Australia[1] means a reduced crop in 2023; Argentina is predicting a 40% decrease; drought in the US plains and Brazil will result in a reduced crop in 2023 – all this along with continued uncertainty with Ukrainian crop production, harvesting and export. This scenario is repeated across a range of commodities such as corn, rice and edible oils. Food import costs are forcing poorer countries to restrict consumption and in rich countries, such as the UK, low-income consumers are cutting back. Global organisations, such as the FAO (Food and Agricultural Organization) and the World Bank, are predicting a series of food shortages and famines in 2023 (Food and Agriculture Organization of the United Nations & World Food Programme, 2022, The World Bank, 2021). Famine is the extreme dimension of food insecurity, but even in countries of the Global North, there is already evidence of rising levels of food insecurity.

As the state of the world food supply changes, along with it is the ability of countries such as the UK to source food globally and use the world as its food bowl when domestic shortages occur. Collingham pointed out that the UK and other countries with colonies moved from a reliance on imports from these countries to a market system based on free trade with few barriers (Collingham, 2017). She classified this as the "hungry empire", and the moves to global markets represents the solidification of the final stage in the change from a reliance on the colonies with taxes and tariffs to trade on the global market with few barriers to trade. This shifted the focus on food policy from protectionism to a concern with global trade with few barriers. These global barriers are controlled and act in favour of the major countries of the OECD. The World Trade Organization (WTO) is the global regulator, and Chang says of it:

> the WTO puts fewer restrictions on trade protection and subsidies for agricultural producers than for manufacturing firms. It is not difficult to guess why – relatively speaking, rich countries have weaker agriculture and poor countries have weaker manufacturing. Or take the WTO rules limiting national governments' ability to regulate MNCs operating within their borders. The WTO bans the use of local contents requirement (that is, a government requiring that MNCs[2] buy more than a certain proportion of their inputs locally, rather than importing them). This rule disproportionately benefits rich countries because most MNCs are from rich countries.

(Chang, 2022, p. 73)

DOI: 10.4324/9781003260301-12

Despite these WTO restrictions, in 2022, many countries limited exports and became focused on developing self-sufficiency, thus limiting the ability of global trading to address food shortages by buying food from other countries (see Chapters 7 and 8). And, as we saw in Chapter 8, the profits of the big transnational companies (TNCs) increased at the expense of the "poor" in many countries, including the UK (Oxfam, 2022).

The UK

In the UK food supply system, similar problems are being encountered. With respect to domestic production, UK farmers are facing problems with increased energy and fertiliser costs. The loss of EU Common Agricultural Policy (CAP) payments and the uncertainty of its replacement (see Chapter 7) have left farmers facing a precarious future. Key among the issues are:

- Subsidies are the difference between profit and making a loss for over 40% of farms (Levitt, 2022).
- The loss of CAP subsidies left farmers 20% worse off in 2021.
- While agriculture and subsidies are a devolved competency, the budget allocations fall far below what was previously allocated from the CAP for both Wales and Scotland.

The National Farmers' Union (NFU) of England and Wales showed that:

- Production costs for growers had risen by 27% in 2022, impacting on the tomato, broccoli, apples and root vegetable growers.
- Energy costs had climbed by 165%, fertiliser by 40%, transport by 28% and labour – where it was available – by 13%.
- £60 million worth of crops was left in the fields due to a shortage of labour and low farm gate prices (Adapted from NFU, 2022).

Lang says: "UK self-sufficiency rose from 50–60% in the post-war period to a heady 80% by the early 1980s (the high point of the EU subsidy regime). It has declined slowly since" (Lang, 2020, p. 100) and later on "[I]mproved UK food security almost certainly means raising UK food production figures from 2018's 53% by value and from 61% 'self sufficiency' to at least 80%, or a level to which the country could resort in crisis" (Lang, 2020, p. 447). Lang says we are currently far from achieving these figures.

The UK food system faces a number of challenges which can be found in disparate polices, both existing and future developments to come. The House of Lords Select Committee on Food, Poverty, Health and the Environment concluded that the evidence received described a:

> food system that is biased towards providing an overabundance of cheap, less healthy food, with adverse consequences for health and the environment. We were told that farmers are trapped in a cycle where there is not enough emphasis or incentive on the need for healthy, environmentally sustainable produce.
> (Select Committee on Food, Poverty, Health and the Environment, 2020)

The negotiated Brexit deal has resulted in no tariffs on food but increases in bureaucracy, lorries queuing at the docks and confusion, all of which add to the cost of food. The paradox is that Brexit, the Food Strategy and even the COVID-19 crisis offer an opportunity to reflect on the adequacy of food systems and to use legislative actions to change them. The problem seems to be a lack of vision, little joined-up thinking and tensions over what is "right to do" and the demands of "Big Food" and consumers. An example of such tensions can be found in consumers' desire for "local food", but also their expectation for a year-round supply of out of season produce, convenience and "cheapness". Some see the solutions to the latter in technological innovations, hence producing healthy ultra-processed foods or moving to plant- and lab-based meat alternatives.

The big mistake lies in viewing these crises as temporary and fleeting and something that cannot be planned for. In terms of the food policy and the food supply system, the various crises exposed existing flaws which have not been tackled and have not gone away or been faced up to or addressed.

At the household level, food inflation and food price rises result in people reporting that:

- Thirty per cent had skipped a meal or cut down the size of their meals because they did not have enough money to buy food in the last month.
- Thirty-two per cent had eaten food past its use-by date at least once in the past month because they couldn't afford to buy more food.
- Eighteen per cent turned off a fridge and/or freezer containing food at least once in the last month to reduce energy bills and save money (Food Standards Agency, 2022).

These findings are repeated by other small-scale and regional surveys and are likely to be even worse in 2023 with real incomes falling behind general levels of inflation (running at 12% between the late months of 2022 and early 2023) and far behind food inflation (running at 15% and for some basic goods as high as 40%). In December 2022, UK households spent £1.1 billion more on food than in December 2021, but the volume of sales was down by 1%. The rise in spending can be accounted for by food inflation. January 2023 data from the Bank of England showed that in the run up to Christmas 2022, credit card borrowing rose to £1.2 billion and the Bank presumed that many households had used credit to finance their Christmas purchases, including food. Food poverty advocates such as Jack Monroe (see Chapter 11) have argued for the establishment of a new food inflation index, which takes not a typical food basket, but one which takes account of the fact that many in food poverty or at risk of it already buy cheaper food products which have increased in price as availability fell. The index will be called the "Vimes Boots Index", in honour of a character in a Terry Pratchett novel *Men at Arms* who set out the "Sam Vimes 'Boots' theory of socioeconomic unfairness". A follow-up report by the Office for National Statistics (ONS) in May 2022 showed that the prices of the lowest-cost grocery items in the UK have not risen faster than average food prices, but there was a disproportionate impact, with a higher impact on low-income households (10.9% for the poorest decile of the population compared to 7.9% for the richest decile). This research took place before the rise in energy cost came into force in October 2022 (Hardie, 2022).

Comprehensive food policy approach

All of the above makes the case for a comprehensive food policy which covers the issues from production to food consumption, the farm to fork approach mentioned in Chapters 2, 7 and 8. Yet, as noted, the government has largely "ditched" or ignored the recommendations put forward in the National Food Strategy (NFS) in 2021 (Dimbleby & Lewis, 2023, Food Ethics Council, 2022, White, 2022). Other countries have implemented policies to ensure future supplies of food such as China and Singapore, setting targets for foods to be grown and restricting exports and imports (Bernaschi & Leonardi, 2022, Lau, 2022, Singapore Food Agency, 2020).

To tackle the immediate crises, others have entered into partnerships with food retailers, such as the Greek government who, in conjunction with supermarkets, have established a core food basket of 51 staples which will be sold at fixed prices. The UK has failed so far to address the issue of food policy comprehensively; we have seen "silo"-based and short-term responses but not overall control or co-ordination. There is no overall policy approach to developing national food security and how this might be tackled by setting targets for domestic agriculture encouraged by subsidies and tariffs, or how changes to farming subsidies post-Brexit and the loss of CAP payments to farmers are being managed to encourage food production. This is being addressed in England by DEFRA through the Environmental Land Management Scheme (ELMS) which has suffered a number of policy U-turns and separately by the devolved administrations in Northern Ireland, Scotland and Wales. Nutrition policy is again devolved and we are seeing different approaches across the UK and the list goes on. Trade deals negotiated in the wake of Brexit seem to place British farming at risk by allowing food imports to have lower standards of production and animal welfare.

The failure of the government to act on the recommendations of the NFS and to introduce an approach to food policy based on a comprehensive overview (see Chapters 1–3 and 7) means that the problems in the UK food chain and system will continue (Adams, 2021, Dimbleby & Lewis, 2023, Lang, 2022, Goodwin, 2022, Yap, 2022). What is needed is an approach to food policy development (as set out in Chapters 2 and 3), whether based on "food in all policies" or a food policy overview regulation and leadership are essential (see Chapter 2 and Table 2.2 for a discussion of models and approaches to food policy). To deliver on health, obesity prevention, procurement policies, sustainable healthy agriculture, circular food economies, equitable food systems, affordable food and comprehensive food welfare policies, both a vision and accompanying policy action are needed.

As we have pointed out throughout the book, the most successful food policy era was that of World War II (WWII) where food control was exercised by the government. Using the Overton Window (see Chapter 2), to analyse this we can see that what was acceptable at that time is no longer acceptable now; the level of control from rationing to buying food on world markets is not feasible in the modern world. However, a new form of food control could be established and exercised by the UK government to ensure food supply is stable, healthy and affordable. As we noted in Chapters 1, 3, 7 and 8, globally and nationally food supply is controlled by a small number of very large corporations; control could be exercised by engaging with regulators at the global level and by ensuring that post-Brexit trade deals do not further weaken the state of UK agricultural production and the livelihoods of farmers. At the UK level, joined-up policymaking is needed to ensure that the food grown, processed and sold meets sustainable and healthy criteria. This latter approach can be achieved through a mix of subsidies and taxes as well as being supported by education and healthy media promotions. Too often, the unhealthy choices are the cheaper choices (Barosh et al., 2014, Which?, 2022). All this is not to advocate a state of no change and protectionism; as we saw in Chapter 7, agriculture will have to adapt to meet greenhouse gas emissions and retail will need to adapt to selling more healthy and less ultra-processed foods. All these are challenges for future food policy and, of course, for growers and food producers. These are in many ways not new; the scale of the problem and the recognition is that we may be entering indistinguishable "permacrises" rather than surviving serial crises. In his 1928 reflection on World War I (WWI), William Beveridge said:

> The main lesson of British food control is that state trading in food is practicable and in times of prolonged shortage is necessary. It is within the wit of man to find an alternative to competitive private enterprise with market forces as a means of obtaining and

distributing food, to replace economic by human laws, to substitute managed for automatic provisioning of the people.

(Beveridge, 1928, pp. 337–338)

A similar sentiment was advocated by Titmuss and Le Gross Clark in 1939 just prior to the declaration of WWII, when they commented:

There are only two further ways of making food more available. The first is to lower the prices of foodstuffs upon the retail market; the second is to provide food to certain sections of the community through the medium of the social services. There is no reason, of course, why these methods should be mutually exclusive …

(Le Gros Clark & Titmuss, 1939, p. 166)

Global impacts from the war in Ukraine, climate and weather crises mean we are entering a new epoch where the challenges for food policy are enormous but also the potential for development is equally challenging and significant, and if we don't get it right, future generations will suffer. We need to take urgent and radical action.

Citizen science

A theme that has run through the various chapters and found articulation in nearly all the chapters is that of citizen engagement and the voices of end users or recipients of any food policy. Such an approach was a hallmark of both world wars in the approach to food control. At the start of WWII, local food committees were established. They consisted of 15 members, of which ten were to be non-trade members, the remaining five were composed of the following: a co-op official; a private butcher; a private grocer; and two retailers. These helped inform local rationing, and through their knowledge of local areas, they helped establish local priorities for rationing. These committees ensured local knowledge and feelings were fed back up the line to policymakers in Westminster. This helped shape the way in which rationing and food price controls were administered and made acceptable for the population (Hammond, 1951). Such involvement now plays an important role in food policy development and is referred to generally as citizen science, lay involvement or often lay experts (Booth, Pollard & Pulke, 2022, Brown & Baker, 2012, Chilton et al., 2009, Gallegos & Chilton, 2019, Reynolds et al., 2021, Wakeford, 2016).

Final thoughts, conclusions and challenges

WWI and WWII introduced a Ministry of Food which oversaw issues related to food from imports to consumption. This resulted in improved health for many sections of the population, but in the post-war period, these initiatives and policies were abandoned as society moved towards more "choice" and the food system became enthralled to free trade and globalisation and largely controlled by big business. The Overton Window helps show us that what was accepted in WWII in terms of self-sacrifice and deprivation in the cause of the greater good is no longer acceptable to the majority of the population, yet we face a new crisis and state of change.

Modern food policy has focused on healthy eating and sustainability and is marked by an approach in government circles focused on choice, consumerism and encouraging the formation of standards in the private sector. This was true of both Labour and Conservative administrations. Food was seen as plentiful and cheap with a Labour Government report in 2008 praising supermarkets for their plentiful supply of "cheap" food (Cabinet Office, 2008). The NFS was the latest to propose a co-ordinated strategy and as we saw in Chapters 2, 4 and 7, this fell at the last hurdle with the government accepting some of the recommendations but in the main ignoring what they did not like and addressing some of the issues through process, and so setting up inquiries or promising to investigate further (Goodwin, 2022, White, 2022). Calls for a comprehensive approach to food policy have not been achieved or even attempted, yet some hope remains in the devolved nations of the UK where food and agriculture are delegated actions and actions around food policy can be seen to be more radical. For example, Scotland is exploring the possibility of a bill to ensure zero waste and circular economy in Scotland; this would contribute to a green economy, livelihoods of farmers, public procurement and health. What is needed is a new form of food control which embraces the range of issues from growing to consumption and the impacts on equity of access, livelihoods, health and the environment.

At times of food crises, both globally and nationally, there is a need to look to the future; history often represents the voices of the powerful and privileged and favours the voices of men and food policy often runs a similar danger (Carr, 1961). Marx asserted that "the philosophers have only interpreted the world, in various ways. The point, however, is to change it" (Marx & Engels, 2004), likewise with food policy, it is not enough to continue to describe it. Much of the contents of this book are aimed at helping an analysis of food policy but an analysis to bring about change (see examples in Chapter 11). We recommend reading the NFS for its breadth and depth of vision (Dimbleby, 2021). The links between agriculture, health and environment are clearly laid out. Even if government decided not to implement its findings, it can help form the basis for a future food system. Additionally (as set out in Chapter 11), the efforts of many of the organisations working around food such as the NGOs and individuals have produced vision statements. We recommend reading documents produced by the Centre for Food Policy on food systems as well as associated work by the Food Research Collaboration (see www.city.ac.uk/research/centres/food-policy). We will provide additional reading and updates on the Routledge website (www.routledge.com/9781032196770) to support the various chapters and to deliver updates on changes in policy.

What is clear is that despite COVID-19 and the war in Ukraine exposing system failures in the food and welfare system, there has been little long-term policy thinking, action or implementation beyond the immediate presenting problems. So, short-term fixes have been the response. Likewise, the retail environment is likely to change as customers demand new services and products, including healthier and more sustainable goods. How companies respond to this will impact on food production and supply systems. Additionally, work in the devolved nations also offers hope for future developments along with food policy initiatives which are designed for local and regional situations, such as the extension of school meals provision in Scotland and Northern Ireland. At an international level reading and keeping an eye on work by FAO, WHO and other global organisations is essential.

Future changes in agriculture, retail and fast food or eating out of home are all potential game changers for food policy. New developments such as home delivery; online ordering; buy now, pay later (BNPL) schemes; and technological developments such as gene editing and lab-based meat are all developments the outcomes of which are difficult to predict and how food policy will deal with them is not yet clear.

Here, we offer a number of challenges which will face food policy in the immediate future:

- Climate change and natural disasters.
- Agricultural production's links to GHG (greenhouse gas) emissions, contribution to UK food security, smart farming and new technologies

- Linking healthy eating and sustainable growing production practices.
- For producers in Northern Ireland, the challenge of providing food choice in an affordable way post-EU Exit grace period.
- Moving to more sustainable practices in respect of encouraging eating with seasonality, increasing expectations for local foods and supporting supermarkets' expectations for volume.
- Changes to food such as plant-based alternatives and lab-based meat, and the associated development of technologies such as nanotechnology.
- Gene-edited foods replacing the concern with Genetically Modified (GM) foods.
- Food supply crises.
- Dealing with consolidated haulage loads and the financial and time costs of doing so.
- Retailers' dominance of the food system and the controls that can be used to control the "Big Food" players in the food system.
- Smart technology and its ability to change purchasing patterns and habits.
- Tensions between demands for healthy and sustainable foods and convenience.
- The ability of different business models/food hubs to introduce their products and produce to new consumer markets at scale.
- Accommodating ever-changing consumer tastes and preferences.
- The development of a food literate population.
- Translation of complex sustainability issues into simple, comprehensible consumer messaging.
- Developing food citizenship and representation at the local and regional levels (like the food committees of WWI and WWII).
- Avoidance of a two-tier system for food, whereby only some consumers can afford to buy food of acceptable quality, standards, sustainability and health.
- The cost of living crisis and rising inflation.
- Free school meal eligibility and the case for universal free school meals.
- Holiday hunger and how it can be tackled in a fair and equitable way.
- Linking healthy diets to incomes and ensuring all households can afford to access food and
- eat healthily.
- The UK's contribution to the development of global food policies which are equitable and harm minimizing.
- Devolved administrations' ability to develop higher standard food policies than those for England.
- Avoidance of regressive trade agreements post-EU Exit that represents a race to the bottom in respect of food standards.
- For Northern Ireland, the post-Brexit talks with the EU over the "Northern Ireland Protocol" and its impact on food supply, agriculture and trade in and for Northern Ireland needs to be kept under review (McFarlane, Lewis & Lang, 2018).
- Prevention of food fraud/crime as a result of any exploitation of any gaps in new trade agreements.
- Attainment of the 2030 Sustainable Development Goal (SDG 2) target(s) for Zero Hunger.
- The continued protection of the exceptionalism of food.
- Pursuance of the right to food.

What would you, the reader, add?

All of the above should have an equity perspective, so that developments in an area do not create new inequalities or enlarge exiting ones. For example, will new smart technology in farming benefit only large farmers due to costs or will the development of lab-based meat contribute to new inequities in the food system? A report from the World Economic Forum highlighted issues around food security and offered a critique of the risks to long chain food supplies and favouring shorter chains (World Economic Forum, 2023).

While writing this book, we saw many U-turns, postponing of policy initiatives, abandonment of others and short-term interventions, the so called "whack-a-mole" approach. Bill Gates, in his book *How to Prevent the Next Pandemic*, recommends that systems be put in place now to monitor changes and that forward planning and action should occur now, not when the crisis happens (Gates, 2022). This is especially pertinent with respect to food policy as the (perma)crises are now.

The challenges facing future food policy are enormous and perplexing. The NFS has been cited throughout the book and the possibilities that it offered to address a comprehensive food policy highlighted (Dimbleby, 2021). Yet government failed to act on the majority of its recommendations. The government response, or lack of a co-ordinated one, led to the lead author and government advisor, Henry Dimbleby, resigning his post and making the following observations:

> The so-called 'Government Food Strategy' that was unveiled in June 2022, in response to my review, is not a strategy at all. It is merely a handful of disparate policy ideas, many of them chosen because they are unlikely to raise much of a media storm. That doesn't mean those ideas are worthless. Some are more interesting and important than might appear at first sight. The government accepted my recommendation to create a Land Use Framework, for example, which is critical to balancing the multiple demands on our land. If they do it right, it will be ground-breaking. But it won't be enough on its own. The government's 'strategy' is far too scant, fragmented and cautious to meet the scale of the problem (page 17).
>
> Having seen progress from the inside, I predict lot of missed deadlines. The policies that are current being pursued are not enough, either singly or together to effect such big changes; and, even if they were, they may be dithered out of existence. It's as if a huge asteroid is careering towards the Earth, and our politicians are working on plans to divert it with a pea shooter.
>
> In some areas of food policy, progress has actually gone into reverse. Having promised to bring in restrictions on junk food advertising and in-store promotions, the government has now 'delayed' this until after the next election. The more chaotic the overall political picture becomes, with recession at home and war abroad, the harder it gets to push through meaningful change.
>
> So we continue to drift towards a future shaped for us by the market. That market has been distorted by two classic system traps. The reinforcing feedback loops within the Junk Food Cycle have led us into *escalation*; our appetite steers us towards junk food, so companies invest more in it, we eat more, they invest more, we get sicker (page 262).
>
> (Dimbleby & Lewis, 2023).

Notes

1 Australia is the second largest exporter of wheat after Ukraine.
2 Multinational companies similarly use the term TNCs, which has been used elsewhere in this book.

References

Adams, J. 2021, "National food strategy: what's in it for population health?", *BMJ*, vol. 374, p. n1865.
Barosh, L., Friel, S., Engelhardt, K. & Chan, L. 2014, "The cost of a healthy and sustainable diet – who can afford it?", *Australian and New Zealand Journal of Public Health*, vol. 38, no. 1, pp. 7–12.

Bernaschi, D. & Leonardi, L. 2022, "Food insecurity and changes in social citizenship. A comparative study of Rome, Barcelona and Athens", *European Societies*, pp. 1–31. https://doi.org/10.1080/146166 96.2022.2115096

Beveridge, W.H. 1928, *British Food Control*, Humphrey Milford, London.

Booth, S., Pollard, C.M. & Pulke, C.E. 2022, "Citizen-Driven Food System Approaches in Cities" in *Environment and Climate-smart Food Production*, ed. C.M. Galanakis, Springer, Cham, pp. 349–381. https://doi.org/10.1007/978-3-030-71571-7_11

Brown, B.J. & Baker, S. 2012, *Responsible Citizens: Individual Health and Policy under Neoliberalism*, Anthem Press, London.

Cabinet Office 2008, *Food Matters Towards a Strategy for the 21st Century*, Cabinet Office, HM Government, London.

Carr, E.H. 1961, *What Is History?*, Vintage, New York.

Chang, H. 2022, *Edible Economics: A Hungry Economist Explains the World*, Allen Lane, Great Britain.

Chilton, M., Rabinowich, J., Council, C. & Breaux, J. 2009, "Witnesses to hunger: participation through photovoice to ensure the right to food", *Health and Human Rights*, vol. 11, no. 1, pp. 73–85.

Collingham, L. 2017, *The Hungry Empire: How Britain's Quest for Food Shaped the Modern World*, The Bodley Head, London.

Dimbleby, H. 2021, *National Food Strategy, Independent Review: The Plan*, https://www.nationalfoodstrategy.org.

Dimbleby, H. & Lewis, J. 2023, *Ravenous: How to get ourselves and our planet into shape*, Profile Books, London

Food and Agriculture Organization of the United Nations & World Food Programme 2022, *Hunger Hotspots: FAO-WFP early warnings on acute food insecurity*, FAO, https://docs.wfp.org/api/documents/WFP-0000139904/download/?_ga=2.123992330.1057690076.1662638953-429207200.1662638953.

Food Ethics Council 2022, *Responding to the government food strategy*, Food Ethics Council, https://www.foodethicscouncil.org/resource/government-food-strategy-response/.

Food Standards Agency 2022, *Latest consumer survey tracks level of worry around the cost of food and its impact on food safety*, Food Standards Agency, https://www.food.gov.uk/news-alerts/news/latest-consumer-survey-tracks-level-of-worry-around-the-cost-of-food-and-its-impact-on-food-safety.

Gallegos, D. & Chilton, M.M. 2019, "Re-evaluating expertise: principles for food and nutrition security research, advocacy and solutions in high-income countries", *International Journal of Environmental Research and Public Health*, vol. 16, no. 4, p. 561.

Gates, B. 2022, *How to Prevent the Next Pandemic*, Allen Lane, London.

Goodwin, S. 2022, "A cursory National Food Strategy lacks substance and joined up thinking on food insecurity", *BMJ*, vol. 377, p. o1549.

Hammond, R.J. 1951, *Food, Volume 1. The Growth of Policy*, H.M.S.O., London.

Hardie, M. 2022, *Measuring the changing prices and costs faced by households*, January 26, Office for National Statistics, https://blog.ons.gov.uk/2022/01/26/measuring-the-changing-prices-and-costs-faced-by-households/.

Lang, T. 2022, "Boris Johnson's food strategy fails to address food poverty and the cost-of-living crisis", *The New Statesman*, [Online], vol. 13 June, 15th June. Available from: https://www.newstatesman.com/environment/food-farming/2022/06/boris-johnsons-food-strategy-fails-to-address-food-poverty-and-the-cost-of-living-crisis.

Lang, T. 2020, *Feeding Britain: Our Food Problems and How to Fix Them*, Pelican, London.

Lau, M. 2022, China can't count on global markets for food security, Xi Jinping says, 7 March, South China Morning Post, https://www.scmp.com/news/china/politics/article/3169467/china-cant-count-global-markets-food-security-xi-jinping-says.

Le Gros Clark, F. & Titmuss, R. 1939, *Our Food Problem: A Study of National Security*, Penguin Books, Harmondsworth.

Levitt, T. 2022, UK organic dairy farmers fear for futures as food prices soar, 16 April, *The Guardian*, https://www.theguardian.com/environment/2022/apr/16/uk-organic-dairy-farmers-fear-futures-food-prices-soar.

Marx, K. & Engels, F. 2004, *The German Ideology*, Lawrence and Wishart, London.

McFarlane, G., Lewis, T. & Lang, T. 2018, *Food, Brexit and Northern Ireland: critical issues*, Food Research Collaboration, Centre for Food Policy, London.

National Farmers' Union (NFU) 2022, *Growers Fear for Future as Rising Costs and Workforce Shortages Impact Horticulture Sector*, Accessed 22nd March, 2023, https://www.nfuonline.com/media-centre/releases/growers-fear-for-future-as-rising-costs-and-workforce-shortages-impact-horticulture-sector/.

Oxfam 2022, *Profiting from Pain*, Oxfam, https://oi-files-d8-prod.s3.eu-west-2.amazonaws.com/s3fs-public/2022-05/Oxfam%20Media%20Brief%20-%20EN%20-%20Profiting%20From%20Pain%2C%20Davos%202022%20Part%202.pdf.

Reynolds, C., Oakden, L., West, S., Pateman, R., M., E., C., Armstrong, B., Gillespie, R. & Patel, M. 2021, "Citizen science for the food system" in *Future Directions for Citizen Science and Public Policy*, eds. K. Cohen & R. Doubleday, Centre for Science and Policy, Cambridge, pp. 55–69.

Select Committee on Food, Poverty, Health and the Environment 2020, *Hungry for change: fixing the failures in food. HL Paper 85*, Parliamentary Copyright, https://publications.parliament.uk/pa/ld5801/ldselect/ldfphe/85/8502.htm.

Singapore Food Agency 2020, *Our Singapore Food Story – The 3 Food Baskets*, Accessed 3rd November, Singapore Food Agency, https://www.sfa.gov.sg/food-farming/sgfoodstory/our-singapore-food-story-the-3-food-baskets.

The World Bank 2021, *Brief: Food Security and COVID-19 (Updated 5th February, 2021)*, The World Bank, https://www.worldbank.org/en/topic/agriculture/brief/food-security-and-covid-19#:~:text=In%20November%202020%2C%20the%20U.N., insecure%20people%20in%20the%20world.

Wakeford, T. 2016, "Signposts for People's Knowledge" in *People's Knowledge and Participatory Action Research: Escaping the White-walled Labyrinth*, ed. The People's Knowledge Editorial Collective, Practical Action Publishing Ltd, The Schumacher Centre, Warwickshire, pp. 113–134.

Which? 2022, *Affordable Food for All: How Supermarkets Can Help in the Cost of Food Crisis*, Which?, London.

White, M. 2022, "Half hearted and half baked: the government's new food strategy", *BMJ*, vol. 377, p. o1520.

World Economic Forum 2023, *The Global Risks Report 2023 18th Edition: INSIGHT REPORT*, World Economic Forum, https://www.weforum.org/reports/globalrisks- report-2023/.

Yap, C. 2022, *Leaked food strategy vs published strategy: a side by side analysis*, https://fixourfood.org/leaked-strategy-vs-published-strategy-a-side-by-side-analysis/.

Index

Note: **Bold** page numbers refer to tables; *italic* page numbers refer to figures and page numbers followed by "n" denote endnotes.

Abel-Smith, B. 67, 221
Aberdeen typhoid outbreak: contaminated water usage 202; policy implications and implementation 203
Accum, F. C. 198
Acheson, D. 49, 177
Adams, C. J. 200
adulteration: The Adulteration of Food and Drink Act, 1860 198; cause of 198; horsemeat scandal 205–208; practices in 199
agriculture industry, UK: conversion ratios of 133; COVID-19 lockdown effect 134; cultivated meat production **137**; digital technologies effect 136; emersions 133; Environmental Land Management Scheme (ELMS) 134; farmland engaged 133; future prospectives 136–137; meat and dairy products 133–134; produce and profit 131; regenerative farming **137**; rewilding/nature recovery **137**; self-sufficiency 131; smart farming 134; trade and agriculture commission report 134–135; Ukraine war impact 134
Aldi, retailer 138
Alexander, S. 220
Anderson, L. **28, 54**
Anti-Microbial Resistance (AMR) 93–96, 97
austerity celebrity 221

Baumgartner, F. **20,** 114
Beardsworth, A. 200, 201
Beaumont, J. 68
Berry, W. 102
Beveridge, W. H.: report 26, 217
Big Food 4, 16–17, 30, 36, 157, 160, 162, 165, 166, 233, 237
The Bill and Melinda Gates Foundation 163; *see also* Gates Foundation
Birkland, T. A. 16

Bitsch, V. 76
Blaiklock, C. **28**
Blumenthal, H. 189
Booth, C. 66
Boswell, J. **21**
Bourdieu, P. 200
Bové, J 158; The World is Not for Sale 158
Bovine Spongiform Encephalopathy (BSE) crisis: consumer perceptions 209–210; Creutzfeldt-Jakob Disease (CJD) 203; devolved nations' policies 204–205; EU import ban on 204; food policy, fundamental disjunction 204; foot-and-mouth disease outbreak 205; labelling, food authenticity and trust 208–209; lack of trust effect 205
Boyson, R. **54**
Bread Scale 59n2; *see also* Speenhamland Scale
breakfast clubs 147, 177, 179, 181, 184
Brexit deal: financialisation 164; Northern Ireland (NI) protocol 35–36; public goods 105
Brief, A. P. 75
British food policy, global context: cheap food 3–4; COVID-19 crises 7–8; CSR commitments 2; cut aid budgets 2; Engel's law 7; equity and food policy 3–4; finance *vs.* well-being 4–5; food control policy, WWII 5–6; food leaders 6; food policy and equity 7; food proofed policies 2; foreign aid importance 2; ghost acres 3; global crises of 7–8; Haber-Bosch process impact 8; health and nutrition focus 3; income elasticity 7; national food education 6–7; price volatility, global crises 7–8; rationing, state-controlled 6–7; silo policymaking 2; state-controlled restaurant 6; Transnational Companies (TNCs) 4; Ukraine invasion impact 2
Brockway, F. 48

242   *Index*

Brundtland, G. H. 93
Brundtland report 93
Buckett, K. **21**
Bull, J. 201
Burnett, J. 198
Buse, K. **20**
Buss, D. H. 49

Cairney, P. **20, 21,** 113
Campbell, L. 75
Cannon, G. 48, 66, 215, 219
canteens **45**, 144, 147, 174, 190
Caraher, M. **20, 21,** 74, 145
Caroline Walker Trust (CWT): establishment
    48–49; health and sustainability 185;
    nutritional standards 175, 176, 217;
    school meals 173; sugar and fibre
    recommendations 177
Carrefour, retailer 130, 138
Cathcart, E. **28,** 52
celebrity chefs 112, 117, 219, 220
Chadwick, E. 27
Chakrabortty, A. 33
Charitable Organisation Society (COS) 66
Child Poverty Action Group (CPAG) 67, 180, 185,
    217, 221
circular economy 191, 236; *see also* closed loop
    economy
Clancy, K. L. 92
Clapp, J. 161, 162
closed loop economy 129, 190, 191
Cohen, B. C. 114
Collingham, L. 3, 175, 231; *see also* Hungry
    Empire
Common Agricultural Policy (CAP) 105, 134,
    136, **140,** 232, 232
contamination: consumer perceptions 209–210;
    E. coli food poisoning 199; fines or
    imprisonment 199; food riots 198;
    privatisation effect, food testing services
    199; Pure Food and Drugs Act (1906) 199;
    types of contaminants 199
cooking skills: community cooking interventions
    224; individual responsibility and
    behaviour 27–29; malnutrition effect 54;
    nutrition standard setting 52–53; school
    caterers 185; school club 177; school
    curriculum 46
Co-Op, food retailers 138, 139, 141
Corporate Social Responsibility (CSR): consumer
    activism model 4; internal policy 30;
    SDG12 161; support to growers 2
COVID-19: childhood obesity 120; cost of living
    crisis 157; financialisation, food 164, 166;
    food insecurity 68–72, **79**; global crises
    7–8, 30; holiday hunger 224; one health
    approach 97–98; school meals 173, 181,

182, 184, 187; supermarkets expansion
    137–138; sustainable diets 105; UC
    uplift 78
culinary deskilling 46, 56
Cullerton, K. **19, 20**
Currie, E. **28**

Davies, D. S. 122
Davis, G. **21**
Dearing, J. W. 114
Deeming, C. 53
Defeyter, M. A. 187
Department for Environment, Food and Rural
    Affairs (DEFRA): food financialisation
    162; sustainable food system 149
De Schutter, O. 74, 76
de Waal, A. 30
Dicks, L. V. 137
Diet for a Small Planet 93
Diet-Related Non-Communicable Diseases (DR-
    NCDs) 2–3
Dimbleby, H. 15, 149, 219, 238
domestic skills 51
double dividend 185
Douglas, M. 200, 202
Dowler, E. 7, 65, 67, 68, 71
Drèze, J. 73
Dufour, F. 158; *The World is Not for Sale* 158

ecological nutrition 32–33
Education (Provision of Meals) Act 1906 44, 171,
    173, **175,** 176
Egger, G. 13, 93
Egger, L. 226
Elliott, C. 205, 207, 208
empire policy 3, 138, 231
Engel's law 7, 66, 83
Environmental Land Management Scheme
    (ELMS) 105, 134, 136, 234
European Commission (EC) 65
European Union (EU) 208; British beef ban
    202–204; commodity concentration **159**;
    common agricultural policy 134; exit
    from 79; food insecurity 65; public goods
    policy 105

fair trade 93, 104
famine 7, 55, 66, 164, 231; end stage 55; global
    food chain disruptions 164; Irish 26
Fanzo, J. **21**
fast food 56, 57, 79, 120, 137, 143–145, 147, 236
Faulkner, W. 25
Fiddes, N. 200, 201
financialisation: algorithmic speculators 162;
    Cargill family 166; control and regulation
    163–164; cut aid budgets impact 165–
    166; food being weaponised 164; food

exceptionalism 166–167; Foreign Direct Investment (FDI) 165; global traders power 163; global trading houses 163; great recession of 2008 162; intensification 162–163; neoliberal trade environments 165; philanthrocapitalism 166; self-sufficiency policy of 164; Tobin tax 163–164; Ukraine war impact 164

food banks: COVID-19 pandemic impact 69–73; emergence 3; emergency food supplies 74; end plan 82; food insecurity 68; food poverty combat **54**; household skills 28; lobby 77; marketing and advertising food 113; policy influencers **225**; successful failures 75

food charity 74

food citizenship **96,** 102–103; sustainable diets 102–103

food contamination 197, 198–199; *see also* contamination

food controller 5

food control policy, WWII: food controller post 5; reasons for 5; subcommittee 6

food crime: Aberdeen food poisoning 202–203; consumer perceptions 209–210; contamination 198–199; harms 197; horsemeat scandal 205–208; labelling and authenticity 208–209; mad cow disease, BSE crisis 203–205; meat and food scares 200–202

food culture 56, 178, 185, 223

food education 6–7; *see also* cooking skills; food literacy

Food Ethics Council 103

food industry, UK: agriculture 131–137; ammonia production 129; circular loop system 129–130; closed loop system 129; dominant food system 130; fertiliser production 129–130; industrialised activities 129; junk food cycle break 131; Mergers and Acquisitions (M&As) 130

food insecurity growth: agreed healthy food basket 84; Charitable Organisation Society (COS) role 66; Child Poverty Action Group (CPAG) 67; COVID-19 impact 68; defined, World Food Summit 65; economic markers, measurement 68–69; Family Resources Survey data 69; food banks 69; *vs.* food poverty 65–66; food poverty impact assessment 73; food workers' concerns 72–73; fourth wave COVID-19 impact 72; health variations 68; Independent Food Aid Network (IFAN) 69–70; measurement of 68–73; modern malnutrition 67; NGO development in 67; Northern Ireland 71; over-nutrition prevalence **67**; poverty line 67;

pre-COVID-19 cohorts 70–71; Protestant work ethic 66; the right to food 73–82; since COVID-19 cohorts 71–72; state guarantee 83; symptoms, food poverty 72; third wave COVID-19 impact 71; Trussell Trust food banks 69–70; under-nutrition prevalence **67**; zero food loss 74

food literacy 58, 225; *see also* cooking skills; food education

food media: agenda-setting 113–115; blogs and vlogs 113; celebrity chefs 112, 117; churnalism 115; digital devices 113; frame contests 113; framing 115–116; journalism's economic model 115; media effects 113; media templates 116; news factors 116; news values 116–117; obesogenic environment 115; ordinary people, reality shows 112; policy responses 121–122; sugar tax 113

food policy: advocacy coalition framework **19**; behaviour change in 27–29; Beveridge report 26; big food 16–17; Brexit deal 35–36; common characteristics of 16; cookery methods impacts 29; cut aid budgets 31; cycle of deprivation 26; definitions **16**; definitions of 16–17; different models 17–18; different types 16; eco-nutrition 32–33; enlightenment model 18; food poverty standards 26; food system *14*; food *vs.* fuel poverty 33; goal numbers of 31; governance change 29–32; group types 13; health inequality 26–27; high-risk strategy 18; historical influences of 25–29; interactive model 18; knowledge-driven model 17; legislation control 29–30; less eligibility principle 25–27; modern malnutrition 26–27; multiple streams theory **19**; narrative policy frameworks **21**; National Food Strategy (NFS) 15, 34; Northern Ireland (NI) protocol 35–36; NOVA classification 14, 32–33; obesity and drip-feed initiatives 15; Overton Window 23–24; policy network analysis **20**; political model 17; population strategy 18; problem-solving model 17; processed culinary ingredients **32**; public health intervention 22; Public Private Partnerships (PPPs) 29–30; punctuated equilibrium theory **20**; responsible production and consumption 31; semi-processed foods **32**; sustainable development goals 31; tactical model 17; two community model 18; Ultra-Processed Foods (UPFs) 14, 32; Unhealthy Commodity Industries (UCIs) 17; unprocessed or natural foods **32**; upstream *vs.* downstream methods 18–22; war of

ideas 23; whack-a-mole model 18; WWI *vs.* WWII 34
food proofed policy 2
food riots 3, 198
food security 1, 2, 5, 6, 7, 31, 34, 35, 50, 58, 65, 66, 68, 69, 70, 74, 75, 76, 80, 81, 83, 134, 135, 136, 149, 160, 165, 166, 167, 175, 176, 189, 202, 204, 210, 232, 234, 238
The Food Scandal 48
food standards: absolute standard, definition 52; domestic education, cooking 52; less eligibility principle 51; nutrition standard setting 52–53; Speenhamland scale 51
Food Standards Agency (FSA) **45, 47,** 69, 95, 141, 182, 189, 202, 218
Furey, S. 70, 72, 74
Future Cook: A Taste of Things to Come 93
future prospects: big business control 235; Brexit deal 232–233; budget allocations 232; challenges 235–238; citizen science 235; comprehensive food policy 233–235; energy costs hike 232; inflation and income decline 233; labour shortage 232; long-term policy 236; production costs hike 232; self-sufficiency 232; subsidies 232; zero waste and circular economy 236

Galtung, J. 116
Gates Foundation 2, 30, 163, 166; *see also* Bill and Melinda Gates Foundation
Geddes, E. 174
George, S. **21**
ghost acres 3
Gilmore, G. 187
Gilson, L. **20**
global food trade: cereals, traders and significance **159**; coffee, traders and significance **159**; commodity trade, main players and significance **159**; concentration of **159**; derivatives markets 161; direct and indirect effect, commodity trade 160; financial trading markets 159; grain storage effect 160; phytosanitary concerns 158; price volatility 158; processed foods consumption effect 160–161; soya, traders and significance **159**; spot markets 161; sugar, traders and significance **159**; vulnerabilities 157
globalisation 3, 55, 105, 157
goal numbers, food system 31
Gopnik, A. 57
An Gortá Mór 5, 26
Gove, M. **28**
the great recession: control and regulation 163; financialisation 164; food-related riots 2; price hikes 162; service cuts 57; Transnational Companies (TNCs) 4

Gross Domestic Product (GDP) 4–5, 134
Guba, E. G. 16
Gussow, J. D. 92

Haber-Bosch process impact 8, 129
Hammond, R. J. 5, 6, 34
Harcup, T. 116, 117
Hassall, A. H. 198
Hawkes, C. *14*, 15, **21**
Health Divide report 48
health inequality, food policy 26–27
Helsing, E. 45
Higgs, J. D. 201
High Fat, Salt, Sugar (HFSS) foods: marketing and advertising regulations 118, 121–123
high-risk strategy, food policy 18
Hilton, S. 115
holiday hunger 173, 181, 187–188, 190, 224, 237
horsemeat scandal, food fraud: authenticity issue 207; complexity, food system 207; consumer perceptions 209–210; disruptive food governance 208; emergence timeline *206*; Food Crime Unit establishment 208; halal labelled product fraud 207; hippography 205; labelling, food authenticity and trust 208–209; positive outcome 208; public attributed responsibility 207; weak points, contamination 207
Huang, T. T. 115
Huisman, W. 197
Hungry Empire 231; *see also* Collingham, L.
Hungry Thirties (30s) 33, 53–55

Iceland, food retailer 138
Ingram, J. **21**
Irish famine 5, 26

James, P. 204
Jarrow March **45**, 174
Jenkins **28**
Johnson, B. 1, 9n1, 123, 150
Johnson, L. 67
Jones, B. D. **20**, 114
Jones, R. 52
Joseph, K. 26, 52
Juniper, T. 136
junk food cycle 1

Kamminga, H. 48
Kapelari, S. 202
Keating, M. **21**
Keil, T. 200
Kickbusch, I. **21,** 93
Kingdon, J. W. **19**
Kirby, J. 27, 53
Kitzinger, J. 116
Kohl, H. 204

labelling and authenticity 208–209
Lambie-Mumford, H. 65, 71
Lang, T. 7, 14, 32, 58, 68, 92, 93, 94, 95, 131, 137, 201, 204, 232
Lappe, F. M. 93
Leather, S. 7, 26, 51, 67, 68
legislation control, food policy 29–30
Le Gros Clark, F. 149, 171, 173, 235
Leith, P. 189, 219
less eligibility: food standards 51–53; historical influences 25–29; the right to food 75; Universal Credit (UC) 78–79; *see also* bread scale; Speenhamland Scale
Lidl, food retailer 138, **206**
Liebig 48
Lindberg, R. **21**
Lord, N. 197
Lyons & Co 138

mad cow disease, BSE crisis: consumer perceptions 209–210; Creutzfeldt-Jakob disease (CJD) 203; devolved nations policies 204–205; EU import ban on 204; food policy, fundamental disjunction 204; foot-and-mouth disease outbreak 205; labelling, food authenticity and trust 208–209; lack of trust effect 205
Maitland, Olga Lady 28
Major, J. 204
Malins, J. 18
marketing and advertising, food: advergaming 119; Advertising Standards Authority (ASA) 122; brand identity 118; campaigns 120–121; colour choices 119–120; COVID-19 pandemic impact 120; digital platforms 120; eavesmining 119; four-stage sequence 119; gamification techniques 121; HFSS (High Fat, Salt, Sugar) foods 118, 121–123; history of 118–120; homebased entertainment 120; logos 119–120; marketing mix 119; multi-platform selling 119; obesity and unhealthy foods promotion 118; paid promotions 119; pester power regulation 118; policy responses 121–122; promotion and placement regulation 118; restrictions and prohibitions 121–122; social marketing 120–121; Voice Activated Personal Assistant (VAPA) 119
Marmot, M. 22
Marsden, T. 208
Marx, K. 236
Mason, P. 14, 32, 58, 92, 95
Maxwell, S. 66
Mayhew, M. 53
Mays, N. **20**
May, Theresa 9n1

McCombs, M. E. 114
McQuail, D. 114
meat, food safety: Aberdeen typhoid outbreak 202–203; CO_2 emissions 202; consumer perceptions 209–210; feast diet 200; Foot-And-Mouth Disease (FMD) 200; horsemeat 202; labelling, food authenticity and trust 208–209; lipid hypothesis 201–202; low cost - mass production 200; protein transition 201
M'Gonigle, G. C. M. 27, 53
Michelini, L. 75, 76, 77
Millennium Development Goals (MDGs) 99
Milo, N. 45
minimum income standard 48, 78
Ministry of Agriculture, Fisheries and Food (MAFF) 15, **47**, 203, 204
Ministry of Food 5, 6, 24, 34, 35, 45, 144, 173, 190, 235
Moleschott, J. 48
Monbiot, G. 136, 137
Monroe, J. 78, 220–221, 233
Morgan, K. 177, 186, 217
Morrison, food retailer 138, 139, 141, 205
Motowidlo, S. J. 75
Muggeridge, M. 53

Napier, A. D. 202
National Food Strategy (NFS) 1, 15, 34, **45, 47,** 65, 79–80, 95, **96,** 130, 145–146, 180, 217, 233
National Health Service (NHS) 50, 178, 179, 188, 189, 219, 224
Netting, F. E **20**
new austerity 57
Newman, G. 29, 52
Nicolson, M. 52, 53
Nixon, L. 35
Northern Ireland: Consumer Council 222–223; food policy, sustainable diet **96**; Future Food Strategy Framework 81–82; key developments 182–184; Nourish NI, charity 223
Northern Ireland (NI) protocol 35–36
Note on the 'wider aspects of food system' 49
NOVA classification 14, 32, 58; *see also* Ultra Processed foods (UPFs)
nutritional standards, school food: age-appropriate calories guidelines 176; Caroline Walker Trust report 176–177; free school milk 175; Social Security Act, 1988 176; socio-economic diet status 177; standard cost set 176; sugar and fibre recommendations 177
nutrition controversy 53
nutrition transition 55–57

Obama, Barack 25
obesity: childhood 122; drip-feed initiatives 15; health care and economic loss 219; holiday hunger 190; hunger-obesity paradox 50–51; interventions *23*; malnutrition effect 67; media framing 113–114; policies past 50 years **47**; rate hike 49–50; school food plan 179; sugar and salt tax effect 147–149; unhealthy foods marketing 118
O'Connor, M. K. **20**
Oddy, D. J. 143
Oliver, J. **28,** 49, 117, 178, 220, 222
One Health 97–98
O'Neill, D. 116, 117
Orr, J. B. 3, 27, 29, 44, **45**, 48, 53, 57, 66, 149
Orwell, G. 53
Overton Window, food policy: impact analysis 24; war of ideas 23

Paoli, L. 197
Parsons, K. 15, 17, **21,** 92, 112
Patten, M. 112
philanthrocapitalism 30
philanthropy 24, 26, 66, 68, 75, 158, 163, 167n2, 174
Phillipov, M. 116
Pickett, K. **21**
Pinstrup-Andersen, P. 15
policy influencers: academic policy influencers 225; Consumer Council for Northern Ireland 222–223; devolved administrations 224–225; the Food Foundation, food insecurity 222; Food Sense Wales charity group 222; groups plugging 221–224; Jack Monroe, poverty premium 220–221; Jamie Oliver, soda tax and school dinners 220; local food projects 223–224; Marcus Rashford, food poverty 220; Nourish NI charity, healthy food 223; Nourish Scotland NGO 222; Sustain initiatives 221–222
Pollan, M. 102
The Poor and the Poorest 67, 221
Poor Law 44, 51, 54, 66, 67; New Poor Law 25–26; Old Poor Law 36n2, 75
Popkin, B. M. 201
Poppendieck 69
Post, F. R. 75
poverty: child poverty 33, 176, 220, 221; food poverty 2, 5, 7, 24–27, 29, 33, 35, 36, 50–51, 54, 57, 58, 65–84, 102, 135, 158, 164, 187, 216, 217, 220, 221, 223
The Press and Foreign Policy 114
Protestant work ethic 66
public goods, sustainable diets 105
public health: downstream 6, 18–22, 33, 46, 74, 103, 150, 198; upstream 18–22, 33, 49, 50, 55, 57, 59, 198

Public Health Responsibility Deal (PHRD) 145–146
public policy: marginalisation 204; media effects 114; policy development **19–21**; state and corporate 157; types 16
Public Private Partnerships (PPPs) 29–30
public procurement 189, 190, 236

The Ragged Trousered Philanthropists 25
Rashford, M. 77–78, 117, 181–182, 191, 220, 222
Rayner, G. 94
Reese, S. D. 116
Reagan, R. 3
Regan, A. 207
retail food industry: annual sales report, volume and value 149; big four 138; Buy Now Pay Later (BNPL) apps 141; calorie labelling 146–147; catering supplies, Ukraine war impact 148; commodity price hike effect of 148; COVID lockdown impact 137; dark kitchens 141; defunct retailers **138**; delivery company 141; desk top eating effect 141–142; diabetes rate hike effect 145; dishes and flavours impact 144; displayed food items 137–138; eating habits changes *142*; energy intake goals 146; expenditure value 137; fast food developments 143–144; food deserts area 145; food swamps 144–145; food value-added chain **140**; grower and employee security 140–141; hospitality 141–143; income inequality impact 145; Just In Time (JIT) retailing 140; nudging method 145; planning and citizen engagement 145; price promotions 138; processed foods 139; public health responsibility 145–146; quick delivery impact 141; regulations, calorie labelling 147; salt and sugar reduction targets 145–146; small chain *vs.* conglomerates 138–139; snack foods delivery effect 144; Soft Drinks Industry Levy (SDIL) 147–148; supermarkets 137–141; takeaway bussiness, elderly people 141; volume promotion restrictions, HFSS 140; voluntary agreements 149; Walmart effect 139
retail price maintenance **45**
Rhodes, R. **21**
Riches, G. 77
the Right to Food 30, 36, 58, 66, 73, 74, 76, 77, 82, 83, 84, 148, 158, 166, 187, 237; Buy Now, Pay Later (BNPL) facility 77; caveat emptor principle 74–75; child food poverty 77–78; food banks proliferation 74; food rescue 75–76; food waste 75; Future Food Strategy Framework, Northern Ireland 81–82; Good Food Nation Bill, Scotland 82;

ICESCR Article 11 73–74; Independent Food Aid Network (IFAN) hierarchy *82*; laissez-faire principle 74–75; Minimum Income Guarantee (MIG) 78–79; National Food Strategy plans, England 79–80; strategic philanthropy 75–76; successful failures of 75; Sustainable Development Goals (SDGs) 74; UNDHR Article 25 73; universal credit payment 78–79; Vimes Boots Index 78; Welsh government development 80–81; Zero Hunger Challenge 74

The Road to Wigan Pier 53
Rockström, J. 95
Rogers, B. 201
Rogers, E. M. 114
Rombach, M. 76
Roosevelt, Franklin D. 3
Roosevelt, Theodore 199
Rose, G. 18
Rose, N. **21**
Rousset, S. 104
Rowntree, B. S. 51, 53, 66
Royal Commission on Poor Laws 44
Ruge, M. H. 116

Sabatier, P. A. **21**
Sainsbury, food retailer 138
Salt tax 146, 149, 150
school food: age-appropriate calories guidelines 176; canteens 174–175; Caroline Walker Trust report 176–177; cash transfers, food parcels 181; central cooking depots 174–175; cheap food culture 178; childcare setting importance 172; commitment, nutritional profile 177–178; competitive tendering 178; compulsory schooling 172–173; curriculum, food and nutrition 179; cutbacks, Geddes axe 174; developments 174–175; double dividend 185; Education Act effect 172; enabling acts 179; energy level report 178; England, key developments 181–182; expenditure analysis 179; expert follow-up and monitoring of 179–180; food ambassadors 186; food parcels 182; four main food groups, Wales 184–185; free school milk 175; great war years 173; green-based closed loop economics 191; health and sustainability 185; Healthy Start Scheme 171–172; holiday hunger 173, 187–188; holiday vouchers 181; hospital food standards panel 188–189; Hull Experiment 178; income eligibility, Wales 185; interwar years 173–174; Jamie's School Dinners 179; lunchtime environment 180–181; monitoring, nutritional standards

180; nutritional standards 175–177; origins of 172–173; policy initiative **175**; powers to innovate 178; privatisation and outsourcing 190; public sector catering 188–189; ration method 174; revised nutritional standards, Northern Ireland 183; the School Food Plan 179–180; Scotland, key developments 182; Social Security Act, 1988 176; socio-economic diet status 177; standard cost set 176; sugar and fibre recommendations 177; summer learning loss 188; universal credit 186; vouchers to low-income women 171–172; Wales, key developments 184–185

Scotland 1, 46, 66, 74, 82, 95, 98, 102, 104, 105, 134, 147, 167, 171, 176, 180, 181, 182, 185, 186, 189, 204, 208, 216, 217, 222, 224, 232, 234, 236
Sen, A. 73
Sert, S. 75
Shaw, B. 75
Shaw, D. L. 114
Shinwell, J. 187
Shoemaker, P. J. 116
silo policy 2
Silvasti, T. 77
Sinclair, U. 199
Smith, B. C. **28**
Smith, D. F. 52, 53, 59, 203
Smith, K. 17, 24
Smith, M. 66
Sobal, J. 200
soda tax 49, 150, 218–219
Sonnino, R. 186
Speenhamland Scale 51; and bread scale 59n2; food standards 51–53; historical influences 25–29; the right to food 75; Universal Credit (UC) 78–79; *see also* less eligibility
Spencer, C. 56
Springsteen, Bruce 3
St Denny, E. **21**
Stewart, C. 201
stigma 25, 69, 174, 175, 190, 226
Subcommittee on Food Policy 66
subsidies 18, 22, 24, 49, 134, 142, 144, 164, 231, 232, 234
successful food policy, government-based: academic policy influencers 225; Consumer Council for Northern Ireland 222–223; Curry Report *vs.* Food Matters 215; devolved administrations 224–225; the Food Foundation, food insecurity 222; Food Sense Wales charity group 222; groups plugging 221–224; Jack Monroe, poverty premium 220–221; Jamie Oliver, soda tax and school dinners 220; local food projects 223–224; Marcus

Rashford, food poverty 220; Nourish NI charity, healthy food 223; Nourish Scotland NGO 222; obesity strategy 219; policy entrepreneurs/influencers 219; salt reduction policy 218; school meals policy 216–218; soda tax policy 218–219; Sustain initiatives 221–222

Sugar, A. 142

Sugar Tax 113, 117, 147, 218

Sunak, Rishi 9n1, 36n1, 150

supermarkets: big four 138; Buy Now Pay Later (BNPL) apps 141; dark kitchens 141; defunct retailers **138**; displayed food items 137–138; food value-added chain **140**; grower and employee security 140–141; Just In Time (JIT) retailing 140; price promotions 138; processed foods 139; quick delivery impact 141; small chain *vs.* conglomerates 138–139; volume promotion restrictions, HFSS 140; Walmart effect 139

super ministry 17

Sustainable Development Goals (SDGs): 17 SDGs **100**, 100–101; financialisation 161; primary objectives, 2030 31; UN progress **99**; Zero Hunger target 237

Swinburn, B. 13

takeaway food 18, 56, 141, 143, 144, 147, 148, 150, 177

taxes: fat 18; salt, soda 149, 150, 216, 219, 225; sugar 15, 49, 113, 117, 146–150, 218

Tedlow, R. 119

Tesco, food retailer 96, 121, 130, 138, 139, *206*

Thatcher, M. 217

Thilsted, S. 95

Titmuss, R. 149, 235

Tobin, J. 163

Townsend, P. 66, 67, 78, 221, 225

Transnational Companies (TNCs) 4, 17, 31, 163, 232, 238n2

Tressell, R. 25, 69

True, J. **20**

Truss, L. 9n1, 150

Tudge, C. 93

typhoid outbreak, Aberdeen 202–203

Ukraine invasion impact 2; *see also* war in Ukraine

Ultra-Processed Foods (UPFs) **32**, 14, 55, 59, 131, 139, 161, 233; *see also* NOVA classification

Unhealthy Commodity Industries (UCIs) 17

Veit-Wilson, J. H. 26

Vernon, J. 26

Virchow, R. 97

Wales 1, 27, 46, 64, **47, 67**, 69, 80–81, 95, **96**, 98, 102, 105, 141, 149, 171, 178, 204, 205, *206*, 208, 209, 222, 224, 234, community cooking interventions 224–225; food poverty policy 80, *81*; Food Sense 222; key developments 184–185; sustainable diet policy **96**

Walker, C. 7, 48, 66, 215, 225

Walmart 130, 139, 150

Walt, G. **20**

war in Ukraine 1, 5, 7, 8, 9n4, 33, 50, 57, 129, 133, 143, 151n1, 157, 164, 208, 235, 235

Waters, Alice 220

Watson II, D. D. 15

Weible, C. M. **21**

welfare capitalism 4, 17, 30, 32, 166

Wells, R. 14, 15, **21**

Widdecombe, A. **28**

Wilkins, J. L. 102

Wilkinson, R. **21**

Willett, W. 95

World Bank 164, 231

World Health Organization (WHO) 2, 12, 13, 17, 50, 93, 97, 98, 163, 166, 180, 236

World Trade Organization (WTO) 231, 232

World War I (WWI) 3–6, 34, **45**, 171, 173, 174, 234, 235, 237

World War II (WWII) 3, 5, 6, 24, 26, 29, 34, 35, 74, **140,** 142, 144, 159, 173–175, 190, 202, 215, 216, 234, 235, 237

Zahariadis, N. **19**

zoonosis 97